Paul VI

PAUL VI

The Divided Pope

YVES CHIRON

Translated by James Walther
Foreword by Henry Sire

Angelico Press

The first edition of this work was published in 1993.
The second revised edition (on which this translation
is based) was published by Via Romana in 2008.
Copyright © Via Romana, 2008
Copyright © Angelico Press, 2022

Photographs for this English edition have been drawn from
Wikimedia Commons and other public domain sources.

All rights reserved:
No part of this book may be reproduced or transmitted,
in any form or by any means, without permission

For information, address:
Angelico Press, Ltd.
169 Monitor St.
Brooklyn, NY 11222
www.angelicopress.com

ppr 978-1-62138-840-1
cloth 978-1-62138-841-8
ebook 978-1-62138-842-5

Book and cover design
by Michael Schrauzer

For Yvette and Marcel Nivoit

TABLE OF CONTENTS

Foreword by Henry Sire xi
Introduction to the Second French Edition xvii
Translator's Note xxv
Abbreviations xxvii
Paul VI Chronology (1897–1978) xxviii

1 The Child of Brescia 1
   A Middle-Class Catholic Family 2
   A Haphazard Education 5
   Birth of a Vocation 8
   The War 13

2 Priest without Having Been a Seminarian 17
   Between Religion and Politics 18
   Towards Ordination 21
   Rome 22
   "Complete Turnaround" 25
   First Voyages 28
   The FUCI 31

3 Between the FUCI and the Secretariat of State 35
   National Chaplain of the FUCI 36
   The Cultural Combat 40
   "Wariness and Prudence" 46
   Pacelli, Secretary of State 48
   The Crisis of 1931 52
   "Resigned" from FUCI 56

4 In the Turmoil of Europe 61
   Between Books and Voyages 63
   Substitute 68
   Towards the War 70
   Pius XII and the War 73
   Diplomacy of the Impossible 77
   Overthrowing Mussolini 85
   Occupied Rome 88

5 The Man in the Shadows 91
   Punishing the Defeated? 91
   Italian Political Games 99
   "Why Go to the Mountain..." 105
   The Non-Cardinal 120

6　*Archbishop of Milan* 129
　　The Capital of the North 132
　　The Mission of Milan 138
　　Pope Roncalli 142
　　Preparation of the Council 147
　　First Session 157

7　*The Pope of the Council* 165
　　Vocabor Paulus 167
　　Resumption of the Council 174
　　First Voyage 181
　　The Pope of Dialogue 186
　　"Black Week" 191
　　Between Doubts and Worries 195
　　Fourth Session 206

8　*Between Reforms and Voyages* 217
　　The Liturgical Reform 217
　　Pursuing Dialogue 222
　　Signs of Crisis 225
　　A "Holistic Humanism" 227
　　From Fatima to Istanbul 229
　　Reform of the Curia and the First Synod 233

9　*From Humanæ Vitæ to the Gates of China* 239
　　"Self-Destruction" of the Church 247
　　The Pope of the "New Mass" 249
　　From Geneva to Kampala 253
　　A Challenged Pope 256
　　All the Way to the Gates of China 260

10　*"The Storm that Batters Us"* 265
　　Peaceful Coexistence 265
　　Political Pluralism 268
　　The "Middle Way" of Paul VI 270
　　The Spirit versus "the Smoke of Satan" 276
　　"The Church of All Ages" 280
　　End of the Reign 288
　　"I did what I could" 292

　　Acknowledgments 297
　　Bibliography 299
　　Index of Names 313

FOREWORD

It is appropriate that the English edition of this biography of Paul VI, which was first published in 1993 and then in a revised edition in 2008, should appear during the pontificate of Pope Francis. The Divided Pope, as Yves Chiron calls his subject, has his counterpart in today's Divisive Pope. We now have a generation of Catholics who, after being lulled by the relative stability of John Paul II's reign and the brief hopes of Benedict's, are horrified by the devastating Modernism that has returned at the head of the Church. Yet the older generation have to tell them that we have been through all this before.

The truth is that, despite the accelerating rate of destruction in Francis's nine years, he has not yet inflicted as much damage on the Church as Paul VI did. On the doctrinal side, Paul began the damage by overturning the conservative plan John XXIII had for his Council, throwing its direction into the hands of a few Western European hierarchies, and allowing Modernist heresy to take control, led by self-promoting Council *periti*. The result, soon seen throughout the Church, was the attack on the most basic tenets of belief, the corruption of the seminaries, and the emergence of a race of renegade priests, by whom the faith of the worldwide laity was ruined. On the liturgical side, Paul VI's work was to hand over the task of "reform" to a clique of revolutionaries and to produce a gutted travesty of Christian worship. Catholics today blame Francis for revoking the toleration of the old Mass granted by Benedict XVI, but it was Paul VI who destroyed it in the first place, and with a totalitarianism more complete than what we are seeing now.

On the other hand, if we compare the personalities of the two popes, the opposition is marked. In behavior Paul VI was correct, cultured, with the personal courtesy of a career diplomat. His tentative confessions to the philosopher Jean Guitton are a world away from the crass distortions of faith and morals that Pope Francis throws around in front of journalists. There are parallels and contrasts. Where Francis has his Becciu, Paul had his Marcinkus, to sink the finances of the Church in scandal, but in Paul's case it was mere naivety — the naivety that made him bring the Mafia banker Michele Sindona with him from Milan — in contrast to the wallowing in grubby financial waters that marked Bergoglio during many years in Buenos Aires.

PAUL VI: THE DIVIDED POPE

Nevertheless, the fact is that Paul VI was the forerunner. It was his reign that saw the unravelling of the tradition which had kept the See of Rome for centuries the rock of orthodox faith. To find the reason for it, we can look to Yves Chiron's analysis of the Divided Pope. A cardinal once said of Paul: "He was a pope who suffered from a dichotomy, with his head to the right and his heart to the left." Paul himself once mused on the question: "Am I Hamlet or Don Quixote?" The division was in his personality itself, but it was also in the intrinsic incoherence of the objective he set himself: to bring modern humanism within the teaching of the Church. This was an ambitious, if not presumptuous, aim, and it called for qualifications that Paul VI did not possess. One of these would have been a grasp of fundamental realities in the world. In a pastoral letter on the eve of the Council, Cardinal Montini, as he then was, assured his flock in Milan: "Today there are no errors in the Church, or scandals or deviations or abuses to correct." He maintained this colossal misreading well after the warning signs that would have alerted more perceptive minds. In the closing months of the Council, in 1965, Paul was still insisting that there was no crisis in the Church. His eyes began to be opened the following year, when he read the report of the French hierarchy on the state of their Church, and began to see that it was much worse than he had thought. By 1968 he was talking, belatedly, of the "self-destruction" of the Church, and he lamented: "No one could have foreseen it after the Council." Wrong: there were many who foresaw it, and many who saw much more promptly.

The closest parallel between Pope Francis and Pope Paul is the manner in which they came to the papacy. Like that of 2013, the Conclave of 1963 was determined by a cabal of radical cardinals. In this book Yves Chiron gives us the narrative of the *sede vacante* period of 1963: Pope John XXIII died on June 3, and the Conclave was called for the 19th. Cardinal Montini remained in his own diocese of Milan until June 16, when he travelled to Rome. He then went to Frascati, to the south of Rome, where, on the 17th, he held a private meeting with five other cardinals — Liénart, Frings, Suenens, König, and Alfrink — all of them leaders of the extreme "progressive" tendency in the Council. What was decided there we do not know, but on the following day, the 18th, the five other cardinals held a meeting in the utmost secrecy, with several more, at nearby Grottaferrata. This meeting had been called by Cardinal Lercaro of Bologna, a prelate who since the election of John XXIII had shown himself the most ostentatious progressive in the Italian hierarchy.

At Grottaferrata the cardinals agreed on a strategy to work for the election of Lercaro himself, or, if that failed, of Montini. To complete the details, the meeting was held in the house of Cardinal Lercaro's secular factotum, the banker Umberto Ortolani, who was later revealed to be a prominent Freemason, and who was sentenced to nine years in prison for the fraudulent bankruptcy of the Banco Ambrosiano.

The two meetings mentioned need to be assessed in the light of canon law forbidding lobbying in a papal election, and declaring null all secret compacts to influence a Conclave. Let us begin with the one at Frascati: this was not a secret meeting (it was held at a Capuchin friary), but it is difficult behavior to reconcile at least with the spirit of canon law; in particular, it was unseemly that a cardinal who, like Montini, was well known to be a leading candidate should have gone to such an assembly (and it also shows how little Montini thought of himself as representing the Church as a whole, as opposed to a party). As to the Grottaferrata meeting, Yves Chiron remarks that Montini "does not seem to have participated" in it, and indeed no writer has suggested that he did. It would be hard to believe, however, that he was unaware of it, and of who its participants were, given that these included all five of the men who were with him at Frascati. This meeting was a much more direct affront to canon law than the now-familiar lobbying of the St Gallen Mafia: it was a meeting held on the very day before the Conclave, in patently underhand circumstances, and with a specific program to manipulate the voting.

The significance of these facts is not just that the election of Paul VI, like that of Francis, took place in conditions of irregularity. It reflects on the whole course of the Church after it. Under canon law, the cardinals who plotted at Grottaferrata ought to have been excommunicated and degraded from their rank. Instead, Paul VI made them the leaders of his revolution. Three of them, Lercaro, Suenens, and Döpfner, were appointed Moderators of the next three sessions of the Council (with a neutral and ineffective fourth, Cardinal Agagianian), and they used their position to slew its program onto the most progressive lines. Several others, including Liénart, Frings, König, Alfrink, and Léger, were standard-bearers of the same tendency.

Especially significant was the career of Lercaro, the organizer of the Grottaferrata meeting and the man who showed most clearly his own ambition. It was this prelate whom Paul VI chose for the most harmful of his legacies, the destruction of the Church's traditional liturgy. The

Council's constitution on liturgical reform *Sacrosanctum Concilium* (which certainly did not mandate the creation of a new liturgy) was given its final vote and promulgated in December 1963, six months after Paul VI's election. To implement it, Pope Paul did not rely on the Council's own Liturgical Commission or on the Vatican's Sacred Congregation of Rites, which had since 1588 exercised oversight in this area. He set up instead a separate "Consilium," under the presidency of Cardinal Lercaro; this choice would have been ominous enough, but in fact Lercaro was the front man for the real maker of the revolution, Msgr Annibale Bugnini, whom he appointed secretary. Bugnini was then given a free hand to pick his own team of supposed experts, all of them of the most radical tendency. One of the more genuine liturgical scholars who were sidelined in this process, Fr Louis Bouyer, later described Msgr Bugnini as "a mealy-mouthed scoundrel" and "a man as bereft of culture as he was of basic honesty."

Over the next five years, Bugnini's men carried on their work in open war with the Congregation of Rites, and even with mounting disregard for the Consilium itself which they were supposed to serve. By 1967 Bugnini had created the Novus Ordo that we know today. The new rite was presented to the Synod of Bishops, the body set up after the Council to introduce collegial government in the Church; the rite was strongly criticized and failed to obtain the necessary majority. Paul VI then ordered the revision of a number of features that he himself personally disliked. Bugnini's strategy was to argue that this implied unqualified approval of all the rest, and with that argument he forced acceptance of it on a reluctant Consilium. No further attempt was made to consult the world's bishops, after the ill-success of the previous year, and a liturgy which was supposed to express the will of the Council, but which was in fact the work of Paul VI's created machinery, was imposed on the Church.

Like the distortion of the Council itself, this mode of proceeding shows us the conflict between Paul VI's professed liberalism and the methods he used. Yves Chiron shows us the origins of Montini's liturgical preferences from an early age, when he was impressed by the simple austerity of the Benedictine liturgy that he encountered in some famous monasteries. That noble simplicity is indeed a valuable strand in the Church's tradition, yet so is the splendor of Baroque liturgy. The balance is given us by the Catholic genius of being true to every human facet, in keeping with the divine balance of Christ, who fasted for forty days in the desert, but immediately afterwards cheered a marriage feast with exquisite wine.

Paul VI thought himself a humanist, but his was not the maxim of Terence, *humani nihil a me alienum puto*. He thought it right to impose his own Lenten tastes in liturgy on everyone, and he maintained his command intolerantly, even after evidence of the hurt it produced and the protests led by Archbishop Lefebvre and others, which Yves Chiron chronicles sympathetically. Pope Paul was ostensibly a liberal, but he thought himself entitled as pope to create a new liturgy and to suppress the old, with an autocracy that no previous pope had dreamt of. It was this break with tradition that troubled Joseph Ratzinger, and moved him when he became pope to soften the harshness of Paul's dispensation and to recognize that the centuries-old liturgy of the Church has a right to exist. We now find ourselves, however, back (as it were) in the worst days of Paul VI, facing a narrowness that pretends to be generous, despotism masquerading as liberalism, and an incoherence that can have no result but to tear the Church apart.

Henry Sire
March 2022

INTRODUCTION TO THE SECOND FRENCH EDITION

IN 2008, THIRTY YEARS ON FROM THE END OF Pope Paul VI's pontificate (1963–1978), a new edition of this biography, first published in 1993, allows for a fresh evaluation. During this pontificate, the Church experienced considerable turmoil, enduring a sort of revolution. If on certain issues (notably priestly celibacy, papal election, birth control, and abortion) the Magisterium maintained its traditional positions in spite of insistent demands for reform, on other issues (liturgy; relations with non-Catholics and non-Christians; the Church's relationship with the world and society) things were said and done that would have been impossible twenty years before, during the pontificate of Pius XII (1939–58). In this light, the short pontificate of John XXIII (1958–63) might seem, in a literal sense, a pontificate of *transition*—a paradigm shift. The Second Vatican Council, which began under John XXIII and was completed by Paul VI, may be considered the essential vector of this revolution.

To be clear: when we speak of the turmoil brought about by the Council, we refer not only to the Council's texts themselves as published — four constitutions, nine decrees, and three declarations — and to the resulting reforms, but also to what one might call the *para-Council*: the declarations, productions, initiatives, and even press campaigns that preceded, accompanied, and followed the Council. From the announcement of the Council (January 1959) until long after its conclusion (December 1965), on the margins of the Council's proceedings, there was a continuous flow of analysis, commentary, policy proposals, and partisanship transmitted in the press, mostly on the part of the cardinals and bishops, but also the *periti* and theologians, who participated in the Council. This para-Council unquestionably had a more immediate influence on the lives of Christians, their conduct, and their ideas than the Council itself did in its promulgated acts.

Paul VI was the pope who saw this council through to the end. He led proceedings without really directing them, but nonetheless succeeded, at certain points, in making his mark and imposing his authority. He had to do it in a "shaken Church," to use the expression of Émile Poulat.[1] It would

---

1 Émile Poulat (1920–2014), French historian and sociologist. He was ordained

PAUL VI: THE DIVIDED POPE

be false to imagine that the Catholic Church entered multiple crises — a crisis of identity, a crisis of faith, a crisis of vocations, a questioning of structures and disciplines — only after the Second Vatican Council. These crises began to manifest themselves before the Council. The Council Fathers had not known how to resolve them. The Council, in certain aspects, only served to reveal this diffuse crisis in the Church, and the way in which the Council was implemented may have amplified this crisis.

Shortly after the death of Paul VI, Émile Poulat summarized his papacy thus: "He died without being able to subdue this dogmatic, disciplinary, and spiritual crisis, without being able to halt the violence of conflicts between peoples."[2]

The last years of his papacy are rather somber. The Italian play on words *Paulo sesto–Paulo mesto* (Paul the Sixth–Paul the Sad) made the rounds. If Paul VI's initial travels, not least to the Holy Land in 1964, generated great international enthusiasm, the difficulties which the pope had to face from the middle of the sixties on cast a long shadow. One year after his death, his successor described the papacy of Paul VI as "a daily martyrdom of worry and labor."[3] A grand memorial to Paul VI, unveiled in 1984 in Brescia, the city where he had spent his childhood and youth, encapsulates this evaluation. The statue, by the sculptor Lello Scorzelli,[4] depicts Paul VI with his head bowed, as though he were burdened by the weight of his duty, supported only by the large crucifix on which he leans or all but holds himself up.

Yet these sorrowful images of a papacy do not suffice to sum it up. Paul VI became pope at the age of sixty-five. The sixty-five years leading up to his ascension to the papacy allow a better understanding of his actions and his decisions as pope. The need for a full biography was obvious in 1993. Such a thing did not yet exist in French.

Sources of information are scattered. Although the Archives collected by the Holy See on the pontificate will not be accessible for decades, we may still consult the cardinals and other churchmen who collaborated closely with Paul VI. Their written and oral testimony has clarified certain details and corrected conclusions that could be drawn about various

---

a priest in 1945 and was active in the worker-priest (*prêtres-ouvriers*) movement. He was laicized and married in 1955. He was a founding member of the Group of Sociology of Religion.
2   Émile Poulat, "Paul VI," *Universalia*.
3   Pope John Paul II, discourse to pilgrims from Brescia, April 1979.
4   Raffaele "Lello" Scorzelli (1921–1997); he also sculpted for Paul VI the ferula-crucifix that became iconic in the hand of Pope John Paul II.

Introduction to the Second French Edition

events. An in-depth interview with the pope's friend Jean Guitton[5] has also revealed memories and frank judgments, which are inevitably more spontaneous than the guarded expressions found in the philosopher's published writings on the pope.

The Paul VI Institute, founded in Brescia in the years after the pope's death to maintain his reputation and publish memoirs and studies on his life and papacy, was also an indispensable resource. In terms of historical research, the French School of Rome's 1983 international colloquium "Paul VI and Modernity in the Church"[6] constitutes a major historiographical turning point.

Since the initial publication of the present work in 1993, historiography on Paul VI and his papacy has been considerably enriched. All the same, subsequent research has not fundamentally altered my initial vision of this churchman and his journey, or my appraisal of his papacy. Beyond some necessary corrections on points of detail, this book remains substantially unchanged. It was useful nonetheless to add some clarifications and fresh points of view that have emerged from studies that appeared after the first edition of this book.

The Institute of Paul VI in Brescia has continued to organize frequent international colloquia and study days whose proceedings are systematically published in short order, producing around thirty volumes to date. No pope has hitherto benefited from such an active posthumous "work of memory": the Institute has considerable financial means at its disposal. Other essay collections, documents, and a review (*Notiziario*) are regularly published, in addition to the abovementioned volumes of proceedings.

Several important colloquia have been organized to study various major aspects of this papacy, notably the definition and application of both episcopal collegiality[7] and ecumenism.[8] During the Institute's most recent colloquium, a communication from Justin Francis Rigali[9] demonstrated how Paul VI, from 1965 onwards, undertook to redefine the

---

5 Jean Guitton (1901–1999) was a French Catholic philosopher and theologian. His religious and intellectual ideas can be largely accredited to a blind priest, François Pouget. He was the first lay person to become an observer at the Second Vatican Ecumenical Council. He wrote approximately fifty books.
6 *Paul VI et la modernité dans l'Église* (Rome: École Française de Rome, 1984).
7 *Paolo VI e la collegialità* (Brescia: Istituto Paolo VI; Rome: Edizioni Studium, 1995).
8 *Paolo VI e l'ecumenismo* (Brescia: Istituto Paolo VI; Rome: Edizioni Studium, 1998).
9 Card. Justin Rigali (1935–) is an American prelate who has worked in various roles in the Curia since the earliest days of Paul VI's papacy, notably as an English interpreter to Paul VI. Since then he has been archbishop of St. Louis (1994–2003) and Philadelphia (2003–2011).

role of the apostolic nuncios so that "they not interfere in the pastoral action of bishops." This directive is found, in the form which applies to this genre of document, in the *motu proprio* entitled *Sollicitudo Omnium Ecclesiarum* (1969).

Amongst the other works published by the Institute is a minutely detailed chronicle of the episcopacy of Archbishop Montini in Milan (1955–1963),[10] featuring a day-by-day listing of all the public activities of the archbishop of Italy's largest city prior to his election as pope.

Amongst the biographical studies dedicated to Paul VI since the first edition of this book, Peter Hebblethwaite's is particularly worthy of note. Initially published in English and translated into Italian, it has not yet been rendered into French.[11] The former Jesuit, who also published a biography of John XXIII in his *sui generis* investigative (and iconoclastic) manner,[12] paints a detailed portrait of the man he considered to be "the first modern pope." Even more substantial is the biography which Eduardo de la Hera Buedo published in Spain in 2002.[13] It is not without merit; all the same, the author's bias is revealed by the fact that he devotes scarcely ten pages to those whom he calls "the crusaders of immobilism" (that is to say, not only Archbishop Lefebvre[14] and the traditionalists, but also members of other diverse "conservative" movements, including those in the Curia). Also noteworthy is that not a single

---

10   Giselda Adornato, *Cronologia dell'episcopato di Giovanni Battista Montini a Milano* (Brescia: Istituto Paul VI, 2002).

11   Peter Hebblethwaite, *Paul VI: The First Modern Pope* (London: Harper & Collins, 1993). Fr Peter Hebblethwaite (1930–1994) was a British Jesuit priest who left the priesthood to become a "Vaticanologist" or journalist who reports on the Holy See and the Roman Catholic Church. He taught French at Wadham College, Oxford, specializing in Georges Bernanos, and served as a correspondent of the *National Catholic Reporter* for the Second Vatican Council.

12   Peter Hebblethwaite, *John XXIII: Pope of the Century* (New York: Continuum, 2000).

13   Eduardo de la Hera Buedo, *La Noche transfigurada: biografía de Pablo VI* (Madrid: B. A. C., 2002). Fr Eduardo de la Hera Buedo is a diocesan priest of Palencia and has a Theology doctorate from the Pontifical Gregorian University. He has published many books about Paul VI.

14   Archbishop Marcel Lefebvre (1905–1991) was a French missionary for the Holy Ghost Fathers (Spiritans) in Gabon, Africa, bishop (then archbishop) of Dakar, Senegal (1947–1962), Apostolic Delegate for French Africa (1948–1959), bishop of Tulle, France (1962), superior general of the Holy Ghost Fathers (1962–1968). He was a leader in the *Coetus Internationalis Patrum* (International Group of Fathers), which comprised many traditionally-minded Council Fathers at Vatican II. He founded a seminary in 1970, which he moved to Écône, Switzerland in 1971. In 1970, he founded the Priestly Society of Saint Pius X (SSPX). He was excommunicated in 1988 for consecrating four bishops without papal mandate.

Introduction to the Second French Edition

chapter of this biography of almost nine hundred pages was devoted to the liturgical reforms initiated by Paul VI.

Much more significant in terms of advancing Spanish historiography on Paul VI's papacy is the very important collection published by Fr Vicente Carcel Orti in 1997.[15] Following on from Study Days dedicated to the same subject by the Paul VI Institute,[16] *Paul VI and Spain* provides a wealth of information and substantial documentation. Numerous episodes and situations relevant to the evolution of the Church in Spain during the papacy of Paul VI are clarified or brought fully to light. For example, the resistance of the Spanish episcopacy to the declaration of religious liberty in the last months of Vatican II is illuminated by the publication of a long letter which the bishops of Spain addressed to Paul VI (October 17, 1965) to express their "profound worry" and their fear of "tragic capitulations in a matter of doctrinal principles." On another front, we see that Paul VI's defiant attitude towards the regime of General Franco[17] endured until its end: for lack of an agreement between the Holy See and the Spanish state, nine dioceses were left without a head for up to two years until the death of Franco, whom the pope considered a dictator.

The Pontifical Commission for Latin America has published the testimonies of 151 Latin American bishops on Paul VI, who was the first pope to visit Latin America and who devoted considerable attention to the problems of development and evangelization on this continent.[18]

The Second Vatican Council has continued to be the focus of countless publications: books of testimonies (private diaries as well as previously published accounts) proliferate even now, as do historical studies.[19] All

---

15 Vicente Carcel Orti, *Pablo VI y España: Fidelidad, renovacion y crisis (1963–1978)* (Madrid: B. A. C., 1997). Fr Vicente Carcel Orti (1940–present) is a Spanish historian and priest. He is the author of works such as *The History of the Church in Valencia* (1986) and *The Religious Persecution in Spain during the Second Republic* (1990).

16 *Pablo VI y España*, Madrid, May 20, 1994 (Brescia: Istituto Paolo VI; Rome: Edizioni Studium, 1996).

17 General Francisco Franco (1892–1975) led the Nationalist forces to victory over the Republicans in 1939 and ruled Spain until his death, providing for the restauration of the monarchy with the coronation of Juan Carlos I.

18 *Papa Pablo VI, profeta de la evangelizacion: Testimonios de obispos latinoamericanos* (Madrid: Edibesa, 2003).

19 Amongst the testimonies, we will only cite the most important ones here: Yves Congar, *My Journal of the Council* (Collegeville, MN: Liturgical Press, 2012); Henri de Lubac, *Vatican Council Notebooks*, 2 vols. (San Francisco: Ignatius Press, 2015 and 2016); Hélder Camara, *Lettres conciliaires (1962–1965)*, 2 vols. (Paris: Cerf, 2006). Amongst the historical studies of the council dominates the five-volume set edited

confirm or clarify what was already known to be the role of Paul VI during the Council.

The influence of the thought of Jacques Maritain[20] at different points during Paul VI's life was emphasized in the first edition of this biography thanks to my findings in various unpublished sources. Soon afterwards, a more systematic study, by Philippe Chenaux, elucidated the connections between "Montinianism" and "Maritainism."[21] The influence of Maritain was also evident in Paul VI's social teaching, particularly surrounding the question of property. Beyond Maritain, the input of the Dominican Father Lebret[22] and the Jesuit Father Pierre Bigo[23] should be noted with respect to the first social encyclical of Paul VI, *Populorum Progressio* (1967).[24] The Roman Franciscan friar, Ermenegildo Lio,[25] should be considered principally responsible for preparing the famous encyclical *Humanæ Vitæ* (1968).[26]

The connections which G. B. Montini always maintained with the politico-intellectual milieu of Italian Christian Democracy have been illustrated by one of his "disciples," Giovanni Battista Scaglia,[27] successor

---

by Giuseppe Alberigo, *History of Vatican II* (Maryknoll, NY: Orbis/Leuven: Peeters, 1995–2006). Its conclusions, however, have been criticized: see notably Agostino Marchetto, *The Second Vatican Ecumenical Council: A Counterpoint for the History of the Council* (N.p.: University of Scranton Press, 2010). An interesting book regarding the history of Vatican II from an eyewitness writing in English is *The Inside Story of Vatican II* (formerly entitled *The Rhine Flows into the Tiber*) by Fr Ralph Wiltgen, SVD (Charlotte, NC: TAN, 2014).

20 Jacques Maritain (1882–1973) was a French philosopher and political critic and a leading exponent of Thomism. He wrote over sixty books, covering a huge philosophical and religious range. He played an important role in helping draft the Universal Declaration of Human Rights of 1948. Pope Paul VI considered making him a lay cardinal but Maritain rejected this proposal.

21 Philippe Chenaux, *Paul VI et Maritain: Les rapports du "montinianisme" et du "maritanism"* (Brescia: Istituto Paolo VI; Rome: Edizioni Studium, 1994). Philippe Chenaux (1959–present) is a Swiss historian who teaches modern and contemporary Church history at Lateran University.

22 Father Louis-Joseph Lebret (1897–1966) was a French Dominican, social scientist, economist, and philosopher.

23 Father Pierre Bigo (1906–1997) was a French Jesuit.

24 Mark G. Etling, *The Relevance of the Property Teaching of Pope Paul VI: An Ancient Teaching in a New Context* (San Francisco: Mellen Research University Press, 1993).

25 Fr Ermenegildo Lio (1920–1992), a highly respected theologian, published *Humanæ Vitæ e Infallibilità: il Concilio, Paolo VI e Giovanni Paolo II* (1986). He was also a university professor at the Pontifical University Antonianum.

26 Roger Aubert, review of *Paul VI: Le pape écartelé* by Yves Chiron, *Revue d'Histoire Ecclésiastique* (January-March 1997): 267.

27 Giovanni Battista Scaglia (1910–2006), was an Italian politician and author, who served in various national governmental positions between 1954 and 1972.

Introduction to the Second French Edition

to Aldo Moro[28] as president of the *Laureati* (Movement of Catholic Graduates), director of Edizioni Studium from 1949 to 1977, and minister in successive Christian Democratic governments during the sixties.[29]

Archbishop Pasquale Macchi, who served as Paul VI's personal secretary for more than twenty years, published a volume seven years ago that he insisted was neither a biography of Paul VI nor "the memoirs of his secretary."[30] Despite this claim, the historian will find useful material throughout the book, in addition to a detailed biographical chronology at the end of the volume, and a minute retrospective account of the teaching of Paul VI.[31]

To conclude, we cite the judgement of the Catholic philosopher Augusto Del Noce.[32] Following the death of Paul VI, he emphasized how this pope had had "to work in one of the most difficult and painful moments of the whole history of the Church," that of "the disappearance of the problem of God." Unlike his predecessors, Paul VI no longer had to confront an aggressive atheism "against God," but an atheism of indifference — a Western society "without God." In these circumstances, Paul VI did not demonstrate hesitance or prudence, according to Del Noce. He remained "inflexible" in the conservation of the faith and in

---

28   Aldo Moro (1916–1978) was an Italian politician and Prime Minister from 1963 to 1968 and from 1974 to 1976; he was assassinated by the Red Brigades, an Italian Communist terror organization. He is remembered for his "Historic Compromise," the political accommodation between the Christian Democracy and the Italian Communist Party in the 1970s.

29   Giovanni Battista Scaglia, *La stagione montiniana* (Rome: Edizioni Studium, 1993).

30   Pasquale Macchi, *Paolo VI nella sua parola* (Brescia: Morcelliana, 2001). Macchi (1923–2006) was the personal secretary of Paul VI from the time of the latter's installation as archbishop of Milan in 1954 until the pope's death in 1978. In 1988, Pope John Paul II consecrated him archbishop prelate *nullius* of Loreto, Italy.

31   Am I permitted to record an anecdote for posterity? An important Italian Catholic publisher wanted to translate the present book. A contract had been signed; an advance had been paid. After a few months the Italian publisher announced that it was canceling the project. In the meantime, I learned from Jean Guitton that Archbishop Macchi, who had read the book in French, had been strongly displeased with it. He judged the tone of the work to be too critical and reproached Jean Guitton, in a long letter, for having made revelations which have been reported in the work. Another Italian publisher, less pusillanimous, asked me to write the chapter on Paul VI in a history of the Church that he was publishing, a translation and continuation of the famous *Histoire de l'Église* of Hubert Jedin. See Yves Chiron, "Il Pontificato di Paolo VI," in *Storia della Chiesa* (Milan: Edizioni Jaca Book, 1995), 10:450–67.

32   Augusto Del Noce, "Il papato che è trascorso," *L'Europa*, August 1978. Reused in *Pensiero della Chiesa e filosofia contemporanea: Leone XIII, Paolo VI, Giovanni Paolo II* (Rome: Edizioni Studium, 2005). Del Noce (1910–1989) was an Italian philosopher who wrote extensively on Marxism and the secularization of the modern world.

reaffirming the principles of Catholic morality, even if this "doctrinal intransigence" was admittedly accompanied by a "broad practical tolerance," the appearance of non-resistance, and overly-rare public reactions to denounce errors or when fundamental principles had been called in question. In sum, Augusto Del Noce deems the pontificate of Paul VI "a pontificate of resistance and watchfulness," a watchfulness more religious than political or tactical "because such a watchfulness in the face of a world, more uncomprehending than hostile, demands a very profound faith." Paul VI gave priority to respecting individual consciences over defending the objectivity of truth, risking the impression that he had ceded ground to subjectivism and relativism; but "in fact, this respect for the individual conscience corresponds to a greater confidence in the truth than in man — the conviction that man, whatever he does, cannot escape the truth."

Yves Chiron
March 2008

TRANSLATOR'S NOTE

POPE PAUL VI IS OFTEN PORTRAYED AS A VICTIM, and some of his statements during the post-conciliar tempest show that he felt himself a victim. In support of this image, it is not uncommon to hear anecdotes such as the pope weeping when he discovered that his new liturgy suppressed the Octave of Pentecost—the implication being that Bugnini and others had duped him into these sweeping reforms. Whatever factual basis such stories may enjoy, the implication is false. Paul VI was, in many ways, his own worst enemy.

Another, and connected, image of the late pope is that he had a sickly nature and yet was a deeply spiritual person, a man who was profoundly misunderstood and who did not have the administrative force to drive against the wind and the waves. But this, too, is a false picture. Although he was excused from the majority of the required priestly formation on grounds of poor health, he certainly showed stamina in the plethora of charitable works, newspaper articles, trips, and political action that he accomplished during those years. In his papacy, we see a strange dichotomy between his authoritarian attitude toward those who could be grouped as conservatives and his endless benevolence and patience with those on the "left." As to his spirituality, his notes and letters show it to be emotional and immature. The glaring lack of solid theological foundation to his spiritual life assuredly goes back to the absence of a seminarian's normal spiritual formation. This void caused him to seek out and follow guides that appealed to his emotional tendencies, instead of enriching and elevating his soul with spiritual meat.

A third common idea about this pope is that the papacy was practically forced upon him. Again, this is believed presumably as a kind of justification for how poorly he handled the ecclesiastical crises after Vatican II. This is a double falsehood. He worked for decades to advance his ecclesiastical career, and it was his own reforms that caused much of the crisis. Now there can be no doubt that grave problems existed in the Church prior to the Second Vatican Council and that not all blame can be laid at Paul VI's feet. Nevertheless, it is equally true that his support of various persons and trends prior to the Council contributed greatly to the chaos that followed it.

With all that said, the purpose of this book is not to vilify Giovanni Battista Montini. As a serious scientific biography by Yves Chiron, an internationally recognized historian, the purpose of this book is to give the reader a true historical appreciation for the man as he was. Mr. Chiron does that in a way that no other biographer has done, by extensive communication with those who knew Paul VI personally. Most notably, he interviewed and corresponded with Jean Guitton, a French thinker and close friend of the pope, who was able to give unique insights into the thoughts and actions of Montini.

Pope Paul VI was badly formed, but he was neither a fool nor a puppet, although some did manipulate him. He was ambitious, but, from all accounts, he truly believed that he was working for the good of the Church and of souls. He defended priestly celibacy and upheld the sanctity of life; yet he simultaneously supported those who opposed the truth, while condemning those who held fast to orthodoxy. In short, he is a complex character, and the divisions in the Church reflect his internal division. Hence, he is rightly called the Divided Pope.

The original title of this biography, *Paul VI: Le pape écartelé*, is more telling than any English translation could be in so few words. Écartelé, in its literal sense, means "quartered," referring to the bloody mediaeval and early modern punishment (usually for high treason) by which a man's limbs were each tied to a separate horse (or team of horses) who then pulled his body apart into quarters. In a figurative sense, it indicates the state of mind of a person who is agonizingly torn between two or more tendencies or alternatives — an apt qualifier for a pope who, as this biography shows, was torn between a commitment to prodigious reform and an attachment to traditional doctrine and piety.

Numerous biographical and bibliographical notes have been added to this English edition. I would like to thank Miss Trinity Pate for her help in researching and writing the numerous biographical notes in this edition.

James Walther
Sexagesima Sunday
February 20, 2022

ABBREVIATIONS

AAS	Acta Apostolicæ Sedis (Acts of the Holy See)
ACI	Azione Cattolica Italiana (Italian Catholic Action)
ACLI	Associazioni Cristiane Lavoratori Italiani (Christian Associations of Italian Workers)
ACO	Action catholique ouvrière (Workers' Catholic Action)
ADSS	Actes et Documents du Saint-Siège relatif à la Seconde Guerre mondiale
AMAE	Archives du ministère des Affaires étrangères
CLN	Comitato di Liberazione Nazionale (National Liberation Committee)
DC	Democrazia Cristiana (Christian Democracy)
FUCI	Federazione universitaria cattolica italiana (Italian Catholic Federation of University Students)
GCI	Gioventù Cattolica Italiana (Italian Catholic Youth)
GUF	Gruppi Universitari Fascisti (Fascist University Group)
ICP	Institut Catholique de Paris
JOC	Jeunesse ouvrière chrétienne (Young Christian Workers)
LCISL	Libera Confederazione Italiana Sindacati Lavoratori (Free Italian Confederation of Trade Unions)
PPI	Partito Popolare Italiano (Italian People's Party)
OFM	Ordo Fratrum Minorum (Order of Friars Minor — Franciscans)
OP	Ordo Prædicatorum (Order of Preachers — Dominicans)
SJ	Societas Jesu (Society of Jesus — Jesuits)

PAUL VI CHRONOLOGY
(1897–1978)

September 26, 1897	Birth at Concesio in Northwestern Italy
Late Summer 1916	Seminary entry
January 18, 1919	Foundation of the PPI
November 21, 1919	Reception of the Cassock
November 30, 1919	First Clerical Tonsure
May 29, 1920	Priestly Ordination
December 9, 1922	Doctorate in Canon Law from the Seminary of Milan
November 1923	Chaplain of the Roman Circle of the FUCI
July 1924	Doctorate in Civil Law from the Lateran University
April 9, 1925	*Minutante* in the Vatican Secretariate of State
Late 1925	Named National Chaplain of the FUCI and Papal Chamberlain ("Monsignor")
February 11, 1929	Lateran Accords ending the "Roman Question"
July 8, 1931	Named Domestic Prelate of His Holiness
March 1933	Forced Resignation from the FUCI
December 1937	Substitute for the Section of Ordinary Affairs in the Vatican Secretariat of State
November 29, 1952	Named Pro-Secretary of State for Ordinary Ecclesiastical Affairs
December 12, 1954	Episcopal Consecration
November 5–25, 1957	Great Mission of Milan
December 15, 1958	Named Cardinal by Pope John XXIII
June 21, 1963	Papal Election
January 1964	Pilgrimage to the Holy Land
November 13, 1964	Resignation of the Papal Tiara
October 4, 1965	Visit to the UN
March 26, 1967	Encyclical Letter *Populorum Progressio*
June 30, 1968	Credo of the People of God
July 25, 1968	Encyclical Letter *Humanæ Vitæ*
April 3, 1969	Promulgation of the New Mass
August 6, 1978	Death at the Vatican

I

The Child of Brescia

THE MONTINI FAMILY, AS THEIR NAME IMPLIES, are mountain people. In the fifteenth century their name first appeared in Brescia, a town at the foot of the Italian Alps, between Milan and Verona. Sons of the prosperous landowners of Olzano, in the Valsabbia valley, they had come down from the hills to make their fortunes in the plain. Soon the Montini were numbered among Brescia's more prominent citizens, as lawyers, doctors, and notaries. Some Montini also entered religious life, as priests, brothers, and sisters.

The future pope's branch of the family was established north of Brescia, at Sarezzo, from the seventeenth century. Over the generations, these Montini mainly practiced medicine. At the beginning of the nineteenth century, Gaetano Montini, also a doctor, moved with his family from Sarezzo to Concesio (about ten miles from Brescia). He was soon successful enough to buy an impressive house surrounded by many fields. This purchase made the Montini the largest landowners in the area. Gaetano commissioned a large family tree that also depicted his lands.[1] At the foot of the tree was the Montini family coat of arms: three mountains topped by three fleur-de-lys. Giovanni Battista Montini would adopt a modified version of this emblem as his episcopal and then papal arms.

In 1830, Lodovico Montini, the grandfather of the future pope, was born at Concesio. Since the end of the Napoleonic wars, Brescia and its surroundings had been subject to Austria. Ludovico actively participated in the two principal uprisings of the Brescians against the Austrians, in 1848 and 1849. But it was not until 1859, and the intervention of the French army along with the kingdom of Piedmont (after their victories at Montebello, Magenta, and Solferino), that Lombardy was freed from Austrian rule. In 1861, Victor Emmanuel II[2] was proclaimed the Italian

---

1   Both the map and the framed family tree still hang today in the Montini house in Concesio.
2   King Victor Emmanuel II (1820–1878) was the eldest son of Charles Albert, Prince of Carignano, and Maria Teresa of Austria. He bore the title of Duke of Savoy until 1849, when his father lost the First Italian War of Independence (1848–1849) against the Austrians and abdicated the throne of Sardinia-Piedmont in favor of his son. He appointed as his Prime Minister Camillo Benso, Count of Cavour, who masterminded

king. The unification of the kingdom of Italy was accomplished in 1870 after the invasion and annexation of Rome and the Papal States.

A MIDDLE-CLASS CATHOLIC FAMILY

Ludovico settled as a doctor in Brescia, and married Francesca Buffali,[3] with whom he had six children. The surviving portrait shows a man with a long face and wide-set ears, characteristics which would be passed further down in the family. He died young, at forty. Francesca provided for the education of their children by herself. She was compelled to sell part of their land at Concesio to support the family and help pay for the children's education. The eldest, Giorgio[4] (father of the future pope), broke with family tradition by studying law instead of medicine.

Giorgio had barely completed his studies when he was asked to edit the city's Catholic newspaper, Il Cittadino di Brescia. He was twenty-one years old. There was a hard battle to be fought against the city's liberal and radical newspapers. The occupation of Rome and the annexation of the Papal States by the kingdom of Italy had not been accepted by the pope. Catholics were given the political keyword: *non expedit* (it is not expedient): Catholics were not to participate, as voters or elected officials, in national political life. To do so would be to recognize the new Italian state.

The pope's prohibition on participating in Italian political life inspired initiatives including the Catholic Movement (*Movimento cattolico*). Since

---

the "Risorgimento" of the Italian unification. Napoleon III of France supported the Second Italian War of Independence which ended in the annexation of Lombardy by Piedmont-Sardinia. From the south, Giuseppe Garibaldi overthrew the Kingdom of the Two Sicilies in the Expedition of the Thousand (1860–1861), giving Victor Emmanuel II the occasion for having himself proclaimed King of Italy by a series of plebiscites in the occupied lands. He did not dare, however, to proceed with the conquest of the Papal States which, thanks to the insistence of the pious Empress Eugène of France, Emperor Napoleon III was protecting. After the French defeat in the Franco-Prussian war, the French forces withdrew and the revolutionary forces entered Rome on September 20, 1870, with Pope Pius IX (Pio Nono) ordering his volunteer soldiers, the Zouaves, to give only a symbolic resistance. It is interesting to note that after claiming the crown of Italy the king did not renumber himself as Victor Emmanuel I of Italy, showing that the "unification" of Italy was rather its conquest by Piedmont-Sardinia.

3   Francesca Montini was the paternal grandmother of the future Pope Paul VI. She was born Buffali and sought to implant a love of Catholicism in each of her grandchildren.

4   Giorgio Montini (1860–1943) was an Italian journalist and politician who was the father of the future Pope Paul VI. He was excluded from government politics in 1926 as he sided against Mussolini and his Fascist party. After this, he moved to Concesio, where he lived out the remainder of his life in private, although he still published some writings on Catholic ideas.

Catholics could not defend their ideas in Parliament, they had to work on the ground, in social, cultural, and educational domains. Giorgio Montini, energetic and enterprising, quickly became one of the principal representatives, or "workers," of the Catholic Movement in Brescia. This involved countering socialist and liberal "philanthropy," and defending the rights of Catholics.

Over time, and with the support of his diocesan bishop, and financial assistance from his friends, Giorgio instituted soup kitchens, the "Saint Vincent Dormitory" for sheltering the destitute, and a consultation office to give legal and administrative advice, provide assistance to workers and peasants, and otherwise attract them away from socialist unions. In the years following his marriage, he would be among the founders of Catholic Labor Unions, a publishing house, a weekly paper for families, and a bank.[5]

Beyond these enterprises, his specifically religious activities included organizing pilgrimages to Castiglione (birthplace of Saint Aloysius Gonzaga) and Rome. During a pilgrimage to the Holy City, he made the acquaintance of Giuditta Alghisi.[6] She was originally from Verolavecchia, a village about twenty miles to the south of Brescia, and had lost her parents at a very young age. She had been sent to a religious boarding school at Milan where, in addition to a solid religious formation, she learned to play the piano, sing, dance, and paint. Also, she had been able to spend summer vacations in Chambéry, where she became familiar with French language and literature. When she and Giorgio met, Giuditta Alghisi was eighteen years old and still under the authority of a guardian. This guardian, a radical, was little inclined to allow her to marry a Catholic of strong convictions like Giorgio Montini.

On July 17, 1895, Giuditta reached the age of majority; on the 18th the marriage banns were proclaimed; on August 1, Giorgio and Giuditta were married. Even as he set about starting a family, Giorgio Montini continued to engage in politics. At last, with the agreement of ecclesiastical authorities, in this same year 1895 an alliance between Catholics and moderates in the administrative elections permitted the former to take their places on the city council of Brescia. Giorgio Montini had been, with Giuseppe Tovini,[7] the leader in the electoral campaign. He

---

5 Antonio Fappani, *Giorgio Montini* (Rome: Edizioni Cinque Luni, 1974).
6 Giuditta Montini (1874–1943) was the wife of Giorgio Montini and the mother of the future Pope Paul VI. Her maiden name was Giuditta Alghisi; they were married on August 1, 1895.
7 Giuseppe Tovini (1841–1897) was an Italian banker and lawyer who cofounded

was among the elected. Two years later, the death of Tovini would make of him the head of the Catholic Movement Party in Brescia.

Paul VI's father was simultaneously a journalist, a politician, and a prominent business leader. As François Saint-Pierre remarked,[8] "Paul VI is the first modern pope to come from a financial and political background." He was born September 26, 1897 in Concesio, on the property which his father had inherited. The first son, Lodovico, had been born the preceding year, and a third was born in 1900.

The child was baptized on September 30 at the church of Pieve di Concesio; the same day that Thérèse of the Child Jesus,[9] for whom he would have a great devotion, died in Lisieux. In honor of his deceased maternal grandfather, he was named Giovanni Battista, but soon the family would typically call him Battista (even as a priest, he would sign his letters "Don Battista"). As was customary with middle-class families in Brescia, the newborn was entrusted to a wet-nurse in the countryside. In Sacca di Nave, near Concesio, with hills covered in vineyards and chestnut trees, he was entrusted to Clorina Zanotti, who already had four children. He stayed with her for fourteen months, until he had learned to walk, then his parents brought him back to Brescia. Of a weak constitution, he gave signs that his health would always be fragile. Sickness would mark all of his childhood and youth.

At Brescia, a city which then counted fifty thousand inhabitants, Giorgio Montini was one of the most prominent citizens. His many activities kept him long away from home. His mother, who lived with the family, and his wife primarily looked after the education of his three sons — an education marked by a triple seal: the sense of family, religion, and culture. From their earliest childhood, the children's education was founded on the stories of the primitive Church and the lives of the martyrs that their grandmother recounted to them. During the summer and at Eastertide, they visited Concesio and Verolavecchia.

At Concesio they had a large two-storied manor house. The main section was reserved for the Montini family, with a more modest wing for the farmers who looked after the estate as well as for the servants. Despite its rustic appearance, the interiors were cozy, with paintings,

---

various Italian banks. He also became a member of the Secular Franciscan Order and was declared as having lived a life of heroic virtue by Pope John Paul II, who declared him Venerable in 1995.
8 François Saint-Pierre (1917–2010) was a French Catholic journalist and writer.
9 St. Thérèse of the Child Jesus and the Holy Face ("The Little Flower," 1873–1897) was a French Discalced Carmelite nun, beatified and canonized by Pope Pius XI in 1923 and 1925, respectively.

beautiful furniture, and decorated ceilings. Servants looked after the family. The great interior courtyard, planted with some evergreens and flowerbeds, offered a view over the orchards and fields of the property, which was surrounded by a distant stone wall. Further away were the pleasant slopes of the Alpine foothills. The Montini family would go there for relaxation and recreation and learnt to love the mountains.

At Verolavecchia, the "Dosso," the property Mrs. Montini inherited, was even more charming. There was a large two-storied square house with lovely arches along the facade. Verolavecchia is on flat land, with rich soil from dried-up swamps. The farms and the vineyard were entrusted to a farmer; the house was looked after by a steward, Giovanni Vergine, of whom Battista would always retain fond memories. In Battista's eyes he personified rustic wisdom. He taught Battista to love nature and to have a precise knowledge of insects, birds, and of mushrooms.[10] Years later, when Cardinal Montini, then-Sostituto (Substitute) for General Affairs to the Vatican's Secretariat of State, learned that his old Vergine was dying, he wrote to him, and asked Pope Pius XII to send him his blessing.

The childhood of a pope should not be idealized more than anybody else's. Lodovico Montini admitted that Battista "had a very difficult character" as a child.[11]

A HAPHAZARD EDUCATION

In autumn 1902 Battista began his studies at the Cesare Arici Institute in Brescia. This Jesuit-run high school had been founded in 1882 by Giuseppe Tovini in opposition to the local state school, the *Arnaldo*. Soon afterwards the government closed the Catholic school; after four years of protracted legal battles, and a journalistic campaign led by Giorgio Montini in *Il Cittadino*, its doors were reopened. The Catholics of Brescia remained close to "their" school; the Montini family would never have dreamed of sending their sons anywhere else.

At school Battista made his first best friend, Andrea Trebeschi.[12] They were born only twenty days apart. A class photograph has survived showing the two boys, side by side, in black smocks. Battista is taller than the other, but sickly in appearance. He grew too fast and developed a heart condition: at the end of two years, Battista would have to interrupt his

---

10   See the few childhood memories recounted by Jean Guitton, *Dialogues avec Paul VI*.
11   Statement quoted by his son, Giorgio Montini, "Mon oncle le pape" [My uncle the pope], *La Documentation catholique*, January 17, 1971.
12   Andrea Trebeschi (1897–1945) was an Italian lawyer and author, born in Brescia. He was regarded as a protagonist of the Resistance.

studies. He lost touch with his best friend Andrea, with whom he would not reconnect until just before the war. Together they would go through the first major intellectual and spiritual experiences of Battista's life.

During Battista's first years at Cesare Arici he became familiar with the Congregation of Santa Maria della Pace (more commonly called "la Pace"). Spiritual descendants of Saint Philip Neri,[13] the fathers of la Pace served several churches in Brescia and in the surrounding region. They were to have a profound impact on Battista's life. The la Pace fathers set up programs that attracted many pupils from the Cesare Arici school. Battista and his brothers eagerly took part. Near the church of Santa Maria della Pace, a large paved area planted with trees provided an ideal playground, equipped with benches, swings, and other amusements. For the older children there were other activities (la Pace owned a gymnasium), but also retreats and conferences were organized, always in the spirit of liberty and non-conformism that characterized Oratorian spirituality.[14]

When Battista was obliged to interrupt his studies for the first time, his mother made him keep up with his academic work at home so that he was not put back a year when he returned to school. Mrs. Montini always followed her sons' studies attentively. She would regularly read them French books aloud; Battista later claimed to have learnt French from *Jeanne d'Arc* by Gabriel Hanotaux.[15] He would also say that he had learned "recollection," the spiritual practice of attending to the presence of God in the soul, from his mother. A devout believer, Third Order Franciscan, and member of several other pious congregations, as well as a daily Mass-goer (along with her husband), Giuditta Montini revealed to her son what the interior life could be.

Battista came into contact with great spiritual writers early. His grandmother was devoted to Saint Francis de Sales, while his mother read writers ranging from Bossuet[16] to Saint Thérèse of Lisieux. At school,

---

13 St Philip Neri (1515–1595) was an Italian priest who founded the Congregation of the Oratory, a society of secular clergy. Known as the "Second Apostle of Rome," he was one of the most influential figures of the Counter-Reformation.

14 Oratorian spirituality is marked by private prayer in common (The Little Oratory), community life, stability, devotion to the Blessed Sacrament and to the Blessed Virgin Mary. An Oratorian does not take vows; promising to live for the rest of his life in the Oratory in which he has entered, he strives after the evangelical counsels of poverty, chastity, and obedience through a voluntary observance.

15 Gabriel Hanotaux, *Jeanne d'Arc* (Paris: Hachette, 1911). Hanotaux (1853–1944) was a French statesman and historian who studied history at the École des Chartres. In 1879, he entered the ministry of foreign affairs and over time rose through the diplomatic service.

16 Bishop Jacques-Bénigne Bossuet, the "Eagle of Meaux" (1627–1704), from Dijon

spiritual exercises were frequently conducted. In the middle of the playground, a statue of the Virgin stands even today, surrounded by a flowerbed. A Marian congregation was organized, to maintain pupils' fervor for the Virgin Mary and discipline their behavior by means of prayer and resolutions. Battista, a pious, serious student (or at least he tried to be), would one day become a Vatican Secretary and Prefect. He lived at school and at home in an atmosphere marked by seriousness, respect, and moderate piety. Among the first written lines from the future Paul VI to have come down to us is a note, written in 1904, for his father's birthday. Battista — he was not yet even seven years old — promised to work hard in school, to "be rude to the domestic servants" no more, to be good with everybody, and not to talk back to his mother.[17]

For the first few years of his formal education, young Montini's academic record, haphazard though it was, seemed encouraging. His report card for the first trimester of the 1909 academic year has been preserved. It shows a hardworking student, with the following results (on a scale of one to ten): 10 in conduct, work habits, courtesy, and catechism; 8 in Italian, Latin, arithmetic, history, and geography; 7 in penmanship. Similar grades merited his inscription on the school's honor roll twice. His classmates nicknamed him "the grind" (le bûcheur, literally the woodchopper — one who has to work hard to get good grades). But his studies had to be intermittently interrupted because of health worries. In June 1910, he was not able to sit for final exams, nor in December of the following year, and in the spring of 1911 he was forced to spend several weeks in the countryside, at Dosso, to rest. His parents decided therefore to withdraw him from school and have him take private lessons so that he might sit his final high-school exams as an independent candidate, which he finally did after some delay.

It is said that as a student, he rarely took part in games during recess, and preferred to withdraw to the chapel to pray; though this is not attested in surviving archival materials. Is this a stereotypical impression of what a future pope ought to be like, or the habitual attitude of a feeble child who was naturally reserved to the point of stuffiness? It is hard to say. Some of his classmates remembered a tall, distant, forbidding boy who spoke "like a dictionary." His brother Francesco[18] attested:

(France), was bishop of Meaux from 1681 and a renowned orator, theologian, and French stylist under Louis XIV. He is particularly remembered for his funeral orations.
17   G. B. Montini, Lettere ai familiari, 2:993. All the other letters to his family which we will cite hereafter are taken from this minutely detailed edition.
18   Francesco Montini (1900–1971) is one of the two brothers of Giovanni Battista Montini. Francesco became a physician.

His great quality is silence, self-mastery, self-control, just like my father. I remember that my mother, who was herself very reserved, would say to my brother Giovanni Battista: "But, Giovanni Battista, say what you think, don't keep silent like you do!"... My brother has always been a silent man.[19]

BIRTH OF A VOCATION

Paul VI left neither a personal diary nor an autobiography, only some stray notes, written irregularly at different periods of his life after his ordination to the priesthood. These permit only occasional glimpses here and there of the state of his soul. It is thus fairly difficult to determine the exact moment when his priestly vocation arose. Was it the fruit of long maturation or was it a sudden decision following some event? According to Jean Guitton, Paul VI claimed to have dreamt in his childhood and adolescence of "all the vocations: lawyer, writer, journalist."[20] The example of his father, an enterprising, energetic defender of the Catholic cause, must have led him to believe that all career paths were potentially open to him.

All the same, he was surrounded by religious sentiments that would have planted the seeds of a clerical vocation. Perhaps the first was in 1903 when Battista heard his parents announce: "The pope is dead." It was Leo XIII.[21] For a child not even six years old, but who was at least aware of a pope, the head of the Church, for whom one prayed at every Mass, this was, he would later say, "profoundly moving." Four years later, in May 1907, he was similarly moved when the whole family went to Rome, visited the catacombs where the first Christians celebrated the Mass, and were received by another pope, Pius X.[22] The

---

19 Quoted by Jean Guitton, *Journal de ma vie*, 555.
20 Quoted by Jean Guitton, in an interview with the author, May 11, 1991.
21 Pope Leo XIII (1810–1903) was the oldest reigning pope and had the third-longest pontificate: February 20, 1878 to July 20, 1903. With the encyclical *Rerum Novarum* (1891), he defined many fundamental worker's rights while supporting free enterprise and property rights, thus opposing both socialism and *laissez-faire* capitalism. Some of his other major encyclicals are *Aeterni Patris* (1879) on Christian philosophy and the restoration of Thomism, *Arcanum Divinæ* (1880) on Christian marriage, *Humanum Genus* (1884) on Freemasonry, *Immortale Dei* (1885) on the Christian constitution of States, and *Providentissimus Deus* (1893) on the study of Sacred Scripture.
22 Pope Pius X (1835–1914) was born Giuseppe Melchiorre Sarto and was head of the Catholic Church from 1903 to 1914. He strongly defended the Church's doctrine against the Modernist heresy. He led the creation of the first central *Code of Canon Law* (published by his successor in 1917) and promoted Thomism as the core philosophical method to be taught in Catholic institutions. He promoted the

following month, Battista made his First Communion at Brescia and was confirmed two weeks later.

Also in 1907, the Montini family packed up and moved to no. 17 via delle Grazie, a beautiful three-storied house, with a large portico at the front featuring an entrance for horse-drawn carriages, and private apartments on every floor, where Battista's paternal grandmother and other members of the extended family would live with the Montinis. One façade of the new house looked out over the Church of Santa Maria delle Grazie. The church was dear to the hearts of Brescia's citizens because it housed a sanctuary of the Virgin where at every moment of the day they loved to come to pray and recollect. The ex-voto offerings attached in the sanctuary bear witness to the fervor with which graces were requested and received. Giuditta Montini would often bring her children, and in particular Battista, to this sanctuary.

The proximity of such a place of fervent piety must have influenced the young Battista's religious development. He was often compelled to stay at home because of the state of his health. One other such place would become, during these years, one of his favorite spots.

At Chiari, fifteen miles to the east of Brescia, a Benedictine community was founded. The monks had been driven from France a few years before by the Third Republic's laws concerning religious congregations. They moved into an old convent — property of the Menna family, friends of the Montinis. The exiled French monks would soon develop strong ties with the Montini family. Even after becoming a priest, then an archbishop, and finally the pope, Battista maintained contact with this monastic community, long after its return to France. According to a well-known anecdote, the religious brother who was in charge of altar boys for solemn ceremonies at the monastery refused to allow Battista to serve because he was "too tall." On the other hand, the young Montini often attended Compline and stayed at the abbey's guesthouse.

In 1973, when receiving some Benedictine abbots at the Vatican, Paul VI confided to them that the seed of his vocation was planted at Chiari. Recalling the pure melodies of the monastic offices' Gregorian chants, he told them: "I was as in ecstasy; it was there, without a doubt, that God planted in my soul the initial yearning for a life consecrated to His service."

---

restauration of Gregorian chant with the instruction *Tra le Sollecitudini* (1903). Some of his major documents against modernism include *Lamentabili Sane* (1907), *Pascendi Dominici Gregis* (1907), and the Oath Against Modernism, *Sacrorum Antistitum* (1910). The obligation for all clerics and Catholic theological and philosophical professors to take the oath was suppressed by Paul VI in 1967.

It is possible to determine with some precision the time when he felt this call to serve God. Ludovico[23] bore witness that it was before the summer of 1913 that his brother had decided to become a priest. This same year 1913, in July, Battista sat his final exams for secondary school at the State High School of Chiari. This school had been chosen to examine him as an independent student, because it had a reputation for being less academically strict than the school in Brescia. Perhaps Giorgio Montini was also less well-known at Chiari as a Catholic public figure, and therefore less susceptible to incurring examiners' prejudice against his son.

At Chiari, Battista stayed with the Menna family. No doubt he must have gone a few times to the monastery. Is it then during this month of July that he first knew his "initial yearning" for a life consecrated to God? Perhaps. Moreover, one of his friends, Lionello Nardini,[24] was going to enter the seminary of Brescia a few months later. The two young men's conversations would not have passed over this event, which might have also made Battista think about his future.

The following September, Giorgio Montini, who was on retreat with the fathers of la Pace near Brescia, wrote to his son counselling him to tell his plans to one of these priests: Father Caresana.[25] Battista, by this date, had therefore already confided in his father, and followed his advice. We know that at one point he wanted to become a monk. He had voiced this desire to the abbot of the monastery of Chiari, Dom Christopher Gauthey, a venerable monk then over eighty years old. He had also talked about it with Father Denys Buenner, one of the father guestmasters who had become his confessor. The two dissuaded the young Battista from entering the monastery; they thought his fragile health would never survive the rigors of the Benedictine Rule. But they encouraged him to persevere in his vocation. Thus, the fathers of la Pace had a determining influence on him in his youth.

Among the fathers of la Pace, Battista's first spiritual director was Father Baroni. A priest with an austere spirituality — he would soon leave la Pace

---

[23] Ludovico Montini (1896–1990; name also often spelled Lodovico) was the elder brother of Giovanni Battista Montini. He was an Italian politician, a Christian Democrat Senator and a member of the Constituent Assembly. In the 1940s, he was sought after by the Fascist police and he sought refuge with his brother in Rome.
[24] Lionello Nardini (1897–1918) was a classmate of Montini's at the Cesare Arici Institute (1913) and entered the seminary. He was summoned to fight in the First World War (1916), but towards the end he became ill and died in hospital.
[25] Fr Paolo Caresana (1882–1973) was ordained in 1906. He founded the diocesan Good Press (1913) and after the First World War focused his efforts on the organization of the female Catholic Youth but had to leave Brescia during the Nazi occupation.

The Child of Brescia

to enter a monastery — he scarcely had time to exercise any influence over the young Montini. This was not the case for Fathers Bevilacqua[26] and Caresana, who would remain his confidants and spiritual directors for decades, right up until the first years of his pontificate.

Father Bevilacqua had completed part of his studies in Belgium and finished a doctorate in political and social sciences at the University of Louvain, where he had been a student of the future Cardinal Mercier.[27] In Belgium, there had also been the Abbey of Mont-César, which had begun to plunge into what is called the Liturgical Movement.[28] Upon his return to Italy, Father Bevilacqua entered the congregation of *la Pace*, in 1906, and was ordained a priest in 1908. Engaged at the same time in the youth apostolate, the Liturgical Movement, and the fight for the defense of the liberty of teaching, he quickly became one of the outstanding figures of Catholicism in Brescia. Sometimes he summed up his program in two words: "Christ and reality."

Father Caresana had entered *la Pace* fairly late, after having ministered as a parish priest. It is not over-analyzing the situation to suggest that, as much as the bonds between all three of these men were tight, Bevilacqua exercised a fundamentally intellectual influence on Montini, while Caresana was his spiritual father (he would serve as his confessor until the end of the 1950s).

It seems certain that Battista did not decide immediately on the secular clergy, even after renouncing his desire to enter a Benedictine novitiate. He felt a certain nostalgia for it, and once he had become a priest, he would again be tempted to become a monk. In 1913, when he felt his first calling to the consecrated life, he was only sixteen years old. Father Caresana, having become his spiritual director, counseled him to reflect calmly on this choice of life and to finish his secondary studies first. But henceforth

---

26 Card. Giulio Bevilacqua (1881–1965) was created a cardinal in 1965 by Paul VI. Another Oratorian and a friend of both, Fr Louis Bouyer, was of the opinion that Father Bevilacqua kept Montini in the secular clergy: see *The Memoirs of Louis Bouyer: From Youth and Conversion to Vatican II, the Liturgical Reform, and After*, trans. John Pepino (Brooklyn: Angelico Press, 2005), 250.

27 Card. Désiré-Joseph Mercier (1851–1926) was a Belgian cardinal and a noted scholar who was the archbishop of Mechelen (1906–1926). He is famous for being an icon of resistance to German occupation in the First World War, encouraging people to remain positive despite the circumstances. He was an active promoter of the ecumenical movement.

28 The leader of the Liturgical Movement at Mont-César was Dom Lambert Beauduin, OSB. For more about the Liturgical Movement, see Roberto de Mattei, *The Second Vatican Council: An Unwritten Story*, trans. Patrick T. Brannan, SJ, Michael J. Miller, and Kenneth D. Whitehead (Fitzwilliam, NH: Loreto Publications, 2012).

his existence would take on an orientation that he did not question again. This vocation was strengthened by new acquaintances and new friendships.

In August 1914, a new pastor arrived at Pieve de Concesio, Father Francesco Galloni.[29] He had just come from seminary and had only been a priest for a month. He soon came into contact with the Montini family, who often attended his church when they were in Concesio. It seems that Battista, dreaming of consecrating his life to God, quickly became friends with this young priest who was no more than seven years his senior. Their common vocation cemented a tight bond between the adolescent and the young pastor. In the first letter which he wrote to Fr Galloni, Montini called him his "older brother."[30]

Another friend: Andrea Trebeschi, with whom he had reconnected. That same year, 1914, Battista told him that he had decided to become a priest. "He presented to me," Trebeschi wrote, "a long story of love and tears: the Redemption. I understood that it was the way, the truth, the life." His own physical sufferings, and human misery in general, appeared to him henceforth in a different light; they were associated with the figure of the "Martyr of Calvary." Battista ended his letter: "I prayed for you this morning to our common friend, Jesus Christ, at the moment of Holy Communion.... Please love me always, your friend Battista Montini."[31]

This letter is not only a testament to a firmly determined vocation (even if it would still take several years to come to fruition), it also demonstrates Montini's spiritual condition at this time: a woe-filled, sentimental, emotionalist Christianity. Also evident is one of his abiding character traits throughout his life, a constant need for friendship and relationships, and to love and to be loved; love of Christ, love of friends, love of the world, love of mankind. At the end of his life, he would say to John Magee,[32] one of his personal secretaries: "I am first of all pardoned by God. I ought never to condemn anyone; I should always be the minister of pardon."[33]

---

29 Msgr Francesco Galloni (1890–1976) was the apostolic delegate to Bulgaria and founded the institute Pro Oriente in Sofia, Bulgaria in 1920.
30 The correspondence G. B. Montini–F. Galloni has been published in *Notiziario* 8 (May 1984): 7–28.
31 G. B. Montini, letter of November 30, 1914, in *Lettere a un giovane amico*, 22–23. All his letters to Trebeschi which we will cite hereafter are taken from this edition.
32 Bishop John Magee (1936–) was the Irish bishop of Cloyne (1987–2010), but he resigned following a scandal. He also served as a missionary priest in Nigeria and remains the only person to have been private secretary to three popes, Paul VI, John Paul I, and John Paul II.
33 John Magee, "La vita quotidiana di Paolo VI," in *Paul VI et la modernité dans l'Église* (Rome: École Française de Rome, 1984), 137.

THE WAR

Battista Montini belonged to a generation of men who reached their twentieth birthdays during the Great War. He himself would not participate in combat; his uncertain health twice delayed his entry into the barracks. When the war erupted in 1914, Italy was one of the only European nations to proclaim itself neutral and stay on the sidelines. Giorgio Montini, in his newspaper, supported this political stance. Battista, however, under the influence of Father Bevilacqua, soon appeared to favor an Italian intervention in the war on the side of the French.

Father Bevilacqua, a supporter of the Belgian side, considered Italian participation in the conflict necessary to repel the invading German force. Moreover, a great number of Italians resented the Austro-Hungarian Empire, which had occupied the north of the country for decades, and still maintained control over the Tyrol. In 1915, in response to treaties with her new allies, Italy finally entered the war. In addition to his brother, Ludovico, many of Battista's friends were mobilized, or else volunteered: Trebeschi, Nardini, Father Galloni, Father Bevilacqua, and others still. He viewed their enlistment with commingled enthusiasm and bitterness, and wrote to them regularly. Yet in a small polygraphed newsletter which he started with some friends during 1915, *Parvæ Favillæ* (Small Embers), the tone was patriotic even if the students who edited it did not take themselves seriously.[34]

The war years were for Montini years not of indecision but of dispersion. There had been the war, its alarms, and the charitable initiatives which it demanded. He had to complete his secondary studies, which he did with difficulty. Not least there was his desire to become a priest, and perhaps his impatience to consecrate himself to God. In August 1915, he went on retreat in a Camaldolese hermitage about a hundred miles from Brescia. Father Caresana and Father Galloni accompanied him. Father Caresana preached on a few occasions. The conversations with the two priests, the solitary meditations, and walks across the magnificent surrounding countryside enthralled him and reinforced his determination.

Upon his return to school, he picked up his solitary studies again with more or less difficulty. They "took a disagreeable turn," he admitted to Trebeschi. One day, overwhelmed by academic work that never seemed to

---

34 Montini consigned one of his first public writings to this ephemeral vacation project. A few months before, in November 1914, he had already published a small newspaper, *Numero unico*, for the inauguration of a travelling library. Fathers Caresana and Bevilacqua, Andrea Trebeschi and others collaborated.

end, he threw his mathematics notebook out the window. He preferred, he wrote to the same Trebeschi, to immerse himself in "the poetry of emotions": the beauty of nature that tells of the work of the Creator, the starry sky or the full moon that speaks to the heart. The states of his soul could be summarized in "a continual thirst for happiness." He would have liked to find the same happiness in the sacrifice of self.

It was not until June 1916 that he passed his *maturità classica* (the equivalent of our high school diploma) at the state school of Brescia, without honors, after a first attempt in February. Illness had kept him these last two years from being able to study consistently. During the following July he spent a few weeks by the seaside at Viareggio with a few other young men under the supervision of one of the *la Pace* Fathers. He spent his time playing in the water (but had to give up on learning to swim because he did not have the physical strength). "The only thing I do not do," he wrote jokingly to his mother, "is do something." He also thought about the young men of his age who were then at the front. "I have for them," he wrote, "a thought of love, of gratitude, of compassion, of prayer." Upon his return, this sickly young man, who had fallen behind in his studies, finally entered seminary.

The Santangelo seminary at Brescia (today the seat of the diocesan pastoral center and of the Paul VI Institute) is a seventeenth-century palace with a sober exterior other than its two beautiful porches and ornate windows. The more solemn interior features a monumental staircase and lovely frescoes from the eighteenth century. The day he entered seminary, Battista wrote to Trebeschi: "This does not change my exterior life in any way."

In truth he was never an ordinary seminarian. The bishop of Brescia and the rector of the seminary exceptionally allowed him not to undergo the usual seminary life by boarding there; his parents made it clear that the state of his health could not take it. It is, therefore, as a day-student that he attended classes, in ordinary street clothes. But soon enough he was not able even to come to seminary. Twenty hours of classes per week, along with preparatory work and the effort of digesting all that information was beyond his strength. Thus, he prepared himself for the priesthood alone at home, with the assistance of various clergy.

To be ordained a priest without having undergone a seminary formation was, at the time, extraordinary. In the intellectual, moral, and religious formation of Montini, the fact is of great importance. He did not receive the Scholastic education which then formed the basis of ecclesiastical learning.[35] Nor did he have any experience of community life, which instills certain lifelong rules, disciplines, and habits; nor had he experienced the separation from the world which years of seminary firmly fixed into one's being. Battista forged his own discipline of life for himself. Intellectually he would remain the autodidact that he had been before he entered seminary; in preparing for the priesthood, he continued to mix personal and profane reading with books of a properly religious nature.[36]

The initiatives Battista undertook during the last two years of the war are characteristic of the tight bonds which he had maintained with society outside the seminary. Battista and his brother, although they were high schoolers at the time, had been part of the Alessandro Manzoni[37] Association, destined to regroup Catholic university students in opposition to another movement of secular inspiration. Battista, from 1917 onwards, was to take active part in the association, substituting for its president, Trebeschi, then far from Brescia.

In February he initiated the project of a "soldier's library," in an "apostolic spirit," he wrote to Trebeschi. The idea was to send good books to soldiers who found themselves on the frontlines, to entertain them during quieter periods, but also to uphold a Christian spirit in an environment where disordered behaviors are frequent and numerous. His father, a member of the administrative council of the *Banco San Paolo* (Bank of Saint Paul), obtained financial aid, and Queriniana Editions gave them books for free or sold them at a discount. The selected works were distributed to the soldiers by members of the association who were themselves on the front. Lectures were organized to collect funds.

Under the circumstances, this seminarian who lived outside the seminary displayed energy and an impressive capacity for organization. Equally,

---

35 Had he methodically read, at this time or later, Saint Thomas Aquinas? Opinions are divided. Msgr Macchi, who was secretary of Paul VI from 1955 to 1978, affirms that, with regard to the *Summa Theologiæ*, "few bishops have read and annotated it the way he did" (quoted by J. Prévotat, *Paul VI et la modernité*, 112). But Msgr Macchi has a "hagiographical" vision of Paul VI... Jean Guitton, on the other hand, says that he realized that "Paul VI had not read Saint Thomas" (interview with the author, May 11, 1991). Clearly, he means "read" in the sense of systematic in-depth study.
36 At the Paul VI Institute in Brescia, the better part of the pope's library has been preserved. From his youth, Montini annotated books as he read them. Upon becoming pope, he continued to read certain works and to introduce handwritten notes in the margins. We have been able to consult the books and notes.
37 Alessandro Manzoni (1785–1873) was an Italian writer and philosopher whose most famous work is *The Betrothed*, a novel generally regarded as one of the masterpieces of world literature. He also was an important contributor to the stabilization of the Italian language.

when regiments of French soldiers came a few months later to the assistance of the Italians after the catastrophic defeat of Caporetto,[38] and the injured and wounded combatants came to Brescia in greater and greater numbers, Battista would be one of the founders of the "House of French Soldiers." In a large room of the Trebeschi family's home, then subsequently in a more convenient location, books, French newspapers, games, a piano, and a bar were placed at the disposal of the foreign soldiers.

In these initiatives Battista demonstrated charity and generosity; but he also felt that the war, as it was then unfolding, called for a new vision of the world, and was going to overturn society. An essay he wrote in 1917 as an entry in a contest organized by the student association of Brescia testifies to this. This relatively long piece of writing, entitled "The Post-War World and the Christian Student,"[39] deserves attention because it allowed the young Montini — he was not yet twenty — an opportunity to reveal what he thought. It is his earliest surviving expository text.

The common sentiment, he explains, is an "indefinable intensity of trepidation, prayer, hope, and pain"; however, after the war, "we can expect a period even more painful than the current moment." He names China, Russia, and Germany among the countries engaged in "a new era of history." Chinese anarchy in the twenties and thirties, the Bolshevik Revolution, and the end of the German and the Austro-Hungarian Empires appear to confirm this analysis. In post-war Italy, he added, the problems to be resolved would be of two types: socioeconomic (care for the orphans, the mutilated, and widows; restarting the economy), and moral. Individuals would want to satisfy their aspirations: combatants would want to "start over." Only the moral principles of Christianity, he concluded, allowed for a resolution, otherwise "we ought to expect after the war a period overflowing with bitterness, disorder, and pain." There again the diagnosis of the young Montini was correct: he had identified the symptoms of the crisis which Italy would soon come to know, and which would soon pave the way for fascism.

---

38 The Battle of Caporetto was fought in present-day Slovenia from October 24 to November 19, 1917 between the Italians and the Central Powers (Austro-Hungarians and Germans) with a decisive victory for the latter. The Italians casualties included 10,000 dead, 30,000 wounded, and 265,000 captured soldiers, while the Central Powers bore a combined toll of 70,000 dead or wounded. Ernest Hemingway gives a vivid description of the bloody aftermath in A Farewell to Arms.
39 Included in Scritti giovanili.

2

Priest without Having Been a Seminarian

THE WAR WAS NOT YET OVER WHEN BATTISTA Montini embarked, with some friends, on an enterprise which would connect him to students' movements, his area of choice for the decades to follow. The Manzoni Association brought together middle schoolers, high schoolers, and college students. It was then independent of the FUCI (*Federazione Universitaria Cattolica Italiana*—Italian Catholic Federation of University Students). The FUCI was organized in circles, with a President at its head (elected by a national council). It was tightly bound to the hierarchy of the Church, which mandated that there be one chaplain per circle and designated the national chaplain (the "Federal Assistant").

In March 1918, Montini undertook a correspondence with the chaplain of the FUCI, Msgr Pini.[1] Montini shared with him his intentions and those of his friends to begin a large, "continuous battle" to defend liberty in teaching. The government and local authorities all too often hindered this liberty which, wrote Montini, "is the key which can open the door to every victory."[2] He and his friends wanted to launch a vast campaign to raise awareness and to mobilize around this theme, directed first towards the circles of the FUCI. Msgr Pini did not discourage this good initiative.

In the month of June, Montini and his friends launched a review under the evocative title *La Fionda* (The Slingshot). Queriniana Editions, again solicited by Giorgio Montini, showed themselves to be a great help. Trebeschi was the director of the new enterprise. The group's profession of faith sounded like an oath: "We want to live out the battles of our homeland and the combats of the Faith, as the youth and for the youth;

---

[1] Msgr Giandomenico Pini (1871–1930) was born in Milan and graduated with a law degree in 1893. He took part in the Second Congress for the Catholic Union (1894) before entering the seminary the following year. He was ordained a priest in 1899. He worked within FUCI to inspire a generation of young Catholic students.
[2] The letters to Msgr Pini have been published in *Notiziario* 15 (November 1987): 7–40.

openly, without cowardice, and without hypocrisy." Battista collaborated from the very first issue with an article entitled "The Fight for School" and published around fifty pieces total in La Fionda; the last was a few years after his ordination. He rarely signed articles with his real name; more often he used only two or three initials (B. M., G. B. M., or even Giovanni Biemme). Sometimes he would even make use of a pseudonym (Vox Clamantis, Omega, Vincenzo Formisano) or an anagram (Nino Tom).

Here Montini demonstrated great maturity of spirit, along with a certain elegance in style. Many of his articles focused on liberty in teaching: as a solution to this problem, he described in detail a Belgian project of "good scholarship," or called again for the creation of a new Catholic university. Occasionally, he launched divisive polemics against those who were partisans of the unified state school system (he thought "the conscience of a perfect imbecile" was the only result to be gained from academic neutrality). Also noteworthy is a long article on Léon Harmel,[3] an industrialist and man of letters who was an important social reformer in French Catholicism. Sometimes Montini also wrote the review's spirituality column In via ("On the Way").

BETWEEN RELIGION AND POLITICS

His status remained ambivalent. Everyone among his friends knew that he was preparing for the priesthood, yet he still declined to take up the cassock; right up until a few months before his ordination, he continued to sign his published articles as "G. B. M., Student." He lacked the strength to survive twenty hours of classes at the seminary every week, but somehow still had enough energy to participate actively in La Fionda and in the activities of the Manzoni Association, and also to give catechism lessons to future first communicants. Finally, part of his time was consecrated to his priestly formation — a very scattered formation.

Father Caresana gave his assurances that the private studies of his protégé covered all the material taught in seminary, but this was obviously fragmented and discontinuous. Battista went several times to Msgr Menna[4] at Chiari. He taught the course of Canon Law at the Santangelo Seminary and gave some private lessons to the young man. Other priests happily provided lessons in theology, philosophy, and liturgy.

---

3 Léon Harmel (1829–1915), a French industrialist, was a supporter of social justice and the rallying of the Catholics to the Republic.
4 Archbishop Domenico Menna (1875–1957) was the Italian titular archbishop of Neopatrasso and bishop of Mantua, appointed by Pope Pius XI. He retired in 1954 to the hermitage of Camaldoli di Gussago.

But Battista's work was mostly solitary, when the state of his health permitted it.[5] The then-famous synopses of moral and dogmatic theology by Tanquerey[6] served as his foundational books. A precise study of the works contained in his library, which he must have read at this time or in the following years, enables us to describe his breadth of knowledge, both religious and profane, as highly eclectic and without anchor point: "varied and heterogenous readings, vast and disorderly."[7]

Private conversations with friends of Giorgio Montini who were visiting the house on via della Grazie also contributed greatly to orienting the spirit of the future priest. A politically active friend of his father's, the lawyer Luigi Bazoli,[8] introduced him to the work of Rosmini[9] (certain of whose books were on the Index). Another friend of the family, Father Semeria,[10] returned to Brescia after the First World War, having been "exiled" to Brussels under Pius X as a result of some of his work on the history of the liturgy. Through this contact Battista acquired a historical conception of the liturgy, completing whatever he had already picked up from Father Bevilacqua on this subject.

Another, more political topic began to dominate the Montini family's conversations from the end of 1918 onward: the formation of a political party. Before the war, the pope, breaking with the non expedit, had authorized certain Catholics to put themselves forward as candidates for the legislature. After the war, but from a different point of view, some Catholics, with the coming elections in mind, began to dream of

---

5   In January 1919, he had to stay at home, without any activity.
6   *Synopsis Theologiæ Moralis et Pastoralis* and *Synopsis Theologiæ Dogmaticæ*, each in three volumes. Fr Adolphe Tanquerey (1854–1932) was a French Sulpician priest who was known for his manuals on dogmatic, moral and pastoral, and ascetic and mystical theology.
7   G. Romanato and F. Molinari, "Le letture del Giovanni Montini," *La Scuola cattolica*, 43.
8   Luigi Bazoli (1866–1937) was a lawyer and one of the founders of the Italian People's Party in 1919. The Bazoli family is well-known for their political involvement: Luigi's sons Stefano and Ercoliano were deputy to the Chamber (1948–1953) and president of the Brescia Province (1951–1970), respectively.
9   Fr Antonio Rosmini (1797–1855) was an Italian priest, philosopher, and theologian, known for his strong patriotism. He specialized in post-Renaissance philosophers and formulated his own ideas about their philosophies. He was best known for his philosophical work on the notion of being and the dignity of a human person. Forty of his propositions were condemned by Pope Leo XIII in a decree published in 1888. In July of 2001, the Congregation for the Doctrine of the Faith published a Note indicating that the censures against Rosmini were no longer of any force.
10 Fr Giovanni Semeria (1867–1931) was an Italian priest known for his sermons and his work with the youth. The works in question were suspected of Modernism.

creating their own political party. Giorgio Montini's Catholic circle in Brescia, which included Longinotti[11] and Grosoli,[12] was among those which most actively participated in this creation. The architect of the work was a Sicilian priest, Father Sturzo.[13]

On January 18, 1919, the PPI (*Partito Popolare Italiano* — People's Party of Italy) was founded. Father Sturzo issued a "call to all free and strong men" to launch the new party's program for the legislative elections which were going to take place in nine months: liberty in teaching, defense of the family, encouraging the formation of agricultural cooperatives, administrative decentralization, adoption of a proportional vote, etc. It is noteworthy that the party did not call for the reestablishment of the temporal power of the Church; nor does the qualification Catholic or Christian appear in its name. The PPI did not want to be a confessional party, and declared itself to be independent of the church hierarchy.

Giorgio Montini would be elected this party's representative three times over. Battista, quite naturally, fully supported its program. On September 3, in an article in *La Fionda* written in the form of an open letter to Trebeschi, he clearly took the side of the PPI:

> We want the entire platform of the PPI, it goes without saying, without any compromises. With this program we want total justice, a fully vibrant Christianity, the complete social Gospel, and the true progress of the people.

The day this edition of *La Fionda* appeared, Battista participated with fourteen other young people from Brescia (among whom were Andrea Trebeschi, and his brother Ludovico) at the first post-war Congress of the FUCI, at the Abbey of Monte Cassino.

The Association Manzoni had been integrated into the FUCI several months earlier. This short stay at Monte Cassino is interesting for more than one reason. In the account which he provided in a letter to his

---

[11] Giovanni Maria Longinotti (1876–1944) was an Italian journalist and antifascist politician. He was a pioneer of the Brescia Catholic movement and was a cofounder of the local Catholic labor unions. He also founded the Brescia branch of the People's Party.

[12] Giovanni Grosoli Pironi (1859–1937) was an Italian Count and politician who was involved in various apostolic activities from a young age. He was known for his organizational ability, motivating people in pursuing their political objectives in the context of religion and helping those in need.

[13] Fr Luigi Sturzo (1871–1959) was an Italian priest and highly prominent politician. He was opposed not only to Fascism but also to the post-war Christian Democrats. He served as Vice-Mayor of his hometown, Caltagirone (1905–1920), Senator (1948–1952), and then Senator for Life. His cause for canonization was opened in 2002.

family, his later reminiscences, and surviving documents, two sides to Montini are visible at this point in time. First there is an active Montini, who directed an agenda to reclaim liberty in teaching: he had the delegates from Brescia adopt it, and ultimately succeeded in putting it forward for a vote by the delegates from other cities. Then there is another Montini, more meditative, admiring the imposing architecture of the abbey and enthusiastically rediscovering monastic chant. In a letter to his grandmother, September 5, he eulogized the Benedictine liturgy, "perfect in the exclusion of everything hyperbolic and artificial that we add to divine worship, because everything is exquisite, precise, and perfect." This taste for a stripped-down liturgy, combined with a desire to see the faithful participate in it, will be seen time and again in the life of Montini, priest, archbishop, pope.

TOWARDS ORDINATION

Two months after these memorable days at Monte Cassino, he finally took up the ecclesiastical habit. It was November 21, 1919. Six months later he would be ordained a priest. During the interval, the reception of minor and major orders[14] was accelerated. This haste was perhaps the bishop of Brescia's favor to an important citizen's son who could not follow the traditional formation at the seminary.[15] But it is also possible that these sacred orders were conferred on him so rapidly because his health gave greater and greater cause for worry. Montini was subjected

---

14 The minor and major orders are the sacramental degrees or steps to the priesthood (see St. Thomas Aquinas, *Summa Theologiæ*, Supplement, Q. 37). In the traditional numeration there are four minor orders (porter, exorcist, lector, and acolyte) and three major orders (subdeacon, deacon, and priest). Bishops were counted apart as the episcopacy is essentially an order of governance, while the other orders are relative to the Sacrifice of the Mass. The episcopacy is now generally considered to be the final order, as the fullness of priesthood, because it is by the episcopal consecration that the power to ordain is transmitted. Paul VI did not consider the minor orders and subdiaconate useful, so he suppressed their conferral in his *Novus Ordo* of the Roman Rite with the motu proprio *Ministeria Quædam* (August 15, 1972). In their place he created "ministries" of lector and acolyte, which are conferred on laymen. All the same, the minor orders and the subdiaconate have never ceased to be conferred in the Eastern Rites (both Catholic and Orthodox) and in the communities which have retained the use of the traditional Roman Rite. For an in-depth discussion, see Peter Kwasniewski, *Ministers of Christ: Recovering the Roles of Clergy and Laity in an Age of Confusion* (Manchester, NH: Crisis Publications, 2021), and James Walther, "*Accipite*: Sacramentality of the Minor Orders and the Subdiaconate," available at www.academia.edu.

15 Nonetheless, in the months preceding his ordination, he made a few stays at the seminary.

to the bare minimum of intervening periods between orders that was stipulated by canon law. He himself underwent the succession of solemn ceremonies in a state of awe.

On November 30, he received the tonsure from the hands of Bishop Gaggia,[16] in the chapel of the Episcopal Palace. This was the official mark of his consecration to God. His family, Trebeschi, and Father Galloni surrounded him. To his father, held back at Rome by the opening session of Parliament, he wrote the same day that he experienced "vertigo and ecstasy" upon hearing the words of the ritual "the Lord will be my inheritance . . ." Interestingly, he added "your work and the very humble spiritual work of my life will be as two forces which, although unequal and different, aim at the same social end: the reign of God."

On February 28, 1920, he received the subdiaconate, the first major order. This was, in his eyes, his true break with the world. On March 3, he wrote to Trebeschi:

> Look at me finally and definitively fixed on the path toward divine election. I am henceforth a subdeacon, after the most fervent days of tranquil and strengthening meditation that I have ever known in my life. I taste the joy of this transformation, which separates me forevermore from the past and its human desires...

One week before ordination, he began a retreat at the Seminary of Santangelo, but he had to interrupt it after three days, because he suffered so much on account of the suffocating heat. On the day of ordination, May 29, he was sick. He would later recount: "At that moment, I didn't even hope to live much longer." Canon law stipulated a minimum age of twenty-four for men to be ordained; it was therefore necessary to request a dispensation.

On May 30, he celebrated his first Mass in the sanctuary of *Santa Maria delle Grazie*; the altar cloth had been cut from his mother's dress. He had ordination cards printed with a quotation from Pius X (who had died only six years before): "Grant, O my God, that all minds may unite in the Truth and all hearts in Charity."

ROME

A young priest, Father Montini was at the service of the bishop of his diocese, Msgr Gaggia, who knew that the weak health of this newly

---

16 Archbishop Giacinto Gaggia (1847–1933) was bishop of Brescia from 1913 until his death in 1933. He was made a titular archbishop in 1930.

ordained priest would not allow him to bear the burden of a parish. He also knew of Montini's taste for intellectual work, writing, and literature. He decided to send him to Rome to continue his studies. He must also have judged that the young priest's formation had been inadequate, and that his knowledge of certain subjects needed to be supplemented. In addition, perhaps his health might have been thought better suited to the climate of the capital than to northern Italy's abrupt changes of temperature.

Many years later, Cardinal Montini would remember his bishop's advice:

> When I was but a young priest, I timidly asked him about the readings best fit to orient my studies, when I was thinking about devoting my attention to the life and history of the Church. He answered right away: "Read the history of the Councils, take Hefele[17] (eighteen large volumes!) and study them: therein you will find everything." That is to say: theology, philosophy, spirituality, politics, humanism, Christianity, errors, discussions, truths, abuses, laws, virtues, and the holiness of the Church.[18]

He arrived in Rome on November 10, perhaps little suspecting that he was going to spend almost his entire life there. He lodged in the Lombard College, which accepted seminarians and priests from dioceses in Lombardy that wanted to continue their studies in the pontifical universities. Father Battista enrolled himself, not only in philosophy at the Gregorian University (which was run by the Jesuits), but also, with the permission of his bishop, in literature, at the state-run university (La Sapienza). Some commentators have wanted to see this double enrollment, in ecclesiastical and lay universities simultaneously, as a mark of absolute originality, a sort of prefiguration of the "openness to the world" that he would later advocate as pope. In reality, this decision, as infrequent as it was, was by no means exceptional. Indeed, one of his fellow students at the Lombard College had also taken classes at the Sapienza for three years before his arrival.

The correspondence he had with his family in Brescia, at the rate of around one letter a week, reveals the strength of those bonds of affection that united him to them. These letters also provide us with some reliable points of reference in terms of reconstructing the life of the young priest until 1943, when his parents died.

---

17 Bishop Karl Josef von Hefele (1809–1893) was a German bishop and theologian. His views tended to be more liberal. He was a member of the commission that prepared for the Vatican Council of 1870.
18 G. B. Montini, lecture given on April 27, 1962, published in L'Église et les conciles, 210.

Even if he regularly attended classes at the two universities — as the surviving certificates of attendance demonstrate — he does not seem to have taken a keen interest in his studies. He preferred personal reading over lecture courses and masses of assigned work. The atmosphere at the Lombard College did not please him either. To Trebeschi, he wrote on November 14: "I find myself well, but fairly isolated, not having been accustomed to living in a disciplined intellectual environment." Out of nostalgia for the student life that he had left behind, not to mention personal conviction, he continued his collaboration in *La Fionda*. If he did not use pseudonyms anymore, he maintained the practice of signing his articles, more often than not, using only his initials. He also tried a new literary genre: fiction. Published in the students' review or in journals destined for families, these fictional stories always ended with a moral.

An important part of his day was devoted to the relationships he maintained with the political friends of his father. Other than Giorgio Montini, Brescia and its environs was represented at the Chamber of Deputies and Senate by men whom Battista had known for years: Longinotti (who was Under-Secretary of State), Grosoli (who was his godfather), and Passerini.[19] Often the father and the son were invited together to lunch. The young priest would sometimes attend sessions of the legislature.

The country was then in the midst of a grave social, economic, and moral crisis; debates were often stormy. In the spring of 1921, the government decided to dissolve Parliament and proceed with new elections in May. Father Montini closely followed the new electoral campaign of the PPI. He is credited with writing some of the campaign speeches of his father. It is not impossible, but no documentary evidence of this has been discovered in the archives to date.

In these elections, The People's Party won 170 seats, a total barely higher than they had accomplished two years before. The Nationalist bloc emerged as the great victor and, for the first time, 35 Fascist legislators, including Mussolini,[20] were elected. Father Battista was very disappointed and compared these results with the disaster at Caporetto. The victors, he wrote to his family, profess an "intellectual and religious skepticism"

---

19 Angelo Passerini (1853–1940) was an Italian entrepreneur and politician from Brescia. He was a civil activist during the First World War and supported Mussolini's regime when he came to power.

20 Benito Mussolini (1883–1945) was the leader of the National Fascist Party and the Prime Minister of Italy (1922–1943) who established a totalitarian state. He was allied with Nazi Germany and aimed to expand the influence of Italian Fascism across the world. He was executed at the end of the Second World War and his body was taken to Milan where it was strung up to deter any remaining Fascists.

which is dangerous for the country; only Christian Democracy would be capable of drawing Italy from "economic materialism which generates hate and corruption."

He passed the summer with his family, at Brescia and various resorts. He returned to Rome in October without enthusiasm. "I feel as though I'm in exile," he wrote to his family, "but I also feel that at Rome is the home of our spirit and hearth of our most dear affections." He was looking to leave the Lombard College. In a few days, the course of his ecclesiastical career was going to change.

"COMPLETE TURNAROUND"

On October 27, he was received at the Vatican, in the company of Longinotti, by Msgr Pizzardo,[21] *Sostituto* (Substitute) to the Secretary of State. The audience was granted through Longinotti's approaches to Cardinal Gasparri,[22] the Secretary of State (and direct superior of Msgr Pizzardo). Pizzardo suggested that the young priest enter the direct service of the Holy See and prepare himself by entering a course of studies with the Academy of Noble Ecclesiastics. This prestigious institution, today called the Pontifical Diplomatic Academy, formed the clerics who were to enter the diplomatic service of the Holy See (nuncios and members of the Secretariat of State). The number of students at this Academy was strictly limited; only five would enter that year. It was the elite of the clergy. In the case of the young Montini, it is evident that he owed his entry into the Academy of Noble Ecclesiastics — he found the name repulsive and always spoke simply of "the Academy" — to the ecclesiastical connections of Longinotti, the friend of his father's who happened to be a member of the government.

Two days after this capital meeting, Father Battista wrote to his mother:

> My life has undergone in an instant a complete turnaround....
> My studies are simply overturned: the literature has been interrupted; the philosophy has been suspended; I am to begin a rudimentary law course. My specialized research, which I

---

21   Card. Giuseppe Pizzardo (1877–1970) was the Prefect of the Congregation for Seminaries and Universities (1939–1968) and Secretary of the Holy Office (1951–1959). He was made a cardinal in 1937.
22   Card. Pietro Gasparri (1852–1934) was a cardinal (elevated in 1907 by Pope Pius X) and a diplomat in the Roman Curia. He also served as the apostolic delegate to Peru (1898–1901) and the Cardinal Secretary of State under Popes Benedict XV and Pius XI. After the First Vatican Council, he was entrusted with the reformation of canon law.

sometimes think of as a form of apostolate, and which for the last year seemed to offer hope for promising results, is now at an end, to make room for practical studies.

He also said that he feared the "terrible responsibilities" which a diplomatic career would entail, but he surrendered himself to Providence.

In November, he left the Lombard College for the Academy. He abandoned his studies in philosophy but enrolled nonetheless in the second year of literature,[23] and had to enroll in canon law at the Gregorian University (by dispensation, he was allowed to enroll directly into second year). At the Academy, he took courses in Latin, Church history, diplomacy, and law. At the end of two weeks of this regime, Father Battista wrote to his family: "I am not certain that his path is for me because it demands too much virtue and Christian fortitude." And concerning his possible diplomatic career, he added: "To interpret the Gospel in this language ought to be possible, but how awfully difficult!" Despite this he completed his course of studies at the Academy and began a long career at the Secretary of State.

Among the young priests who were students at this academy, two would remain his friends from now on: Antonio Riberi[24] and Mariano Rampolla del Tindaro.[25] Rampolla, before having been ordained a priest, had studied Sanskrit. Montini admired his vast erudition and would later ask Rampolla to work for him. After he became pope, he remembered the Academy he knew as "a *cenacolo*[26] of ideas and discussions, of reading above all, and of meditations."

Nonetheless, he did not forget the world of Brescia. One of his high school classmates, Carlo Manziana,[27] came to Rome to continue his

---

23 In June and October, he successfully passed the five exams of the first year, in History, Paleography, and Christian Archeology.

24 Card. Antonio Riberi (1897–1967) was a Monegasque diplomat of the Holy See. He was consecrated a titular archbishop in October 1934 and was assigned as the Apostolic Delegate to Eastern Africa. He also served as Nuncio to China (1949–1958), to Ireland (1959–1962), and to Spain (1962–1967). Paul VI created him a cardinal in 1967.

25 Mariano Rampolla del Tindaro (1893–1945), the identically-named nephew of the better-known Secretary of State of Leo XIII, was a highly cultured Indologist who taught Sanskrit in Rome and published a grammar of it (written in Latin).

26 From the Latin word *cenaculum*, the word used to describe the "upper room," the place of the Last Supper.

27 Bishop Carlo Manziana (1902–1997) was the bishop of Crema, appointed in 1963 by Pope Paul VI. During his youth, he became close friends with the future Pope Paul VI. As bishop of Crema, he steered the diocese according to the new ideas brought forth from the Second Vatican Council.

studies in literature at La Sapienza. Fr Montini kept in close contact with him, thus staying in touch through him with the world of lay students. Beyond this, the student of the Academy maintained a regular correspondence with his Brescian mentors, Fathers Caresana and Bevilacqua. The latter had published a book during the preceding year entitled *La Luce nelle Tenebre*[28] (The Light in the Darkness). In it he recounts conversations about God and the meaning of life that he had conducted during the war with his fellow prisoners. Montini read the work; in early 1922, he published a review of what he regarded as "a book of contemporary mysticism."[29] Fr Montini's commentary reveals an intellectual and spiritual orientation he would maintain throughout his life, continuing through to the end of his pontificate. He invokes the novelty of the modern soul, and its "chaotic complexity." For this modern soul, religion is no longer "the one necessary thing"; also, to make him rediscover the Gospel he needs "conversations more than discussions; a truth expressed more by artistic words than by perfect words; prayer more than logic."

Young Fr Montini took this language of the "heart to heart," which Bevilacqua had taken from Saint Augustine,[30] and made it his own. From hence he drew his great attentiveness to other people, their sentiments, and their opinions — his extreme sensitivity. We find this sensitivity again at the beginning of this same year 1922, when Benedict XV[31] died. On January 23, Don Battista went, amid the Roman crowds, to bow before the mortal remains of the deceased pope, lying in state in the middle of the gold and marble of Saint Peter's Basilica. That very day, he wrote a long lyrical letter to his family recounting the story. The crowds "pass and speak no more, so as to not wake the Sleeper. Peter, why are you sleeping?" Then, "at last, with forehead pressed to the frozen marble, we pray, the *Credo* comes upon our lips; the *Credo* over the tomb of the Apostle who planted the Cross, the pole of humanity, of the ages of History . . ."

---

28 Giulio Bevilacqua, *La Luce nelle Tenebre* (Rome: Studium, 1946).
29 G. B. Montini, *Riflessioni su "La Luce nelle Tenebre" di P. Bevilacqua* (Palombara Sabina: Edizioni La Fionda, 1922). The study has been republished in *Scritti giovanili*.
30 St Augustine (354–430) was bishop of Hippo Regius in Roman-occupied North Africa. His work in theology, including *The City of God*, was so instrumental in the development of Western Christianity that he is regarded as a foremost Father and Doctor of the Church.
31 Pope Benedict XV (Giacomo della Chiesa, 1854–1922), from Genoa; he was Undersecretary of State (1901–1907), archbishop of Bologna (1907–1914), and successor to St. Pope Pius X in 1914. He led the Church through the First World War, worked to improve Vatican-Italian relations, revitalized foreign missions, and promulgated the 1917 Code of Canon Law.

On February 2, Achille Ratti,[32] archbishop of Milan, was elected pope and took the name of Pius XI. Ten days later was the long and solemn ceremony of the coronation; Don Battista was there. On March 6, the new Sovereign Pontiff granted an audience to the students of the Academy, including Montini.

FIRST VOYAGES

A few months later, Fr Montini's academic year ended with examinations in Italian and Latin Literature at La Sapienza, a Diploma in Philosophy that he received from the Roman Academy of Saint Thomas Aquinas,[33] his second-year examinations in Canon Law, and then his Licentiate in the same. "Hard studies, a bit old," he wrote at that time to Father Galloni. Literature, contemporary religious essays, and history attracted him more.

After a few weeks spent with his family, he made a month-long journey through Austria and Germany. He lodged, more often than not, in Benedictine monasteries, where he found again a liturgy which pleased him. Thus, he managed at low cost to traverse the Tyrol, Bavaria,[34] and the Rhineland, and made it as far as Berlin. On the way, he came across two priests from Brescia who continued the journey with him; then his friend Rampolla came to meet up with him. Finally, on July 30, he joined his father in Vienna where, with other Italian representatives, he participated at an international convention of Democratic-Christian members of parliament. With them, Fr Montini went on the Danube to Budapest.

Upon returning to Italy, he rested four months at Brescia or at Verolavecchia to rest and study. Before leaving Rome, Msgr Pizzardo had asked him to finish his studies in canon law "as quickly as possible." A doctorate in this subject was necessary, not merely for the remainder of his studies at the Academy, but especially for his future career in diplomacy or the Secretariat of State. Thanks to some dispensations from examinations in

---

32   Pope Pius XI (Ambrogio Damiano Achille Ratti, 1857–1939), from Milan, and pope from 1922–1939. He concluded a record number of concordats, and during his pontificate the hostility with the Italian government over the status of the papacy and the Italian Church was more or less resolved with the creation of the Vatican City-State in 1929.
33   It was not a doctorate in philosophy, as has been written here and there, but a diploma obtained after two years of studies. The candidate was interrogated on one of forty theses which formed the basis of instruction.
34   In Bavaria, he attended the Drama of the Passion which is performed, once every ten years, by the inhabitants of Oberammergau. In an article for La Fionda on this Passionsspiele, written upon his return, Fr Montini noted that he had been impressed by this theatrical representation but unsatisfied on the spiritual plan ("God is inaccessible," he concluded).

certain disciplines, Don Battista was able to enroll in the College of Law at the Seminary of Milan on November 21 and, by December 9, obtain a doctorate in Canon Law (with 32 out of 40 in the written and oral exams).

As soon as he returned to Rome, January 4, 1923, he was summoned by Msgr Pizzardo, who instructed him to be ready to serve the Holy See in the near future. Various possible assignments were discussed in short order: the nunciatures of Poland, of Peru, then of Hungary. To prepare himself for his upcoming appointment, he supplemented his Academy courses with those of the "Studio," which was attached to the Congregation of the Council, where young clerics familiarized themselves with the administrative and juridical work of the Vatican's congregations.

The prospect of moving overseas for an undetermined period of time and of leaving his relations displeased the young Montini. He would have preferred to return to his diocese of origin. Interestingly, it seems that during the years 1921–1923, he again felt a twinge of nostalgic longing for a monastic vocation. Little satisfied with the formation he was receiving in multiple universities, and uncertain of the future that awaited him upon his departure from the Academy, he regularly visited the Abbey of Saint Paul Outside the Walls, whose abbot, Ildefonso Schuster,[35] became his confidant. Don Battista again seems to have revealed his desire to become a Benedictine monk. But he was turned away yet again: his health would not permit this. Still, Abbot Schuster happened to be another important influence on the theological formation of the future pope. An eminent liturgist, he published, in nine volumes, the *Liber Sacramentorum* (1923–1932), an extensive historical and liturgical commentary on the Roman Missal. Fr Montini would possess all nine volumes and read them attentively.[36]

In May 1923, Don Battista learned that he had been assigned to the nunciature of Warsaw. After passing a few days at Brescia, he left Italy for Poland at the beginning of June. The situation in the country was immensely difficult in many respects. Three years before, Poland had had to drive out the Bolshevik Red Army, and the government continued to be seriously unstable. In terms of religion, there had been rivalries between

---

35   Card. Alfredo Ildefonso Schuster, OSB (1880–1954) was an Italian Benedictine elevated to the cardinalate by Pope Pius XI shortly before being consecrated archbishop of Milan. The English translation of his great work on the liturgy, *The Sacramentary*, has been republished in five volumes by Arouca Press of Canada.

36   Fr Montini had contact with another Benedictine liturgist, Father Emanuele Caronti (1882–1966; an Italian and the first director of the liturgical review *Rivista liturgica*, founded in 1914), who preached a retreat in April 1923 at Brescia. Montini had already read some of his works with great attention. He took part in this retreat and afterwards kept in regular touch with Fr Caronti, mainly through letters.

the Uniates[37] and the Roman Catholics with the need to reconstruct an ecclesiastical hierarchy, which until then had been divided in three separate countries.[38] It has been written that Fr Montini had been named to Poland to be the nuncio's "adjunct." Msgr Lauri[39] is supposed to have asked for a trustworthy man to be sent to him to help negotiate the concordat then in preparation between the Holy See and Poland. This is yet another out-of-proportion exaggeration meant to embellish the youthful career of Paul VI. In reality, when Fr Montini arrived, the nunciature of Warsaw was already staffed by an auditor and a secretary (in addition to the nuncio himself). The numerous letters which Don Montini sent to his family demonstrate that his position was far beneath that of *attaché* to the nunciature: he had no official title and he received no salary. To cover his basic personal needs, he had to ask his parents to send him some money, and his protector, Msgr Pizzaro, to procure Mass stipends for him.

After a month in Poland, he wrote to Trebeschi: "Morally, it is a trial; professionally, nothing extraordinary — an office life"; and he asked Msgr Pizzardo to return him to Rome! While awaiting a response, he tried to learn Polish. He contacted the student movements which were much more numerous and better-organized than in Italy. To distract himself, he wrote some articles, both pseudonymous and unsigned, for his father's newspaper, in addition to others under his own name in *La Fionda*. Thanks to the newspapers as well as letters from his father, he was able to follow the political situation in Italy closely.

From October 1922, Mussolini was in power. Certain members of the PPI had agreed to help form his first government. While Don Battista was in Warsaw, an electoral plan had been presented to the House of Representatives proposing to give two-thirds of all seats to the party that would win the next elections (Mussolini thought it would be the Fascist

---

37 The term "Uniates" was once used to refer to Eastern Catholics generally, because they had belonged to one of the Orthodox Churches before reuniting with the Catholic Church while preserving their distinctness in rite. In this case, it is referring principally to the Ukrainian Greek Catholics.

38 The Commonwealth of Poland had been divided and annexed by Austria, Prussia, and Russia in 1795, which led to the division of the Ruthenian Uniate (Catholic) Church. It regained its independence with the Treaty of Versailles in 1918. The reconstitution of the country required the parallel reconstitution of a national hierarchy. The presence of both Latin and Eastern Rite Catholics created a difficulty concerning territories and jurisdiction.

39 Card. Lorenzo Lauri (1864–1941) was elevated to the cardinalate in 1926 and served in the Major Penitentiary (1927) and as Camerlengo (1939–1941). Born in Rome, he studied at the Pontifical Roman Seminary, where he then taught until 1910, also the year he was raised to the rank of Domestic Prelate of His Holiness.

Party). The PPI was divided on the attitude to adopt. Father Sturzo had had to resign from the party leadership, following pressure from the Vatican's Secretariat of State, which did not want to see Christian-Democratic representatives enter into conflict with the government while negotiations to resolve the "Roman Question"[40] were ongoing. When he learned the news from the papers, Don Battista wrote a long political letter to his father in which he analyzed the Italian situation.

Fascism had imposed itself on the country, he explained, because it had successfully guaranteed the support of certain members of the PPI. This was an unnatural alliance.[41] And if the party was divided over the electoral law with regard to having to support the Fascist regime, it was because it had become

> merely a secular party, which has possibly forgotten its duty to provide a calm and patient example of honesty, integrity, and adherence to higher ideals in the face of the Byzantinism and commercialism of the other parties...; our militantly Catholic character no longer has any consistency.

During the summer, he visited some beautiful sites: Oświęcim, Krakow ("beautiful, graceful, much more interesting than Warsaw," he wrote to his family; "there are monuments everywhere, of Poland's heroic history and of Italian art"), the Marian sanctuary of Częstochowa, Poznań, and Gniezno. Then on October 2, when he had given up hope, he received a telegram from Msgr Pizzardo authorizing him to return to Rome. Once again, the steps taken by the parliamentarian Giorgio Montini with the Secretariat of State and Msgr Lauri, who had visited Rome in September, had been effective. He had made them understand that the health of his son would not hold up well in the Polish winter.

THE FUCI

Having returned to Rome, Don Battista resided again at the Academy where he continued to take classes. In addition, he audited some courses

---

40 The "Roman Question" refers to the unsettled dispute regarding the temporal authority of the pope after the conquest of the Papal States by King Victor Emmanuel II in 1870. Thus, Popes Pius IX (since 1870), Leo XIII, Pius X, Benedict XV, and Pius XI (until 1929) had spent their papacies as "prisoners of the Vatican." It was settled by the Lateran Treaty in 1929.

41 In an article for *La Fionda*, published at the same time, in which, while ostensibly writing about Poland, he was in fact covertly discussing Italian politics, he opposed the "barbarian" conception of patriotism (that of Fascism) to the unitary, "synthetic, Latin" conception of Catholics.

in Civil Law at the Pontifical Lateran University.[42] He happily rejoined his friends Manziana and Rampolla and had barely resumed his normal life when he was entrusted with a pastoral duty, which this time corresponded perfectly with his tastes and his capacities. At the end of November 1923, he was named the Chaplain of the Roman Circle of the Italian Catholic Federation of University Students (FUCI). Msgr Pizzardo, aside from his functions as Substitute to the Secretary of State, was the *Assistente Ecclesiastico Generale* (General Chaplain) of Italian Catholic Action (*Azione Cattolica Italiana*, or ACI), of which FUCI was a branch. He had thought that his protégé Montini would be the ideal man to direct the Roman Circle spiritually: not only did he have connections with the FUCI going back several years; he had also spent some time in Roman universities, and was surely familiar with students' preoccupations. Once again Msgr Pizzardo's choice would determine Fr Montini's destiny, associating him for at least twenty years with university life, while his previous decision to enroll him in the Academy would permit the young priest simultaneously to climb the ranks within the Secretariat of State. As pope, Paul VI would describe Msgr Pizzardo more than once as his "master." The term is perhaps exaggerated if interpreted as denoting intellectual influence; more properly it may be understood as recognition of a superior.

Father Montini was named Chaplain of the Roman Circle to establish a bit of order. It was a matter of high priority to tighten the bonds between the FUCI and the ACI while depoliticizing its activities. The first contact that Father Battista had with the Roman Circle revealed to him its chronic agitation, "with a parody of parliamentary intrigue and gossip," he wrote to his parents. The Circle had its headquarters near the State University. In concert with the national chaplain of the FUCI, Msgr Piastrelli,[43] he set about reorienting the life of the Circle towards cultural and religious activity.

It is true that Italian political life in these years was entering a perpetual climate of fever and uncertainty. At the beginning of 1924, the House of Representatives was dissolved; elections (according to the new voting system) were scheduled for the month of April. The PPI was divided in three currents: partisans of an alliance with Fascism, partisans of a

---

42 After one scholastic year, in July 1924, he obtained a doctorate in civil law. His preceding studies in canon law had permitted him to skip steps...
43 Fr Luigi Piastrelli (1882–1975) was a priest of Sant'Agata from 1908–1975 who actively promoted the Faith by educating generations of young university students in Catholicism. He promoted the Perugia section of the FUCI and became close with Giovanni Battista Montini.

firm independence, and partisans of a union with the Socialists. Giorgio Montini, and his son with him, wished for the party to preserve its freedom. Don Battista, yet again, followed the electoral campaign very closely. On March 17, he wrote to his father, who was battling against the Fascist candidates at Brescia: "The parade of heroic figures is pitiful, when one thinks of the miserable personal virtues and the egotistical ideas they are founded upon." At Brescia, the PPI lost half of its seats, but Giorgio Montini was reelected. All told, the PPI did not have more than forty elected officials in the new Assembly. In June, the Socialist leader at the Assembly, Giacomo Matteotti,[44] who had pronounced a violent denunciation of Fascism, was kidnapped and assassinated. On June 27, the representatives of the opposition decided to stop taking their seats in Parliament. It is what has been called, in reference to antiquity, the "Aventine Secession"[45] But the PPI and the others of the opposition did not remain inactive as a result. They held endless demonstrations of protest, distributed tracts, and addressed a letter of protest to King Victor Emmanuel III[46] asking him to disavow Mussolini.

During these dramatic weeks, Don Battista left Italy on July 18 to spend a month and a half in France.[47] First he stayed for about ten days at the Abbey of Hautecombe, where the monks he had known at Chiari had moved two years before. He renewed his acquaintance with some men who had been close to him, and he immersed himself keenly into this Benedictine environment he loved so much, savoring again, as he wrote to his family, "the magnificent, austere, melodious office." Then he left for Paris. He lodged at the guest house of a Benedictine convent situated at rue Monsieur, in front of the publisher of Études.[48] He also

---

44 Giacomo Matteotti (1885–1924) was an Italian antifascist, socialist politician who openly spoke out in Parliament, claiming the Fascists had been acting fraudulently. This led to his assassination eleven days later by the Fascists. He opposed Italy's entry to World War I and boldly spoke against Mussolini.

45 The Aventine Hill is southernmost of the seven hills of Rome. In antiquity the Roman commoners would leave the city *en masse* as a sort of general strike against the patricians (aristocrats). This was known as the *secessio plebis* (withdrawal of the commoners). The second (449 BC) and fifth (287 BC) secessions were to the Aventine Hill.

46 Victor Emmanuel III (1869–1947) reigned as king of Italy (including the Papal States that his grandfather Victor Emmanuel II had annexed) from 1900 until his abdication in 1946, Emperor of Ethiopia from 1936 to 1941, and King of the Albanians from 1939 to 1943.

47 By mistake, in his famous *Dialogues avec Paul VI* [Dialogues with Paul VI], Jean Guitton — and therefore countless subsequent authors — had the pope say: "In 1926 I spent a few months in Paris" (p. 129). In 1926, he only spent a few days in Strasbourg.

48 *Études* is a monthly journal of contemporary culture founded by the Jesuits in

took courses at the *Alliance Française* in the Boulevard Raspail, to perfect his grasp of a language that he always enjoyed. He was taught by René Doumic,[49] whom he would remember with great affection. Doumic had, he told Jean Guitton some forty years later,

> a highly agreeable voice, a great deal of knowledge, and above all authority, and a gift of profound clarity. I will always remember the courses he gave us on Baudelaire, Flaubert, and Maupassant:[50] he specifically read us the short story "Le Petit Fût." I knew Verlaine very well; Doumic gave me even more reasons to admire Verlaine.[51]

He also visited the Louvre several times, went to Versailles and Fontainebleau, and made a pilgrimage to the tomb of Thérèse of the Child Jesus at Lisieux.[52]

During this Parisian visit, he read numerous French authors (Barbey d'Aurevilly, Huysmans, Bourget,[53] etc.). Before leaving Paris on August 30, he received a diploma: "Abbé Jean Montini has taken a course during the summer of 1924 at the *Alliance Française*. He was awarded first place in the Certificate of Proficiency, with first-class honors."

On several occasions, before the Second World War, he would return to France, but these first weeks spent in Paris during August would leave him with his fondest memories.

1856. It played an important role in the reforms surrounding Vatican II by providing a platform for the distribution of progressive thought.

49   René Doumic (1860–1937) was a French teacher of rhetoric at the Collège Stanislas de Paris. He is best known as the independent literary critic of the *Revue des Deux Mondes*.

50   Charles Baudelaire (1821–1867) was a French Decadent poet, art critic, philosopher. His most famous work was *Les Fleurs du mal* [The Flowers of Evil]. The sensuality of his works earned him sharp criticism. Gustave Flaubert (1821–1880) was a French realist and romantic novelist, known especially for *Madame Bovary*. Guy de Maupassant (1850–1893) was a French realist short-story author, journalist, and protégé of Flaubert. One of his most popular works was *Pierre et Jean* [Peter and John].

51   Jean Guitton, *Journal de ma vie*, 150. Paul Verlaine (1844–1896) was a poet of the Symbolist and Decadent movements. He left his wife to have an affair with a young man, whom he shot in a drunken rage. Claude Debussy set his poem *Clair de Lune* to music.

52   Beatified the previous year, she would be canonized in 1925.

53   Jules-Amédé Barbey d'Aurevilly (1808–1889), French late-romantic novelist and short story writer, known for mystery stories and "dandyism." He was a convert to Catholicism. Charles-Marie-Georges Huysmans (pen name: Joris-Karl Huysmans, 1848–1907) was a French novelist and art critic. His later works reflect his personal conversion to Catholicism. Paul Bourget (1853–1935), French novelist and member of the Académie française. He was a convert to Catholicism and a monarchist.

3
Between the FUCI and the Secretariat of State

WHILE HE WAS STILL IN PARIS, DON BATTISTA received a letter from Msgr Pizzardo informing him that the pope had authorized his entry into the Secretariat of State. Thus began a thirty-year career in one of the most important institutions of the Roman Curia. The Secretariat of State, directed by Cardinal Gasparri, was then divided into two sections: Extraordinary Affairs, which was specifically in charge of the Holy See's diplomatic relations and their political implications, and was run by a Secretary, Msgr Borgongini Duca;[1] and Ordinary Affairs, which was devoted mainly to the Church's internal affairs, and was headed by the Substitute, Msgr Pizzardo.

Don Battista began work on October 24 as a functionary at the lowest level of the hierarchical ladder. Yet for the first time in his life, at twenty-seven years old, he was able to support himself financially. First he had to familiarize himself with the tasks to be accomplished, the specialized language to be used, and the formats of various documents. After several months of apprenticeship he was officially named, on April 7, 1925, a *minutante* ("minute-taker"—the lowest secretarial rank), whose duty it was to edit drafts of documents, official correspondence, bulletins, and the guidelines circulated by various departments, in accordance with official instructions. He was assigned to Ordinary Affairs, under the authority of Msgr Pizzardo. This was a modest post, requiring only that he edit documents diligently and faithfully carry out orders without taking personal initiative. A few years later, when he became *primo minutante*, he had more input into texts prior to their circulation, and could be consulted for his opinions by the Substitute or the Secretary of State himself.

During those years, the Secretariat of State employed several priests who then held modest posts but would eventually occupy important

---

1 Card. Francesco Borgongini Duca (1884–1954) was ordained a priest in 1906 and taught theology at the Pontifical North American College and Pontifical Urbaniana Athenæum de Propaganda Fide (1907–1909). He also served as the Apostolic Nuncio to Italy (1929–1953) and was created a cardinal by Pius XII in 1953.

positions in the Church: Alfredo Ottaviani,[2] Domenica Tardini,[3] Francis Spellman,[4] Antonio Bacci.[5] In this milieu there was daily contact with the Church's most powerful authorities, and frequent encounters with Italian state officials and foreign diplomats. This was a world of rumors, political maneuvers, holy projects, and ambitions both high and low.

NATIONAL CHAPLAIN OF THE FUCI

Fr Montini's nomination to the Secretariat of State had in no way interrupted his apostolate with Catholic students in Rome. His days were divided in two: until midday, office work at the Vatican; throughout the late afternoon and into the evening he kept up a constant presence at the headquarters of the University Circle, in the heart of Rome. He wrote to his parents: "The young people distract me a great deal, but as a consolation I can work directly on consciences, not just indirectly through mere paper."

For the roughly eighty students who frequented the Circle, he organized conferences, invited dignitaries who were visiting Rome (notably the Patriarch of Jerusalem), and himself offered a series of lectures on Christian morals.[6] He also had the students participate in *ritiri minimi* ("mini-retreats") at the Abbey of Saint Paul outside the Walls. From Saturday evening to Monday morning, participants would follow monastic life, attend the Offices, and hear sermons from Don Battista, or from the Father Abbot himself. The students also organized the "Conference of

---

[2] Card. Alfredo Ottaviani (1890–1979) was born in Rome and elevated to the cardinalate in 1953 by Pius XII. He was Secretary of the Holy Office in the Roman Curia (1959–1966) and was widely regarded as a central figure of the Church in his time. At the Second Vatican Council he was one of the most prominent conservative voices.
[3] Card. Domenico Tardini (1888–1961) was an Italian curial prelate who served as Secretary of State for Pope John XXIII (1958–1961).
[4] Card. Francis Spellman (1889–1967) served as archbishop of New York (1939–1967) and was created a cardinal in 1946. He was one of the most influential American prelates of twentieth century.
[5] Card. Antonio Bacci (1885–1971) was an Italian who served as Secretary of Briefs to Princes (1931–1960) and was elevated to the cardinalate in 1970. *The Short Critical Study of the New Order of Mass* (1969), which he signed along with Cardinal Alfredo Ottaviani, is his most famous intervention, but it is also noteworthy that the initial reason he was invited to join the Secretariat of State (1922) was his exceptional knowledge of Latin. See *With Latin in the Service of the Popes: The Memoirs of Antonio Cardinal Bacci (1885–1971)*, trans. Anthony Lo Bello (Waterloo, ON: Arouca Press, 2020) and *Antonio Cardinal Bacci: Essays in Appreciation of His Life, His Latinity, and His Books*, ed. Pier Carlo Tagliaferri, trans. Anthony Lo Bello (Waterloo, ON: Arouca Press, 2021).
[6] This first series of lectures, presented in 1924–1925, was published under the title *La Via di Cristo* (Rome: Editrice Studium, 1931).

Saint Vincent" to offer regular alms and care packages to the homeless who lived in shelters at Porta Metronia.

Some of the students whom Don Battista met at the Circle would become friends for life, and would advance in their careers under his protecting wing: Ugo Piazza became Fr Montini's personal physician when he was appointed Substitute to the Secretary of State, and would remain one of his intimate friends to the end of his life; Federico Alessandrini[7] became the Editor of L'*Osservatore Romano*, the Vatican newspaper, then the Vice-Director and, during the sixties, Director of the Press Office of the Holy See.

During the spring of 1925, Fr Montini had his first serious clash with his superiors. He had organized a week of social science lectures for the students. He had invited, amongst other lecturers, his brother Lodovico, who then taught Economics and Social Sciences at the Catholic University of Milan. The daily paper of the PPI, reporting on this conference, praised "the Montinis," associating their father in their homage. Some ecclesiastical factions accused the University Circle of "participating in political games" to make Catholic Action dependent on the PPI. Cardinal Pompilj,[8] Vicar General of Rome, addressed his protestations to Msgr Pizzaro, Fr Montini's superior in both of his official roles. Fr Montini was compelled to defend himself. In a letter dated May 11, the Chaplain of the Roman Circle disassociated himself with his own youthful political agitations:

> The young people whom I would describe as the most active in the Circle desire passionately to participate and immerse themselves in politics; all my efforts aim at diminishing this passion..., at keeping them away from political agitations because of their affiliation with Catholic Action, and at educating and instructing them as well as possible...[9]

If it is true that Father Battista did not incite the youth of the Circle to direct political action, nonetheless the simple facts of his having a

---

7   Federico Alessandrini (1905–1983) was an Italian editor of the Vatican City's newspaper L'*Osservatore Romano* and directed the Holy See Press Office (1970–1976). His writings were very popular and were often quoted as insights into the thinking of the Church's hierarchy.
8   Card. Basilio Pompilj (1858–1931) was created cardinal in 1911 and became Vicar General of Rome (1913–1931). Before becoming a cardinal, he held several other ecclesiastical roles, such as auditor of the Sacred Congregation of the Council (1891) and protonotary apostolic (1899).
9   Letter published in Andrea Riccardi, Roma "*città sacra*"? [Rome, "Holy City"?] (1979).

politically committed father at the PPI, along with his frequent meetings with other party members with whom he shared convictions, would have allowed him countless opportunities to discuss politics with his students. In subsequent years, he would be accused again and again of politicizing his apostolate.

The matter did not rest there. More serious incidents arose thereafter, including a clash between Fascist students and members the Circle during the *Corpus Christi* procession;[10] several people were injured. The letters Fr Montini wrote to his parents during this period reveal that Msgr Pizzardo was thinking about sending him abroad again, perhaps to ease tensions. In July, the young priest sent a formal letter to Cardinal Pompilj resigning his position as the University Circle's Chaplain, giving his health as an excuse. His resignation was refused. Instead, in the ensuing months, he was entrusted with even greater responsibilities at the heart of the Catholic youth movement.

In September, FUCI held its National Congress at Bologna; Fr Montini did not participate. The National President of the movement, Pietro Lizier,[11] and the General Chaplain, Msgr Piastrelli, sent the Congress's compliments by telegram to King Victor Emmanuel III. At the Vatican this was considered a serious political error: the "Roman Question" had not been resolved and the Holy See still kept its distance from Italian institutions; this message to the king could have been interpreted as a polemical gesture against Mussolini's government, which often maintained frosty relations with the sovereign.

When, a few days later, President Lizier and Msgr Piastrelli arrived in Rome, with a delegation of the FUCI, to be received in audience, the pope refused to see them. He sent Fr Montini to go inform them of his refusal. The following October, Msgr Piastrelli and Pietro Lizier were finally removed from their positions and replaced respectively by Fr Montini and Igino Righetti,[12] who had thitherto been the vice-president of the Roman Circle. The Sovereign Pontiff had the right to name the General Chaplain of the FUCI; on the other hand, until then, the National President had always been elected by the movement's national council. By imposing Montini and Righetti to head the movement, Pius

---

10 Thursday, June 11, 1925.
11 Pietro Lizier (1896–1973) was an Italian politician who was a member of the Christian Democracy party. He founded the local party newspaper, *Popolo del Veneto* [People of Veneto] in 1945. He had a degree in journalism and teaching.
12 Igino Righetti (1904–1939) was an Italian lawyer and president of the FUCI (1925–1934) who would help to establish the *Laureati* in 1933.

XI would maintain closer control over the Circles of Catholic students while territorial treaties with the Italian State, as well as a concordat, were in the midst of negotiations. This appointment, which was presented as provisional, but was in fact permanent, displeased Fr Montini at first, because he was replacing, on the orders of his superiors, a priest who, in his eyes, had not been at fault;[13] also, his instructions from the Vatican would inevitably clash sometimes with his convictions, not to mention his other commitments. Notably, it was undesirable for the FUCI and Catholic Action in general to appear associated with the PPI any longer.

To grant more authority to the new national chaplain, who was otherwise still *minutante* at the Secretariat of State, he was named a Supernumerary Privy Chamberlain — a title corresponding to no precise function, but which gave him the right to be called "Monsignor." As often as he could, Msgr Montini tried to avoid using the title, preferring the more technical but less clerically honorific "Ecclesiastical Assistant" (*Assistente Ecclesiastico*). For his parents, he remained Don Battista; for his students he soon acquired the nickname "Don Gibiemme" (from his initials GBM).

At the heart of FUCI, he and Righetti met with opposition that was more or less open for several months. They were regarded as "the men of the Vatican." Several directors of provincial Circles were frankly hostile to the central authority's directives. Msgr Montini had been specifically asked to separate male and female students, so that the young ladies would form another organization, independent of FUCI. The national chaplain insisted that the directive be obeyed, but allowed mixed groups under some circumstances. In general, Righetti and Msgr Montini imposed a predominantly cultural and spiritual program on the movement and held meetings in a more academic style than had previously been the case. Numerous provincial circles, jealous of their autonomy, protested. There were the beginnings of a schism. To ease tensions, Msgr Montini made himself freely available to everybody, writing to all provincial directors who seemed recalcitrant or disillusioned, or were tempted to resign.[14] He visited several provincial towns to explain and convince.

---

13   Fr Montini stayed in close contact with his predecessor, keeping up a regular correspondence with him for a few years. Cf. F. Fonzi, ed., *La Testimonianza di Luigi Piastrelli*.
14   Part of this correspondence for normalizing the FUCI has been published in *Notiziario* 4 (April 1982): 20–48.

THE CULTURAL COMBAT

Conflicts between Catholic and Fascist students became more and more frequent. At the beginning of 1926, Msgr Montini wanted to reopen the church of Sant'Ivo alla Sapienza for worship. Sant'Ivo was next to the university La Sapienza and was then being used as a warehouse. The Fascist press attacked the proposal; students of the GUF (*Gruppo Universitario Fascista* — University Fascist Group) treated this initiative as a provocation. Nonetheless, Mussolini's government authorized that the church be returned to use for Catholic worship. Msgr Montini celebrated the first Mass on March 21. The official chaplain was Msgr Amleto Cicognani,[15] professor at the Pontifical Athenæum of San Apollinare. Sant'Ivo became the main parish for Catholic students. On May 1, a bulletin appeared, *La Sapienza*, advertising itself as the "newspaper of opinion for the Catholic university students of Rome." Montini collaborated from the very first printing. This inaugural issue contained an anonymous article recalling how, in 1898, Pope Leo XIII had defended Catholic associations against attacks by the anticlerical government of that time in his encyclical *Spesse Volte*.[16] The parallels to the present situation were self-evident and hinted at a veiled accusation against the current pope who, this time, did not intervene. The article's insinuations caused a scandal. The affair made it as far as Pius XI himself, who summoned Msgr Montini. The pope demanded that he reveal the identity of the anonymous article's author. It was Alcide De Gasperi,[17] one of the leaders of the PPI.

Msgr Montini did not reveal Gasperi's name but managed to evade being held responsible. Still, the bulletin decisively changed direction editorially, only to disappear the following year.

Msgr Montini's period as national chaplain of FUCI was plagued with conflict because of growing hostility between Fascist groups and a Catholic group presumed to be hostile to the Fascist regime. In August 1926 the National Congress of FUCI was held at Macerata; this was the

---

15 Card. Amleto Cicognani (1883–1973), Italian, served as Vatican Secretary of State (1961–1969). From 1972 until his death, he was also Dean of the College of Cardinals. He was appointed Apostolic Delegate to the United States, which he remained for 25 years, serving as liaison between the Vatican and the American hierarchy. He was made titular archbishop of Laodicea in Phrygia (1933).
16 Pope Leo XIII issued the encyclical *Spesse Volte* in Italian on August 5, 1898, as a protest against the violent oppression of Catholic associations in Italy and as a call to action by peaceful and non-political means of resistance.
17 Alcide De Gasperi (1881–1954) was among the founders of the PPI in 1919 and then of the DC during World War II. He served as Prime Minister from 1945 to 1953, during which time the crippled Italian monarchy was overthrown.

first in which Msgr Montini participated as the national chaplain.[18] On the first day of the congress, young Fascists and "Fucini" (members of FUCI) fought in the streets; some were wounded. At night the Congress's attendees felt compelled to leave the city and seek refuge in Assisi.

A few months later, some Fascist militants sought to avenge the attempted assassination of Mussolini (October 31). At Brescia the headquarters of Il Cittadino was sacked and burned; Giorgio Montini sent his family to the country, out of harm's way. There were similar incidents in other cities. Msgr Montini was afraid that FUCI's publications would be suspended. Writing to his family on November 4, he blamed the government of Mussolini for the chaos and violence:

> evidently the goal is to provoke a purge: it is a means of chaining the minds that seek to escape it.... What is painful is that the Italian people thus come to receive the mortal example of loquacity and disturbance and that they are continually troubled, not restraining themselves within reasonable limits but unleashing themselves in improvised brutality....

Following this failed assassination, the one hundred and twenty Opposition legislators (including Giorgio Montini) who had refused to take their seats in Parliament since 1924 lost their mandates.

It should be noted that after the assassination attempt on Mussolini failed, the president of the ACI, Luigi Colombo,[19] addressed an official message to the Duce to express relief that he had escaped death. Evidently the Catholic movements were not unanimously anti-Fascist. The Church, in its highest authority, the pope, sought above all to defend the religious rights of the faithful and maintain social harmony. For this reason, the Catholic movements were directed to keep away from political activities and agitations. Under orders from the Secretariat of State, Msgr Montini asked all members of FUCI to leave the UGI (Unione Goliardica Italiana — Italian Union of Student Fraternities), which had been recently created as an alliance between Catholic, Socialist, and Liberal students who were hostile to the regime.

---

18 He had spent the preceding month in France to study German in Strasbourg. On his way back he stopped in Paray-le-Monial, for a pilgrimage to the tomb of Saint Margaret Mary Alacoque (1647–1690; canonized in 1920 by Pope Benedict XV).
19 Luigi Colombo (1886–1973) was a lawyer and a leading exponent of Catholicism. At just eighteen years old, he became the secretary of both the Diocesan Council of Catholic Action and the Diocesan Federation of Economic and Social Works.

The national chaplain and the president of FUCI increasingly adopted a policy of tactical retreat, avoiding public demonstrations and writings that would irritate authorities. They would not confront the regime directly or engage with Fascist ideology; instead they would engage in cultural combat, reinvigorating Catholic culture while aiming at forming an elite. Few students were members of the FUCI;[20] but this minority, formed in a spirit of renewal, would inherit the leftist Catholicism of the now-voiceless PPI and be in a position to take up the torch at the opportune moment. Subsequent events have demonstrated the soundness of this strategy: the leaders of the Christian Democratic movement, who would lead Italy from the post-war period through to the 1990s, almost all came from the pre-war PPI (De Gasperi) or from Montini's FUCI (Guido Gonella,[21] Aldo Moro, Giulio Andreotti,[22] etc.).

To develop this cultural and religious formation of the Catholic élite of the future, Msgr Montini reinvigorated the movement's review, *Studium* (which was transferred to Rome): soon a publishing house of the same name was founded, along with a bimonthly journal, *Azione fucina*. Very often he collaborated in these publications himself, contributing in-depth editing on some articles, writing book reviews, and composing essays that originated in the religion classes he conducted on Saturday evenings for his students. At the end of the 1920s he conducted extensive research into the life and teaching of Christ in the New Testament; these studies likely spread out over many months, and even years. In total, Msgr Montini filled five large notebooks with meditations and commentaries, in Latin, on the Gospel of Saint Luke, and five others, in Italian, on the letters of Saint Paul.[23] These studies were used, in part, in the religion lessons for the students and the articles published in *Studium*.

---

20 A total of 2,370 enrolled throughout Italy for the academic year 1928–1929: that is to say, less than six percent of all university students. Numbers established by Renato Moro, *La Formazione della classe dirigente cattolica* (1929–1937).
21 Guido Gonella (1905–1982) was an Italian politician from the Christian Democracy who was also Minister of Public Education (1946–1951) and Minister of Justice (four terms in office, between 1953 and 1973). He was suspected of having antifascist views and so was closely watched by the Fascist hierarchy.
22 Giulio Andreotti (1919–2013) was a right-wing Italian statesman who served in numerous senior ministerial roles and was the forty-first Italian Prime Minister, in office three times between 1972–1992. He is widely regarded as one of Italy's most powerful post-war politicians. As a student, he joined FUCI, meeting the future leader of the Christian Democratic Party and eventually becoming the FUCI president in 1942.
23 Daniel-Ange is wrong to date these "large volumes" to the fifties, during his episcopacy in Milan (*Paul VI, un regard prophétique*, 2:230). Archbishop Montini would not have had the time then to dedicate himself to personal studies of such magnitude.

Montini's writings from the twenties and thirties bear witness to an interiorist conception of religion ("the prayer of the soul where one can meet God"), as well as an optimistic vision of the world in which the Christian life should be a "witness."[24] They also betray considerable interest in modern culture. Aside from the numerous biblical references, contemporary writers in literature, religion, and history are much more frequently cited than classical authors on these subjects. Msgr Montini believed that a new religious culture appeared during the twenties and thirties, so that a "work of intellectual apostolate" was possible, where questions might be considered in a new light. This new religious approach would rarely cause any open conflict with traditional Catholic culture, which would take no notice of it, or pass over it in silence. Msgr Montini wanted to promote what he would later call "a new humanism." A humanism nourished by multiple sources: the Gospel, a new conception of the liturgy and prayer, and finally, contemporary Catholic culture.

With regard to this "new humanism," it is important to note that during this period he developed an interest in two authors in particular: Fr Maurice Zundel and Jacques Maritain. He had met the former during his stay in Paris in 1924. When, two years later, Zundel published his book *Poème de la sainte liturgie* [Poem of the Holy Liturgy],[25] Msgr Montini not only reviewed it in *Studium*, but ensured its translation into Italian. In this volume, Zundel developed a poetic and mystical vision of the liturgy: liturgy treated as a symphony, rather than as an orderly ritual. Msgr Montini also published in the review a text of Zundel titled "Caro verbum factum est," an inversion of the famous gospel phrase: Et *Verbum caro factum est* ("the Word was made flesh," John 1:14). Some theologians were alarmed by this reordering of sacred words.

The interest in Maritain began almost simultaneously. The first book of the famous philosopher that Msgr Montini read seems to have been the Italian translation of *Introduction générale à la philosophie*.[26] He read the volume attentively at some point in 1925; his personal copy contains

---

24 See, in particular, the two series of articles "La preghiera dell'anima" and "Le idee di S. Paolo," of the years 1930 and 1931, re-edited under the title *Colloqui religiosi*. There is still lacking a study of the body of Montini's works of this period.
25 English version: Maurice Zundel, *The Splendor of the Liturgy*, trans. Edward Watkin (London: Sheed & Ward, 1945). Maurice Zundel (1897–1975) was a Swiss priest and theologian whose doctoral thesis in philosophy explored the influence of nominalism on Christian thought. In 1972, Paul VI invited Fr Zundel to preach the traditional Lenten retreat at the Vatican.
26 English edition: Jacques Maritain, *Introduction to Philosophy*, trans. E. I. Watkin (London: Sheed & Ward, 1930).

numerous handwritten notes. That same year, Maritain's *Trois Réformateurs* appeared in France. Msgr Montini no doubt learned about it during his visit to Strasbourg in 1926; in December of that year he wrote to Maritain, asking if he could translate the work into Italian. Maritain accepted. Msgr Montini's translation was published in 1928 by Morcelliana Editions.[27] It was preceded by a long preface, signed simply "g.b.m."

In this preface, Msgr Montini praises Maritain for having retraced "the origins of contemporary subjectivism" as expressed through the work of three "reformers": Luther (in religion), Descartes (in philosophy), and Rousseau (in the sociopolitical domain).[28] What all three men had in common was that each promoted "individualist relativism" in his discipline. Despite this, the author of the preface does not defend tradition. He also denigrates the Neoscholastics[29] (in his eyes Maritain is not one of them): "Ancient Thomism needs revision," he writes, and he stigmatizes certain Catholic philosophers of the day (without naming them) "who crush their adversaries under the weight of their Thomistic manuals without recognizing that the manuals were conceived not for crushing one's neighbor, but to be read and meditated upon." In this same preface there is also a criticism of Fascism (not directly named either, but the allusion is clear) which he blames for having broken with the tradition of Christian humanism to promote "the insolent and adventurous liberty of the egoists and revolutionaries."[30]

---

27 Jacques Maritain, *Tre Riformatori*, trans. G. Battista Montini (Brescia: Morcelliana, 1928). English edition: *Three Reformers* (London: Sheed & Ward, 1950).

28 Fr Martin Luther (1483–1546) was a German Augustinian monk, priest, and theology professor, who inaugurated the Protestant Reformation by rejecting several Roman Catholic teachings and practices. Because of his controversial writings, he was excommunicated by Pope Leo X in 1521. René Descartes (1596–1650) was known as a groundbreaking mathematician and philosopher of nature who was credited as a co-framer of refraction theory. Among other influential works, he published *Treatise on Light*, *Discourse on Method*, and *Meditations on First Philosophy*. Jean-Jacques Rousseau (1712–1778) was a philosopher, writer, and composer from Geneva whose theories in political philosophy, economics, and education were influential in the European Enlightenment and in the unfolding of the French Revolution.

29 On August 4, 1879, Pope Leo XIII issued the encyclical *Aeterni Patris* on the importance of following the philosophy of St. Thomas Aquinas to avoid the pitfalls of modern philosophical errors. That encyclical gave rise to neoscholasticism (otherwise known as neoscholastic Thomism or neo-Thomism), named after the medieval school of philosophy based on the moderate realism and critical reasoning of Aristotle, of which St Thomas was the preeminent figure. Maritain is often considered a Thomist, but his reinterpretation of Aquinas in the light of humanistic and personalist perspectives has led some more traditional Thomists to exclude his thought from the school.

30 Fairly regular epistolary ties must have been established because Maritain wrote articles in *Azione fucina* in 1930 and 1931. The Maritain Archives (Kolbsheim) have not preserved any of the correspondence of this period.

This preface is dated Epiphany 1928. On this same day Fr Bevilacqua left Brescia and moved to Rome, to live in the same house as Catholic Action's chaplains and Msgr Montini. Fr Bevilacqua was ordered to leave the city by Cardinal Laurenti,[31] Prefect of the Congregation of Religious, after he was repeatedly denounced by the Fascists of Brescia in the wake of recent clashes. The Congregation, in calling him to Rome, focused as much on protecting him as on calming tempers. Fr Bevilacqua's arrival in Rome was going to stimulate Msgr Montini all the more to take the path less trod. A few months later, on October 31, the two priests left the common residence of the Catholic chaplains and rented a large house, on the Aventine hill. A major reason for Msgr Montini's decision to live in this neighborhood was the proximity of the Benedictine Abbey of Sant'Anselmo: he would be able to attend the monastic offices frequently and to keep in regular contact with the religious there, who had been carrying out liturgical research for decades.

This interest in liturgy, along with the idea that it could be renewed through a simplification tantamount to purification, and through greater participation by the faithful, only grew stronger in Msgr Montini. Three months before moving to the Aventine, he had made another tour of various abbeys, as he often enjoyed doing.[32] His travel companion was Msgr Grazioli, chaplain of the FUCI circle of Verona, who happened to have been the first man to introduce Italians to the Liturgical Movement that arose at the Abbey of Maria-Laach as a result of Dom Casel's work.[33] After a day-long visit to Paris and then to Reims, they visited Belgian and German abbeys throughout July and August: Maredsous, Saint-André-de-Lophem, Mont-César, Maria-Laach, Beuron. At Maredsous, where they spent five days, they had several conversations with the young director of the *Révue liturgique et monastique*.[34] All the monasteries they visited during this

---

31   Card. Camillo Laurenti (1861–1938) was an Italian cardinal, elevated in 1921 by Pope Benedict XV. He studied at the Pontifical Gregorian University and received doctorates in theology and philosophy. He was chosen to be pope in the 1922 election, but he refused to accept the election and instead became Prefect of the Sacred Congregation of Religious (1922–1928), then Preface of the Sacred Congregation of Rites (1929–1938).
32   In preparation for this trip, Msgr Montini had taken German lessons with Fr Damasus Winzen, OSB, a monk of the abbey of Maria-Laach who was then studying at Sant'Anselmo (letter of Fr Petrus Novack to the author, March 17, 1992), and who later founded Mount Savior Monastery in Elmira, New York.
33   Dom Odo Casel (1886–1948) was a German Benedictine monk whose theology of mysteries would play a role in the liturgical reform movement of the twentieth century. Pope Pius XII (1947) incorporated some of his ideas into the official teaching of the Catholic Church.
34   The *Révue liturgique et monastique* was published by the Abbey of Maredsous from 1919 to 1940.

summer tour shared in common the trait of having participated or participating in the Liturgical Movement, with personalities of repute including Dom Lambert Beauduin, OSB[35] and Dom Gaspar Lefebvre, OSB.[36] This Movement was aimed at encouraging the faithful to participate more deeply in the Mass, publishing translations of the Missal, and encouraging liturgical "experiments." The reforms that Montini would initiate as pope were inspired by these experiences of the 1920s.

Father Bevilacqua's presence in Rome renewed Msgr Montini's acquaintance with his main intellectual influence, with whom he had so much in common intellectually. Msgr Montini's surviving correspondence demonstrates how these men's house on the Aventine became a frequent meeting place for numerous anti-Fascist Catholics, who had been reduced to public silence or at least a prudent reserve: Longinotti, Dalla Torre,[37] and still others. In this milieu, the Lateran Accords[38] were dismissed or only half-heartedly accepted.

"WARINESS AND PRUDENCE"

When Mussolini came to power in 1922, he quickly voiced his desire to see the "Roman Question" resolved after it had been hanging in the air for half a century. Pius XI had received the proposition favorably; the first discreet contacts were established between the Italian government and the Holy See before Cardinal Gasparri, the Vatican's Secretary of State, opened official negotiations. The "Roman Question" combined several questions: what territorial sovereignty should be accorded to the Vatican State; what financial indemnities should be granted to the Vatican to compensate for territories lost in 1870; and what should the status of the Catholic religion be in the Italian state? The papacy wished to see its rights to rule a temporal and sovereign state recognized (albeit with its territories drastically reduced), and also wished to preserve the

---

35 Dom Lambert Beauduin (1873–1960) was a Belgian monk who founded Chevetogne Abbey in 1925. He was a leading member of the Liturgical Movement that originated in the nineteenth century. Beauduin encouraged the people's active participation in the Mass.
36 Dom Gaspar Lefebvre (1880–1966) was a French churchman who studied at the abbey school of Maredsous and was ordained a priest in 1904. He dedicated his life's work to liturgical theology and was heavily influenced by Dom Guéranger.
37 Giuseppe Dalla Torre del Tempio di Sanguinetto (1885–1967) was an Italian journalist who was active in the ACI and was the director of L'Osservatore Romano from 1920–1960.
38 The Lateran Treaty, often referred to as the Lateran Accords, was the treaty between the Holy See and the Fascist Italian State (still technically a kingdom) that put an end to the Roman Question concerning the mutual recognition of the two countries.

Church's full liberty to assure her spiritual mission in all its aspects. Mussolini agreed to recognize Catholicism as an essential component of the Italian national tradition and strove to win the favor of Italian Catholics while simultaneously affirming the need for the Fascist state to control all engines of society, including the education of the young. It was on this particular question that they encountered the greatest difficulties with negotiations, "to the point of suspending them twice and seriously jeopardizing them."[39]

On February 11, 1929, they finally concluded negotiations and signed the Lateran Accords. At his modest post in the Secretariat of State, Msgr Montini was obviously not directly involved with the negotiations; at most he might perhaps have been informed of developments through conversations with his superiors. On January 19, in a letter to his parents a month after the signing of the Accords, he shared his skepticism with them, writing: "This could be amongst the greatest events of our history and even the most beautiful," but he was afraid that the pope, and still more the faithful, might lose their spiritual liberty. Further, he suspected Mussolini and the Fascist negotiators of having "anything but good faith." Once he was fully aware of the content of the Accords, he privately made clear his extreme reservations about the whole agreement, and his criticism of certain specific points. The Accords consisted of a treaty in which the Vatican and Italy mutually recognized one another as sovereign states;[40] a financial convention through which the Italian state paid damages to the Holy See for its losses; and finally a concordat which notably recognized Catholicism as the state religion.

At the hour of the signing, Pius XI announced the event, declaring his great satisfaction with it; L'Osservatore Romano boasted a full-page headline: "Italy has been returned to God and God to Italy"; the church bells of Rome rang; the streets were decked with flags. Msgr Montini and his friends of the Christian Democracy did not feel the same enthusiasm. That very evening, in the Aventine house, De Gasperi (freed from Fascist prison a few months before), Dalla Torre and others met with Fr Bevilacqua and Msgr Montini to discuss the event. A student of the FUCI, who was present at the meeting, reports that the discussion was lively.[41] Some were fiercely hostile to the new "reconciliation," others including Msgr

---

39 Georges Jarlot, Pie XI, 151.
40 A reduced sovereignty for the Vatican over the 109 acres (0.7 mi. sq.) that surround Saint Peter's basilica, plus the domain of Castel Gandolfo and a few other religious sites.
41 Giuseppe Cassano, "Testimonianze," Notiziario 4 (April 1982): 63–69.

Montini shared the "deepest reservations." That the Church had officially renounced the exercise of temporal power in Italy seemed beneficial in his eyes; on the other hand, he was afraid that the Church would never be forgiven for having obtained an advantageous situation (concordat, financial indemnity) from the hands of an authoritarian regime.

One week after the Accords were signed, he wrote to his parents: "Wariness and prudence should never cease, that is the conclusion; only the superficial and irresponsible can, shamefully, feel complete joy." He and his friends thought that there was nothing left to do but remain patient. Shortly afterwards, thanks to steps taken by Longinotti and a few political friends, De Gasperi found an ideal refuge: the Vatican. Employed officially in the Vatican Library, he was able freely and fearlessly to meet with friends and read the foreign press, which was sometimes banned from distribution in Italy by the Censor.

This wait-and-see form of opposition was by no means common to all Catholics. At the legislative elections the following May, the President of Catholic Action encouraged voting for Fascist candidates. At the heart even of FUCI, not all students were anti-Fascists. The signing of the Accords could be considered a reconciliation between Church and State; it seems that Catholic organizations saw an influx of new members in the ensuing months. Msgr Montini, in a confidential circular letter addressed to FUCI leaders, complained that FUCI's atmosphere had been "gradually modified by the influx of new and diverse people"; he also criticized "the conciliatory attitude" towards the regime adopted by many Catholic students since February 11.[42] Instances of double membership, in both FUCI and the University Fascist Group (GUF) multiplied. Righetti and Msgr Montini quickly decided to exclude students who did not want to abandon the GUF.

PACELLI, SECRETARY OF STATE

A few months after the signing of the Lateran Accords, Cardinal Gasparri considered his work to have been completed and relinquished his position as Secretary of State. Pius XI chose Cardinal Pacelli[43] to replace

---

42 Circular letter of October 2, 1929, cited in a note in *Lettere ai familiari* 2:618.
43 Eugenio Pacelli (1876–1958) was head of the Catholic Church and Sovereign of the Vatican City State under the name Pius XII (1939–1958). He served in various ecclesiastical roles before becoming pope, including Papal Nuncio to Germany (1920–1930) and Cardinal Secretary of State (1930–1939). During his pontificate, the Catholic Church passed the Decree against Communism, declaring that Catholics who professed the Communist doctrine were thereby excommunicated.

him. This cardinal had been nuncio in Germany, first at Munich, then at Berlin, for about ten years. At a banquet given in the cardinal's honor at the Ecclesiastical Academy, a few days after the official nomination, Msgr Montini met for the first time the man who was to be his superior for decades to come. His first impression, recorded in a letter to his parents on January 27, 1930, reveals how he felt from the beginning of their acquaintance; his feelings would not change when the cardinal rose from the Secretariat of State to become pope nine years later. "He is someone who genuinely inspires admiration," wrote Msgr Montini to his family. In career and personality, Cardinal Pacelli was brilliant: he was a polyglot intellectual who had rapidly climbed the ranks of the Secretariat of State before embarking on a diplomatic career that had now led him to the second-highest post in the Church. It is not unthinkable that, at this date, Msgr Montini recognized that he shared certain of these traits with the new Secretary of State and could dream of following in his footsteps.

The nomination of Cardinal Pacelli had been preceded by some assignment changes within the Secretariat of State — not to mention promotions: Msgr Ottaviani was named Substitute, while Msgr Pizzardo became Secretary of Extraordinary Affairs, of which department Msgr Tardini (until then the *primo minutante*) became the Under-Secretary. Msgr Montini remained in Ordinary Affairs, with the title of *primo minutante*. The arrival of Cardinal Pacelli at the head of the Secretariat changed the rhythm of work. His predecessor had counseled him not to deal in person with any but the most important questions, leaving the others to his subordinates. Cardinal Pacelli acted in completely the opposite manner. One of his collaborators reported:

> He wanted to be kept up to date on everything.... He was an eminent master and a sure guide for his subordinates. He closely supervised even the style of texts to be transmitted and the exterior presentation of the typed sheets. If he found a small error, he would return the documents to the person responsible and would not place his signature until after the correction. He always behaved with graceful good manners, never making a reproach or manifesting the least irritation. But his acts were more eloquent than his words. Every evening we sent him a large leather folder containing the documents to be signed (there were sometimes almost a hundred), and the next day the folder would be returned to our offices. It contained two pockets: in

one, the cardinal placed the signed documents; in the other, those which had not been signed.[44]

In spite of the added responsibilities and the greater workload which his new post had earned him, Msgr Montini continued his apostolate with the students of the FUCI, often traveling throughout the regions of Italy for meetings, or to preach retreats. Thus, during Holy Week of 1930, he preached the Spiritual Exercises at Frascati. One of the participants has kept a "precise, localized and even acoustic memory of the pathos and the characteristic voice, incisive and almost strident, in which he discussed the *Improperia* of Good Friday and the parable of the Prodigal Son."[45] Msgr Montini, official at the Secretariat of State, students' chaplain, and priest, did not fulfil these three functions with equal pleasure. The letters he continually wrote to his parents show us that his work at the Vatican did not enthrall him. His FUCI activities, the provincial visits entailed by his duties, his visits to Brescia to see his family, and his holidays,[46] made his absences frequent.

Although he sometimes doubted the effectiveness of his ministry with young people, he does not seem to have felt any similar reservations about his priestly vocation. For the tenth anniversary of his ordination, he made a retreat at the Abbey of Monte Cassino, in the company of Fr Bevilacqua. There he renewed his acquaintance with the Benedictine *ora et labora* which he so admired. During this retreat he meditated on the *Pontificale Romanum*,[47] which includes directions for the rites of ordinations. In a notebook he wrote down his daily reflections on this liturgical reading.[48] One meditation ends with long notes on the priesthood: "The priest should imitate Christ... copy morally his virtues. Desire holiness. The virtues of Jesus: a) in the period of his family life: humility and

---

44   Domenico Tardini, *Pie XII*, 91.
45   Nicola Ciancio, *Vita con don Bosco*, 35. The *Improperia* or Reproaches are sung during the rite of the Adoration of the Cross during the Mass of the Presanctified on Good Friday. They are a series of complaints that Our Lord is portrayed as addressing to His Chosen People, asking them what among His blessings is the cause of their turning against Him: *Popule meus, quid feci tibi? Aut in quo contristavi te? Responde mihi*... (O my people, what have I done to you? How have I offended you? Answer me!...)
46   During the summer of 1930, he made another visit of around ten days to France: a week in Paris (with outings to Amiens and Reims) then a quick tour of Chartres, Solesmes, Angers, Tours, and Lourdes.
47   The *Pontificale Romanum*, last edited under Pope John XXIII in 1961, is the book that contains the texts of the sacraments (e.g., confirmation and ordination) and rites (e.g., the consecration of chalices and churches) normally celebrated by a bishop.
48   Text published in *Notiziario* 11 (November 1985): 7–23.

silence and obedience; b) in his public life: strength and meekness." In the Church the priest "ought to know and to feel principally member and son, rather than superior."

This conception of the priesthood allowed him to consider his apostolate amongst the students as a work of "formation of consciences." The expression is employed by Montini himself in a work he published this same year 1930, *Coscienza universitaria*,[49] a collection of articles which had previously appeared in *Studium*. This formation, he explained, ought to enable students to acquire a sense of the responsibilities, difficulties, and rules of life. The Christian student should also consider study as a passionately enamored search for the truth. His conscience should become critical. In a lyrical flight, Msgr Montini defined the formation received at FUCI as unique and separate:

> Against the senile formalisms in which the wilted modern soul vegetates; against the commercial imperialism of today's professional formation; against the pedantries and compulsions of certain methods of teaching and discipline; against the dangers and monstrous melancholy of certain romantics: we want to preserve for the souls of students a spontaneity of thought, of action, and of sentiments which will be their own and will reform them; with the confidence that this will give a strong encouragement to the personal activity of the young people and guide them in the path of Christian optimism and hope.

It is important to note that the veiled criticism in these words is directed not merely at secular Fascist education but simultaneously at traditional Catholic education as well. During this period, Msgr Montini thought that religious and cultural activities ought to be combined, that cultural activity possessed a "great potential for conquering." Some reproached his activism — his faith in an apostolate through culture, including Fr Giuseppe De Luca,[50] historian, translator of Saint Augustine, Saint Francis de Sales, and Saint Bonaventure, and learned connoisseur of French literature, who had collaborated for several years in the activities of FUCI, writing in the movement's journals, participating in its meetings,

---

49 G. B. Montini, *Coscienza universitaria* (Rome: Studium, 1930). Republished in 2014 by the same publisher.
50 Fr Giuseppe De Luca (1898–1962) was an Italian priest and publisher. He began his studies with the Jesuits in Ferentino (1909). He was ordained in 1921 and had many roles in ecclesial positions such as archivist at the Congregation for the Oriental Churches, and displayed religious activism by committing to the Catholic Action movement.

and giving talks. In November 1930, he decided that he would no longer participate in the lectures and meetings of the movement, because he was not attracted to the "commando" style of the "conquest projects" being enacted. He preferred to spend his time on in-depth personal projects. Msgr Montini was hurt by this departure, and wrote to De Luca, not without some pretention:

> If your solitude were a simple tactical retreat — and certainly it is — and a pure fidelity to your work — and it is — then I would have no right to make any complaint. But you seem to announce it as a theory, a theory which cuts the shabby worn threads with which we believed we would be able to weave again the robe of charity which should clothe the Church of Christ with youthfulness and glory in this century. Maybe we are in a hurry, and it is too bad. But charity presses us onwards, and our awkwardness hopes to find itself somewhat softened by our zeal. Take care that your wisdom does not cool love, does not eliminate sacrifice, does not fracture the body of Christ. You have chosen your books; I would choose souls instead.[51]

The break between the two men was not total; they continued to maintain contact. But De Luca's departure heralded some increasingly sharp criticisms leveled against Msgr Montini's apostolate at FUCI. They came from multiple directions.

THE CRISIS OF 1931

In 1931, the government of Mussolini and the Church entered into conflict. Full rupture was averted only by concessions made on both sides. At the same time, Msgr Montini became the object of serious misgivings; the only reason he was not forced to leave his post as national chaplain is that his superiors did not want to weaken a movement that was already in decline, as other Catholic organizations also were, on account of the government's hostility.

FUCI did not directly provoke the grave crisis that arose between the government and the Church. It was a circular of March 19, 1931 of the GCI (*Gioventù Cattolica Italiana* — Italian Catholic Youth), signed by the President of the Roman Federation, which set off the explosion. It called for the creation of a "secretariat of workers" in each Circle, to

---

[51] Letter of November 19, 1930, published in Romano Guarnieri, "Notizia bio-bibliografica di Don Giuseppe De Luca," *Rivista di storia della Chiesa in Italia* (January-April 1963): 39.

promote charitable works and to undertake "every activity that could be an aid and encouragement in society." In the following days, several Fascist newspapers learned of this circular and denounced it as part of a plot to create rival organizations to the Fascist unions. Attacks were soon directed against all branches of Catholic Action, including FUCI. The Fascist press published lists of the leaders of Catholic organizations who were current or former members of the PPI. Skirmishes between young Fascists and militant Catholics multiplied. A regional congress of FUCI that should have been held at Padua was suspended by order of the government, and relocated to Pavia, where it was ultimately banned for fear of potential consequences. For several weeks in April, *Azione fucina* was prevented from appearing. While the Fascist press continued attacking Catholic Action, clashes became more and more frequent. In Rome some young Fascists invaded and wrecked a church; there was violence in Venice, Florence, Milan, and Genoa. On May 29, finally Mussolini ordered the prefects to close all Circles of the GCI and to dissolve FUCI and confiscate its property. The next day members were locked out of FUCI headquarters, in the presence of Msgr Montini and Righetti. They were banned from the chapel of Sant'Ivo.

Twice, on May 28 and 29, the apostolic nuncio in Rome, Archbishop Borgongini Duca, sent a letter of protest to the Minister of Foreign Affairs. Rumors ran wild of a rupture of the concordat and a breakdown in diplomatic relations. Msgr Montini wanted such a rupture; on May 30 he wrote to his family: "Everyone has the feeling that something at first terrible, and ultimately providential, is about to happen."

Pius XI responded with sang-froid. He asked that all the Italian bishops take Catholic Action under their protection in their diocese and control its movements directly; he also suspended solemn processions in Rome and Italy. From the whole world, messages of sympathy and affection arrived at the Vatican. The pope chose to not provoke irreversible actions, while standing firm on the spiritual rights of the Church. He wrote a long encyclical, not in Latin as is the tradition but in Italian: *Non Abbiamo Bisogno*. Championing the "sacred and inviolable rights of souls and the Church," he denounced the dissolution of the Catholic youth movements which had no other goal, he wrote, than "to rip young people, all young people, from Catholic Action, and thence from the Church." He accused the Fascists of wanting

> to monopolize all young people ... for the full and exclusive advantage of a party, a regime, on the basis of an ideology which

explicitly falls into a true and proper pagan statolatry, in full conflict as much with the natural rights of the family as with the supranatural rights of the Church.

The state cannot claim the education and formation of young people for itself alone. But Pius XI did not want, for all that, to incite rebellion against the government: "the battle we are fighting today is not political, it is moral and religious: specifically, moral and religious." He did not make a global condemnation of Fascism, as is explicitly stated in the conclusion: "We have not aimed to condemn the regime and the party as such."

This encyclical was dated June 29 but was not made public until a few days later. Pius XI feared that its circulation would be forbidden in Italy. Also, in the days preceding its publication, he took the precaution of sending the text discreetly to the nuncios of various foreign countries. From his correspondence with his parents, we know that Msgr Montini was charged with carrying the encyclical to the nuncios of Berne and Munich.[52] Thus, when *L'Osservatore Romano* published the encyclical on July 5, the newspapers of France, Germany, the United States, Switzerland, and elsewhere were also able to publish the text on the same day. Msgr Montini had a copy of the Vatican newspaper sent to every member of FUCI.

The government and the Fascist press reacted violently to the papal protestation: membership in any movement of Catholic Action was banned for the adherents of the National Fascist Party; the "unheard-of alliance between the Vatican and Freemasonry" was denounced. Pius XI did not wish, however, to reignite polemics and violence. On July 23, he convoked the cardinals to the Vatican and proposed that an emissary be sent to the government to try to find a solution to the crisis. The majority of the Sacred College pronounced in favor of this initiative. On the following day, a Jesuit, Fr Tacchi Venturi,[53] went to Mussolini, bearing a verbal message from the pope. Secret negotiations were opened, with Fr Tacchi serving as intermediary between Pius XI and the Duce. Msgr Montini was kept entirely out of these transactions and did not even know that they were taking place. While he was on vacation with

---

52 It is doubtless in recompense for this service that he was named, on July 8, a Domestic Prelate of His Holiness, an honorific title which changed nothing in his functions but which, in the subtleties of ecclesiastical hierarchy, was a personal mark of thanks.

53 Fr Pietro Tacchi Venturi, SJ (1861–1956) was a historian by profession and a highly influential diplomat by trade. Although he had no official role in the Vatican Diplomatic Corps, he was known for his friendship with Mussolini and his ability to get things done between the unfriendly parties of the Holy See and the Fascist regime.

his family, he heard that an agreement had been signed on September 2 between the Church and the government. In what has been called the "second conciliation," the Church made many concessions. She was going to assure that no leader of Catholic Action was politically linked to the PPI. If the circles of FUCI were again authorized, it was henceforth under the name of "University Associations," with greater dependence on the general direction of Catholic Action. Thus, Msgr Montini and the direction of the ex-FUCI had to leave their rooms at Piazza di S. Agostino, near the state university, a few weeks later, to move to Largo di Cavalleggeri, in the rooms of Catholic Action, near the Vatican. To be closer to the new headquarters of his movement, Msgr Montini solicited, and after a few months obtained, a large seven-room apartment in the Belvedere Palace, in the heart of the Vatican.[54]

Msgr Montini was disheartened by the accords, as all his correspondence from this time attests. To President Righetti, on September 15, he described them as a "scarcely dignified epilogue, hardly reassuring" but also asked him to accept them with "obedience and loyalty."[55] Even if henceforth only "university associations" existed, and FUCI was officially no more, Msgr Montini, Righetti and all the students retained the old name nonetheless. The reviews of the movement could be published again; meetings resumed in December. Also, at the end of 1931, Msgr Montini was entrusted with a new responsibility: to give a course on the history of Holy See diplomacy at the Pontifical Lateran University. For several years, he took on this supplementary post, with interest it seems.

In 1931, the National Congress of the FUCI had not taken place; nor did any of the three planned regional reunions. In August 1932 the student movement was able to hold a National Congress again, at Cagliari. To go there, Msgr Montini took, for the first time in his life, a plane (he wrote to his family of being "deliciously stunned by the simplicity and security of this new and very convenient mode of transportation"). The congress was closely supervised by the police. Former members of FUCI there decided to create a new movement, that of the "Laureati" ("graduates"). Regrouping former members who had entered into active life, it promoted an intellectual and spiritual formation in line with what the student movement had previously provided. Msgr Montini fully supported this initiative. It was approved by the Vatican, and the next

---

54   Fr Bevilacqua who, until then, had lodged with him, also received an apartment in the Vatican but decided after a few months to return to Brescia. "I find myself very alone spiritually," wrote Msgr Montini to his family, on November 16, 1932.
55   Letter cited in Moro, *La Formazione*, 193.

year the Laureati were able to hold their first congress. Msgr Montini, even after he was separated from FUCI, remained in close contact with the Laureati and participated in their activities.

"RESIGNED" FROM FUCI

Over the course of the crisis of 1931, the first signs of hostility towards Msgr Montini became apparent, in the heart of the Vatican and in some Roman circles. This hostility, which would only grow, was stoked by significant facts as well as rumors, and would lead, two years later, to his expulsion from FUCI.

In May 1931, a new Cardinal Vicar was named: Francesco Marchetti Selvaggiani.[56] This cardinal, in charge of the diocese of Rome, named Msgr Ronca[57] the chaplain of the Roman Circle of FUCI. His ideas of a youth apostolate were radically different from those of the national chaplain Montini. Discord soon arose.

On the preceding March 1, in the run-up to Easter, Msgr Montini had addressed a circular letter to all the chaplains of FUCI circles, giving them some recommendations. He counseled them

> not so much to preach as to converse: fraternal dialogue, based in profound convictions, [but] not academic or rhetorical in style which easily exposes itself to young people's irony. Let us avoid vague subjects; themes of purely natural ethics; overly specialized themes. Let us avoid general allusions to the sciences — facile sweeping condemnations as well as servile flatteries.

But he also stigmatized the "pilgrimages of the devout before cardboard statues" and asked that "the useless and unhealthy multiplicity of candelabras, palms, flowers, etc."[58] be removed from the altars. The text, which Msgr Ronca found without a doubt amongst the papers of his predecessor when he took up the position, scandalized him. He shared this with the Cardinal Vicar but did not want to aggravate FUCI's situation with an intervention, when the government was on the verge of banning it.

---

56   Card. Francesco Marchetti Selvaggiani (1871–1951) was an Italian cardinal, elevated in 1930, serving as, inter alia, the Secretary of the Congregation for the Propagation of the Faith (1922) and Vicar General of Rome (1931–1951).
57   Archbishop Roberto Ronca (1901–1977) was an Italian archbishop affiliated with the University of Brescia. He founded Civiltà Italica (1946), a Christian, anti-communist political movement, which he led until 1955. He was a conservative at the Second Vatican Council and opposed Cardinal Montini even after he became Pope Paul VI.
58   Text cited by M. Marcocchi, "G. B. Montini, scritti fucini," *Notiziario* 21 (June 1991): 33.

At the same time, another fact likely poisoned the situation. Msgr Montini wanted to publish a book of the religion lessons he had given to the students of FUCI over the years; some had already appeared in the review *Studium*. To be published, the book, *La Via di Christo*[59] [The Way of Christ], had to pass scrutiny by the diocesan censor of Brescia, where Msgr Montini was still officially incardinated. The ecclesiastical censor of Brescia, Fr Ernestus Pisani, whose duty was to check that the doctrine being expounded was orthodox, apparently raised several objections. Msgr Montini likely had to justify himself in writing or orally. The *nihil obstat* was granted with great reluctance in April 1931. On August 9, when the work had finally appeared, Msgr Montini wrote to his family that it had cost him "more controversy to have it published than study to write it." The reluctance manifest at Brescia regarding the moral teaching of Msgr Montini must have been known in Rome.

In addition, a rivalry arose in 1932 between FUCI and the Jesuits, who also had apostolate groups for high school and college students — the Marian Congregations. In their university, the Gregorian, they created a Superior Institute of Religious Culture intended to provide courses in doctrine and spirituality for students. These two activities, carried out in a traditional spirit, came into competition with FUCI's activities in the same field, which were conducted in a much more self-consciously innovative manner.

For Easter 1932, Msgr Montini published a circular identical to the one he had sent the preceding year. The climate of suspicion against him, in certain Roman circles, intensified in the following months. He complained to Archbishop Pizzardo, who was in charge of Catholic Action. Still other difficulties arose. The new style that Msgr Ronca introduced in the Roman "university association" — one which Msgr Montini described as "an authoritarian manner deprived of elementary understanding of young people's souls" — provoked conflict within the core group, which had known the Montinian style. A veritable revolt arose against the chaplain of the Roman Circle. Soon, some at the Vatican accused Msgr Montini of being the instigator. Again, the Easter circulars were brought up; their "liturgism" was censured; they were spoken of as disrespectful toward Marian piety. Had Msgr Montini not also written, in the *Studium*, an article in which he affirmed that the liturgy is "preferable to all other customary

---

59 G. B. Montini, *La Via di Christo: Schemi di lezioni sui precetti della morale cattolica per gli studenti di scuole superiori* [The Way of Christ: lesson plans on the precepts of Catholic morality for college students] (Rome: Studium, 1931).

or innovative forms of piety"?[60] That could appear as a criticism of individual devotions that were independent of liturgical ceremonies, such as the Rosary, the veneration of saints, or devotions to the Sacred Heart.

In February 1933, Msgr Montini had to explain himself in turn to Archbishop Pizzardo, Cardinal Pacelli, and Cardinal Marchetti Selvaggiani. The first two, he wrote, seemed satisfied with the justifications and the explanations he provided, although the second made "a few observations."[61] The Cardinal Vicar judged Montini's apostolate entirely unfavorably. On March 12, an anonymous article in *Azione fucina* published a letter from Archbishop Pizzardo announcing the resignation of Msgr Montini from his duties as national chaplain of the Catholic university associations. The stated motive was overwork as a result of his position at the Secretariat of State. No one, of course, was deceived. Had Msgr Montini resigned in the interests of the student movement, or had his resignation been forced? Evidently a number of prelates and religious judged him to be suspect, and asked that he be removed from his position. The final decision lay with the pope. It is reasonable to assume that he asked Montini to resign to calm the waters, while losing none of the esteem in which he held the national chaplain. This seems clear from Msgr Montini's subsequent career.

This forced resignation was painful for Msgr Montini. He wept over it. Was he distanced from Rome for a time, as some have said? It is difficult to be certain; however, he was absent from mid-February to the end of May, in convalescence or for a holiday, either with his parents in Brescia or at some other location. At the end of May, he made a visit to Castel Gandolfo, south of Rome. Emilio Bonomelli,[62] who had worked closely with Giorgio Montini in the PPI, had been asked by the pope, after the Lateran Accords, to restore the pontifical domain that dominates Lake Albano. As the pope was there only during the summer, Bonomelli often hosted Msgr Montini and other political friends throughout the rest of the year.

Msgr Montini, while having been distanced from FUCI, did not break off all contact with the student milieu. Although he no longer wrote in

---

60 "Per la vita spirituale dell'università," *Studium* (August-September 1929): 307.
61 A long letter of Msgr Montini to the bishop of Brescia, dated March 19, 1933, in which he justified himself. Published by A. Fappani and F. Molinari, *G. B. Montini giovane*, 285–91.
62 Emilio Bonomelli (1890–1970) was a leading figure of the twentieth-century Catholic laity. He is well-regarded for his services to the Holy See and the pope for forty years.

Azione fucina, he soon resumed contributing to *Studium*, signing his articles with a pseudonym (SATOR), or with his initials if it was only a book review. Above all, he remained in contact and in correspondence with the lay leaders of the movement, giving them advice, and continuing spiritual direction with some of them. He also created a new Conference of Saint Vincent, to reunite those who were particularly attached to him in charitable enterprises. The meetings took place in the small church of Saint Anne, within the Vatican walls; alms were distributed to the poor in Primavalle, a suburb of Rome. Lastly, he took particular interest in the activities of the Laureati movement and took part in their meetings for several years.

At the end of 1933, on December 8, a group of Fucini and Laureati were reunited around their former chaplain at the Benedictine Abbey of Santa Priscilla in Rome, for a feast celebrated in his honor. According to people who were present, during the sermon he gave that day for the Mass he celebrated in the church of the catacombs, he angrily, frustratedly refuted some of the accusations against him: "It has been said that we never spoke of the Virgin Mary: it is not true!" At the meal which followed, the young friends of Msgr Montini offered him a chalice with this pregnant phrase of Saint Paul's engraved on the base: "The Word of God is not bound" (II Tim. 2:9). The photograph which was taken in souvenir of this reunion shows a Msgr Montini still stricken by melancholy, and almost visibly bitter.

Can it be claimed that after ten years spent at the helm of FUCI, he had given it an impulse it had never known? With regard to membership numbers, we cannot say. When he left the leadership of this Catholic movement, there were hardly three hundred more members than at his arrival; proportionate to the total number of Italian university students, the Fucini now represented only 4.6% — a decreased percentage. As far as concerns the impact he made on the souls of the thousands of young people who visited, read, or listened to him, one can conclude that his tenure marked an important step in the evolution of Italian Catholic youth movements. Some of those whom he formed in FUCI found themselves in years to come in important posts of Catholic Action, numbering amongst high-ranking political leaders, or even included in the ecclesiastical hierarchy.

4
In the Turmoil of Europe

WITHOUT DOUBT, IF MSGR MONTINI HAD maintained control of FUCI, he would not have been able to do so for much longer. He was entrusted with increasing responsibilities at the Secretariat of State that would have prevented him from devoting so much time and energy to his apostolate with the students.

The period following his departure from FUCI coincided with Hitler's[1] rise to power in Germany, and the beginning of turmoil throughout Europe. Msgr Montini became increasingly involved in these matters. In July 1933, von Papen[2] came to Rome to sign the concordat which Hitler's Germany was concluding with the Holy See. This concordat guaranteed freedom of worship, freedom of education, and freedom for Catholic youth movements, but Hitler would ignore these promises soon enough. Msgr Montini was present for the signing of the document. The official photograph of the event shows us the Secretary of State Pacelli seated at the signing table, his two Substitutes Archbishop Pizzardo and Msgr Ottaviani standing at either side of him; Msgr Montini stands further back, as is appropriate for an Undersecretary.

What did he know about National Socialism at this time? Nothing in his writings allows us to judge just how much he knew about Nazi ideology, the programs of the National Socialist German Workers' Party (NSDAP), or the problems which Germany was facing. Was he even interested in international questions? This is a matter for speculation. When, a few months

---

1   Adolf Hitler (1889–1945), Austrian by birth, was the head of the German National Socialist (Nazi) Party. He was appointed Chancellor of Germany in 1933 and then Führer in 1934. He successfully brought an end to the economic depression which had plagued Germany since World War I. His invasion of Poland on September 1, 1939 set off World War II. He committed suicide on April 30, 1945 to avoid capture by the Soviet Red Army.

2   Franz von Papen (1879–1969) was a conservative German politician and diplomat who was the Chancellor of Germany (1932) and then Vice-Chancellor, beneath Hitler (1933–1934). After the Second World War, he was charged in the Nuremberg war criminal trials but was acquitted of all charges. A denazification court found him guilty in 1947 and sentenced him to an eight-year prison sentence. He was released on appeal after two years.

after the signing of the concordat with Germany, Giorgio Montini alerted his son to a long article by Robert d'Harcourt[3] on the Hitler Youth that appeared in La Revue des Deux Mondes[4] (the Montini family had subscribed to this august journal for decades), Msgr Montini read this piece, but with "more repugnance than interest," he noted to his father.

All the same, he grew increasingly interested in international questions. One man, in particular, would have an important role in this respect: Guido Gonella, former member of FUCI, who had studied philosophy and law, and edited *Azione Fucina* and *Studium*. *L'Osservatore Romano* was looking for a commentator on foreign politics. Msgr Montini suggested the name of Gonella to Giuseppe Dalla Torre, editor of the daily paper, who was one of his political friends. Gonella was hired; from May 6, 1933 to May 1940 he wrote, under the title *Acta Diurna*, a widely read chronicle. Two facts explain why Gonella's articles struck a chord with readers: firstly, thanks to his contacts in the Secretariat of State (who were themselves informed by diplomats, and by briefs received from the nuncio), he could circulate original, unfiltered information; secondly, in an Italy where news was subjected to strict censorship, *L'Osservatore Romano* was the only newspaper able to maintain editorial independence. Guido Gonella was to become one of Msgr Montini's confidants and could enlighten him on problems of international politics.

But between 1933 and 1936, Msgr Montini was not necessarily yet the diplomat that some would find brilliant in the forties and fifties. After his nomination as Substitute in 1937 he seemed to blossom. In the meantime, he remained but a modest functionary in the Secretariat of State who was far from passionate about his work at the Vatican and had been deprived of his principal preoccupation thitherto, the youth apostolate. On September 30, 1934, when he had returned after his vacation to what he called — in French — the *corvée* (chore), he wrote to his parents: "This thing is beginning to weigh me down, not so much by fatigue as by my growing need for study, regularity, solitude, and freedom." He wanted to quit his post. Passing moment of depression, or flight of fancy? A few months later, he wrote to his family: "I have finally found a way to entertain myself: I too am in possession of a radio . . ."

---

3 Robert d'Harcourt (1881–1965) was a French academic who focused his attention on German culture and is known for his very strong anti-Nazi views. He published many articles critical of the Nazi regime; his best-known work was *The Gospel of Might*.

4 Robert D'Harcourt, "Jeunesse Hitlérienne," *Revue des Deux Mondes* 18.3 (1933): 514–43.

In 1934, his spiritual director, Fr Caresana, was moved to Rome as Procurator General[5] of his religious congregation and pastor of Chiesa Nuova.[6] He would remain there for twenty years. Msgr Montini could thus see him more frequently and find in him comfort and aid.

BETWEEN BOOKS AND VOYAGES

After his departure from FUCI, he devoted his ample leisure — his duties at the Secretariat of State were hardly overwhelming — to intellectual work. He continued, until 1937, to teach his course on the history of pontifical diplomacy at the Lateran University. At the same institution, he was asked to provide a course of "Introduction to Catholic Dogma" for lay students; this was an indication that he was not universally considered suspect in ecclesiastical circles. In 1933 and in 1934 as well, he published La Vita di Cristo and Introduzione allo studio di Cristo[7] for his FUCI students, and completed a translation of Fr de Grandmaison's[8] Personal Religion, a defense and demonstration drawn from the mystics on the value of mental prayer. This translation was published by Morcelliana Editions, which had published Msgr Montini's translation of Maritain, in the collection significantly entitled "Modern Catholic Thought." This publishing house, which he had helped to found in 1925 at Brescia with Fathers Bevilacqua, Manziana, and Cottinelli,[9] published important translations of European Catholic authors throughout the thirties, including works that inspired particular streams of the Liturgical Movement, such as Sacred Signs and The Spirit of the Liturgy by Romano Guardini,[10] and Liturgy and Personality

---

5   The Procurator General represents the interests of the confederation of Oratorian Congregations to the Holy See.
6   Santa Maria in Vallicella, also known as the Chiesa Nuova, is the principal church of the Oratorians. Founded in 1561 by St Philip Neri, it faces the main thoroughfare of Rome, the Corso Vittorio Emanuele, about a mile to the east of the Vatican.
7   These two texts are included in the book Paul VI, Scritti fucini: 1925–1933 (Brescia: Istituto Paolo VI; Rome: Edizioni Studium, 2004).
8   Fr Léonce de Grandmaison (1868–1927), ordained in 1898, was a French Jesuit priest, theologian, and spiritual writer. He wrote La religion personelle which was published in Etudes in 1927. It was translated into English in 1929 by Algar Thorold.
9   Fr Giuseppe Cottinelli was born in Brescia in 1891 and was also a founding member of the Alessandro Cottinelli Foundation for children in need.
10 Fr Romano Guardini (1885–1968) was a German-Italian priest, author, and academic, widely regarded as one of the most crucial figures in Catholic intellectual life of the twentieth century. His influential books often dealt with the ways in which Christians approached present-day challenges to traditional themes. His first major work, The Spirit of Liturgy, was published during the First World War (1918). English translations: The Spirit of the Liturgy, trans. Ada Lane (London: Sheed & Ward,

by Dietrich von Hildebrand;[11] but also works of what was starting then to be called the "new German theology," notably those of Karl Adam.[12] A childhood friend of Msgr Montini, Mario Bendiscioli,[13] was the translator of Adam's *The Spirit of Catholicism, Christ our Brother, Jesus Christ,* and *The Christ of Faith.*[14] Msgr Montini attentively read at least the first three works, as can be seen from his surviving personal copies; he quoted them repeatedly in his religion courses. The Holy Office worried about the doctrine expounded in these works. Karl Adam's writings were subjected to examination; there was a rumor that certain of his books were going to be included in the *Index of Forbidden Books*. When he heard of it, Msgr Montini wrote to Bendiscioli on May 6, 1934 to express his "stupor and regret." Finally, when *The Spirit of Catholicism* was banned from sale, Msgr Montini hid the remaining copies in his apartment in the Vatican! The book was thus able to retain its influence, as it was passed under the table. Msgr Montini did not want open opposition. In another letter to Bendiscioli, he rejected the formula that was gaining popularity in some circles: "Work for the Church, if necessary by opposing the Church." He clearly explained his attitude, which seemed wait-and-see to some: "I think, I pray that the eternal renovation that the Church needs will germinate from within . . ."[15]

It is also worth noting that, during the summer of 1934, Msgr Montini took one of those cultural and religious voyages he liked so much. His traveling companion this time was his friend Msgr Rampolla del Tindaro.

1930), republished several times thereafter; *Sacred Signs*, trans. Grace Branham (St. Louis, MO: Pio Decimo Press, 1956).
11   Dietrich von Hildebrand (1889–1977) was a renowned German Catholic phenomenological and personalist philosopher who influenced John Paul II and Benedict XVI. He was strongly opposed to how the Second Vatican Council was implemented, especially in liturgical matters. Thus, he played an active role in the promotion of the Traditional Latin Mass, helping to found Una Voce America. English translation: *Liturgy and Personality* (Steubenville, OH: Hildebrand Project, 2016).
12   Father Karl Borromäus Adam (1876–1966), Bavarian theologian and member of the Nazi party.
13   Mario Bendiscioli (1903–1998), a Catholic historian who worked at the University of Pavia, founded the Mario Bendiscioli Collection which contains about 5,300 volumes, including works on the history of Christianity and the relationship between religious conscience and democracy in Italy. Many works in the collection were either authored or collaborated on by Bendiscioli himself.
14   English editions: Karl Adam, *The Spirit of Catholicism* (London: Sheed & Ward, 1928); *Christ our Brother* (London: Sheed & Ward, 1931); *Jesus Christ* (Düsseldorf: Patmos, 1933); *The Christ of Faith: The Christology of the Church* (London: Burns & Oates, 1957).
15   Quoted in M. Bendiscioli and M. Marcocchi, "La censura del S. Ufficio a 'L'essenza del Cattolicesimo' di K. Adam," *Studi e memorie* 7 (1979).

In the Turmoil of Europe

They left Rome for Marseille on July 19, and visited Notre-Dame de la Garde, the famous Marian sanctuary which overlooks the city. Then, after a brief stay in Paris, they embarked at Le Havre for England. They stayed first on the Isle of Wight, at the Benedictine Abbey of Quarr, which depended on Solesmes at the time. Then they were guided around the British Isles by Msgr Riberi. He had been Msgr Montini's fellow student at the Academy and was then Auditor at the nunciature of Dublin. He showed them the prehistoric site of Stonehenge, Shakespeare's house at Stratford-upon-Avon (Msgr Montini had often read Shakespeare in his youth), and the Gothic cathedrals of Winchester, Salisbury, and Wells. A quarter-century later, in an emotional address on "The Secret of the Cathedral," he evoked the "sad" impression left by the "splendid but empty" Anglican cathedrals:

> too often chronically empty of faithful, and always empty of that heart which is for us the tabernacle; empty of the mystical body and the real body of Christ; but in the evenings they were filled with very sweet chants. From whence came these chants? I do not know; but it seemed to me that the cathedral herself chanted, as a violin without a musician, soft melodies, sometimes melancholic as lamentations issuing from the statues and tombs, sometimes serene and joyous as the voices of invisible angels flying under these very high Gothic spires.[16]

They stayed also for a few days in London, lodging at St Peter's Italian Church. On July 25, in Austria, the Nazis attempted a *coup d'état*, killing Chancellor Dollfuss.[17] Msgr Montini and his friends went to the House of Commons the day when the British Minister of Foreign Affairs communicated the news of this tragic event. In London, did they also meet with Father Sturzo, who was still there in exile? There is no evidence to affirm this, but it is not impossible. At Rome, Msgr Montini was in regular contact with several personalities of the PPI, notably Longinotti and De Gasperi. It is almost unthinkable that in London he would not have at least carried their friendly greetings to the exiled leader.

They continued on their trip, visiting Cambridge, Lincoln, York, and Edinburgh. Then they stayed a few days at the Benedictine Abbey of Fort

---

16   Discourse pronounced in the cathedral of Crema, in April 1959, published in *L'Église et les conciles*.

17   Engelbert Dollfuss (1892–1934) was the Austrian Chancellor from 1932 until his assassination by a failed Nazi coup attempt in 1934. He rose to power during a crisis in the conservative government and quickly shut down parliament, assuming control and suppressing the socialist movement in early 1934.

Augustus, in Scotland, near Loch Ness (Msgr Montini wrote to his family on August 2: "Instead of the monster, a sweet and green landscape can be seen, poor in sunlight and heat, but beautiful in vegetation, the panoramas..."). They completed their tour in Ireland, where they resided for a week at the nunciature of Dublin.

Throughout much of the year 1935, Msgr Montini was absent from Rome, for health reasons. In January, he contracted a severe influenza, which led to complications and kept him away from the Secretariat of State until August. In February, he went to convalesce by the seaside, at Nettuno, in the rest house kept by religious sisters; his superior, Msgr Ottaviani, had had him admitted there. At the beginning of March, he tried to go back to work at the Secretariat of State but, after a check-up and an X-ray, his doctor, who also diagnosed a generalized asthenia, recommended complete rest. Thus, from the end of March until June, he went to rest at Gardone Riviera in a house kept by German religious sisters. During his brief stay in this health resort near Brescia, he received frequent visits from his family and friends. He also made some outings to the surrounding areas. The fair climate, the vegetation rich in cypress, citrus, and olive trees, and the magnificent landscape encouraged him to prolong his stay more than seems necessary. In June, Msgr Ottaviani, in the name of the Secretary of State Pacelli, let him know that his return to the Secretariat of State was desired. But with the help of a new medical certificate, he was allowed to continue his convalescence. In mid-June, he returned to Brescia for a few days, then left for three months in the mountains, at Aprica, where his parents usually took their vacations. He passed all these months reading and keeping up a voluminous correspondence with his friends. His mood was rather somber. To Fr Caresana, for example, on July 5, he expressed his "habitual perplexity." He also continued to follow the activities of FUCI. Several letters survive from this period that were addressed to Giovanni Ambrosetti,[18] who had succeeded Righetti as president of FUCI a few months earlier. Msgr Montini lavished him with encouragement, and above all practical advice (on electoral maneuvering!) to help orient and control the Catholic student movement.

At the end of September, he went to Venice with his father and brothers, and did not return to Rome until the middle of October. He resumed his class on pontifical history; on the other hand, he left the class on

---

18 Giovanni Ambrosetti (1915–1985) was an Italian president of FUCI between 1934–1941. He was also a university professor for much of his career.

Christian doctrine to Msgr Rampolla. At the Secretariat of State, it seems that his long absence, even if it was medically justified to some degree, harmed his career. When Msgr Ottaviani, his immediate superior at the section of Ordinary Affairs, left the Secretariat of State for the Congregation of the Holy Office where he became Assessor, it was not Msgr Montini that was called to replace him as Substitute, but Msgr Tardini, who had occupied an equivalent post in the section of Extraordinary Affairs.

As zealous as he was, he evidently did not display the enthusiasm which would have been necessary for a rapid promotion. In the letters he wrote to his family, he often complained of the "drudgery" to which he was bound (official ceremonies, receptions) and of the little interest which he had for his work. Thus, on March 13, 1937: "I work detachedly, as usual, without the satisfaction of being engaged in any vaguely constructive activity: it is a sore point, and sometimes I am confronted with my own solitude." When, a few months earlier, he and seven other monsignors had been granted purely honorific titles as Referendary Prelates of the Tribunal of the Apostolic Signatura, he promptly reassured his father: they were a "batch" to fill the empty seats, "the thing signifies nothing, and does not involve, I hope, new duties" (September 18, 1936).

The growth of religious culture and the activities of Catholic movements interested him much more. He attentively followed the development of the Laureati and participated actively in the first "week of religious culture" they organized in a Camaldolese monastery at Camaldoli, in the province of Arezzo, in September 1936. There he gave a lecture on "God in the New Testament." These "weeks of Camaldoli" were held even during the war years and represented an original initiative. They helped enrich the Laureati's religious culture with weeks devoted to the study of a single theme: "God in the New Testament" the first year, "Jesus Christ" the second, "Man" the third, etc. In addition to Msgr Montini, Fr Bevilacqua, and Fr Primo Mazzolari,[19] some young theologians participated in these weeks: Fathers Mariano Cordovani,[20] Charles Boyer,[21] Carlo Colombo,[22] and

---

19   Fr Primo Mazzolari (1890–1959) was an Italian Catholic priest who also went by the name "Don Primo." He was well-known for his strong sympathy for the poor and disadvantaged and for his aversion to violence and war.
20   Fr Mariano Cordovani (1883–1950) was an Italian Dominican, a prolific Thomist writer and critic of the *nouvelle théologie*.
21   Fr Charles Boyer (1884–1980) was a historical author and priest who is known for creating an International Association for the Unity of Christians.
22   Bishop Carlo Colombo (1909–1991) was ordained a priest of Milan in 1931 and became the auxiliary bishop of Milan in 1964, which he remained until he retired in 1985.

Giuseppe Siri,[23] who went on to have prominent careers. The Laureati who received this formation (one hundred and thirty people the second year) were often active after the war in politics and culture.

Msgr Montini, through the Laureati, kept contact with university life. Through the review *Studium*, to which he began to contribute again from 1936, it is clear how much his interest for intellectual life, Italian as well as foreign, remained strong. For example, he published, under the pseudonym of Sator, an article on *The Diary of a Country Priest*, which he had read in its French edition. His verdict was mixed. He found the novel of Bernanos "strong (even if it is not beyond criticism)," but he regretted that sin was presented in too seductive a manner, and that the female characters, by contrast, were all depicted in an unfavorable light.[24]

SUBSTITUTE

Notwithstanding his resistance, Msgr Montini's superiors decided to entrust him with more important responsibilities. During the thirteen years that he had spent in subordinate posts at the Secretariat of State, his qualities could be assessed. In December 1937, Archbishop Pizzardo was created cardinal and relinquished control of the section for Extraordinary Affairs. This led to successive nominations: Msgr Tardini returned to Extraordinary Affairs, as Director this time, while Msgr Montini replaced him at Ordinary Affairs as Substitute (on the proposition of Msgr Tardini it seems). A letter to his parents (December 15) hints that Msgr Montini tried to refuse this promotion, arguing that his weak health could not sustain the increased workload that his new function entailed, but Cardinal Pacelli and Pius XI were evidently not convinced; on December 17, *L'Osservatore Romano* publicly revealed the nominations of Monsignors Tardini and Montini. This promotion focused attention on him from diplomats stationed in Rome. Sir D'Arcy Osborne,[25] Envoy Extraordinary and Minister Plenipotentiary of Great Britain to the Holy See, would

---

23 Card. Giuseppe Siri (1906–1989) was archbishop of Genoa from 1946 to 1987. He was renowned for his staunch defense of Catholic Tradition throughout his life and was a member of the Cœtus Internationalis Patrum at Vatican II.

24 Georges Bernanos (1888–1948) was a French fiction writer known for his many novels, such as *Journal d'un curé de campagne*, in English *The Diary of a Country Priest*, trans. Pamela Morris (London: Boriswood, 1937). A fervent Catholic and monarchist, he was no stranger to controversy. He turned down a post in De Gaulle's government, as well as the Legion of Honor and a seat in the Académie française. Montini's review was published in *Studium* (September 1937): 529–31.

25 Sir Francis D'Arcy G. Osborne (1884–1964) was the twelfth Duke of Leeds and a diplomat. He was originally from Yorkshire in England.

henceforth include Msgr Montini in the list of "Leading Personalities at the Holy See" which he addressed each year to his government. The notice on Msgr Montini was significant: "He is a man of intelligence, culture, and charm and he does not show himself inclined to submit to Fascist enthusiasm."[26]

This nomination to the important post of Substitute was accompanied by a suite of complementary duties: on December 24 Msgr Montini was named Consultor of the Consistorial Congregation and also of the Congregation of the Holy Office.[27] An equally short time later, he left the Belvedere Palace to lodge on the second floor of the Apostolic Palace, under the offices of the Secretariat of State. This apartment, which looked over Saint Peter's Square, was spacious and richly furnished, with a large terrace where Msgr Montini kept many green plants and enjoyed receiving his friends.

His new functions made him accelerate his work. He had to abandon his classes on the history of papal diplomacy; soon he would frequently complain in his letters to his parents that he no longer had the time to read. Responsible for a department that at that time had an ecclesiastical staff of fifteen or so, he also had to fulfill the directives that came mainly from the Secretary of State, though sometimes from the pope himself. Msgr Montini would remember Pius XI with awe. To Jean Guitton he later recounted:

> I would often stay two hours with him, and it made me think of those words of the *Dies Iræ*: *Rex tremendæ majestatis*, king of tremendous majesty. Pius XI would unfold his phrases slowly, like a plane circling the runway before landing, like a silkworm weaving its silk. Watching Pius XI search for the most exact expression of his thoughts, slowly meditating what he wanted to express, was deeply moving. His thoughts seemed to be born before my eyes.[28]

The Substitute was in charge of Ordinary Affairs, i.e., of the Holy See's relations with the large organizations of the Church; he usually had recommendations and directions to transmit on behalf of the superior authority. But he also played an intermediary role in collecting information and opinions from the personalities who came to visit, and on the

---

26 Archives of the British ministry of foreign affairs, FO 371/22441.
27 This last assignment was going to permit him, in the years to come, to intervene successfully in favor of certain authors held in suspicion by the Holy Office.
28 Guitton, *Journal de ma vie*, 549.

other hand in making known to these personalities the point of view of the Holy See. It was in his power to introduce occasional personal nuances to this information. Any diplomatic questions in principle concerned the Section of Extraordinary Affairs. But circumstances often demanded Msgr Montini's involvement in aspects of foreign policy; he worked in tandem with Msgr Tardini. The Substitute also happened to be secretary of the code office, responsible for the service whereby sensitive or confidential messages were encrypted and deciphered.

The Substitute's working day followed an unchanging pattern: at the start of each day he studied files, then he was received by the Secretary of State for one or two hours (he remained standing before Cardinal Pacelli). Then he reread the documents prepared by his subordinates,[29] correcting them as needed, and having them copied before being sent to the superior authority. From 11:00 am to 2:00 pm he granted audiences. He received cardinals, Italian and foreign bishops, diplomats, foreign personalities, but also leaders of FUCI and the Laureati, who always found a warm welcome. About these many visits, Msgr Montini would later say: "To know how to listen to others: that seems so easy, when in fact it is often difficult . . . because it is boring, because it seems to consume both time and energy in the detours of the conversation and the thoughts of the other."[30]

TOWARDS THE WAR

The year 1938 saw the threats of war multiply. In March, Nazi Germany invaded Austria and annexed it, without protest from Italy, despite the fact that Mussolini had amassed troops at the Austro-Italian border and threated to intervene against Germany when they attempted to annex Austria in 1934. This *Anschluss* gave way to a lively controversy between the *L'Osservatore Romano* and *Il Regime Fascista* of Farinacci.[31] The articles of the Vatican newspaper were signed "t"; in fact, they were the work of the editor, Giuseppe Dalla Torre, Msgr Montini's friend. The Substitute soon wrote to his parents about this controversy: "It was done with

---

29 Amongst these was a young Frenchman who had entered the Secretariat of State the preceding year: Father Jacques Martin. He was to have a successful career; Paul VI would name him prefect of the Papal Household.
30 Preface to R. Spiazzi, *Padre Mariano Cordovani*, 1:16.
31 Roberto Farinacci (1892–1945) was a prominent Italian Fascist politician and a member of the National Fascist Party before and during the Second World War. He was infamous for being antisemitic during Mussolini's regime and was executed by Italian partisans in 1945.

full knowledge of the situation, and after calculating possible dangers, which at least involved no violence." Throughout the course of the war, which was just about to break out, the Holy See, in its public acts and declarations, would always try prudently not to exacerbate situations while trying to protect the rights of Catholics and save lives.

The Church's judgment on Nazi ideology was well known, most famously from the encyclical *Mit Brennender Sorge*[32] which Pius XI had published in March 1937 (and in which Cardinal Pacelli had collaborated). National Socialist doctrines on race and the totalitarian state were explicitly condemned. When, in May 1938, Hitler came to Rome on an official visit, Pius XI left the Vatican and retired to his residence at Castel Gandolfo. He would later tell of his pain at having seen flying over the Eternal City a "cross which was not that of Christ."

From the following May 25 to 30, the Thirty-Fourth International Eucharistic Congress was held in Budapest. Fifteen cardinals and some three hundred archbishops and bishops were present. The pope sent Cardinal Pacelli as legate, and also sent a delegation with Msgr Montini at its head. On the 25th, Cardinal Pacelli pronounced a memorable discourse on the persecutors of the Church, intending both the Soviet Union and Germany:

> The apostles of the negation and hatred of God may proscribe the work and even the name of Christ, may banish from the land confessors of the Faith as enemies of the state; the arsonists may profane and reduce to ashes the churches and chapels, may deprive Jesus Christ of his houses of stone.... Christ will continue to be the victor.

Msgr Montini wrote to his parents: "Our cardinal made a magnificent impression." On the evening of the 26th, a splendid Eucharistic procession took place near the Danube, "in the midst of a fantastic myriad of lights and chants and a calm and collected crowd," he wrote.

In Europe and in Italy tensions worsened. The Mussolini government prepared a law "for the defense of the race" which, albeit much less severe than the anti-Semitic legislation enacted by the Germans, was no less discriminatory. This instigated another verbal clash between the Holy

---

32 *Mit Brennender Sorge* [With burning concern] was promulgated on March 14, 1937 against the errors and abuses of the Nazi government. Notably, the original language of this encyclical was German rather than Latin. The document was smuggled into Germany, printed and distributed in secret, then read from every Catholic pulpit in Germany on Palm Sunday.

See and the government. Giulio Andreotti remembers that the leaders of FUCI received instructions from Msgr Montini during an audience to protest these laws during their next national congress.[33]

The annexation of the Sudetenland[34] by Germany spread the fear of impending war. On August 18 the ambassador of France to the Holy See, François Charles-Roux,[35] came to see the Substitute and asked for an intervention of the pope to ward off the danger of a conflict. On the 21st, in an address, Pius XI called for peace and denounced "exaggerated nationalism." On September 28, while Mussolini, Hitler, Chamberlain,[36] and Daladier[37] were meeting in Munich to negotiate a solution with regard to the Sudetenland, Pius XI addressed a message on Vatican Radio to the faithful of all nations, asking them to pray "for the conservation of peace, in justice and charity," and offering his life to God "for the salvation, for the peace of the world."

The peace was saved at Munich by the abandonment of the Sudetenland to Germany, but war was not definitively ruled out. In January 1939 at Rome, the British Prime Minister Chamberlain and his Minister of Foreign Affairs Viscount Halifax[38] held talks with the Italian government. At the Vatican, after being received in audience by an aging and ill Pius XI, they were offered a luncheon. Msgr Montini was present at this official reception. The conversations were pessimistic.

---

33 Giulio Andreotti, "G. B. Montini, aumônier des universitaires et des licenciés," in *Paul VI et la modernité dans l'Église* (1984), 34.
34 The Sudetenland was the German name for those regions of the modern-day Czech Republic which were predominately German-speaking. After World War II, these German-speakers were expelled.
35 François Charles-Roux (1879–1961) was a French businessman, historian, and diplomat who chaired the Catholic Relief Agency after World War II. He was also strongly in favor of keeping intact the French colonial empire and was the chairman of the Central Committee of the Ministry of Overseas France (1948–1956). He served as the French ambassador to the Holy See from 1932.
36 Neville Chamberlain (1869–1940) was the Prime Minister of the United Kingdom in the years before and at the beginning of the Second World War (1937–1940). He is known for his policy of "appeasement" towards Adolf Hitler and Nazi Germany.
37 Édouard Daladier (1884–1970) was a Radical Socialist politician who served as Prime Minister of France on three different occasions (1933, 1934, 1938–1940). He was realistic about Hitler's aims with regard to Continental domination.
38 Edward Halifax (1881–1959), formally known as the Earl of Halifax, was a British conservative politician who held several major ministerial roles, most notably Viceroy of India (1925–1931). He worked with Neville Chamberlain in the policy of appeasement toward Hitler before the Second World War, but as Hitler's power in Europe increased, Lord Halifax pushed for a more aggressive approach.

PIUS XII AND THE WAR

On February 10, Pius XI died. Msgr Montini, as also Cardinal Pacelli and Msgr Tardini, was present for the pope's last breath. A conclave was organized to pick his successor. Msgr Montini was among those who supervised the material organization of the space — rooms where the cardinals were to meet to elect the new pope, while maintaining the obligations of secrecy and no contact with the outside world, until the new pope was elected. Writing to his family, Msgr Montini described the fascinating contrast between the magnificent rooms, resplendent with history and art, where the cardinals were going to meet, and "the very modest iron beds" that were set up in them in case the conclave lasted several days.

On the first day of the conclave, March 2, Cardinal Pacelli was elected. He took the name Pius XII. A few days later he named Cardinal Maglione,[39] former nuncio to Switzerland and to France, as his Secretary of State. On account of the numerous issues to be addressed, Msgrs Tardini and Montini often dealt directly with Pius XII concerning the various dossiers that they had to handle. As the war loomed close, under the orders of Pius XII a triumvirate of sorts was set up; however, to respect the hierarchical order, Msgr Tardini and Msgr Montini would generally keep Cardinal Maglione informed of their actions and the documents they sent out.

Contact between the Substitute and the new pope grew still closer. On May 2, Msgr Montini wrote to his parents: "Almost every day I have the opportunity... and the anxiety of an audience with the Holy Father, who is always very kind and goodly towards me and all."[40] "Anxiety" and admiration in the presence of Pius XII would never leave Msgr Montini. Anxiety because he was a demanding master who wanted work to be executed perfectly, and was also committed to producing documents that were faithful to the teaching of the Church, in the most precise terms possible. Msgr Montini remembered: "He venerated details. There were words in the language that he did not allow, so much that I made

---

39   Card. Luigi Maglione (1877–1944) was an Italian who served from 1939–1944 as the Vatican Secretary of State during Pope Pius XII's pontificate. He had been Nuncio of Switzerland (1920) and then Apostolic Nuncio to France (1926). Due to his excellent relations with the French government, he was rumored to have been involved in the formation of the Hoare-Laval Pact (1935).
40   For the feast of Saint John the Baptist, Pius XII sent him five bottles of excellent Mass wine. When he became pope in his turn, Montini would multiply such gestures of thoughtfulness and friendship towards his friends and subordinates.

myself a small lexicon of the words that had thus been proscribed, so that I would never use them in the documents I submitted to him."[41]

The war would inevitably intensify Pius XII's collaboration with the clerics in charge of the Secretariat of State, and necessitate countless messages, documents, memorandums, and notes.[42] To know the precise positions of the Holy See before and during the war, the communications and actions of the pope and of his collaborators must be consulted.

Before the war had even begun, the Holy See, because of its moral authority, was approached from all sides to try to maintain peace and to find solutions to the tragic problems that were beginning to arise in Europe. In July and August 1939, Dr Manfred Kirschberg[43] of Paris wrote several times to Msgr Montini about what seemed to be a personal project to enable the Jews of Europe to flee the persecution by allowing them a territory in Angola, which was then a Portuguese colony. Kirschberg hoped that the Holy See might take steps to facilitate this arrangement with the Portuguese government. The project was studied but determined to be unrealistic for a number of reasons. A negative response was regretfully sent to Dr Kirschberg. Other similar projects were submitted to the Holy See during the war, all inspired by the same generous sentiments, but all equally unrealistic.

On August 23, the Molotov-Ribbentrop Pact was signed, which paved the way for the German invasion of Poland soon afterwards. At midnight that night, in a letter to his family, Msgr Montini said: "I think of you every hour, even though I am always very busy in these days of grave preoccupations" and he made his recommendation: "Have the children pray." The next day, the pope made a final plea for peace on Vatican Radio. It has been established that Pius XII asked Msgr Montini to submit a draft message to him; some passages of the message are the Substitute's work.[44] "Being above public contestations and passions," as the pope said, he appealed to governments and peoples alike, asking heads of state to renounce "the accusations, threats, and causes of mutual mistrust" and to attempt to "resolve current disputes by the only appropriate means, that

---

41   Quoted by Guitton, *Journal de ma vie*, 549.
42   These have been published by Fathers Blet, Graham, Martini, and Schneider in a monumental edition: *Actes et Documents du Saint-Siège relatif à la Seconde Guerre mondiale*, 11 tomes in 12 vols. (Vatican City: Libreria Editrice Vaticana, 1965–1981); henceforth, ADSS.
43   Dr Manfred Kirschberg was a French medical doctor.
44   B. Schneider, "Der Friedensappell Papst Pius XII vom 24. August 1939," *Archivum historiæ pontificiæ* 6 (1968).

is to say mutual understanding." "The danger is imminent," he added, "but there is still time. Nothing is lost with peace. Everything can be lost with war." On August 29, Pius XII again approached Fr Tacchi Venturi, who had previously been entrusted with more than one confidential message for Mussolini, and sent him to ask Mussolini to intervene in favor of peace, either by approaching Hitler, or at least by keeping Italy neutral if Germany declared war.

Mussolini had already warned Hitler that Italy was not ready for war. Neither the appeal of the pope, nor the procrastination of Mussolini himself prevented Hitler from acting on his threats. On September 1, Germany invaded Poland; on the 2nd, Italy proclaimed its neutrality; on the 3rd, England and France declared war on Germany, opening what Msgr Montini called, in a letter to his parents, a "new drama of blood."

On September 3, Guido Gonella was arrested by the Fascist police on account of his *Acta Diurna*, which were judged contrary to the interests of Italy. Msgr Montini intervened to have him liberated, and had him live at the Vatican so that he would not be subjected to police checkpoints. Eventually diplomats from the allied countries, and then refugees and political dissidents, would find sanctuary within the walls of the papal city.

The Holy See decided rapidly to set up a new service that was going to prove invaluable: The Information Office.

> Its functions were highly specific: to facilitate liaisons between prisoners of war, or those incarcerated civilly, and their families, and thus they involved transmitting to families or friends, by post or radio, the names of prisoners of war or those missing in action. The office also transmitted messages from their families to prisoners. This operation, relying on the voluminous lists furnished by military authorities, demanded great precision to avoid confusions in identifying prisoners.[45]

The Information Office was subordinated to the second section, that is to say, placed under the responsibility of Msgr Montini. Msgr Evreinoff[46] was charged with setting up and managing the new pontifical organization. Prelates who were previously assigned to foreign nunciatures but had to be recalled to Rome because of the circumstances were reassigned to this office; among these was Msgr Montini's friend Archbishop Riberi.

---

45 ADSS 6:8.
46 Archbishop Evreinoff (1877–1959) was a well-known Russian political figure, born in St Petersburg. He was ordained a priest in 1913 and became the titular archbishop of Parium in 1947.

During the ensuing months and years of the war, millions of requests for information would come to the Vatican, from all over the world. The Substitute would try to respond by contacting, or sharing information with: the nuncios or apostolic delegates of the countries at war; the bishops of the whole world; religious orders; chaplains in the prison camps; major charitable organizations (such as the Red Cross); and by asking for the collaboration of governments (only Germany and the Soviet Union refused). Beginning in 1942, a monthly review, *Ecclesia*, circulated information on the activities of the service.

A few weeks after the annihilation of Poland by the combined forces of the Wehrmacht and the Red Army, new alarms began to spread about the fate of the Polish military, the clergy, and civilians at the hands of the Nazis. When this information had been received and confirmed, Pius XII asked Msgr Montini, in January 1940, to circulate it by Vatican radio in German and other languages. The announcement denounced the "inexcusable excesses" and "state of terror, brutality, and barbarism." English radio picked up these statements, adding political and military commentary. On January 27, the Counselor of the German embassy to the Holy See, Fritz Menshausen,[47] demanded to be received in audience by Msgr Montini. He protested against these broadcasts and threatened the Holy See with a press campaign. Msgr Montini referred the matter to the Cardinal Secretary of State and the pope. Then on the 29th, he informed Menshausen that the management of Vatican Radio had received the order, in accordance with the Holy Father's wishes, to suspend these broadcasts on Poland.[48]

It would be wrong to see negligence on the part of the Holy See, a first "silence" of Pius XII. Rather, it should be seen as an attempt by the Holy See to not aggravate the already existing situation or provoke reprisals against a population that had already suffered terribly. As the historian Léon Poliakov[49] noted: "Experience demonstrated on the local level how public protestations would immediately be followed by pitiless reprisals."

---

47 Fritz Menshausen (1885–1958) was counsellor of the German Embassy to the Holy See during the Second World War. He wrote various letters defending German policy and claiming that some of the broadcasts of the Vatican Radio provoked an anti-German attitude in the world press.
48 ADSS 3:208–9.
49 Léon Poliakov (1910–1997) was a French historian born into a Russian family that lived in various European countries. He was of Jewish descent and wrote extensively about the Holocaust and antisemitism.

DIPLOMACY OF THE IMPOSSIBLE

On May 10, 1940, Germany invaded Belgium, Holland, and Luxembourg, three countries that had demonstrated no intention of going to war against Hitler. Immediately Pius XII ordered a telegram of condolence to be sent to the sovereigns of the three invaded countries. This gesture of support was interpreted as a provocation by some Fascist leaders while Italy was preparing to go to war. The militants of the National Fascist Party prevented L'*Osservatore Romano* from being distributed at newsstands for several days. Ambassadors to the Holy See from the invaded countries were invited to come reside in the Vatican shortly afterwards.[50]

The situation of the Holy See was delicate. Officially neutral, it could not come down in favor of either opposing side. When Italy entered the war on the side of Germany, on June 10, the situation became still more difficult. The Vatican could not cause harm, by its declarations, to the country that surrounded it. For this reason Guido Gonella had to abandon his chronicle of foreign politics. A general directive was issued to writers for the Vatican newspaper instructing them to keep henceforth to matters of a religious character.

On June 14, German troops entered Paris. That very evening, Msgr Montini took up his pen to write a compassionate note to the only Frenchman in his service, Father Martin:

> Dear and Reverend Friend,
>   I had no time today to see you and speak with you of the very hard trial to which your great county has been subjected at the moment. I would have wanted to tell you how close I am to you, and how much I pray that the Lord may change your homeland's bitter sufferings into blessings for herself, for the Church, and for the world. I wish and I hope that it will be so, and I tell you with all my heart, that you may know as well the friendship of your
>
>   G.-B. Montini.[51]

During the war, the Secretariat of State received a never-ending stream of diplomats, offering explanations for their countries' attitudes, or asking what the Holy See's position was, or soliciting a service or public

---

50 On May 28, Wladimir d'Ormesson succeeded Charles-Roux as ambassador of France to the Holy See.
51 Jacques Cardinal Martin, "Journal," extract published in L'*Osservatore Romano* (French ed.), September 24, 1991.

intervention, or protesting something. Other than the ambassadors of Germany, Italy, and France to the Holy See, Msgr Montini and the other officials of the Secretariat of State often received Myron C. Taylor,[52] personal representative of President Roosevelt[53] of the United States, and Sir D'Arcy Osborne, Envoy Extraordinary and Minister Plenipotentiary of Great Britain to the Holy See. Frequent visits of Allied diplomats to the Secretariat of State, and the residence of some at the Vatican itself, incited repeated attacks from the Fascist press, who feared a conspiracy of the Allies and the Vatican against Italy. It will be seen that, with respect to the Substitute at least, there really was a conspiracy, beginning in the summer of 1942.

At the end of September 1940, in the middle of the assault on England, Msgr Montini manifested his pessimism in an audience with Wladimir d'Ormesson. He believed that England was "at the end of its resistance" and that the Axis powers would soon share Europe and Africa. Received afterwards by Msgr Tardini, d'Ormesson heard a contrary analysis of the situation: Great Britain would hold fast.[54] History has proved the second right.

Msgr Montini and his colleagues at the Secretariat of State were permanently on duty. In addition to the audiences granted to diplomats, there were the activities of the Information Office, which continued to expand. Receiving up to one thousand people per day, the Office soon counted more than eight hundred employees. There was also the distribution of aid to prisoners or to civilian populations: this was funded by various sources, then distributed in many instances through the Red Cross. Msgr Montini's ongoing correspondence with his parents shows that, although he was all but overwhelmed by the sheer range of responsibilities, he took his duties to heart and eventually seemed to blossom as a result of them. His actions, and the dispatches he had to write, aimed at a concrete result: the daily exercise of charity in a

---

52 Myron Charles Taylor (1874–1959), an American industrialist, served as personal envoy of American Presidents Franklin D. Roosevelt and Harry S. Truman from 1939 to 1950.
53 Franklin Delano Roosevelt (1882–1945) was a Democratic President of the United States of America from 1933 until his death, making him the only president to take office four times. He is especially remembered for his New Deal aimed at ending the Great Depression and for bringing the US into and through most of World War II.
54 Report of W. d'Ormesson dated September 20, 1940, Archives du Ministère des Affaires étrangères [Archives of the Ministry of Foreign Affairs of France], Europe/Saint-Siège, 559, 149; henceforth these unpublished archives will be cited as AMAE.

dramatic situation. At the end of October 1940, Wladimir d'Ormesson left the French embassy; he was replaced by Léon Bérard.[55] D'Ormesson addressed a long report to the French Minister of Foreign Affairs at the conclusion of his mission. It featured a portrait of Msgr Montini, based on several months of frequent meetings; not all the details are flattering:

> The pope holds him in such affection that Msgr Montini seems to have a halo. He is a bit of a choir boy or favorite child[56] for the Holy Father, and this reputation, which he upholds with a pious authority, allows him special consideration. Emotional, fickle, and uncertain in his judgements, he is at the same time easy to like, very sincere, very open, and yet inscrutable. That he has been profoundly formed to the Secretariat of State's ways is tangible. The balance between his natural temperament, which enables him to maintain some independence of spirit, and the nature of his duties, enables a sort of spontaneous equilibrium in him. And it is at the very moment when one believes one has discovered a friend that one finds oneself before an impenetrable bureaucrat.
>
> This sketch would be incomplete if one did not add Msgr Montini's indisputable fondness for France, his sense of justice (the current news causes him great sorrow) and his professed horror for the methods of the Nazis. But all that does not push him all the way to action. Speaking one day in front of me about the atrocities which the Germans were committing in Poland, he had this to say: "Is there no one to condemn these crimes?" The day when he becomes pope — for everyone agrees in predicting that Msgr Montini will one day be pope (which is obviously dangerous for him), he will ask himself, I fear, the same question, without realizing that he himself is the answer...[57]

Returning as ambassador of France to the Holy See in 1948, Wladimir d'Ormesson would spend time with the Substitute again and ultimately form a different judgment on him, but it is remarkable that, already in 1940, a diplomat would announce that Msgr Montini would one day become pope. It is a sign that in his position as Substitute and through the trials of war, the former chaplain of FUCI had grown in authority.

---

55   Léon Bérard (1876–1960) was a French politician, lawyer, and member of the Académie française. He served as Ambassador from the Vichy government to the Holy See until 1945.
56   The French makes a play on words: "l'enfant de chœur — ou de cœur."
57   Unedited. Report of October 28, 1940, AMAE 1373, 159.

The last weeks of the year 1940 and the beginning of 1941 saw the Italian army in difficulty. On two fronts, in Egypt and Albania, it suffered reversals and had to retreat; "sad weeks," Msgr Montini could not resist writing to his family. Although a convinced anti-Fascist, he thought of the Italian soldiers who were engaged in these battles, and also of his friends who had been mobilized (Fr Bevilacqua and Msgr Pignedoli[58] were both chaplains in the Italian Navy).

In the ensuing weeks, his well-known anti-Fascism gave rise to two diplomatic incidents. At the end of April, he was accused of having spread an anti-Fascist tract during a public audience accorded by the pope to Catholic Students and the Laureati. Minister Ciano[59] brought the matter to the attention of the Apostolic Nuncio in Rome. Fifteen hundred copies of the typed sheet were allegedly distributed. Informed of the complaint, Cardinal Maglione summoned Msgr Tardini and Msgr Montini. The latter denied having been responsible for the act. An investigation was held. The Italian police were unable to find a single copy of the distributed tract. A few weeks later, new accusations were brought against the Substitute. A note which had been sent to different diplomatic representatives to the Holy See also fell into the hands of the Secretary of State. It claimed that Msgr Montini had presided on the preceding May 14 over an "anti-Fascist" meeting in one of the apartments of the Vatican. In supposed attendance were the diplomats Osborne (for Great Britain) and Tittmann[60] (for the United States); Dalla Torre, director of L'*Osservatore Romano*; and Msgr Kaas,[61] former director of the German Catholic Party, now residing in Rome. Farinacci devoted several articles in Il *Regime fascista* to the affair. Because diplomats and a confidant of

---

58   Card. Sergio Pignedoli (1910–1980), an Italian cardinal, was a close collaborator and supporter of Paul VI. He was a leading candidate for the papacy in both conclaves of 1978. He was also the President of the Secretariat for Non-Christians (1973–1980).
59   Galeazzo Ciano (1903–1944) was an Italian statesman who became a figurehead of Mussolini's Fascist regime after marrying Mussolini's daughter (1930). He is known for influencing Italy's entrance into World War II. In 1934, he became a member of the Fascist Grand Council which was a highly important group that determined the party's policies. Although initially wary of Hitler's lack of communication when invading Poland, he urged Mussolini to enter the war when France fell.
60   Harold H. Tittmann (1893–1980) was a soldier during the First World War, before joining the Foreign Service Office and becoming an American delegate to the Vatican.
61   Msgr Ludwig Kaas (1881–1952) was a German prelate, parliamentarian, and head of the German Center Party before the War. He had been an advisor to Pacelli, then Nuncio to both Bavaria and Germany, and helped to negotiate a concordat with Prussia in 1929.

the Holy Father were implicated, this time there were official denials, in a letter from the Secretary of State to the Ambassador of Italy, and during a visit of the Apostolic Nuncio to the Italian Minister of Foreign Affairs. Il *Regime fascista* nonetheless persisted in its personal accusations against Msgr Montini for several weeks, and the Secretary of State had to intervene again to defend his collaborator.[62] A police report also survives dated March 12, 1941, accusing Msgr Montini of having distributed a text hostile to Fascist Italy and the Axis, demonstrating how the totalitarian state is contrary to Christian doctrine; this was alleged to have occurred on the preceding February 25 during a papal audience with priests charged with preaching Lenten retreats.[63]

Are all these accusations against Msgr Montini baseless? Are they possibly maneuvers of the German or Italian secret services looking to weaken the cohesion of the Holy See?[64] That is not impossible. Hard evidence is lacking to implicate Msgr Montini in anti-Fascist and anti-Axis propaganda during this period, though his personal sympathies are undeniable.[65] When, in the near future, he did act, he did so far more discreetly.

The month of June 1941 saw Germany invading Russia. The official position of the Holy See's impartiality was not modified. The Church, through the encyclical *Divini Redemptoris* of March 1937, had renewed its condemnation of Marxism, denouncing "the inventions and directives of Communism" and describing "the means of defense which must be put into action." However, now that Nazi Germany had attacked the USSR, the Church did not believe it right to bless its armies. Pius XII refused to support the "anti-Bolshevik crusade" as some wished. On the other hand, he looked for every means to provide aid for all the victims of this new front. In September 1941, the Holy See was informed that the bishop of Estonia (invaded by the USSR in 1940) had been deported towards the Urals. As the Church had no diplomatic relations with the USSR, Pius XII asked Msgr Montini to write a memorandum on the subject and to give it to the American representative so that his country

---

62 All the protestations of the Secretariat of State were published in ADSS, vol. 4.
63 Riccardi, Roma "Città Sacra"?, 200.
64 It is known that Allied as well as Axis spies were operating in Rome throughout this period; see, for example, R. Graham, "Espions Nazis au Vatican pendant la Deuxième Guerre mondiale," *La Documentation catholique*, April 5, 1970.
65 Following the first controversy, C. Senise, the Italian chief of police, received orders from Mussolini to have Msgr Montini arrested. When it turned out that there was no proof, the order was suspended.

might intervene in favor of the persecuted bishop. The Information Office also tried, the following months, to obtain information on the German, Italian, French, etc. soldiers who were prisoners of the Soviets in Russia. Msgr Montini had the International Red Cross, the apostolic delegate in London, and the American diplomatic services intervene. It was without result.

The requests for aid, help, and information that came to the Holy See were countless. Even before the war, "beginning in the spring of 1939, the Vatican registers make mention of innumerable cases of intervention by the pope in favor of the Jews, particularly in Germany, and of monetary aid provided for Jewish refugees."[66] In the first months of 1940, American Jews had sent seventy-five thousand dollars to the Holy See to aid the "non-Aryan" refugees in Europe; this gift, added to other sums provided by the Church, enabled payment for thousands of immigration visas for the Americas; funds were sent elsewhere for more direct action. In June 1940, money was sent in aid of French refugees. Still other examples of the charitable action of the Holy See could be cited. In November 1941, on the model of the Information Office, the Vatican decided to create an "Aid Commission" to centralize and organize distribution. Msgr Montini was again responsible for supervising operations. In addition to financial assistance, this commission also sent packages of books and medicines to prisoners, whether or not they were Allied.

Beginning in 1942, there was a proliferation of increasingly alarming reports on what Germany intended to do with the Jews of Europe: mass deportations, followed by executions. The Secretary of State tried to intervene in each case that came to his attention. In March of that year, the Grand Rabbi of Budapest gave a memorandum to the Apostolic Nuncio in Hungary on the situation of the Jews of Slovakia and asked him to intervene to stop their deportation. The nuncio, Msgr Rotta,[67] transmitted the file to the Secretariat of State. Msgr Montini and Cardinal Maglione took care of it. On March 25, the Secretary of State noted the decision that had been ordered by the pope: "I called the minister [diplomatic representative of Slovakia in Rome] and asked

---

66 R. P. Leiber, "Pie XII et les Juifs de Rome (1943–1944)," *La Documentation catholique*, April 2, 1961, col. 465.
67 Msgr Angelo Rotta (1872–1965) was an Italian prelate who, as the Apostolic Nuncio to Hungary (1930–1945) by the end of World War II, was directly involved in rescuing Jews in Budapest from Nazi persecution and the Holocaust. He was noted as a highly important Catholic figure of resistance to the Nazis.

him to intervene immediately with his government to prevent such a horror."⁶⁸ The deportation was suspended. The same month, the Secretariat of State intervened with the Italian government in favor of Yugoslavian Jews incarcerated in an Italian concentration camp. The general direction of the police responded that "every individual request presented by the interested parties will be taken into benevolent consideration, and the confiscated money will be duly returned." There were also interventions in favor of German Jews, but in most cases they proved ineffective. On June 24, 1942, Msgr Orsenigo,⁶⁹ nuncio to Berlin, wrote to Msgr Montini that the steps taken so far to assist the Jews (even those who had not yet been deported) were useless. He even specified: "They are not well received; on the contrary, they end up alienating the authorities."⁷⁰

On its own, this remark, from a nuncio at the heart of the European drama, suffices to explain the attitudes of the Secretariat of State and the pope, as the head of the Church, during this war. In the sixties, a notorious stage play (Rolf Hochhuth's *The Deputy*) depicted Pius XII as "indifferent" to the fate of the Jews; it fixated on his "silence," and attacked him for not denouncing Nazi atrocities. Certainly, the pope knew of the scale of German persecutions against the Jews and other populations; the sheer profusion of reports from the nuncios in Europe and from other sources of information made clear that there were mass deportations and massacres. At the end of 1942, around ten telegrams in a row were sent to the pope from the Jewish communities of South America, the Jewish organizations of the United States and Egypt, and the Grand Rabbi of the British Empire, all asking him to intervene on behalf of the Jews of Eastern Europe, who were threatened with annihilation. The pope intervened as he could. In his traditional Christmas message to the whole world, he called for an awakening of every conscience, referring clearly to the massacred Jews: "Humanity owes this pledge," he said, "to the hundreds of thousands of persons who, without any fault on their part, for the singular fact of their nationality or their race, have been sentenced to death, or to a progressive extermination." At the same time, he attempted to make his

---

68 ADSS 8:475.
69 Msgr Cesare Orsenigo (1873–1976) was Germany's Apostolic Nuncio (1930–1945) and was the direct link between the pope and the Nazi regime. He supported the Italian Fascist ideal and hoped the Nazi regime would follow suit, making him a controversial figure who was seen to "compromise and conciliate" with the Nazis.
70 ADSS 8:570.

condemnation known through the intermediary of the Polish bishops. Father Dezza,[71] who preached a retreat to the pope and the cardinals of the Curia, recounted:

> I had a long audience during the course of which the pope spoke to me of the Nazi atrocities in Germany and other counties. He expressed his pain, his agony, because, he told me, "it is deplorable that the pope does not speak. But the pope cannot speak. If he speaks, it will be worse." He then told me that, recently, he had sent three letters in which he denounced the Nazi atrocities: one to "the heroic archbishop of Krakow," as he called him, the future Cardinal Sapieha;[72] the other two to other Polish bishops. "They responded by thanking me," he told me, but added that "they could not publish these letters because it would aggravate the situation."[73]

In intervening more forcefully, that is to say by publicly denouncing Germany and especially Hitler, the pope would have incited reprisals: against German Catholics and Catholics in countries occupied by Germany, and obviously against the Jews themselves. With regard to the Jews of Germany and Europe, Pius XII and the Secretariat of State preferred to act through diplomacy, saving those who could be saved without the risk of making matters even worse. On the subject of the pope's actions on behalf of the Jews, a report has been compiled by Pinchas Lapide,[74] who became the consul of Israel in Milan after the war: "I can affirm that the pope personally, the Holy See, the nuncios, and the whole Catholic Church saved between one hundred and fifty thousand and five hundred thousand Jews from certain death."[75]

---

71 Card. Paolo Dezza (1901–1999), ordained a priest for the Jesuits in 1928. He led the Pontifical Gregorian University during Pope Pius XII's pontificate and was a confessor to Pope Paul VI and Pope John Paul I. He was elevated by Pope John Paul II to the cardinalate in 1991.
72 Card. Adam Stefan Sapieha (1867–1951) was bishop of Krakow from 1911 until the see was elevated to an archbishopric in 1925. He continued to govern it as metropolitan archbishop until his death. Pius XII made him a cardinal in 1946. He ordained Karol Wojtyła in 1946.
73 P. Paolo Dezza, "Le silence de Pie XII," La Documentation catholique, July 1964, cols. 1033–34.
74 Pinchas Lapide (1922–1997) was an Austro-Israelian Jewish theologian and historian. His book Three Popes and the Jews (1967) was written in response to Hochhuth's play, The Deputy.
75 Cited by Alexis Curvers, Pie XII, le pape outragé, 44.

OVERTHROWING MUSSOLINI

The Fascist press was not wrong to see Msgr Montini as the most antifascist of the Vatican prelates. On the other hand, they lacked secure proof, and made accusations that were not always justified. Not until the summer of 1942 was Msgr Montini verifiably at the heart of a plot to overthrow Mussolini. Diplomatic documents published by the Holy See indicate simply that on September 3, 1942, the Princess of Piedmont, Maria José of Savoy,[76] daughter-in-law of King Victor Emmanuel III, was received in audience by Msgr Montini. He wrote an account of this meeting for his superiors. The princess, explained the Substitute, thought that the Italian people were ready to abandon the Fascist regime, that a change of government was possible, that men were ready to take up the torch, and that a separate peace could then be concluded with the Allies.[77] This account was not dishonest, but incomplete and imprecise. Nonetheless it enables dating of the beginning of a process that ended, less than a year later, in the expulsion of Mussolini. Around forty years after the events, an interview with the Princess of Savoy revealed the exact role played by Msgr Montini — a role of which his superiors had very scanty knowledge.[78]

Princess Maria José had met with Marshal Badoglio[79] during the summer of 1942. He assured her that he was ready to overthrow Mussolini in a military *coup d'état*. It would still be necessary to contact the Allies for reassurance of their goodwill towards a future non-Fascist government. Would they be ready to make peace with it? For this reason, the princess contacted Msgr Montini, through the intermediary of Guido Gonella. He was ideal for the situation for two reasons: he was in regular contact with the leaders of the anti-Fascist Christian Democracy;[80] also, through his functions at the Secretariat of State, he could meet with the Allied diplomats daily.

---

76 Maria José de Savoy (1906–2001) was born a Princess in Belgium but was the last Queen of Italy by marrying into the House of Savoy. Her tenure was very short, only 35 days, hence the nickname "The May Queen."
77 ADSS 5:662.
78 Interview granted to *La Repubblica*, September 7, 1983.
79 Pietro Badoglio (1871–1956) was the twenty-eighth Prime Minister of Italy, elected at the fall of the Italian Fascist regime (1943). During both World Wars, he was an Italian general, but he was never tried for war crimes committed in Africa since the British government felt he imposed an anti-communist atmosphere in post-war Italy.
80 De Gasperi met frequently with Msgr Montini at Castel Gandolfo, at the home of Bonomelli. Further, according to the testimonies of his letters to his family, the Substitute repeatedly went to the country home of Longinotti.

The meeting of September between the Substitute and the princess, which was followed by many others, were exchanges of general points of view, but also the beginning of a concerted action. Msgr Montini shared his project with the Allies, through the intermediary of the diplomats Tittmann and Osborne. The Allies were favorably disposed, declaring themselves ready to defend the Italian borders and aid the country militarily if the county was attacked by Germany. The composition of the government which would succeed Mussolini was also studied. The princess gave the names of suitable people to Msgr Montini, and he asked the Allies "if they were inclined to accept them." King Victor Emmanuel was ready to be done with Mussolini, but through constitutional means rather than a *coup d'état*. The "conspiracy" thus took longer than expected.

On the other hand, the Allies had a battle plan on the continental level and could not modify their strategy for a coup that appeared rather risky. In November 1942, they landed in French North Africa. The front approached the Italian peninsula. From the month of December, the Secretariat of State undertook efforts with the Fascist government to declare Rome an "open city" and tried to persuade Allied governments not to bombard the Eternal City. The government of Mussolini only partially demilitarized the Italian capital and Roosevelt assured for his part: "Our aviators have been informed of the location of the Vatican and it has been specified that they should not bomb it." The Vatican was not all of Rome. So, when the Allies landed in Sicily on July 10, 1943, there was some doubt whether Rome would escape the fate of the other great cities of the peninsula.

In fact, on July 19, a first Allied bombardment struck the Italian capital. From the end of the morning for several hours, hundreds of planes flew over, releasing bombs which reached not only their objective (the train lines to the southeast of Rome) but also a neighborhood. There were more than a thousand dead, and the cemetery of Campo Verano and the Basilica of Saint Laurence outside the Walls were gravely damaged. Immediately after the bombardment ended, Pius XII left the Vatican, taking with him all the liquid cash available in the Vatican, and went to the site, accompanied by Msgr Montini. The photos taken in these tragic instants show the crowd pressing around the pope. He knelt in the midst of the rubble to pray, then he distributed aid. That evening, the terrified inhabitants of that neighborhood and others came to find refuge before the Basilica of Saint Peter, under Bernini's colonnades. The pope had food distributed to them.

The approach of the Allies rattled the government and the Fascist hierarchy. The plan prepared by the princess of Savoy could take place, even if it was under a "constitutional" form to satisfy the desire of Victor Emmanuel III. On the night of July 24, the Fascist Grand Council voted down Mussolini and voted for a motion presented by Dino Grandi[81] restoring to the king his full constitutional authority for the remainder of the war. On the 25th, in the early hours of the morning, Alberto De Stefani,[82] one of those who had supported Grandi's motion (*Ordine del giorno Grandi*) asked Msgr Montini to come and see him. He explained the night's events and wished that the Holy See serve as a mediator between the Allies and the new government which was going to be formed.

The same day, the king asked Marshal Badoglio to form a government. One of the first decisions of Badoglio was to have Mussolini arrested. On July 26, the Holy See asked the new government to declare Rome an "open city." It agreed in principle a few days later but delayed the announcement, perhaps wishing to obtain guarantees from the Allies first. On August 13, another bombardment hit Rome, in the middle of the day. The train stations of Saint-Laurence and Littorio were targeted but, yet again, houses were hit. Pius XII, accompanied by Msgr Montini, went to the sites to comfort the population. At the Basilica of Saint John Lateran, he prayed with the fearful crowd. The next day the Badoglio government proclaimed Rome an "open city."

In the weeks preceding the fall of Mussolini, clandestine reunions of Christian Democratic opponents to the regime were more frequent. The PPI was going to reconstitute itself under the name "Christian Democracy" around Alcide De Gasperi. A clandestine newspaper, Il *Populo*, had been launched in April, directed by Guido Gonella. One meeting place for the dissidents was the home of Msgr Montini's friend Msgr Rampolla. Documents and sums of money were hidden there. Did Msgr Montini participate in these meetings? We do not know. On the other hand, he knew of their existence. His brothers, Francesco and Lodovico, were closely associated with the resurrection of the Christian Democratic party.

---

81 Dino Grandi (1895–1988) was an Italian Fascist politician who held various ministerial roles. He was an ally to some of the most radical Fascist groups but towards the end of World War II he voted in a motion that removed Mussolini from office and negotiated a truce with Italian left-wing movements, supporting resistance against Nazi Germany. He was sentenced to death for treason by an alternate Italian Fascist government when the Allies occupied southern Italy.

82 Alberto De Stefani (1879–1969) was an Italian politician and economist who favored laissez-faire ideals and policies. Mussolini appointed him as finance minister in 1922.

PAUL VI: THE DIVIDED POPE

The fall of the Fascist regime again permitted the party to come out of hiding. The very day of Mussolini's removal from office, the Laureati, reunited for their annual "Week of Camaldoli," agreed on the "principles of social order" to be put in place in the newly liberated Italy. This text, known under the name of the "Code of Camaldoli," had among its writers the young Aldo Moro, Msgr Montini's associate. Soon all the former opposition parties, from the Christian Democrats to the Communists, regrouped in a CLN (*Comitato di Liberazione Nazionale* — National Liberation Committee).

OCCUPIED ROME

On September 8, 1943, an armistice was signed between the Allies and the Badoglio government. Two days later the German army occupied northern Italy and entered Rome. The Badoglio government and the king fled the city. Mussolini was liberated by an S.S. commando and created, in the North, the Italian Social Republic. The Eternal City was going to be occupied by the Germans for almost one year. The Christian Democracy and the CLN had to return underground. Many found refuge in religious houses, in convents, and even within the walls of the Vatican and in the papal residence of Castel Gandolfo. The Lateran Seminary, under orders from Msgr Ronca, sheltered, among others, De Gasperi and the socialist leader Nenni.[83] Giorgio La Pira[84] hid in the home of Msgr Rampolla and, for a time, also at that of Msgr Montini. Lodovico Montini found refuge in the apartment of his brother and made use of a false identity (Martini).

The danger was still greater for Jews who found themselves in Rome. On September 20, the leaders of the Roman Israelite community were summoned to the general quarters of the S. S. and ordered to collect fifty kilos of gold, or else two hundred Jews residing in Rome would be arrested and deported. Only a part of the required weight was collected. The Chief Rabbi of Rome, Zolli,[85] appealed to the pope to find the fifteen

---

83 Pietro Nenni (1891–1980) was a socialist Italian politician who, as a figurehead of left-wing Italian politics, was awarded the Stalin Peace Prize (1951). When Italy surrendered to the Allies (1943), he became one of the officials of the National Liberation Committee.

84 Giorgio La Pira (1904–1977) was an Italian politician with numerous roles including deputy of the Christian Democrats and Mayor of Florence for two terms, between 1951 and 1965. He was known for his strong advocacy of peace and fought to better the lives of the poor and disenfranchised.

85 Eugenio Pio Zolli (born Israel Anton Zoller, 1881–1956) was the Jewish head rabbi of Rome during its Nazi occupation. When he converted to the Catholic Faith

missing kilos. Pius XII gave the order to do what needed to be done. In the following days, with the help of various Catholic communities, the whole amount was gathered. The persecution, however, did not cease. Beginning in the month of October there were unending roundups to take the Jews away from Rome. Thousands were able to find a refuge in the religious communities of the city: convents, seminaries, parishes, and monasteries (some even wore the religious habit). A few were even taken into the Vatican and the Lateran seminary.

The German troops stopped at the Piazza of Saint Peter's, the limit separating the Vatican State from Italy. The sovereignty of the Holy See was respected. Nonetheless, in the first weeks, an intervention by the German troops in the papal city was feared. Diplomats who had found refuge there began to burn their papers. The order was given to particular members of the Secretariat of State to be ready at all times to accompany the pope if he should be obliged to leave the Vatican. Were there plans on the part of the Germans to kidnap the pope, or remove him from Rome by force? It seems so, but they were not executed because the Nazi leaders held highly divergent opinions on the subject.[86]

These fears did not prevent the services from functioning. The Aid Commission continued to distribute subsidies, most often through the intermediary of existing operations: the General Chaplaincy of Prisoners, led in France by Father Rodhain;[87] the Swiss Catholic Mission; also Father Anton Weber's Mission of Saint Raphael, which specialized in smuggling refugees overseas: through this organization, fifteen hundred Jews from Rome were able to find refuge in America. There was also the Information Office, which handled tens of thousands of cases per month. Msgr Montini was particularly concerned to obtain news of the seventy thousand Italian prisoners of war in the Soviet Union; he did

---

after the war, he took Pius XII's baptismal name for his own. See *Before the Dawn: Autobiographical Reflections by Eugenio Zolli, Former Chief Rabbi of Rome* (San Francisco: Ignatius Press, 2008).

86 Fr Robert A. Graham, SJ, "Hitler voulait-il éloigner Pie XII de Rome?," *La Documentation catholique*, May 7, 1972, cols. 427–34.

87 Msgr Jean Rodhain (1900–1977) was a priest who had been entrusted especially with youth ministry before the War. Seeing that there was a void to be filled, in 1940 he dubbed himself the Chaplain General of Prisoners of War. The Vichy regime tacitly approved of his ministry. In 1940, de Gaulle confirmed him as Chaplain of Prisoners and the Deported and named him Catholic Chaplain General of the Armies of France. He held this office until 1946. Afterwards, he founded *Secours catholique* in France. In 1965, he led the federation of such national Catholic charitable organizations into *Caritas Internationalis*.

not succeed. He intervened, when he could, on behalf of his political friends. In January 1944, Giulio Andreotti, new president of FUCI, came to express his fears concerning the creation, in Rome and other cities in the North of Italy, of tribunals destined to judge the "anti-Fascists." Msgr Montini asked the ambassador of Germany in Rome, Ernst von Weizsäcker,[88] to be the intermediary between the Holy See and the Italian Social Republic to avoid score-settling and vigilantism.

In May 1944, the Allied offensive against Rome began. The Holy See succeeded with the German military authorities and the Allies in protecting Rome from becoming the field of a land or air battle. Through the good sense of both sides, between June 4 and 5, the German troops evacuated the city and the Allied troops entered without any major combat. The civil population was spared; there was no destruction either. On June 5, the Roman population crowded into Saint Peter's square to acclaim Pius XII "Defender of the City." The war was not over. Only in April 1945 was Italy entirely freed.

Without question, this war was a turning point in the life of Msgr Montini. It made him come out of himself, as it were. His nomination as Substitute before the conflict, then the agonies of the war itself, led him to exercise greater and greater responsibilities. His collaboration every day with Pius XII brought him into greater proximity with the pope, even if it would be inaccurate to speak of intimacy between these two churchmen. Yet the last years of the war were a trial for him. In January 1943 his father died; his mother the following May. In 1943–1944 three of his friends, Fathers Marcolini[89] and Manziana, and Andrea Trebeschi were deported to Germany; Trebeschi died in the concentration camp at Gusen. In 1944 as well, Longinotti, who had done so much for his career, died in a car accident.

For a man who had already been thought of as a future pope as early as 1940, the post-war period would open a decade during which he would work to give a new face to the Church — often in the shadow of the pope, and sometimes in direct opposition to his authority.

---

88   Ernst von Weizsäcker (1882–1951) had been a naval officer during World War I before he was the German Secretary of State at the Foreign Office (1938–1943) and then Ambassador to the Holy See until 1945.
89   Fr Ottorino Marcolini (1897–1978) was an Italian priest, born in Brescia, who devoted much of his life to teaching. He took charge of the Arnaldo School and became an assistant of FUCI. During the Second World War, he became lieutenant chaplain in the Air Force, but he was captured and sent to a Nazi concentration camp.

5

The Man in the Shadows

ON AUGUST 22, 1944, A FEW WEEKS AFTER THE liberation of Rome, Cardinal Maglione died suddenly of a heart attack. Pius XII decided not to name a new Secretary of State. The post could have gone to Msgr Tardini or Msgr Montini. Perhaps the pope did not want to offend one of the two by choosing the other. Perhaps also, in not naming anyone, he maintained the possibility of directly controlling the Secretariat of State himself.

The temperaments and styles of the two assistants of the pope were very different. A "Vaticanologist," who had known both of them well, has outlined their differences and their complementarity: Msgr Tardini had "rough and frank manners..., his pitiless judgments spared neither men nor events"; he was "small and heavy, worrying little about his appearance." Msgr Montini had a "prudent, controlled style," "tall and thin, always attentive to his appearance."[1] Their points of view were also different. In certain areas, we will see that the pope often had to choose between contrary opinions expressed by his two subordinates.

PUNISHING THE DEFEATED?

The history of the attitudes of the Holy See in the immediate post-war remains to be written. When, as was done for the war, the official "Acts and Documents" are published, we will better understand what the pope and his collaborators thought and did in their secretive diplomacy, while half of Europe, freed from Fascist and Nazi totalitarianism, began to restore (and purge) its democratic regimes, and the other half fell under the yoke of Soviet totalitarianism. For now let it suffice to observe Msgr Montini's attitudes in different circumstances as they can be studied in the French diplomatic archives and other unpublished sources.

Even before the French State (État Français–Vichy France[2]) had come to an end, General de Gaulle,[3] in the name of the Provisional

---

1 ADSS 11:336–37.
2 Vichy France (1940–1944) refers to the French state led by Marshal Pétain during the German occupation. Pétain tried to retain a level of autonomy in the governance of a portion of France and the French colonies despite German interference.
3 Charles de Gaulle (1890–1970) was a French soldier, statesman, and writer,

Government that was still in Algeria, contacted Pius XII. On May 29, 1944, he sent him a letter in which he assured the pope that "from the moment of deliverance, the spiritual interests of the French people will regain their primacy, which is endangered by the oppression of the enemy." On June 30, a few weeks after the Germans had left Rome, while Paris was not yet freed, he was received at the Vatican. Nothing is known about this meeting beyond what he said in his *War Memoirs*: "Pius XII judges each thing from a point of view which surpasses men, their undertakings, and their quarrels." Was there already question of the purging of the French Bishops' Conference (which was guilty of having been, on the whole, too favorable to Marshal Pétain[4]), or recalling the nuncio in France, who had continued his diplomatic mission at Vichy? Apparently not; but soon afterwards these questions would become the subject of discussions between the French authorities and the Holy See.

The Provisional Government authorized Hubert Guérin,[5] counselor of the French embassy in Italy, to discuss these matters with the Holy See. The Vatican did not recognize his authority in this role until September, after the dissolution of the Vichy government. But from the month of August, even before the government of De Gaulle was installed in Paris, Guérin was received at the Vatican. At the beginning of the month, he had received a memorandum from Pierre Bloch[6] concerning the bishops to be purged.[7] On August 10, first Msgr Tardini, then Msgr Montini, granted Guérin an audience. At this date he did not broach the question of episcopal purges; he awaited the files which

---

but most notably, he crafted the constitution of the Fifth Republic government in France. He was inaugurated as the Fifth Republic's first president (1959) and due to the constitutional amendment (1962), he became the first French president to be elected by popular vote since 1848.
4 Philippe Pétain (1856–1951) was a Marshal of France and hero of World War I. He governed what was left of France during German occupation after the prime minster, Paul Reynaud, resigned. De Gaulle vilified him as a Nazi cooperator in part to divert attention from the fact that De Gaulle had abandoned his command and fled to England.
5 Hubert Guérin (1896–1986) was a military officer and French diplomat who served as ambassador to various countries and during the Second World War represented the French Committee of National Liberation.
6 Pierre Bloch (1905–1999) was a French Resistant of the Second World War and an activist; in support of this activism he was a president of the International League against Racism and Anti-Semitism. He worked alongside General de Gaulle from London for many years in various war efforts and was arrested by the opposition multiple times.
7 AMAE, 1374, ff. 28–29.

The Man in the Shadows

Massigli,[8] commissioner of Foreign Affairs of the Provisional Government of the French Republic (*Gouvernement provisoire de la République française*, GPRF) would send him, "files," wrote Massigli, "which will permit you to discuss various specific cases over the course of your meetings."[9] It seems that Guérin had delayed bringing up this delicate question.

On August 25, during an audience with Pius XII, he heard the pope state his intention of maintaining Msgr Valeri[10] as nuncio in Paris. In Paris, on the other hand, quick action was desired, all the while respecting the Holy See's right of nomination. Since September, Massigli and Georges Bidault,[11] president of CLN, agreed on the extent of the episcopal purge: three cardinals and thirty bishops.[12] But the question was approached indirectly. In October, Msgr Valeri officially shared the aims of the French government with the Holy See: renewal of the entire diplomatic corps accredited to the French State, including the nuncio; and changes in the French episcopacy, without specifying how many bishops. Finally, it was a bishop who had been imprisoned by the Germans, Msgr Théas,[13] who was sent to the Vatican to find common ground. On November 25, he was received by Msgr Montini. After the hour-long interview, Msgr Théas noted: "Strong impression: courteous, intelligent, of a supernatural outlook, desiring a resolution." The pope was more intransigent. On the 27th, Pius XII received Msgr Théas. Concerning the change of the nuncio, the pope "stated his displeasure with the attitude of the French government, which he regards as offensive, discourteous, injurious. He will change

---

8 René Massigli (1888–1988) was a French diplomat who had several secret meetings with German officials after the First World War, on behalf of the French government. He was very senior in the Quai d'Orsay (the French Foreign Ministry) and was a leading member of the "Protestant Clan" that dominated the Quai d'Orsay.
9 AMAE, 1374, f. 21 and f. 37.
10 Card. Valerio Valeri (1883–1963) had been the Apostolic Delegate to Egypt and Saudi Arabia, before serving as Nuncio to France (1936–1944). He had just been received into the Legion d'Honneur before his removal was requested by de Gaulle.
11 Georges Bidault (1899–1983), a soldier in both World Wars, a member of the French resistance, and president of the Provisional Government of the French Republic from June 24 to December 16, 1946, held various government offices until he was deemed a traitor for organizing a resistance movement to defend French Algeria.
12 André Latreille, "Un évêque résistant: Mgr. P. M. Théas," *Revue d'histoire ecclésiastique* (April-June 1980): 284–321.
13 Bishop Pierre-Marie Théas (1894–1977) made himself known during the War for his resistance to Nazism and his denunciation of Jewish deportations. His fire from the pulpit earned him ten weeks in a concentration camp. Pius XII named him bishop of Tarbes and Lourdes (1947–1970).

the nuncio because he has become *persona ingrata*, but he will not do it without pain or protest." As for purging the episcopacy, he declared: "There can be no question of changing the bishops. That has never been done. That will not be done. That would be an injustice. That would be without precedent. That is inadmissible."[14]

Finally, a new nuncio was named to Paris: Msgr Roncalli,[15] until then apostolic delegate in Turkey. Was his name suggested by Msgr Montini? This is possible: the men had known each other for twenty years. Concerning the French bishops to be purged, while Pius XII did not force the departure of any, he immediately accepted the resignation of three of them. Three others were to resign later.

In January 1945, Jacques Maritain was named ambassador of France to the Holy See, to replace Hubert Guérin. This was an unexpected choice: the philosopher had no diplomatic experience. This appointment could only satisfy Msgr Montini, who saw the advent of a man whose work he admired. But the pope was reticent, and made it known in Paris, through Msgr Tardini, that he "would prefer a person who had not been implicated in partisan public controversies."[16] In 1944, Maritain had made a controversial lecture tour in South America on human rights. The nuncios in Argentina and Chile felt compelled to inform the Holy See.

The pope could not refuse the ambassador that France had sent him. In May, Jacques Maritain presented his credentials to the pope. He would retain this post until 1948 and maintained a privileged relationship with Msgr Montini.[17]

The French government planned to monitor closely who would replace the bishops who had resigned. Maritain wrote, early in the process: "If the purge, limited to six sees because of Rome's stubbornness, ends today, the question of the nomination of bishops continues to remain open."[18] Msgr Tardini oversaw the French episcopal nominations; in his reports to Quai d'Orsay, Maritain did not conceal that he was in conflict with

---

14 Latreille, "Un évêque résistant," 311–12; and Pierre Blet, "Pie XII et la France en guerre," *Revue d'histoire de l'Église de France*, 231.
15 Archbishop Angelo Giuseppe Roncalli (1881–1963) had served the Secretariat of State in various roles since 1925. He would be made Patriarch of Venice and a cardinal by Pius XII in 1953. As will be recounted below, he was pope under the name John XXIII from 1958 to 1963. Fr Bouyer will later say that he was not the revolutionary that he is made out to be (*Memoirs*, 236).
16 ADSS 11:679.
17 A special edition of the *Cahiers Jacques Maritain* (no. 4bis, June 1982) contain the official documents of this embassy. We will refer primarily to other documents preserved in public and private archives.
18 AMAE, 538, f. 159.

him. He would have preferred to deal with Msgr Montini, with whom he dealt on other questions, hoping that through him the Holy See could be led to modify other positions, particularly with respect to Germany.

Since the end of the war, the pope had been exhorting the German people to reject "the satanic spectacle of National Socialism" (address of June 2, 1945). Yet he did not regard the German people as collectively responsible for the tragedy which had beaten down Europe and he believed that a spiritual revival was possible in Germany, led by German Catholics.

Jacques Maritain did not agree. On December 9, 1945, he wrote a memorandum for Msgr Montini on the subject. The pope, he wrote, should publicly recognize the "responsibility of the German people as a people" in the Second World War. The spiritual renewal of the German people seemed to him impossible, because "they are not a political people: there is too much dreaming and too much brutality for that, too much apolitical passive obedience." In moral reparation for the crimes it had committed, Germany should pronounce a collective and solemn *mea culpa*. Regarding its political future, Maritain concluded that only the division of Germany into several independent countries could guarantee future peace in Europe.[19] Msgr Montini did not apparently respond in writing to this memorandum. Yet he spoke in person to the ambassador and must have explained the position of the Holy See in greater detail. Was this what he himself thought? No surviving texts or witnesses contradict the possibility. On April 12, 1946, Jacques Maritain addressed a second memorandum on Germany to the Substitute. More moderate in tone than the previous one, it referred frequently to the pope's pronouncements on the subject, while still retaining the notion of the "collective responsibility," of the German state and people.[20]

More pragmatic considerations determined the attitude of the Holy See with regard to Germany after the war. The situation in the conquered country and in the countries liberated by the Red Army soon raised alarm in the Secretariat of State. The information relayed by the nuncios, and local ecclesiastical hierarchies, was often shocking. Yet again, as the Holy See could not intervene directly with the Soviet authorities to protect the rights of people, and of Catholics in particular, Western powers were approached in the hope that they could intercede with the USSR. During the months that followed, Msgr Montini addressed multiple reports to the Western diplomats on the situation in Eastern

---

19   Unedited memorandum of December 9, 1945 (Archives J. Maritain).
20   Unedited memorandum of April 12, 1946 (Archives J. Maritain).

European countries occupied by the Red Army. "These reports," according to recent historians, "comprised a long list of horror: confiscations of property, deportations; a growing number of abortions as a result of rapes committed by Soviet soldiers; dysentery and other illnesses due to a policy of deliberately starving the population."[21]

As during the war, the Holy See acted with the only means at its disposal: diplomacy and humanitarian aid. The Information Office continued to function until 1947. It kept families informed about the liberated prisoners, but also about new political prisoners, and "displaced persons" (Italians, Germans, and Poles who had been forced from their homes in the tens of thousands after borders were redrawn). In November 1944, after a visit to Rome by Father Rodhain, Msgr Montini wrote him a long letter on the subject of an international charitable project to be established post-war to care for these "displaced persons." A service specializing in assistance for immigrants was set up within the Secretariat of State at the end of 1946, under the supervision of Msgr Montini. Its duty was to collect all available information and coordinate the efforts of various national committees. Later, under the guidance of Msgr Rodhain, this would result in the creation of *Caritas Internationalis*.

From summer 1946 until 1949, pontifical charitable organizations sent convoys of trucks, then nearly a thousand loaded train cars, to provide essential aid for the residents of a ruined Germany. An American bishop of German origin, Bishop Aloisius Muench,[22] accompanied the first convoy. Pius XII had named him the Apostolic Visitor in Germany, with a duty to report on the moral, religious, and material situation of the devastated country. Thousands of tons of foods and clothing were brought to the German population.

This attitude was sometimes misunderstood. Many thought that the pope should also make a solemn declaration regarding the Jews as the first and principal victims of the war. Jacques Maritain wrote another memorandum for Msgr Montini on this subject. His suggestion was, he specified, not that of the government he represented: he spoke, not as an ambassador, but as a friend. "During this war," he wrote, "six

---

21 M. Aarons and J. Loftus, *Des Nazis au Vatican* [Nazis in the Vatican], 35. This work, which relies on numerous sources from diplomatic archives and files of secret services, must be used with great caution, on account of its uncritical use of sources and the incoherence of its arguments.

22 Card. Aloisius Muench (1889–1962) was an American prelate who served numerous roles within the Catholic Church. From 1935 to 1959, he was the bishop of Fargo and, in addition, from 1951 to 1959, the Apostolic Nuncio to Germany. He was created a cardinal in 1959.

million Jews have been *liquidated*," as if the people of Israel had been "thrown onto the road to Calvary and conformed to the sufferings of its Messiah in spite of itself." He suggested therefore that the Church make a sovereign declaration. The pope "should bear witness to his compassion for the people of Israel, renew the Church's condemnations against anti-Semitism, and remind the world of the doctrine of Saint Paul, and the teachings of the faith on the mysteries of Israel."[23] Msgr Montini shared this with the pope. A few days later, Pius XII received the ambassador in audience; he reminded him of the statements he had already made on the subject, notably on November 29, 1945, when he received a group of Jews who had returned from the concentration camps. Maritain's request found a response almost two decades later when the Second Vatican Council, under the impulsion of John XXIII and Paul VI, elaborated a declaration on the Jews.

Did the Church also worry about the fate of those "politically conquered" during the war — the militants and leaders of the Nazis, Fascists, or the Axis countries? Did she help some of them flee Europe? Some authors affirm that Msgr Montini aided the secret "exfiltration" networks, directed by German and Croatian priests. These writers allege that at Rome, in the Vatican itself, a sanctuary was given to "war criminals," where they were supplied with false identification papers and helped to escape into Latin America.[24] The same authors even affirm that Msgr Montini was recruited by the American secret services. In these two cases, these claims lack adequate proof, and tend to betray the authors' weak understanding of the Vatican and its functioning. Msgr Montini's reports to American or English diplomats do not prove that he worked for the secret services of either country. As Substitute, he addressed this type of report to numerous other organizations, public and private alike, and to individuals as well. As for the personal testimonies presented as evidence, none features an adequate guarantee of authenticity. The American archives of the Military Information Services certainly contain a few files on Msgr Montini, but they are without interest, and riddled with errors.[25] One of them, in 1952, presents him as a "cardinal," which he was not at the time, and as "assistant of Cardinal Tardini," which was also not true at the time (and Tardini was not yet cardinal at this date)... Such errors cast extreme doubt on the suggestion that Msgr Montini could have been an operative of the CIA.

---

23   Unedited memorandum of August 12, 1946 (Archives J. Maritain).
24   M. Aarons and J. Loftus, *Des Nazis au Vatican*.
25   Archives of the Department of Defense, FOI/Privacy Office, S-12803.

During and after the war, Rome and the Vatican, like all European capitals, were crawling with spies and informers, among whom were undoubtedly members of the clergy. The most well-known case is that of Fr Félix Andrew Morlion,[26] who had worked for the OSS (ancestor of the CIA) during the war. He was active in Rome from 1944, and was in contact with Maritain, and likely with other ambassadors to the Holy See as well. Maritain asked Paris for information on him. He was sent the following note: "Fr Morlion is a Belgian Dominican and not a Franciscan. The activity of Fr Morlion took on a particular extension in South America and North America where he was before coming to Rome."[27]

Fr Morlion created the "CIP," the Pro Deo Information Center (*Centre d'information et de publication* Pro Deo), headquartered in New York, and the Pro Deo University for Social Studies of Rome. All this was the cover for a private espionage service, financed by American and Italian industrialists, that sold its information to the American and Italian secret services.[28] Fr Morlion researched and sold all information that might shed light for Western governments on Vatican politics both in Italy and abroad. For that he "recruited" several clerics, amongst whom were Igino Cardinale[29] and Angelo Dell'Acqua,[30] of the Secretariat of State. He contacted Msgr Montini. What were their relations in the years after the war? We do not know. The only trace of a direct contact between the two men shows that Msgr Montini was not in favor of Fr Morlion's activities. In 1954, Fr Morlion looked to obtain a canonical recognition of his private university Pro Deo. Msgr Montini, who had become Pro-Secretary of State, refused it on the grounds that he had not "clearly defined the nature and the ends of the institution." In 1960, Fr Morlion would be ordered by Cardinal Pizzardo, Prefect of the Congregation of Seminaries and Universities, to leave Rome. But it would be only to return, in triumph, in 1962.

---

26 Fr Félix Andrew Morlion (1904–1987) was a Belgian scholar, theologian, diplomat and social reformer. A self-proclaimed atheist until the age of 21, he then converted to Catholicism and became a Dominican priest. He actively helped Jews escape Nazi persecution, causing the Gestapo to place a million-dollar bounty on his head.
27 Note of September 1945, AMAE, 538, p.84.
28 Sandro Magister, "I servizi segreti italiani spiano Paolo VI," pts. 1–3, L'*Espresso* (February 15 and 22, May 21, 1976).
29 Archbishop Igino Cardinale (1916–1983) spent his career in the diplomatic service of the Holy See. He became archbishop and apostolic nuncio from 1963 until he died in 1983.
30 Card. Angelo Dell'Acqua (1903–1972) was an Italian cardinal who also served as the Vicar General of Rome (1968–1972). He was appointed titular archbishop of Chalcedon by Pope John XXIII (1958) and Pope Paul VI named him Cardinal-Priest of Ss. Ambrogio e Carlo (1967).

ITALIAN POLITICAL GAMES

In the aftermath of the war, the internal situation of Italy was as serious a preoccupation for the Vatican as was the division of Europe. Msgr Montini would play a determining role in the evolution of post-war Italian politics in the fifties.

Upon the liberation of Rome, the Committee of National Liberation had reemerged from the shadows to form a coalition government, led by Bonomi,[31] a liberal politician from the pre-Fascist era. In July 1944, De Gasperi was appointed Political Secretary of the Christian Democratic Party. Other new parties, claiming a "Christian" label, appeared: the Christian Left (made up of Communist Catholics coming from the resistance movements) and a Christian Social Party. At the Vatican, opinions were divided. The opinions of Pius XII's two top assistants were diametrically opposed on this subject, as on others. Msgr Tardini was favorable to this Christian pluralism of parties; Msgr Montini was opposed, and wanted to regroup all the Catholics into a unitary party that could be more easily controlled: he was afraid that the parties to the left of the Christian Democrats would not favor the emergence of another Catholic party to their right. Msgr Montini succeeded in imposing his views. By the end of 1945, the Christian Left had disappeared from lack of visible support from the Church. Its members rejoined the Italian Communist Party. In 1946 the Christian Social Party faded out. Some years later, Church figures including Msgr Ottaviani and Msgr Ronca would try to establish a Catholic party on the right, sometimes called the "Roman Party," but nothing came of the idea.

Montini had considerable influence. Almost all the leaders of Christian Democracy had either been associated with his father before Fascism and subsequently become his own friends, or had been guided by him in FUCI and the Laureati. Msgr Montini united the old generation and the new generations. At the end of 1945, De Gasperi was asked to form a government. The Christian Democrats would lead the government, sometimes in coalition with other parties, until 1979. The first government of De Gasperi also included some Socialists and Communists. The heads of these two parties occupied key posts: the Socialist Nenni was Deputy Prime; the Communist

---

31 Ivanoe Bonomi (1873–1951) was an Italian statesman affiliated with the Italian Socialist Party. He served terms of office as the Italian prime minister both before and after Mussolini's Fascist regime. He played a significant role in the Treaty of Rapallo which reestablished normal relations between Germany and the Soviet Union after the First World War. He also led the anti-fascist movement in World War II.

Togliatti[32] served as Minister of Justice, at a time when the purge was in full swing. Some would have preferred the Vatican to denounce this governmental alliance, but, according to the former Prime Minister Spadolini,[33] Msgr Montini acted effectively to assure its continuation. Referring to the bond between De Gasperi and the Substitute, the Prime Minister wrote that the latter "had protected him [De Gasperi] against the initial attacks, marked by an intransigent anti-Communism."[34] Msgr Montini and the pope did not oppose this coalition because they did not want to destabilize Italy coming out of the war. But they did not let their guard down either. The ambassador of the United States to Rome informed the American authorities that the Jesuits "have the task of organizing and running, through all the members of the Society of Jesus dispersed throughout Italy, a meticulous information service on the clandestine activity and the relations of Italian Communism with Moscow."[35] From whom had they received the order? Doubtless from the pope himself.[36]

In 1946 came the hour of the choice of the country's political regime. Some wished for the abolition of the monarchy, which they blamed for having permitted Mussolini to govern for over twenty years; others supported the monarchy, fearing that a republican regime would destabilize the country even further. On June 2, the Italians were called to a double vote: an institutional referendum (for or against retaining the monarchy) and the designation of a Constituent Assembly to write the country's new constitution. The Holy See closely followed this double ballot. Msgr Montini was ordered by Pius XII to mobilize the laity.[37] He did so by giving very precise instructions to Vittorino Veronese,[38]

---

32   Palmiro Togliatti (1893–1964) was a founding member of the Italian Communist Party and became a citizen of the Soviet Union. He held various Communist Party offices both in Italy and internationally.
33   Giovanni Spadolini (1925–1994) was Prime Minister of Italy (1981–1982) and President of the Italian Senate (1987–1994).
34   G. Spadolini, "Paolo VI e l'Italia," *Stampa sera del lunedì*, August 7, 1978.
35   Report of February 1, 1946 cited by Andrea Riccardi, Il "*Partito romano*" *nel secondo dopoguerra (1945–1954)*, 47.
36   In 1955, following this first initiative, the Jesuits would create a *Centro Studi* intended to combat Communism in every diocese through lectures and seminars.
37   J.-D. Durand, "Pie XII et l'Italie," in *Pie XII et la cité* (Paris: Téqui; Aix-en-Provence: Presses de l'Université d'Aix-Marseille, 1988), 145–80.
38   Vittorino Veronese (1910–1986) was a lawyer and Catholic Action leader. He played important roles in several of Fr Montini's works until his removal by Pope Pius XII from the presidency of Italian Catholic Action in favor of Luigi Gedda in 1952. He became involved in UNESCO, which he directed from 1958 to 1961. Thanks to Montini he was to have a role at Vatican II and to hold several offices in the post-conciliar Curia.

one of the leaders of Catholic Action (Msgr Montini had known him at FUCI before the war) and Msgr Borghino,[39] General Vice-Director of the movement. The movements associated with Catholic Action were permitted to advocate for electoral liberty on the referendum, but they were advised to cast votes for the Christian Democratic candidates on the constituent elections. Only the Christian Democratic candidates agreed with the Church on certain important points: respect for the Concordat, protection of the family and the Christian school, and defense of private property. Members of Catholic Action were authorized to present themselves as candidates on Christian Democratic lists but as private individuals. This was how Giulio Andreotti and Aldo Moro, two former leaders of FUCI during the war years, and Lodovico Montini, all began in politics.

Catholic Action campaigned hard and was financed in part by the Holy See: there were systematic visits of the dioceses, rallies, campaign signs, and widespread distribution of tracts. Meanwhile the bishops, who were divided between maintaining and abolishing the monarchy, also generally advised voting for Christian Democrat candidates. The republican constitution defeated the monarchy, by about two million votes, and the Christian Democrats came ahead in the legislative elections with 35 percent of the votes. During the drafting of the Constitution, the Vatican, through the intermediary of Msgr Montini again, pressed the Assembly to enshrine the Lateran Accords in the Constitution (art. 7). Although he held strong reservations about these accords at the time of their signature, Msgr Montini, in this instance, faithfully represented the will of Pius XII.[40]

But this quasi-unanimity would not last. In 1947, De Gasperi decided to form a new government without the Communists. The country then fell into chaos. Armed bands of Communists became active in numerous regions of the country. After the adoption of the Constitution, which went into force on January 1, 1948, the first legislative elections were set for April 18. The breaking of the coalition government born in the aftermath of the war made the stakes of these elections particularly high. Socialists and Communists united themselves into a "Popular Bloc," campaigning for the institution of a "socialist society." For the Italian voters, this choice of society was linked to a choice of

---

39   Msgr Giuseppe Borghino was the general ecclesiastical assistant (1943) of Catholic Action.
40   J.-D. Durand, "Pie XII et l'Italie."

international politics for the country: to insert itself into the Western bloc then in formation, to maintain a strict neutrality for Italy, or to move closer to the Soviet camp. The Christian Democrats, united in their choice of society, were divided on the attitude to adopt on international politics: the "Atlanticists" (De Gasperi) opposed the "neutralists" (Dossetti[41]). It was decided to mute these divisions to win the battle. Numerous Catholics feared a victory of the Popular Bloc. One of the leaders of Catholic Action, Luigi Gedda,[42] with the support of various members of the hierarchy (Msgr Ottaviani, Msgr Ronca, Msgr Tardini), founded "Civic Committees" aimed at reorganizing the right (including monarchists and nationalists) to block the Socialists and Communists, by calling for votes for the Christian Democrats. There was a chance to form a new party, to the right of the Christian Democrats; De Gasperi was hostile to it; again Msgr Montini supported him. The Christian Democrats carried these elections with 35 percent of the vote and were able to maintain power; De Gasperi formed his fifth government. But as political strife among the hierarchy intensified, Msgr Montini made some choices which met with increasing opposition.

The following year, the creation of NATO again divided the Secretariat of State. De Gasperi wanted Italy to enter the North Atlantic Treaty, and officially consulted the Holy See. Msgr Tardini was opposed to NATO and thought that Italy should remain neutral. Msgr Montini was of the contrary opinion, judgin g that the Holy See was not to pronounce on a matter of external affairs as long as it did not contradict the interests of the Church. Pius XII, with different arguments, favored Italy's joining NATO.

Msgr Montini succeeded equally well in having his views on trade unions prevail. After the war, the unions that had been eclipsed by Fascism decided to form a single organization (the CGIL, *Confederazione Generale Italiana del Lavoro* — Italian General Confederation of Labor), which was dominated by Communists and Socialists. At the Vatican, some wanted to create an independent Catholic union. Msgr Montini was opposed, thinking that the unions' unanimity should not be broken. Yet

---

41 Fr Giuseppe Dossetti (1913–1996) was an Italian theologian and politician who became a Catholic priest in 1958. At a young age, he joined Catholic Action and, due to his strong political and moral beliefs, joined the Italian Resistance. At the Second Vatican Council, he helped turn the council in a progressive direction.
42 Dr Luigi Gedda (1902–2000) was an Italian doctor, activist, and publisher. He was the central president of the Italian Youth of Catholic Action (1934–1946), and then of the Men of Catholic Action (1946–1949), until finally becoming president of the entire association (1952–1957).

he was among those who influenced (notably through his friend Vittorio Veronese) the creation of the ACLI, the Christian Associations of Italian Workers (*Associazioni Cristiane dei Lavoratori Italiani*) at the end of 1944. His brother Lodovico also played a significant role in the foundation and leadership of the movement. Not a union as such, but an "expression of the Christian movement" in a single union, ACLI members were to provide a doctrinal formation for workers and promote various charitable activities. In the spirit of Msgr Montini, they should also be a sort of liaison with the DC. The Church structured the movement through chaplains and the Holy See furnished financial support. Msgr Luigi Guardi, a friend of Msgr Montini since the twenties, was named the General Chaplain.[43]

Pius XII had authorized the members of the ACLI to continue membership in the union on the condition that it "confine itself to its essential aim of representing and defending the interest of workers and the work contract" (address to ACLI, March 11, 1945). It was a warning against the politicization of the unified union. During 1948, following the political crisis of the preceding year, the union fell increasingly under the control of the Communists. In July, the CGIL organized insurrectional strikes all over Italy, with occupation of factories and occasional outbreaks of violence. Some members of the ecclesiastical hierarchy decided that the moment had come to create a Catholic union. In ACLI itself, some members hoped for the transformation of the movement in this direction. Msgr Montini made the president of ACLI, Ferdinando Storchi[44] (who had discussed the possibility of an autonomous union since May) see the value of a different policy. Yet again, he was opposed to affirming Catholic identity, preferring the creation of a non-confessional union. Pius XII supported this point of view, while also entertaining other arguments. Msgr Montini was charged with explaining to Cardinal Ruffini,[45] archbishop of Palermo, one of the most fervent partisans of the creation of a Catholic union: "The formation of a neutral union may be the most efficient means

---

43 Its membership would grow from forty-six thousand in 1945 to six hundred thousand in 1948.
44 Ferdinando Storchi (1910–1993) was a member of the DC and had been part of ACI before heading the ACLI from 1945 to 1954.
45 Card. Ernesto Ruffini (1888–1967), Italian, served as archbishop of Palermo (1945–1967) and was elevated to the cardinalate by Pius XII in 1946. He spent a lot of time in academia, both studying and teaching, and founded the Medical Biological Union of St Luke (1944), which looked at the relationship between science and Catholicism. He also participated in the 1958 papal conclave that elected Pope John XXIII.

of isolating Socialism/Communism, because it can more easily polarize all the forces of labor that reject the revolutionary principles and violent methods of Communism."[46] In September 1948 was created the organization that became the CISL (*Confederazione Italiana Sindacati Lavoratori* — Italian Confederation of Trade Unions).

In political questions as in questions related to the unions, Msgr Montini supported organizations that were officially independent of the Church. It was what he called "promoting the autonomy of the laity," which did not prevent, however, the exercise of more or less direct influence in certain circumstances. One of the leaders of Catholic Action has noted: "The intellectual Catholic laity had learned to see Msgr Montini as 'the new man of the Church,' severe and audacious, prudent but equally ready to encourage all that could be important for the future of new generations."[47]

At the Secretariat of State, Msgr Montini was particularly occupied during this period by Italian internal affairs; Pius XII reserved most foreign policy matters for himself, particularly the dramatic ones: the Sovietization of the Eastern countries; the expansion of Communism in the rest of the world; persecutions of the Catholic hierarchy and faithful in all these countries. Pius XII multiplied his encyclicals and addresses on the subject. Msgr Montini appears to have played no part in putting together these solemn interventions. Nor was the Secretariat of State consulted by the Holy Office during the preparation of its famous decree on Communism (promulgated on July 1, 1949). Catholics were forbidden, on pain of excommunication, to join a Communist party "or to favor it in any manner," to read the Communist press, or write for it. There was a simple answer to the question: "Do the faithful who profess the materialist and anti-Christian doctrine of Communism, and above all, do those who defend or propagate it, rightfully, as apostates of the Catholic Faith, incur the penalty of excommunication reserved to the Holy See?" The answer was: "Yes."

While Msgr Montini had not taken part in putting together this decree, as consultor he was present at the plenary meeting of the Congregation that had approved the text. Having in view the documents he would publish later on the subject, as pope, it seems fair to claim that in 1949 he already did not agree with this type of condemnation and would have preferred to formulate a rejection of Communism in less abrupt terms.

---

46   Letter of September 24, 1948, cited by F. M. Stabile in *Le Chiese di Pio XII* (Bari: Editori Laterza, 1986), 387.

47   Mario Rossi, "Mes rencontres avec Mgr. Montini," *Témoignage chrétien* (June 1963).

"WHY GO TO THE MOUNTAIN..."

By virtue of his position, Msgr Montini could often be considered the official interpreter of the thoughts of Pius XII. In the name of the pope, he wrote letters, messages, and other communications addressed to individuals and organizations alike: international Catholic societies, Catholic Action movements in various countries; the Secretary General of the Leagues of the Sacred Heart; even the President of the UFCS (*Union féminine civique et sociale* — Ladies' Social and Civic Union). Although signed by the Substitute, these official texts, which were meant for publication, are today collected among the "Papal Documents" of the reign of Pius XII, because they are rightly considered to be expressions of this sovereign pontiff's positions, as he was the one making this delegation. Much of Msgr Montini's time was taken up with editing encyclicals (ten or so during the reign of Pius XII), and other important pontifical texts, and putting together public letters to bishops and speeches to all the increasingly numerous groups that solicited a papal audience. The Secretariat of State was entrusted with composing minor documents, which sometimes carried some importance. Traditionally these were ultimately the Secretary of State's responsibility. When Cardinal Maglione died, and was not replaced, the duty was delegated to Msgr Montini.[48] The seventy-four letters he signed date mainly to his last years at the Secretariat of State. They included messages destined to be read during the course of a conference or an exceptional meeting; they could also be responses to requests made to the Holy Father. Can Msgr Montini's own ideas and preoccupations be glimpsed in these texts he signed? Until the relevant archives are open for study, it will be difficult to determine his role in the final versions of texts. It seems reasonable to assume that these texts, drafted at the Secretariat of State, were prepared in accordance with the pope's own instructions. Msgr Montini had these messages drafted, revised them himself as needed, then submitted them for the pope's approval, and further possible corrections, before sending them.

Certain documents, such as the letters sent each year to the various *Settimane Sociali* (Social Weeks conferences) in Italy, France, or Canada,

---

[48] During the lifetime of Cardinal Maglione, only one of these pontifical documents was signed by Msgr Montini: a letter to Father Gemelli, rector of the University of the Sacred Heart of Milan, March 15, 1944, on the occasion of a "University Day." It is undoubtedly in consideration of the longstanding relationship between Msgr Montini and Father Gemelli that the pope entrusted him with writing this letter.

were a reminder of the important principles of the social doctrine of the Church. Others were more delicate and were composed with careful attention to the terms used. Thus, in 1951 when Joliot-Curie,[49] president of the Soviet-inspired World Peace Council, addressed a letter to the pope,[50] Msgr Montini had the duty of responding to him. The response was surely outlined by Pius XII himself. Joliot-Curie wanted the pope to encourage countries to reduce their stockpiles of weapons; the official response was that "true peace" has its source "in the doctrine taught by Our Lord Jesus Christ." Another delicately worded reply was addressed to the Orthodox archbishop of Athens who, for the nineteenth centenary of Saint Paul's arrival in Greece, wanted representatives of the Catholic Church to participate in the celebrations. Msgr Montini was delegated to refuse the invitation, "given the current conditions confronting the Holy See in the Hellenic nation" (no diplomatic relations then existed between the Holy See and Greece) and "abstracting from other considerations" (the participation of Catholic representatives at Orthodox ceremonies).

The personal opinions of Msgr Montini at this time will not be found in these official texts, but in the statements of those with whom he met. All bear witness to a man "open" to innovative and audacious theological currents, with a simultaneously accommodating and prudent nature. During the post-war period he very soon became conspicuous as having a different sort of spirit at the heart of the Vatican. It has been noted: "Each *ad limina* visitor bearing a thorny dossier knows that it is better to begin the Roman tour with him rather than with someone else . . ."[51] The office of the Substitute was also open to entreaties from condemned theologians, theologians who risked condemnation, ecumenists who wanted the Church to soften her positions, and also diplomats who sought to defend authors who were at risk of seeing their books put on the *Index*, or else had other favors to ask.

In 1946, Jean Bourdeillette, chargé d'affaires of the French embassy to the Holy See, came to complain to Msgr Montini of articles published in

---

49 Frédéric Joliot-Curie (1900–1958) was a French physicist who, in collaboration with his wife Irène, discovered artificial radioactivity. He was a Communist and kept his Soviet colleagues informed of his research.
50 Although not known at the time, the letter was in fact written by the Dominican theologian Chenu and simply signed by Joliot-Curie (Chenu, *Un théologien en liberté*, 162–63).
51 Étienne Fouilloux, "G. B. Montini face aux débats ecclésiaux de son temps (1944–1954)," in *Paul VI et la modernité* (Rome: École française de Rome, 1984), 89.

a Catholic newspaper in Rome, Il Quotidiano, that were hostile to French policies. The Substitute promised to intervene.[52] He was able to do so all the more easily as the director of the paper was Federico Alessandrini, whom he had formed at the FUCI.

Sometimes Msgr Montini intervened directly in situations, other times he knew merely to give advice, act as an intermediary, or else counsel prudence and recommend patience. An untranslatable play-on-words soon spread in well-informed ecclesiastical circles: "Why go to the mountain [Pius XII] when you can pass by Montini?"[53] One of the first to take this route was Father Yves-Marie Congar.[54] He had published with Fr Henri-Marie Féret,[55] in the review La Maison-Dieu, a harsh critique of the new Latin translation of the psalter. Pius XII, who had this work done by a commission overseen by his confessor, Fr Augustin Bea,[56] a German Jesuit, was upset at the two Dominicans' criticisms. Fr Congar visited Msgr Montini for the first time on May 21, 1946, and learned that a memorandum in defense of the Psalter, undoubtedly written by members of the commission, was in circulation. The Substitute counseled him to respond. Frs Congar and Féret did so a few days later after obtaining a copy of the memo in question. During the same visit, Msgr Montini and Fr Congar spoke of ecumenical questions. The Substitute seemed well informed about these questions and subscribed to the bulletin of the SOEPI (Service œcumenique de presse et d'information — Ecumenical Press and Information Service), a publication that was then all but unknown in Catholic circles. But Fr Congar noted in his journal that Msgr Montini seemed reticent to draw nearer to non-Catholics "without a sufficient doctrinal foundation, neglecting principles."[57] Father Congar

---

52   Report of J. Bourdeillette to G. Bidault, August 22, 1946, AMAE, 538, 142.
53   The saying is a play on words. The mountain refers to Pius XII because there is a mountain in his coat of arms; Montini is the diminutive form of "mountain" in Italian.
54   Card. Yves Congar (1904–1995) was a French Dominican known for his works on ecclesiology and ecumenism. He was created cardinal by Pope John Paul II in 1994.
55   Fr Henri-Marie Féret (1904–1992) was a French Dominican, theologian, and Church historian who wrote The Apocalypse of St John, among other works.
56   Card. Augustin Bea (1881–1968) was a German Jesuit priest and scholar at the Pontifical Gregorian University whose research centered around biblical studies. He was confessor to Pope Pius XII (1945–1958), who recommended appointing him to the College of Cardinals (1946). He was eventually created cardinal in 1959 and then consecrated a titular archbishop in 1962. He was highly influential at the Second Vatican Council.
57   Étienne Fouilloux, Les Catholiques et l'unité chrétienne du XIXe au XXe siècle, 898; Yves Congar, "L'oecuménisme de Paul VI," in Paul VI et la modernité, 807.

offered Msgr Montini one of his own books on ecumenism, Chrétiens désunis,[58] which he had written before the war. Msgr Montini read it attentively. Thereafter, he transmitted the files and memoranda that were sent to him by Father Congar and his ecumenist friends to the relevant Vatican dicasteries.

At that time, the doctrine of the Church on relations with non-Catholics was as follows: the Catholic Church is the only Church willed by Christ; those who have separated themselves from her in past centuries (Orthodox, Protestants, etc.) should convert and return to the Catholic Church. Before the Second World War, particularly in France, a movement arose to speak no longer of individual conversions, but of seeking the "unity of the Churches" by moving closer together and initiating dialogue between the different Christian confessions. Fr Couturier,[59] founder of the Week of Prayer for Unity, and Fr Congar, with the work mentioned above, were the principal representatives of the Ecumenical Movement. Msgr Montini, in 1945, encouraged an ecumenical initiative by a French professor of theology at the Gregorian University, Fr Charles Boyer, who created an International Association for the Unity of Christians (called Unitas). Msgr Montini helped to set this up and to obtain for it papal approval.[60] He always paid close attention to Fr Boyer's work, and would appeal to him hereafter.

Another person with whom Msgr Montini met and to whom he gave his support was Fr de Lubac.[61] What was then called the nouvelle théologie (new theology) was severely criticized by prominent Thomistic theologians.[62] The pope himself, in an audience on September 17, 1946 with the participants of the General Congregation of the Jesuits that had just ended in Rome, issued a severe warning:

---

58   Yves Congar, Divided Christendom: A Catholic Study of the Problem of Reunion, trans. M. A. Bousfield (London: Geoffrey Bles, 1939).
59   Fr Paul Couturier (1881–1953) was a French priest of the Society of St. Irenaeus. His Week of Prayer for Christian Unity corresponds with the Octave from the old Feast of the Chair of St Peter in Rome to the Feast of the Conversion of St Paul (January 18–25).
60   Charles Boyer, SJ, "Le Pape Paul VI," Esprit et Vie (December 11, 1978): 692.
61   Card. Henri de Lubac (1896–1991) was a French Jesuit who, despite repeated disciplinary action and censorship, was a prolific author whose works had an influence on much of conciliar theology. Paul VI wanted to make him a cardinal but he refused it. In 1972, he founded the theological journal Communio along with Joseph Ratzinger and Hans Urs von Balthasar. He accepted the red hat in 1983 from Pope John Paul II.
62   Above all, Fr Garrigou-Lagrange in the review Angelicum and Frs Nicolas and Labourdette in the Revue thomiste.

> Let no one disturb or overturn what must not be changed. Too much has been said and in a careless manner on the subject of the "new theology," which must evolve as all things evolve, to be in perpetual development without any stability. If such an opinion should be embraced, what will become of the immovable dogmas of the Catholic Church? What will become of the unity and the stability of the faith?

Fr de Lubac, who participated in this General Congregation, felt singled out by this admonition. He had just published an audacious work, *Surnaturel*,[63] in which he criticized the notion of "pure nature" and argued that man, by his very nature, had an innate desire for the beatific vision, a supernatural desire. At the French embassy, Jacques Maritain and his canonical advisor, Fr Delos, counseled Fr de Lubac to go see Msgr Montini. It seems that he almost miraculously procured some appeasement to the situation. Sometime afterwards, at the request of his superiors (and on the advice of Msgr Montini), Fr de Lubac wrote a "Theological Examination of Conscience," to prepare himself for the possibility of the condemnation of his book.[64]

Although in Italian affairs he was proactive in certain things and the promotor of certain positions, with regard to theological and political questions of foreigners he got involved almost exclusively because they asked him to do so. For some people, he was the point of reference, a choice contact, and a precious counsel. Thus, in the spring, some South American politicians (notably Eduardo Frei,[65] future president of Chile in the sixties) set up a Christian Democratic movement that had a double peculiarity: it wanted to be both international and directly inspired by Maritain's thought in *Integral Humanism*.[66] He planned to fight "against the growing dangers of neo-Fascism, Communism, and the Capitalist counterreaction." Maritain briefed the Substitute on this incipient movement; soon afterwards he could inform his Latin American disciples that

---

[63] Henri de Lubac, *Surnaturel: Études historiques* (Paris: Aubier, 1946). A new edition was published by Desclée de Brouwer in 1991.

[64] Henri de Lubac, SJ, *Mémoire sur l'occasion de mes écrits*.

[65] Eduardo Frei (1911–1982) was a Chilean conservative political leader. During his career, he was President of his Christian Democratic Party and the twenty-eighth President of Chile (1964–1970). His oldest son also became the Chilean President (1994–2000).

[66] Jacques Maritain, *Integral Humanism*, in *The Collected Works of Jacques Maritain*, vol. 11, *Integral Humanism, Freedom in the Modern World, and A Letter on Independence*, rev. ed., ed. Otto Bird, trans. Otto Bird, Joseph Evans, and Richard Sullivan (Notre Dame, IN: University of Notre Dame Press, 1996).

Msgr Montini was "very well disposed" toward them even if "they must expect a very adverse reaction on the part of a few Chilean bishops."[67] During a second meeting, Msgr Montini expressed his desire that a "doctrinal control of the fundamental ideological program"[68] be exercised.

At the beginning of June 1948, Jacques Maritain left the French embassy to the Holy See for Princeton University, where a chair of philosophy awaited him. The ties between the embassy and the Substitute were not weakened on that account. The chargé d'affaires Jean Bourdeillette served during the interim. He had an opportunity to intervene effectively with Msgr Montini. In June, Msgr de Solages,[69] rector of the Catholic Institute of Toulouse, came to Rome. He was an object of suspicion for some theologians on account of his support for the ideas of Fr Teilhard de Chardin.[70] Pius XII refused to receive him in audience. Bourdeillette then went to the office of the Substitute and made him see that this rejection would leave an unfavorable impression once it became known in France. Msgr Montini promised to intervene. Eventually he succeeded in having Pius XII change his mind.[71]

On September 1, Wladimir d'Ormesson took over as French ambassador to the Holy See, occupying the post until July 1956. He resumed the position he had already occupied before the war, and so was already familiar with the Substitute. From the month of the following November, he interceded with him in favor of a work of Maxence Van der Meersch[72] on Saint Thérèse of Lisieux that had been submitted for examination to the Holy Office. Already his predecessor, Maritain, had similarly noted that if the work were included in the *Index* of forbidden books, it would

---

67 Letter of J. Maritain to Alceu Amoroso Lima, June 13, 1947 (Archives J. Maritain).
68 Letter of J. Maritain to A. A. Lima, June 18, 1947 (Archives J. Maritain). Cf. also P. Letamendia, "Eduardo Frei et Jacques Maritain," in *Jacques Maritain et ses contemporains* (Paris: Desclée, 1991).
69 Msgr Bruno de Solages (1895–1983) directed the Institute from 1931 to 1964. In 1932 he was made a Protonotary Apostolic.
70 Fr Pierre Teilhard de Chardin (1881–1955) was a French Jesuit priest who worked as a paleontologist and geologist and wrote as an evolutionary philosopher. He had taught at the ICP in the early 1920s. He was a part of the expedition that discovered the Peking Man and was implicated in the Piltdown Man Hoax. His written works interpret revelation and theology from an evolutionary viewpoint, which led to contradictions with such doctrines as Original Sin, the Incarnation, and the Redemption. Several of his works were condemned by the Holy Office in 1962; more recently, they have received renewed interest because of rehabilitative gestures by Benedict XVI and Francis.
71 Report of J. Bourdeillette to G. Bidault on June 18, 1948, AMAE, 539, ff. 49–56.
72 Maxence Van der Meersch (1907–1951) was a French Catholic writer whose work was marked by Christian humanism. He also wrote about St. Jean Vianney.

provoke a strong protest in France where Van der Meersch enjoyed notable fame. Msgr Montini then showed himself "sensitive to these arguments and let it be understood that he would do everything possible to avoid ecclesiastical censure against the book." D'Ormesson renewed his efforts because a harsh critique of the book by Fr Cordovani had recently been published in *L'Osservatore Romano*. Msgr Montini renewed his assurances;[73] the book was not condemned.

In March 1949, Msgr Montini met Roger Schütz[74] and Max Thurian,[75] the two leaders of a Protestant monastic community that had been founded in 1940 at Taizé.[76] Cardinal Gerlier,[77] archbishop of Lyons, had sent them to the Substitute; he had also prepared for them interviews with Msgr Ottaviani of the Holy Office, with Fr Boyer, and for an audience with Pius XII. With Msgr Montini they found the warmest welcome. They complained of the publication of a *monitum* of the Holy Office that had appeared the preceding year when the World Council of Churches[78] had been created which forbade Catholic participation in it. Msgr Montini led them to understand that participation would be possible in the future; he explained that the document was aimed at those "unsolid ecumenical groups where a distorted charity risked to compromise both the Catholic truth and its clear and authentic profession."[79] He also gave advice to his two visitors with regard to their meetings with the pope on the following day, counseling them "not to try to approach the pope on a doctrinal and theological level, because Pius XII

---

73   Report of W. d'Ormesson to G. Bidault on November 11, 1948, AMAE, 539, 71.
74   Roger Schütz (1915–2005) was a Swiss Protestant monk and first prior of the Taizé ecumenical monastic community in Burgundy, France. He was murdered in 2005 and his funeral was celebrated by Card. Walter Kasper, President of the Council for Promoting Christian Unity.
75   Max Thurian (1921–1996) was the first subprior of the Taizé community. Pope Paul VI invited him to participate in the liturgical reform of the Catholic Mass after the Second Vatican Council. He was known for believing that Protestants could receive Holy Communion along with Roman Catholics.
76   Beginning in 1969 the community of Taizé welcomed Catholic brothers. In 1987 Max Thurian would be ordained a priest by the archbishop of Naples. Cf. Yves Chiron, *Frère Roger* (Paris: Perrin, 2008).
77   Card. Pierre-Marie Gerlier (1880–1965) was a French cardinal who served as archbishop of Lyons (1937–1965). He was a cardinal elector in the 1963 conclave that chose Pope Paul VI.
78   The World Council of Churches (WCC) is an international organization founded in 1948 to promote the unity of Christian bodies, of which it comprises some three hundred and fifty. Notably, the Catholic Church is still not a member, although several Orthodox communities are.
79   Account written by Max Thurian, Archives COE (Geneva).

was a theologian, and at that level he had a very precise point of view. But he was also a pastor and, as a pastor, he could listen."[80] Lastly he outlined for his interlocutors a program of true ecumenical dialogue: "The great difficulty will remain that of the Credo: the Church cannot retreat from its dogma. But there is another area where the Church can show more openness. She must firstly recognize the faults of her members, both in history and today."[81] It is interesting to glimpse in this initial statement one of the keys of ecumenism as practiced by Paul VI: to ask pardon from Protestants and Orthodox for the harm done to them in the past by the Church. Roger Schütz and Max Thurian would remain in close contact with Msgr Montini in years to come, during his episcopacy in Milan, and when he became pope.

The year 1950 was, in many senses, one of the most important years in the papacy of Pius XII. He published the encyclical *Humani Generis* condemning various contemporary theological and philosophical currents; and he promulgated the dogma of the Assumption. This was also a "Holy Year," a Jubilee year, which came every twenty-five years; during these, the pope could accord a plenary and general indulgence[82] under the condition of certain sacramental and devotional practices.

Pius XII wanted it to be "the year of the great return, the year of the great pardon, to the degree that our recent past has been a time of offence and desertion of God." The pope put Msgr Montini in charge of the material preparations for this Holy Year. Millions of pilgrims were expected in Rome. It was necessary to allocate times for major national pilgrimages at intervals throughout the year, to establish the calendar of public and private audiences, and to supervise the possibilities of lodging as well. In these duties, the Substitute was assisted by Msgr Pignedoli, whom he had known during the war through his articles in *Azione fucina*.

A few months before the inauguration of the Holy Year, Msgr Montini was asked to introduce it in a speech given to the political and civil authorities of Rome, as well as the diplomats on duty in the capital. In the solemn setting of the Ruspoli palace, in the audience's first row, the Prime Minister De Gasperi and several ministers were present, surrounded

---

80   K. Spink, *Frère Roger de Taizé*, 67.
81   Statements reported by M. Thurian, "Paul VI et les observateurs au concile Vatican II," in Paolo VI e I *problemi ecclesiologici al Concilio* (Brescia: Istituto Paolo VI; Rome: Edizioni Studium, 1989), 250.
82   A plenary indulgence is the complete remission of the temporal punishment due to sin the guilt of which has already been forgiven. A person can do the prescribed works and prayers to merit the indulgence for himself or for a soul in purgatory.

by numerous cardinals of the Curia. The ambassador of France, in a report to the French Foreign Minister, has described what a strong impression Msgr Montini made on this occasion:

> He is a prelate-diplomat who is only seen and heard between the baize walls of his office. He never shows himself in public, but keeps himself, discreetly, in the shadow of the pope. Perhaps this was the first time that circumstances led him to pronounce a grand discourse before a large audience; yet he did it as a master. What was most striking was the fire that animated him, his force of persuasion, the authority that flowed from his person. He was able to develop an entirely banal and common theme with such a real talent that not for an instant, during almost an hour, was interest weakened or attention distracted. Everyone was impressed. The speech ended with uniform exclamations and praise on all sides. I would wager that this was a red-letter day in the destiny of the pope's right hand (or his left). I heard people saying among themselves, that evening: "We have heard a future pope." Let us hope so for the Church...[83]

Did this success surprise Msgr Montini? Perhaps not: he was aware of his value. At the beginning of the Holy Year and in the wake of this memorable evening, although not looking to profit from it, Msgr Montini helped in the foundation of the "Roman Circle." Two of his personal friends, Dalla Torre, editor-in-chief of *L'Osservatore Romano*, and Veronese, director of International Catholic Action, created a sort of salon where diplomats posted in Rome and figures from politics and culture could all meet. The atmosphere was not strictly Catholic: there were Protestant, Buddhist, and Muslim diplomat members. Its goal was to promote public talks and informal discussions on various subjects, and to organize receptions to welcome visitors of distinction who were passing through Rome. All the prominent Christian Democratic leaders of the time (including De Gasperi and Fanfani[84]) would repeatedly give talks there.[85]

---

83   Report of W. D'Ormesson to R. Schumann, dated May 27, 1949, AMAE, 540, E 190.
84   Amintore Fanfani (1908–1999) was the thirty-second Italian Prime Minister who served for five separate terms between the years 1954–1987. He also served in several different ministerial positions within the Italian government. He was in addition Secretary of the Christian Democracy and he worked to decrease its strong dependence on the Catholic Church.
85   Report of W. d'Ormesson to P. Mendès-France, dated November 12, 1954, AMAE, 540, ff. 213–15.

The year 1950 also saw several French theologians sanctioned or threatened with sanctions. The "new theology" had already been denounced by Pius XII in 1946. It was targeted again: this time, attention was directed towards the Jesuits of Fourvière and some Dominicans at Le Saulchoir.[86] Some of them, Fathers de Lubac, Congar, and Chenu, who were associated with Msgr de Solages, aimed to produce a comprehensive theological treatise in six volumes, "conceived in another spirit and following a different order than the manuals still in use."[87] The sanctions and condemnations did not expressly target this project, but they kept it from seeing the light of day.

In June, because of "pernicious errors on essential points of dogma," five Jesuit professors of Lyon were removed from teaching; among them was Fr de Lubac. On August 12, the encyclical *Humani Generis* was published; it focused on "some false opinions which threaten to ruin the foundations of Catholic doctrine": relativism in the exposition of dogmas; immanentism, idealism, and existentialism in philosophy; irenicism in relations with non-Catholics, polygenism in anthropology, and still other errors.[88] This encyclical, however, did not discourage healthy intellectual research or the legitimacy of multiple theological "schools."

The encyclical struck like a bolt of lightning. Several theologians felt themselves targeted by one or another passage of the encyclical, even if the pope had not cited any specific names or titles. Msgr Montini, in his conversations with diplomats and visitors, strove to minimize the

---

86 Fourvière is the common name for the Jesuit house of studies in Lyon, taking its name from the surrounding district of the city. Le Saulchoir is the name given to the French Dominican house of studies while the Dominicans were in exile in Belgium after the separation of Church and State in 1905. Upon returning to France in 1939, the name was retained for the new house of studies. These two houses of studies were hotbeds of the *nouvelle théologie*: from Fourvière came Fathers Henri de Lubac and Jean Daniélou and from Le Saulchoir came Fathers Marie-Dominique Chenu, Yves Congar, and Edward Schillebeeckx.
87 de Lubac, *Mémoire*, 144.
88 Relativism denies absolute truth. Immanentism is a philosophical school holding that human experience is the ultimate source of verification. Idealism, as presented by Immanuel Kant, holds that man cannot know things as they really are but only as they appear to us according to our subjective sensibility. Existentialism is the philosophical movement that holds that one's lived experience as a thinking, feeling, and acting individual forms one's essence (existence precedes essence). Irenicism is the error of attempting to foster peace and unity by compromising doctrines of the Faith. Polygenism is the theory that the human races descend from multiple origins, as opposed to monogenism in which there is an original first couple from which all men descend. Monogenism is a divinely revealed truth and necessary for the transmission of original sin.

weight of the encyclical. In a conversation a few weeks later with the philosopher Jean Guitton he explained:

> the encyclical never speaks of *errores*.... It speaks only of *opiniones*. That indicates that the Holy See aims not at condemning errors, but at condemning modes of thought that could lead to errors, but in themselves remain respectable.... The French are wrong to interpret as condemnation what is merely a warning — an appeal to prudence, to gradualness, to maturation.[89]

It has been written that Pius XII caught wind of the Substitute's appeasing statements and was irritated. He is alleged to have sent a letter to the editor of *La Civiltà Cattolica*, the famous Italian Jesuit journal, to complain of the efforts made in various ways to reduce the impact of his encyclical. There is nothing to these rumors.[90] If he was hurt to see the cold reception his warnings received in certain circles, he found enough theologians and journals to defend and explain his thought in good faith.

Sometime after the encyclical, several works of Fr de Lubac (*Surnaturel*, *Corpus Mysticum*,[91] *De la Connaissance de Dieu*),[92] and books by other targeted authors, were removed from stores and libraries. Msgr Montini took advantage of a visit to Paris by one of his French colleagues, Msgr Veuillot,[93] giving him a message for Fr de Lubac. Msgr Veuillot was asked to reassure the sanctioned theologian of the Substitute's esteem "not only for your person but for your work."[94] Three years later, when Fr de Lubac published *Méditation sur l'Église* [Meditations on the Church],[95] Msgr Montini read it immediately and ordered several copies to distribute to his friends.[96] These minor details illustrate

---

89 Guitton, *Dialogues*, 27–28.
90 Letter of Giacomo Martina, SJ, to the author, June 26, 1992.
91 Henri de Lubac, *Corpus Mysticum: The Eucharist and the Church in the Middle Ages*, trans. Gemma Simmonds, Richard Price, and Christopher Stephens (London: SCM, 2006).
92 An expanded version of this work was translated as Henri de Lubac, *The Discovery of God* (Grand Rapids: Wm. B. Eerdmans, 1996).
93 Cardinal Pierre Veuillot (1913–1968) was graced with a post in the Secretariat of State thanks to then Nuncio to France Roncalli in 1949. He was made a prelate in 1953, bishop of Angers (1959–1961), Coadjutor of Paris (1961–1966), and then archbishop of Paris until his death. He helped to send the worker-priests back to work with the consent of Paul VI in 1965 and would be created cardinal in 1967.
94 de Lubac, *Mémoire*, 144.
95 Henri de Lubac, *The Splendor of the Church*, trans. Michael Mason (San Francisco: Ignatius Press, 1986).
96 Msgr P. Veuillot, preface to Msgr Montini, *L'Église et les conciles* (Paris: Éditions Saint-Paul, 1965), 8.

the capacity for thoughtful loyalty of "the left arm of the pope."

The proclamation of the dogma of the Assumption was one of the other great events of the year. The world's bishops had been consulted by the pope about this solemn promulgation of a very ancient and widespread belief. The responses had almost all been favorable. The Protestants on the other hand criticized it. A few months before the proclamation, Roger Schütz and Max Thurian asked to be received by Msgr Montini. They undoubtedly hoped that the proclamation could be avoided. They explained to the Substitute how this new dogma was doubly unacceptable in the eyes of Protestants: not only did it attribute a supplementary privilege to the Virgin Mary that was not historically attested, but the pope was going to proclaim it infallibly, and papal infallibility was another dogma rejected by non-Catholics.[97] Concerning Marian piety, Msgr Montini wished "a greater discipline and a text specifying the purity of the doctrine."[98] He also counseled his interlocutors to prepare a text on these questions of infallibility and Marian dogma, and to take it to the pope. Pius XII received the two visitors but did not change his mind.[99] The proclamation of the Assumption took place on November 1, in the presence of 622 bishops and a large crowd.

That Msgr Montini believed personally in this new dogma cannot, of course, be doubted. On the other hand, it is also certain that his whole life he feared excessive emphasis on Marian devotion, and the possibility of its degenerating into "Mariolatry." His warm reception of Jean Guitton, in this same year 1950, is, in this regard, significant.

During the previous year, Jean Guitton had published a work on the Virgin Mary, *La Vierge Marie*. Before making the acquaintance of the writer, Msgr Montini had already read several of his books, notably his famous *Portrait de monsieur Pouget*.[100] He had also read *La Vierge Marie* and greatly appreciated it. He would say to Guitton: "Since the pages of Newman[101] in his famous letter to Dr Pusey, I believe I have never

---

[97] In the Taizé journal, *Verbum Caro*, Thurian wrote, after the proclamation of the Assumption: "The dogma of the infallibility [of the pope] posed only a theoretical question, because the pope had not yet used his power. The recent promulgation reveals in a magisterial and significant way where his power can lead the Roman Church: to the affirmation of a doctrine without historical foundation."
[98] Thurian, "Paul VI et les observateurs," 242.
[99] Chiron, *Frère Roger*, 128–32.
[100] Jean Guitton, *Portrait de monsieur Pouget* (Paris: Gallimard, 1941).
[101] Card. John Henry Newman (1801–1890) was an English Anglican cleric who, after his conversion, was ordained a Catholic priest and was elevated to the cardinalate in 1879 by Pope Leo XIII. He was also a theologian, poet, and evangelical

read pages which have so satisfied me on the subject of the Virgin."[102] However, an article in a French review, then very widely spread in the Roman circles, had expressed "the strongest" reservations with regard to certain pages of the book and wished "to warn" its readers.[103] The Holy Office had taken up the affair and proceeded to a scrupulous examination of the work under suspicion. One passage above all was in contradiction with the doctrine of the Church, in which Guitton explained that at the moment of the Visitation, the Virgin did not know that she was going to give birth to the Son of God. The book was at risk of being condemned by the Holy Office. On his own initiative, Msgr Montini, even before meeting Guitton, made an effort to check its condemnation; he even wrote a letter praising the book and had it signed by Pius XII.[104] This letter, undoubtedly shown to the theologians of the Holy Office whose duty it was to examine the work, prevented its inclusion on the *Index*.

The nuncio in Paris, Msgr Roncalli, had counseled Jean Guitton to contact Msgr Montini to save his book. When, on September 8, 1950, Guitton met the Substitute, it appeared that a great deal had already been done for him. Yet Msgr Montini was not omnipotent; the work was not beyond reproach. A few months later, a second highly critical review of the work appeared in France.[105] The next year, Cardinal Pizzardo severely criticized *La Vierge Marie* in *L'Osservatore Romano*; the Holy Office obliged Jean Guitton to make some corrections to his book in subsequent editions.[106]

The work pleased Msgr Montini because of its strong insistence on the distinction between "faith" and "devotion"; also, it had been written in an ecumenical spirit (it was dedicated "to our Protestant, Anglican, and Orthodox brothers"). September 8, 1950 marked the birth of a great friendship between the two men. Msgr Montini had Jean Guitton promise two things: that each year, on September 8, he would come to visit him, and that he would always tell him the truth. Jean Guitton was

---

academic of Oxford University. As leader of the Oxford Movement, he influenced a number of Anglicans who wanted the Church of England to readopt many Catholic beliefs and liturgical rituals. He was canonized in 2019.
102 Guitton, Dialogues, 21.
103 *Revue des Cercles d'études d'Angers*, July 1950.
104 Interview of Jean Guitton with the author, May 11, 1991.
105 *Revue des Cercles d'études d'Angers*, December 1950.
106 The second edition of the book, in 1953, was effectively a "corrected" edition. On the other hand, the latest re-edition, in the collection *Oecuménisme* (Paris: DDB, 1986), reused the original text.

faithful to these two promises, even after the man who had "saved him from the scourges of the Inquisition" became pope.

To see Substitute Montini in these years as only occupied in interceding for someone or other, playing the intermediary, would be caricatural. He welcomed and listened to many people in his office. In spring 1947, for example, he received Fathers Roguet[107] and Martimort,[108] the two heads of the *Centre de Pastorale Liturgique* (Liturgical Pastoral Center) that had been established in Paris a few years before. This center helped drive liturgical reform. From this first meeting, its leaders were sure that Msgr Montini would support them. One of them wrote:

> During the conversation the question of liturgical language arose: Msgr Montini expressed the opinion that one day the celebration of the whole "didactic part" (according to his expression) of the Mass in the language of the people should arrive. I remarked that it might well require a hundred years for that evolution. "No," he replied, "an evolution that previously might have required a century can nowadays be realized in twenty years."[109]

In fact, twenty years later, the Substitute, as pope, would make Mass in the vernacular language spread throughout the churches of the entire world.

During this period there was another important meeting, with Fr Lebret,[110] who had founded *Économie et Humanisme* (Economy and Humanism)[111] during the war. He came to explain his ideas to the Substitute: integral development and economy at the service of men. Fr Lebret toured the world to spread these concepts and help plan projects of microdevelopment on all continents. These ideas inevitably harmonized with the intuitions of Msgr Montini and are repeated in the encyclical *Populorum Progressio* (1967) which he promulgated about fifteen years later.

---

107 Fr Aimon-Marie Roguet, OP (1906–1991) was the author of several books, including *Christ Acts through the Sacraments*. He was advisor to the Catholic Center for Cinema and Radio, particularly responsible for the radio components.
108 Fr Aimé-Georges Martimort (1911–2000) was a Catholic priest and liturgist, with a doctorate in theology. He was the co-director of the Liturgical Pastoral Center (1946–1948).
109 A. G. Martimort in *Le rôle de G. B. Montini–Paul VI dans la réforme liturgique* (Brescia: Istituto Paolo VI; Rome: Studium, 1987), 59.
110 Louis-Joseph Lebret (1897–1966) was a French Dominican and philosopher who is known as a pioneer in the ethics of development. He focused much of his career on understanding the problems that fishermen faced and how to provide solutions.
111 *Économie et Humanisme* was founded in 1941 to promote Lebret's concept of human economy.

The Man in the Shadows

Another visitor was Dom Hélder Câmara,[112] who was made auxiliary bishop of Rio de Janeiro in 1952. During a visit to Rome, he explained to Msgr Montini: "You know, in Brazil we have a chance to create an almost ideal model for relations between Church and state. In our country, Catholicism does not have the status of official religion. But there is a great mutual respect between the Church and the government, and we work together in loyal collaboration."[113] Such a position was highly attractive to a man who had been hostile to the Italian concordat. The Brazilian bishop also suggested the creation of an episcopal conference in Brazil. Even if the authority to create it did not rest with Msgr Montini, the idea was kept in mind until the Substitute found occasion to bring it to fruition and create the National Bishops' Conference of Brazil, in which Bishop Hélder Câmara would serve as Secretary for twelve years, and which would serve as a model for the creation of episcopal conferences in other countries.

Msgr Montini was also interested in pan-European politics; he supported the Schuman Plan[114] and then the European Defense Community,[115] hoping to strengthen ties between Germany and the other Western Bloc countries. In August 1951 he traveled to the United States, in the footsteps of Cardinal Pacelli, who had toured the American continent for a month in 1936. But the future Pope Pius XII's voyage was official, while the Substitute's trip was private.[116] He stayed in Washington, Denver, Chicago, Detroit, Pittsburgh, and New York. In Washington, he was received by Msgr Cicognani, whom he had often visited in Rome before the war, until Cicognani was named Apostolic Delegate to the United States. He also met the archbishops of the major metropolises.

---

112   Archbishop Hélder Câmara, OSF (1909–1999) was an auxiliary bishop of Rio de Janeiro from 1952, then archbishop of Olinda e Recife (Brazil) from 1964 to 1985. He was a self-identified socialist and an outspoken proponent of the Liberation Theology that fueled the armed revolutions across Latin America in the 1970s and '80s. His cause for canonization was opened in 2015.

113   Cited by J.-A. Meyer, "L'Amérique latine" in *Histoire du Christianisme*, vol. 12 (Paris: Desclée; Paris: Fayard, 1990), 985.

114   The Schuman Plan was the 1950 proposal of the French Minister of Europe and Foreign Affairs Robert Schuman, which set in motion the economic integration of France and Germany, leading to the European Economic Community and eventually the European Union.

115   The European Defence Community was a proposed military pact between Belgium, France, Germany, Italy, Luxembourg, and the Netherlands, which would have been formed by the Treaty of Paris in 1952. The treaty, however, went unratified in France and Italy and so never took effect.

116   Several authors (Lesourd, Pallenberg) and biographical notices inexplicably place this voyage in 1931.

Cardinal Spellman, archbishop of New York, was a friend: the cardinal had worked at the Secretariat of State from 1925–1932. American Catholicism interested Msgr Montini because of its originality: in the United States, Church and state have always been separate; religious liberty (of which the American bishops were the principal champions at Vatican II) was a longstanding reality.

Msgr Montini then passed a few days in Canada. The French embassy to the Holy See was particularly interested in this phase of the Substitute's journey. They learned that at Ottawa the Substitute had lunched with the Canadian Prime Minister Louis St. Laurent.[117] They discussed the exchange of diplomatic representatives between the Holy See and Canada. The next day Msgr Montini met with the French ambassador to Canada, Hubert Guérin, whom he had come to know in Rome throughout 1944 and 1945.

THE NON-CARDINAL

It is difficult to ascertain precisely why Pius XII never created Msgr Montini a cardinal, and ultimately sent him away from Rome. Yet some educated guesses can be made. Jean Guitton who, in the course of time, became a confidant of Msgr Montini's, later acknowledged that a shadow hung over this situation. "There are things I know that are difficult to say. Certainly, it was dramatic. At some point, Pius XII began to distrust Montini. He understood that it was his duty to prevent Montini from becoming pope."[118] When this distrust began is hard to determine. Yet clearly there were some in Rome who wished for his removal from the Secretariat of State. From the end of 1948 onwards, there was a rumor that he was going to be removed from Rome and named to the then-vacant patriarchal see of Venice. To Fr Bevilacqua, who expressed concern about such a distant removal from Rome, Msgr Montini replied that it was a "most unlikely supposition."[119]

Whether Pius XII envisioned this nomination remains unknown, but the simple fact that the rumor circulated at all enables speculation that some parties in Rome were maneuvering to make this a reality. In late 1948, the supporters of the "Roman Party" could reproach Msgr Montini for repeatedly advocating political choices contrary to their own

---

117 Louis St. Laurent (1882–1973) served as the twelfth Prime Minister of Canada from 1948 to 1957. Although the Holy See had had a diplomatic delegation to Canada since 1899, ambassadors were not exchanged until 1969 under Paul VI.
118 Interview of Jean Guitton with the author, May 11, 1991.
119 Letter of December 30, 1948, published in *Notiziario* 3 (May 1981): 15.

during the previous year, including: unity of Catholics in the Christian Democratic Party; distrust towards the Civic Committees of Gedda; and hostility to the creation of a Catholic labor union.

In 1952, new opposition arose between the "Roman Party" and the tendency represented by Msgr Montini. At the beginning of the year, Vittorio Veronese, president of the then-influential Italian Catholic Action, friend of Msgr Montini and of the Prime Minister De Gasperi, had to cede his post to Luigi Gedda, friend of the "Roman Party." Gedda wanted to spur growth in the ICA by making it a movement of the masses, a vanguard for defending the interests of the Church, and a force for electoral maneuvers, as needed. He was appointed to this position partly in anticipation of important elections. Municipal elections for administrative positions were to take place in a few months in Rome and several other large cities; these would serve as a rough electoral index for the legislative elections that would take place during the upcoming year throughout the peninsula. A victory for the left was feared in Rome. "Operation Sturzo" was launched, named in honor of the historical founder of PPI who, after exile in England and then the United States, had returned to Italy after the war and been named a Senator. At the request of various individuals in the Vatican, and with the support of Pius XII, Father Sturzo made himself the mediator between the Christian Democrats and the parties of the right and center, with the aim of creating a "civic list" in Rome to enable an assembly of all political forces hostile to Communism. The new head of Catholic Action was also deeply involved in this attempt to put together a unified list of candidates. But De Gasperi was hostile to this strategy, which would feature Christian Democrats, moderates, monarchists, and nationalists all standing side-by-side during the campaign. He protested to the Vatican, with the support of Msgr Montini. Luigi Gedda then considered presenting an independent list of candidates to compete against the Christian Democrats; finally, he was asked by his superiors to jettison the idea. It was another victory for the Montinian side — one of the last.

Incontestably Msgr Montini was increasingly out of step with the Vatican. Two other facts make this clear. A few months after *Humani Generis*, Fr Congar published a work, *True and False Reform in the Church*,[120] in which he claimed that as the "perfect hierarchical society" the Church has an obligation to be more "pastoral," less separated from the world.

---

120 Yves Congar, *True and False Reform in the Church*, rev. ed., trans. Paul Philibert (Collegeville, MN: Liturgical Press, 2011).

To do so, a "reform" of her spirit, her action, and certain of her institutions was needed. In February 1952, the Congregation of the Holy Office took various measures against the author and his book. *True and False Reform in the Church* was in the process of being translated into different languages; a new French edition was planned. All that was forbidden. Fr Congar was ordered to submit all his future writings to the Master General of his order, Fr Suarez.[121] These measures were not made public but soon became known in interested circles.

The Substitute presented two faces with respect to this affair. In front of his visitors, he forced himself variously to defend the measure, to minimize it, or to express his regrets regarding it. To Bishop Blanchet,[122] rector of the Catholic University of Paris (*Institut catholique de Paris* — ICP), he explained: "What is hypothesis in Paris, is theory in Madrid, and doctrine in Buenos Aires. We also have responsibilities in Buenos Aires." A short while later, in April, when Msgr Richaud,[123] archbishop of Bordeaux, came to him to plead in favor of the book, he explained that the sanctions were not to be interpreted as a condemnation but simply as a "measure of caution."[124] And to the French ambassador, Wladimir d'Ormesson, he said that he was "fatigued and annoyed" and wished "that the error committed be undone."[125] But at this date he had not yet read the book. He procured the work two months later from Father Congar himself, by having one of his subordinates at the Secretariat of State, Msgr Veuillot, order it. He read the book attentively, as the copy preserved in his library indicates. Later events demonstrate that he found ideas in this book that conformed with his own views.

The "Moral Re-Armament" affair reveals the divide between Msgr Montini and other Vatican officials. The Moral Re-Armament (MRA) was a movement founded by a Protestant pastor, Frank Buchman,[126] and

---

121 Fr Emmanuel Suarez (1895–1954) was born in Spain and committed to the Dominican Order at a young age. He was the 80th Master General of the Order of Preachers, elected in 1946. He died in a car accident.

122 Bishop Émile Blanchet (1886–1967), ordinary of Saint-Dié in the Vosges region (1940–1946) then rector of the ICP until 1966.

123 Card. Paul-Marie-André Richaud (1887–1968) had been an auxiliary in Versailles (1934–1938), then ordinary of Laval (1938–1950), before becoming archbishop of Bordeaux (1950–1968). He would be raised to the scarlet by John XXIII in 1958.

124 Statement quoted by Étienne Fouilloux, "Recherche théologique et magistère romain in 1952," *Recherches de science religieuse* (April–June 1983): 278–79.

125 Statement cited by Fouilloux, "G. B. Montini," 95.

126 Frank Buchman (1878–1961), an American Protestant preacher and missionary, was founder of the Oxford Group in the early 1920s. He changed the orientation of

had its headquarters in Switzerland, at Caux-sur-Montreux. Its goal was to "re-arm" society with moral values including honesty, purity, and selflessness. It also relied on prayer and did not observe confessional distinctions. Each summer, large gatherings were organized at Caux; these attracted a highly diverse public: financiers, diplomats, politicians, and laborers alike came from around the world. From 1946, a number of bishops promulgated warnings against this movement, which attracted some Catholic priests even though it practiced religious indifferentism. When he was Apostolic Delegate for French-speaking Africa, Archbishop Lefebvre asked during a visit to Rome for the Holy Office to issue an official condemnation of the movement. He was concerned that some African leaders had gone to Caux. Among the prelates with whom he discussed the question was Msgr Montini. The Substitute was hostile to a condemnation of the movement, arguing: "One must not always condemn. Otherwise, the Church would seem like a cruel mother."[127] The Holy Office nonetheless published a warning against the Moral Re-Armament in 1955, on the grounds that it presented "a danger of syncretism and religious indifference."

In the Moral Re-Armament affair, as in that of *True and False Reform in the Church*, he showed hostility to the very idea of condemnation. This does not necessarily imply approval of all the ideas manifest in the movement or expressed in that book.[128] Above all it was his mindset that made him react as he did. Was it this mindset that deprived him of the cardinal's hat at the end of 1952? This cannot be the only reason.

According to Msgr Tardini, Msgr Montini's alter ego at the Secretariat of State, already by May 1952 Pius XII proposed to create both of them cardinals at the next consistory, but the two men refused. "There was gossiping on this subject," he wrote.

> Some say that Pius XII only made the offers to us *pro forma* without any insistence. Others supposed that we had renounced the

---

the group towards a politico-religious movement in 1938, the Moral Re-Armament, as it was known until 2001. Today the movement is known as Initiatives of Change.
127 Archbishop Lefebvre, unpublished speech, August 20, 1976.
128 Msgr Montini also demonstrated endless compassion for individuals, with only rare exceptions. In March 1946, he sent a priest to the dying Ernesto Buonaiuti (one of the pillars of Italian modernism, who had been excommunicated, and whose classes he may have attended while he was a student at the University of Rome). In December 1950, on Christmas Eve, he charitably made a visit to Carlo Falconi, who had worked under him at the Secretariat of State, and who had just left the priesthood, eleven years after ordination.

> red hat so as not to separate ourselves from the pope. The truth is that, as always, Pius XII acted with goodness and decency. Not only did he offer us the rank of cardinal, but he insisted on it for several months, to make us accept it. His idea was to leave us in the same positions as before: "We will change nothing," he said. "You will only have the red hat in addition." And he laughed good-naturedly when he heard us respond that we would be highly content to remain as before, but ... without the red biretta.[129]

This version of events is hardly satisfying. Why would the two main prelates in the Secretariat of State refuse this rank? Humility? But they allowed themselves to be created cardinals after the death of Pius XII, under John XXIII. To stay close to the pope? But Pius XII, according to Msgr Tardini, had promised to maintain their positions. Might this therefore be seen as some political or bureaucratic maneuver? Some have suggested that Msgr Tardini declined the red biretta to oblige his peer, nine years his junior, to refuse it as well, or that Msgr Tardini, in refusing the title of cardinal, allowed Pius XII not to offer it to Msgr Montini, whom he did not want to see enter into the Sacred College.

In November 1952, Pius XII announced that he would hold a consistory in the coming weeks. At the same time, he accorded the title of "Pro-Secretary of State" to Msgr Tardini and Msgr Montini both. This honorific title involved no supplementary responsibility. On the following January 12, during the consistory to welcome twenty-four new cardinals, he mentioned the two absentees in an unusual manner:

> Our intention had been to bring into the Sacred College the two distinguished Prelates responsible for each section of the Secretariat of State; their names were the first two inscribed on the list of cardinals to be designated that We had prepared. But these two Prelates, in a sign of their outstanding virtue, beseeched Us so insistently to let them decline this high charge, that We thought that We should acquiesce to their repeated supplications and prayers. While doing so, We wish nonetheless to compensate their virtue in some way; thus, We have promoted them, as you know, to a higher post of honor, better-suited to the scope of their hard work.[130]

---

129 Tardini, *Pie XII*, 138.
130 Pope Pius XII, Discourse, January 12, 1953, in AAS 45 (1953): 66.

This 1953 consistory is revealing in terms of the concerns that animated Pius XII. Among the twenty-four new cardinals, two were archbishops persecuted by Communist governments: Stepinac,[131] archbishop of Zagreb, who lived in "supervised residence" after having been condemned to forced labor in 1946; Wyszynski,[132] archbishop of Warsaw, who had been prevented by the Polish government from coming to Rome to participate in the consistory and who, a few months later, was arrested. There were the prelates whom the pope appreciated because they were defenders of the integrity of doctrine: Ottaviani, assessor of the Holy Office, and Siri, archbishop of Genoa, who, at forty-six years old, became the youngest cardinal in the Church. Though Roncalli, apostolic nuncio to Paris, was created cardinal, Pius XII also named his predecessor, Valerio Valeri, a cardinal, to compensate for the offensive way in which he was rejected by the French government in 1944–1945. There were the metropolitan archbishops from sees that traditionally received the cardinal's hat, such as Feltin,[133] from Paris. Did Msgr Montini have a place amongst these eminences? Pius XII had decided: no.

As compensation, to protect him from public insult, the pope named him Pro-Secretary of State. Was Msgr Montini hurt to be excluded from promotion to the cardinalate? Undoubtedly, just as he would be pained, two years later, at being sent to Milan. During a reception after the consistory, he is alleged to have said with regret "that he had missed the bus going up,"[134] up to the papacy. But, according to another, more hagiographic, entirely contradictory anecdote, when someone remarked to him "that he had missed the bus going up," he replied: "This is possible, but in compensation I have perhaps taken up the wood that will lead me to paradise."[135]

The problem of worker-priests dominated the year 1953. This experiment of priests in factories, which was started principally because of the war effort, incited more and more concerns as it continued after the war. Msgr Montini was interested in the matter not merely because

---

131   Card. Aloysius Stepinac (1898–1960) was the Yugoslav archbishop of Zagreb from 1937 until his death. He never was able to go to Rome to receive the red hat. He was beatified by Pope John Paul II in 1998.
132   Card. Stefan Wyszynski (1901–1981) was the archbishop of Warsaw and Gniezno (1948–1981) and Primate of Poland. His cause for canonization was opened at the behest of Pope John Paul II.
133   Card. Maurice Feltin (1883–1975) was the French archbishop of Paris from 1949 until he resigned in 1966. Pope Pius XII elevated him to the cardinalate in 1953.
134   L. Dorn, Paul VI, portrait familier en 100 anecdotes, 67.
135   G. Huber, Paul VI, 117.

it was his job to be concerned, but because he was preoccupied by the general phenomenon of dechristianization. In May 1951 he met Fr Jacques Loew,[136] a Dominican, who worked as a longshoreman. He had given Msgr Montini a note on his experience as a worker-priest, expressing various disagreements with the other worker-priests and fearing the influence of Marxism among them. Refusing to adopt an analysis based on class conflict, he concluded all the same that working in a factory was the best method of evangelizing the working class.[137]

Msgr Montini also read a number of French works that enjoyed a brief vogue and discussed questions of manual work and of the evangelization of the "masses": *Au cœur des masses* by René Voillaume (founder of the Little Brothers of Jesus), published in 1950;[138] and *Pour une théologie du travail* by Fr Chénu, published in 1952.[139]

When a series of prohibitions was announced in succession in 1953, he approved wholeheartedly, because he was aware that the worker-priests, overall, were on a dangerous path. In July, Cardinal Pizzardo, prefect of the Congregation of Seminaries, banned seminarians from doing work placements in factories; in August the "worker-religious" were ordered to leave the factories; finally, in September the nuncio in Paris communicated the instruction of the Holy See to the French bishops that worker-priests were to quit their jobs. All these measures were justified out of concern for maintaining the special identity and mission of the clergy; also, too many worker-priests were engaging in political activity. Three French cardinals traveled to Rome to try to make Pius XII reconsider these measures. He allowed the experiment to continue only

---

136 Fr Jacques Loew (1908–1999) was a French Dominican worker-priest, ordained in 1939. Alongside various lay people and priests, he founded the Mission Worker Saints-Pierre-et-Paul (MOPP), an organization whose goal was to unite the parish churches and remove unjust burdens thrust upon the poor.

137 F. Leprieur, *Quand Rome condamne* [When Rome condemns].

138 René Voillaume, *Au cœur des masses: La vie religieuse des Petits Frères du père de Foucauld* [At the heart of the masses: the religious life of the Little Brothers of Father de Foucauld] (Paris: Cerf, 1952). Fr Voillaume (1905–2003) founded several groups based on the spirituality of Charles de Foucauld. This work was translated into Italian in 1953. Voillaume asked Msgr Montini to write the preface. He agreed, then changed his mind, finally explaining to the author that his position did not allow him to dedicate himself to such important work. Yet his preface had been drafted (M. Guasco in *Le Chiese di Pio XII*, 106). Was Msgr Montini unsatisfied with it, or did he fear provoking controversy by prefacing such an innovative work? Later, after becoming pope, he invited Fr Voillaume, in 1968, and Fr Loew, in 1970, to preach the Vatican's Lenten retreat.

139 Marie-Dominique Chenu, *The Theology of Work: An Exploration*, trans. Lilian Soiron (Chicago: H. Regnery Co., 1963).

under strict conditions: work in a factory would be limited to three hours a day; all political activity and involvement in labor unions was forbidden. Only in 1959, under John XXIII, was there a total ban on the movement.

In an audience with Wladimir d'Ormesson in the following October, Msgr Montini justified these decisions:

> From the beginning, this initiative had a bad start; the first priests who offered themselves for this enterprise were unbalanced in mind. From the outset Rome was troubled by this possibility.... Some of these worker-priests increasingly misunderstood the basic spirit of Christianity until they had become Marxists.[140]

A short time later, the Pro-Secretary of State received a letter from his friend Maritain that confirmed him in his opinions. The philosopher then at Princeton judged that the crises involving the worker-priests had "revealed grave inadequacies in the formation of clergy," and he provided his correspondent with a long report "on the reform of current methods in use in ecclesiastical teaching." The worker-priests had committed errors, he explained, "because they were not *prepared*"; their formation at seminary, "all formulas and clichés," had rendered them vulnerable to Marxist ideology. He suggested a reform of ecclesiastical studies by "an absolutely frank and loyal open-mindedness to the greatest extent possible ... to the 'outside intellectual world'"; he suggested, for example, that "Protestants, Jews, Muslims, and Hindus come to explain their thoughts in the seminaries."[141]

When he became pope, Paul VI decided that the reform of the seminaries to be undertaken after Vatican II would better prepare seminarians for this sort of apostolate, so in 1965 he reauthorized priests to become factory-workers.

The concept Msgr Montini had of the priesthood during the 1950s is developed in a long preface he composed for a book by one of his collaborators in the Secretariat of State: *Notre sacerdoce*,[142] by Msgr Veuillot. This collection of pontifical texts on the priest had undoubtedly been made to reaffirm the sacerdotal identity after the crises of the worker-priests. The priest, wrote Msgr Montini, is "a human being for

---

140 Leprieur, *Quand Rome condamne*, 294.
141 Letter of March 12, 1954 and report (Archives J. Maritain).
142 Pierre Veuillot, ed., *The Catholic Priesthood According to the Teaching of the Church*, trans. John A. O'Flynn (Dublin: Gill and Son, 1964).

whom to live is to offer worship to God, to look for God, to serve God. He is a religious man, a sacred man. He is the intermediary between God and men, he is the bridge." But Msgr Montini did not look to define the priesthood in theological terms; instead he developed a concept he referred to as "a sort of apostolic relativism":

> The priesthood is a social service. The priest exists for others.... The words issue unendingly from the pen: apostle, missionary, father, pastor, master, brother, servant, and victim. Whence he is well-suited to distinguish himself and involve himself, to influence and suffer, to speak and listen. He is light, he is salt.... Artist, specialized worker, essential doctor, invited to the subtle and profound phenomenologies of the spirit: a man of study, a man of speech, a man of taste, a man of tact, a man of sensibility, of finesse, of strength...[143]

In depicting the priest in this way, was Msgr Montini painting a self-portrait? At least he described the ideals he aimed at, although his diplomatic functions could often mask them.

---

143 Preface of P. Veuillot, *Notre sacerdoce* (Paris: Fleurus, 1954), II–XVII.

6

Archbishop of Milan

IN AUGUST OF 1954, CARDINAL SCHUSTER, ARCHbishop of Milan, died. Shortly thereafter, Pius XII announced to Msgr Montini that he was thinking of entrusting him with the pastoral charge of this illustrious metropolis. This nomination would have pleased any prelate. Milan was one of the principal cities of Italy. Its archiepiscopal see had been covered with glory and holiness by Saint Ambrose,[1] then by Saint Charles Borromeo.[2] More recently, an archbishop of Milan, Achille Ratti, had become pope, under the name of Pius XI.

All the same, Msgr Montini considered this promotion to be a sanction. The pope was pushing him away from Rome; the fact caused him great pain. His nephew stated: "It was a drama for him in every sense of the word, particularly the emotional sense: at that time I saw him with tears in his eyes."[3] On November 1, the nomination was officially made. *Le Monde*, in commenting on the news, asserted that he would soon be named cardinal and that one could already inscribe him on the "short list" of the *papabili*. The prediction was half right. Pius XII created no more cardinals during his lifetime. He did so to avoid having to elevate Msgr Montini.

Several weeks after the official announcement of his nomination (or disgrace?) he was still mortified, as a letter to his old teacher Fr Bevilacqua shows. Montini opened his heart to him: "I am bewildered, dazed; as yet no peace, no trust, no abandonment; an impression of invasion, of vexation by things which are immensely greater than I. . . . The temptation of pusillanimity assails me."[4]

---

1 St Ambrose of Milan (340–397) unexpectedly became the archbishop of Milan (374) and is recognized today in Western Christianity as both a saint and one of the four traditional Doctors of the Church. Due to his popularity, gained from donating his money and land to the poor, he had political leverage, even over the emperor.
2 Charles Borromeo (1538–1584) was the archbishop of Milan from 1564–1584. Descended from nobility, his family line was one of the most prominent and wealthy of Lombardy. Borromeo also played a crucial leadership role within the Counter-Reformation combat against the Protestant Reformation when he created seminaries for the education of priests.
3 G. Montini, "Mon oncle le pape."
4 Letter of November 18, 1954 published in *Notiziario* 3 (May 1981): 19–20.

There are several possible explanations for this nomination. The most flattering and hagiographical: Pius XII named Msgr Montini to Milan to give him the experience of overseeing a large diocese, thus preparing him then to take on the whole Church. But this explanation does not stand up to scrutiny: the pope did not make him a cardinal, so Msgr Montini had no immediate chance of succeeding him. Another, more psychological, explanation takes into consideration that at the beginning of the year (from January to March) Pius XII was so ill that he had to refrain from most of his customary activities:

> Montini thus virtually oversaw the Church by himself for several months; it is possible that Pius XII, who liked to discuss different facets of problems with him to clarify them, realized during this period that the prelate had trouble settling questions and making rapid decisions, and thus, in spite of his great qualities, was not meant to become pope.[5]

According to still other sources, Msgr Montini made contact (via an intermediary) with Soviet authorities, without the knowledge of Pius XII, to try to improve relations between the USSR and the Vatican; when the pope learned of this, he was scandalized.[6] Such contact is not unimaginable: Cardinal Siri, whom no one can suspect of communist sympathies, revealed that he was approached by Soviet diplomats near the end of Pius XII's reign. Without informing the pope, he had maintained contact with them through a cleric of his diocese.[7] In Msgr Montini's case, the sources contradict one another, and do not agree on the names of intermediaries, nor on the dates when these contacts are supposed to have taken place.

At last there is the most convincing explanation, which involves ecclesiastical politics. The head of the Italian Youth of Catholic Action, Mario Rossi,[8] was closely connected to Msgr Montini. Rossi wanted to retain freedom of movement from interference by ecclesiastical authorities and, following Montini's methods at the FUCI, to form the elites both

---

5   R. Aubert, "Paul VI, 'Un pontificat de transition,'" *Revue nouvelle* (December 1978): 614.
6   Msgr G. Roche and P. Saint Germain, *Pie XII devant l'Histoire*, 440; R. Raffalt, *Wohin steuert der Vatikan?* (Munich, 1973), 124–27; A. De Quarto, "Il Segreto del Vaticano," *Il Borghese* (August 15, 1976); H. Monteilhet, *Paul VI ou l'Amen Dada*, 25; M. Martin, *Les Jésuites*, 78.
7   Benny Lai, *Les Secrets du Vatican* (Paris: Hachette, 1983), 103–4.
8   Mario Rossi (1925–1976) was an Italian physician who led the Youth branch of the ACI from 1952 to 1954.

intellectually and spiritually. This policy put him in conflict with the president of the ACI, Luigi Gedda, to whom he reported. Rossi decided to resign in April 1954. He wrote a letter and gave it to Msgr Montini, intending for it to be published in L'*Osservatore Romano*. The Pro-Secretary of State, hoping perhaps to convince Rossi to reconsider his decision, kept this letter to himself and did not transmit it to the Holy Father as he should have done. When the news of the resignation of the president of the Catholic Youth began to spread, Msgr Montini was accused of having "hidden information from the Holy Father."

Whatever the reason, or more likely the reasons, that incited Pius XII to distance himself from Msgr Montini,[9] the latter had to put on a brave face. From the first days of November, Milanese ecclesiastical authorities came to visit him, including Msgr Bernaneggi, auxiliary bishop, Msgr Schiavini,[10] Vicar General, and Msgr Giovanni Colombo,[11] rector of the seminary. They organized the practicalities of his official entry and of his installation in Milan. Msgr Montini also let them know that he wanted a secretary who was not merely acquainted with French language and culture but had also been formed theologically by francophone authors. A young priest was chosen, Father Pasquale Macchi, who had lived in Paris for a few years to prepare a thesis on Georges Bernanos,[12] and who taught French at a Catholic college in Milan.[13]

On November 6, Msgr Montini gave a farewell discourse to members of the diplomatic corps accredited to the Holy See. He did not allow any pain or bitterness to show. But no one was fooled. Wladimir d'Ormesson bluntly informed his government: "He had exercised a power of 'resistance,' opposing with discreet tenacity, but not ineffectively, the power of the zealots." The "reactionary" clan had obtained his transfer.[14]

On December 12, the episcopal consecration was held in Saint Peter's Basilica. Pius XII was not able to carry out the consecration himself due

---

9 His collaborator, Msgr Angelo Dell'Acqua, replaced him as Substitute at the Secretariat of State.
10 Archbishop Giuseppe Schiavini (1889–1974) was the auxiliary bishop of Milan (1913–1974) and was appointed the titular archbishop of Famagusta (1963).
11 Card. Giovanni Colombo (1902–1992) was major rector of the seminaries of Milan from 1953. He was made auxiliary bishop of Milan in 1960 and succeeded Montini as archbishop in 1963. He was elevated to the cardinalate in 1965.
12 Published as Pasquale Macchi, *Bernanos e il problema del male* [Bernanos and the problem of evil] (Varese: La Lucciola, 1959).
13 Card. G. Colombo, *Ricordando G. B. Montini*, 11–12.
14 Report of W. D'Ormesson to P. Mendès-France, November 5, 1954, cited by A. Riccardi, Il *Potere del Papa da Pio XII a Paolo VI*.

to illness. Nonetheless, he had written a message to be shared during the ceremony, granting blessing to his "faithful collaborator, who has today become his brother in the episcopal order." The new bishop had had to choose a coat of arms and a motto. He adopted the arms of the Montini family: three *fleurs-de-lys* above six stacked mountains. For a motto he had initially chosen, in reference to the gospel scene of the Transfiguration, but also to his name(!): *Cum ipso in monte*. It was pointed out to him that this motto expressed too great a "contemplative" intention, so he chose another: *In nomine Domini*, in the name of the Lord, which placed greater emphasis on the roles of pastor and teacher that he would have to assume.

THE CAPITAL OF THE NORTH

At 3.2 million inhabitants, the diocese of Milan was the most populous in Italy. The city itself was the financial capital of the country, and one of its largest industrial centers. A great city of business, technological research, and culture, during the fifties Milan saw considerable growth and development. Tens of thousands of people, from the South of Italy and from neighboring agricultural regions, arrived each year in the "Capital of the North" to try their luck. This massive influx of Italian migrants, accelerated industrialization, and the haphazard construction of new buildings were changing the physiognomy of the city. There were also cultural and religious upheavals: dechristianization; a growing rootless population; the rapidly increasing influence of Communism over the working class of the city; the liberalization of morals throughout the entire population. The new archbishop was going to be confronted with countless problems. Having never been in charge of a parish himself, he was going to find himself at the helm of a diocese with more than nine hundred highly diverse parishes: ancient and well-endowed parishes downtown; poorer parishes of the disadvantaged neighborhoods in the city's outskirts; parishes in the large agricultural towns of the rich plain of the Po, contrasting with those of villages hidden in the mountains. Fr Bevilacqua told him: "You have moved from diplomacy to brutality."

On January 4, 1955 after celebrating Mass at the altar of Saint Pius X in Saint Peter's basilica, Archbishop Montini left Rome by train. He stopped at Lodi, south of Milan. The bishop of the city, the Vicar-General of Milan, and the civil authorities awaited him. He took his seat in a car that was to take him into his diocese. The sky was gray; the countryside, misty. Near Melegnano, a marker indicated the separation between the dioceses of Lodi and Milan. It was pointed out to the archbishop. He stopped the cortege of cars that formed his escort. He knelt on the damp ground, recited a few prayers, and kissed the ground of his new diocese. It was the first spectacular "gesture" of an archbishop who loved to multiply them.

He made a short retreat in a religious college, at Rho, then on January 6, the Feast of the Epiphany, he made his solemn entry into Milan. Welcomed by the mayor and all the civil and religious authorities of the city, standing up in an open car at the head of a long line of official vehicles, he traveled the main roads of the city to the Duomo, the cathedral, greeting and blessing the large crowds that had gathered on the roofs or applauded him from balconies, in spite of the battering rain. When he arrived at the Duomo, he pronounced his first discourse, which was a sort of statement of his episcopal platform, hesitating between firmness and openness. Archbishop Montini straightaway announced that he would refuse to follow the "zealous and imprudent" who think that Christianity "must submit to the principles and methods of new times, and must bend to exterior transformations in the forms of her action, or interior transformations in her beliefs and discipline"; our Catholicism must "be holistic and authentic," he specified; but at the same time he planned to work "for the conciliation of the Italian Catholic tradition with the wholesome humanism of modern life." He also wished to say "a special word to workers." He invited them to raise their heads "above material and earthly work" and "open themselves to the winds of the Spirit." He also assured them that he would bring, "when there is suffering, or injustice, or legitimate aspiration to social improvements, a clear and solid defense as pastor and father."[15] Soon he would acquire a flattering reputation as a "bishop of the workers."

For the first time in his life as a priest, in a pastoral duty entrusted solely to him, he had to make decisions on his own and have them applied by his collaborators. In the first days after his installation in Milan, he received countless people in audience: bishops of the region; ecclesiastical leaders of his diocese; Fr Gemelli,[16] founder and rector

---

15 Discourse of January 1, 1955, published in *Rivista Diocesana Milanese* (1955): 9–22. From 1955 to 1962, more and more of his discourses and writings will be translated into French and published, in whole or in part, in *Le Monde*, *La Croix*, and *La Documentation catholique* — a sign of the growing attention which was being given him abroad.

16 Fr Agostino Gemelli (1878–1959) was an Italian Franciscan friar, physician,

of the illustrious University of the Sacred Heart; directors of Catholic Action; and various laymen[17] (including financiers and bankers with ties to the diocese). Soon a small number of men began to be formed into an inner circle of those whom he regularly consulted: Carlo Colombo, professor of theology of the seminary of Milan, whom he had met during the Weeks of Camaldoli, and who was going to become his private theologian; Giovanni Colombo, rector of the seminary, whom he received every Wednesday; Fr Manfredini,[18] professor of philosophy in a modest college, to whom he was going to give responsibilities of increasing importance at the head of the diocese's Catholic Action group from 1956 on, and who would help the archbishop carry out various projects and initiatives. Msgr Montini also corresponded regularly with Fr Caresana, who was still in Rome, and often received visits from Fr Bevilacqua from the neighboring diocese of Brescia. The archbishop sought his advice for an "intelligent, careful, and pious" ceremony for the first Easter celebrated in his diocese.

From the first days following his arrival, he frequently received local deputies and senators. Shortly thereafter, the president of the Chamber of Deputies[19] came from Rome to see him, as did Camille Chamoun,[20] the President of Lebanon, who was then on an official visit to Italy. These political visits were numerous and soon the former prefect of Bologna signaled in a report to Rome that the archbishop of Milan was very implicated in political affairs and wanted "to control and direct all the politics of the DC" in the valley of the Po.[21]

His contacts with civil society were not, of course, limited to political figures. In the following April, he visited the Milan International Fair,

---

and psychologist; his Institute of Psychology was the most prominent in Italy of its time. He is also notable for being the founder and first rector of the Catholic University of the Sacred Heart (1921).
17   A chronology of the audiences of the archbishop has been published in *Notiziario* 14 (May 1987) and 18 (August 1989).
18   Bishop Enrico Manfredini (1922–1983) was ordained a priest in 1945 before graduating in philosophy from the Catholic University of the Sacred Heart. He became the bishop of Piacenza (1969) and was entrusted with the pastoral care of the archdiocese of Bologna by Pope John Paul II (1983).
19   The President of the Chamber of Deputies (*Presidente della Camera dei deputati*) at this time was Giovanni Gronchi (1887–1978), a Christian Democrat.
20   Camille Chamoun (1900–1987) was the President of Lebanon from 1952–1958 and one of the country's most prominent Christian leaders during the civil war (1975–1990). He founded the National Liberal Party which allowed him to be elected to the National Assembly multiple times.
21   Cited by G. Battelli in *Le Chiese di Pio XII* (Bari: Editori Laterza, 1986), 269.

one of the principal trade fairs in Europe. He was the first archbishop to tour the exhibitors' stands and to ask questions; he was awed by the technological progress on display. After his visit, he invited the exhibitors to a Mass at the Duomo and gave an ardent sermon on the Gospel and scientific progress. His visits and the subsequent Mass became annual.

He also multiplied visits to hospitals, parishes, and the religious communities in Milan and around his diocese, systematically taking the measure of the needs of his diocese. He had studies conducted. Many recently built neighborhoods lacked churches; other edifices of worship in Milan and in the cities and towns were in need of repair. Soon an "urban-religious plan" would be established to organize the work to be done. By the time he left his diocese, he had built seventy-two churches, with another twenty or so under construction. The donations of the faithful did not suffice, of course. The archbishop appealed to the generosity of a few industrialists and businessmen, and also to the savoir-faire of a banker, Michele Sindona,[22] who would later be embroiled in papal finances.

To be archbishop was also to worry about the faith of the faithful, the growing dechristianization of the population, and the welcoming of new arrivals in the parishes. Archbishop Montini paid particular attention to these newcomers and advocated an expanded conception of the parish. He explained to a meeting of priests that, in addition to the place of worship, it must include "a hall for shows, then a sports field, here and there a pool, headquarters of Catholic associations, a day-care, works of charity, and lastly schools." At the diocesan level, the archbishop also insisted on a new conception of what was "pastoral." In a few months, new organizations were created: an "Office of Studies," to promote modern methods of catechesis among the clergy, and publish liturgical manuals; an "Office of Social Ministry" focusing specifically on immigrant neighborhoods and churches, and an "Office of Social Assistance" to distribute aid and resolve situations of distress.

The magnitude of his duties, but also his inexperience in managing the diocese, not to mention his fragile health,[23] obliged him to appoint two supplementary auxiliary bishops. To Bishop Bernareggi,[24] already

---

22 Michele Sindona (1920–1986) was a Sicilian Freemason and banker for the Mafia.
23 Two months after his arrival, exhausted by intense activity, he had to rest for a while, far from Milan, at Venegono, seat of the diocesan seminary.
24 Archbishop Adriano Bernareggi (1884–1953) was ordained a priest in 1907. After studying canon law at the Pontifical Gregorian University, he taught it in

in post as auxiliary bishop under his predecessor, was added Bishop Pignedoli (who had already worked under his orders at the Secretariat of State) in April 1955; in May Bishop Schiavini, until then Vicar General, was promoted. These three auxiliary bishops permitted him to not be overwhelmed by his duties as archbishop, which were so radically different from his activities for over thirty years in the offices of the Secretariat of State.

Other than the exceedingly few people whom he received regularly in audience, Archbishop Montini habitually communicated with his collaborators through the intermediary of "notes," written in haste. Wishes, suggestions, requests, and (rarely) orders were written on small pieces of paper and sent or carried to the interested party. These "Montini Notes" would become famous in the chancellery of Milan.

Archbishop Montini was not fully at peace in his position. "In Milan, he suffered martyrdom," remembered Jean Guitton.[25] He was effectively in exile, far from Rome, center of decisions for all ecclesiastical affairs, and had also lost contact with the diplomats whom he had entertained for so many years. As a result, he invited theologians, and bishops of other large cities, to Milan so he could stay informed of what was being said, done, and written elsewhere. Fr Congar was invited twice to Milan and also exchanged letters with Archbishop Montini.[26] The archbishop welcomed Fr Bouyer, a convert from Protestantism, who was now professor at the Institut Catholique de Paris, for a conference on "Word, Church and the Sacraments in Protestantism and Catholicism."[27] When he could, he still tried to thwart some Roman decisions. Thus, when Fr de Lubac wanted to have his work *Mystère de l'Église* translated, and the vicariate of Rome refused to grant the *imprimatur* because the author was then under a cloud of suspicion, Archbishop Montini granted the *imprimatur* himself and allowed the

---

Milan. Pope Pius XII promoted him to the archbishopric in 1952.
25 Jean Guitton, interview with the author, May 5, 1991.
26 "When we approached him to kiss his ring, he quickly withdrew his hand," remembered Fr Congar, *Une vie pour la vérité*, 117.
27 The conference took place on February 3, 1958. In 1955 Archbishop Montini had attentively read *Du Protestantisme à l'Église* [From Protestantism to the Church] by Fr Bouyer. Fr Louis Bouyer (1913–2004) was a French Lutheran minister who, in 1939, was accepted into the Catholic Church. As a scholar, he published several noteworthy writings on Christian spirituality and its history. The Vatican consulted him throughout his career. Pope Paul VI chose him and others to start the International Theological Commission (1969). His posthumously published memoirs have been referred to several times in the notes.

translation to be printed in Milan. He cited the book repeatedly in his discourses and, on occasion, distributed copies to priests of his diocese.[28]

He also welcomed Roger Schütz and Max Thurian, of the community of Taizé, more than once. Other visitors included Anglican clergy who wanted to visit a Catholic diocese. They were guests of the diocese for a week. Archbishop Montini summoned Fr Boyer, of Unitas in Rome, to show them around.

Bishops who were to play an important role in the Council got in touch with him during these years.[29] Bishop Roy,[30] of Quebec, and Bishop Suenens,[31] then auxiliary bishop of Malines, were his guests in Milan. Bishop Suenens had published L'Église en état de mission [The Church in a state of mission],[32] which was translated into several languages. For the Italian translation archbishop Montini wrote a preface in which he provided a melodramatic impression of the situation:

> The moment seems apocalyptic, and it is. The central phenomenon involves the anguish of Christ — in his Church — in the midst of the legalistic tortures of persecutions, of the sarcastic imprecations of its adversaries, in the midst of the abandonment of its disciples, who hold the attention of a few people at best...

A "general mobilization" of the Church was necessary to "repair the losses, defend the positions, recuperate lost members, and win new ones." He therefore concluded that it was imperative to adapt Church institutions "to the spiritual needs of our era," "reform" them, and "modernize" them.[33] These terms of adaptation, reform, and modernization would become, in the following years, the marching orders of a large number of bishops.

---

28 Henri de Lubac, SJ, Mémoire sur l'occasion de mes écrits, 77.
29 The visits of Cardinal Roncalli were also frequent. But they often annoyed Archbishop Montini because they wasted his time: the patriarch of Venice spoke too much trivia and nonsense (Jean Guitton, interview with the author, May 11, 1991).
30 Card. Maurice Roy (1905–1985) was the archbishop of Quebec (1947–1981) who became a cardinal in 1965. When Quebec's ecclesiastical rank was elevated (1956), he was also appointed the Primate of the Canadian Church.
31 Card. Léon-Joseph Suenens (1904–1996) was auxiliary bishop of Malines (Belgium, 1954–1962), then the first archbishop of Malines-Brussels and Primate of Belgium until his retirement at the age of 75 in 1979.
32 Léon-Joseph Suenens, The Gospel to Every Creature, trans. Louise Gavan Duffy (Westminster: Newman Press, 1956).
33 The preface of Archbishop Montini was included beginning with the fourth French edition of the book (Paris: DDB, 1958).

THE MISSION OF MILAN

After midnight, in the early hours of January 5, 1956, a bomb exploded under the windows of the archiepiscopal palace, causing only material damage. Emotions ran high in Milan;[34] the newspapers ran headlines about it for several days. Countless telegrams of solidarity were sent to Msgr Montini, including one from Pius XII.

The archbishop was surprised by all this attention, which arose one year to the day after his arrival in Milan, just when he was going to announce, on the feast of the Epiphany, his great pastoral project: the "Mission of Milan." He had not known that he personally inspired such strong feelings. In fact, this stupid and isolated act was not the expression of a growing aversion to Archbishop Montini. He did not appear, at this date, to be the man of a party. And his public declarations, always very balanced, often had enough to satisfy some while reassuring others.

A few weeks after the attack, he published a Lenten pastoral letter on the "Duties of the Christian before the Evolving Social and Religious Crisis of the Modern World." It was essentially a vigorous warning against Marxist ideology:

> Social evolution had no need of being penetrated by an ideology so troubled that it turns it, not towards the needs of true and human society, but towards a fearsome crisis, towards materialist systems, such as Communism and Socialism, which compromise the whole patrimony of the civilization of the spirit, and principally the natural profession of religion.

And faithful to the teaching of *Divini Redemptoris*, the archbishop of Milan went to the heart of the question:

> Two features make the Communist threat even worse: the propaganda of its ideas, and the strength of its organization. The phenomenon becomes stable and deep-rooted. Its trickery is not therefore lesser, but rather it shows itself to be contrary to every reasonable expectation: contrary to our history, to our doctrines, to our needs, to our interests...

The Church must react, he concluded, by building "a new society," and propagating her social doctrine.[35]

---

34 In December 1957, the penal tribunal of Milan condemned three far-right sympathizers for this act.
35 Pastoral Letter of February 19, 1956.

This doctrinally anti-Communist discourse was accompanied by an extreme sensitivity to the sufferings of the working classes, a sort of exacerbated compassion which could lead the archbishop of Milan, on some occasions, to pronounce words in which emotion overwhelmed reason, as when, a few months later, a mining disaster killed hundreds of victims in Belgium. In honor of the dead and afflicted he composed a long litany which he had published in the Catholic daily of Milan and in the diocesan journal:

"Let us pray for the victims of labor, for their families, for the workers, for justice and peace...." "Lord, have mercy on our brothers buried in the mines of Belgium; have pity on their fate; pay attention to the bitterness, the risk, the insufficient defense of their fatigue..." These litanies were criticized for appearing to contain a veiled accusation of the mining industry. The labor unions' leftist parties had formulated identical censures.

To avoid the impression of being compassionate only towards some victims of misfortune, and also because of his profound convictions, he held a funeral service, organized a procession of penitence, and asked for a day of mourning and prayer when, the following November, the Hungarian rebellion against Communism was crushed by Soviet tanks.

Throughout the archbishop's first years at the head of the diocese of Milan, he seems to have worried obsessively about not being close enough to the residents of his diocese, whether or not they were believers. Reserved in nature, and preoccupied with the magnitude of his duties, he did not demonstrate the warmth that would have made him instantly sympathetic in a first impression. But he was restlessly eager, in all situations, to demonstrate his own closeness to the concerns of people, and his attention towards his collaborators and his friends (for example, already from Rome and then from Milan he sent a telegram of best wishes to Maritain for the feast of Saint James), and also to make himself loved. It was the same desire as a priest and then as a bishop to not be indifferent to any pain or aspiration, to understand and not condemn, that will push him to passionate declarations and spectacular "gestures." Thus, in October 1957, during the Second World Congress of the Apostolate of the Laity in Rome, he gave a long speech on the Christian mission. "It is not directly political, neither social nor economic. It considers man in regard to his supreme end..." The speech included a warning: "We will be vigilant so that our attitude of love and respect, vis-à-vis those who are not Catholic, does not degenerate into indifference, eclecticism, lenience, defection." And he concluded with a flight of lyricism:

> We will love our homeland; we will love that of others. We will love our friends; we will love our enemies. We will love Catholics, we will love schismatics, Protestants, Anglicans, the indifferent, Muslims, pagans, and atheists. We will love all social classes, but above all those who are in the greatest need of aid, of help, of promotion. We will love children and the elderly, the poor and the sick. We will love those who mock us, those who ridicule us, those who oppose us, and those who persecute us. We will love those who deserve to be loved and those who do not. We will love our adversaries: they are men, and we do not want to hold any as enemies. We will love our times, our civilization, our technology, our art, our sports, our world. We will love in forcing ourselves to understand, to be compassionate, to respect, to serve, to suffer. We will love with the heart of Christ...

The same spirit prevailed throughout the Great Mission which was inaugurated on November 5, 1957 and ended on November 24. The idea had been suggested to the archbishop a few months after his arrival, during a meeting of priests at which he presided. Announced at the beginning of 1956, it was carefully planned over the course of several months. Limited to the city of Milan itself, this Mission, in accordance with the will of Archbishop Montini, was aimed towards the *lontani*, towards those who were far away from the Church. To his "missionaries" he said, "It is not enough for the pastor to ring the bell and wait. He must hear the factory sirens, in those temples of technology in which the modern world is born and lives; he must go out search for the strays and the tormented, the lost and the lonely."

To prepare for the event, multiple gatherings had been organized in the preceding months; books of songs and prayers were printed by the hundreds of thousands.[36] To supplement the local clergy, he appealed to those of other dioceses. In total: two cardinals (Siri from Genoa and

---

36 Notably *Il rituale della famiglia* [The ritual of the family], published from 1956. This booklet had been suggested by Msgr Montini, then in Rome, in a letter to Fr Bevilacqua on December 19, 1951: he requested a "liturgy of the family," containing "prayers and small rites for the sanctification of family life (blessing of children by their parents; common family prayer; blessing of meals; prayers for the sick, prayers for particular circumstances of family life, etc.)." Letter published in *Notiziario* 3 (May 1981): 17.

Lercaro[37] from Bologna), twenty-four archbishops and bishops, and more than a thousand priests (both secular and religious), preached in locations all over the city: churches, but also public places, shops, factories, hospitals, schools, government offices; the central theme of the preaching was "God the Father."

Mobilizations of clergy on this scale are rare in the history of the great dioceses, particularly since World War II. At the height of the mission, Archbishop Montini, in a letter to Cardinal Roncalli, revealed the scale of the effort to return the Milanese to the faith and religious practice: "Things are moving; but, *by human sight*, it gives the impression of barely scratching the surface of the religious indifference and hostility that has spread over this land of Catholic tradition."[38] Archbishop Montini had asked preachers to favor "goodness" over "polemic": "Let this preaching offend no one, satirize no one, attack no one; instead, let everyone be invited, informed, almost called and awaited." Among the preachers were several of Archbishop Montini's personal friends, including the Swiss theologian Charles Journet,[39] and Fr Bevilacqua; there was also at least one priest, Fr Primo Mazzolari, who had just been condemned by the Holy Office. Father Mazzolari, pastor of Bozzolo, in the diocese of Milan, was the founder of *Adesso*, which promoted a "Christian revolution." Because he had preached collaboration between Catholics and Communists, in 1954 he was forbidden to preach outside of his parish, and in January 1956, the Holy Office banned him from continuing to write in the journal. In spite of these condemnations, Archbishop Montini wanted to include him in the great preaching mission in Milan. He had known Father Mazzolari since before the war; they met during the Weeks of Camaldoli. He did not want him to be left out of such a major event for the Church.

A few months later, from June 26 to July 1, 1958, Archbishop Montini went on pilgrimage to Lourdes with 4,500 of the faithful of his diocese. The archbishop and the pilgrims wanted to make this pilgrimage to

---

37   Card. Giacomo Lercaro (1891–1976) was an Italian prelate, created cardinal in 1953 by Pope Pius XII, who also served as both the archbishop of Ravenna (1947–1952) and the archbishop of Bologna (1952–1968). At Vatican II, he served on the Board of Presidency. Afterwards, he was president of the Consilium (1966–1968) and so one of the key architects of the liturgical reforms.
38   Letter of November 12, 1957 published in *Giovanni e Paolo: Saggio di corrispondenza* (1925–1962) (Brescia: Istituto Paolo VI; Rome: Edizioni Studium, 1982), 96.
39   Card. Charles Journet (1891–1975) was also a close friend of Jacques Maritain, with whom he founded the theological journal *Nova et Vetera* in 1926. He was consecrated a titular archbishop and made a cardinal in 1965.

celebrate the centenary of the Marian apparitions at Lourdes and give thanks for the "good fruits" of the Mission.

Archbishop Montini then spent several weeks of August on retreat in two Swiss Benedictine abbeys: Einsiedeln, then Engelberg. A letter written to Maritain from the latter reveals something of the state of his soul: "The pastoral mission, which weighs on my shoulders, is so heavy that it robs me of all freedom."[40]

The disillusionment was not long in coming. In Milan, after a brief eruption of fervor, the results of the Great Mission were profoundly disillusioning. The religious and moral situation of the city deteriorated. The archbishop complained of it bitterly. In 1960, when the meeting of an ecumenical council was announced, with the declared objective of realizing an *aggiornamento* ("bringing up to date"), did Archbishop Montini see another chance for the Church to go towards the world, with other methods than those which had failed during the Mission of Milan?

POPE RONCALLI

Some have said that after his departure for Milan, Archbishop Montini never saw Pius XII again. That is evidently not quite true. From May 1, 1955, the archbishop of Milan was briefly in Rome at the head of a pilgrimage of the ACLI. A photograph exists of the public audience the pope granted to Archbishop Montini and his faithful. The look on Archbishop Montini's face looking at Pius XII reveals his great admiration for the pope as well as a sort of sorrowful incomprehension. Certainly, that day there was no private audience. It seems there were none right up to the death of Pius XII, despite many short visits to Rome by the archbishop of Milan.

A few months before the death of the pope, Archbishop Montini published a text which seems, in some passages, to criticize various aspects of the pontificate that was drawing to a close. The Pontifical Pastoral Institute held its eighth Week of Pastoral Adaptation from September 22 to 26, 1958 in Milan. In anticipation of the event Archbishop Montini wrote a letter, entitled "The Pastor in the Face of Contemporary Disbelief," which was reproduced in the review of the diocese but also in other publications, in Milan and elsewhere. Archbishop Montini discussed the "relativism" which the Church should attempt. This term, "relativism," was close to his heart. As an example of this relativism, he cited the famous encyclical of Pius XII: "Even in the encyclical *Humani Generis*, which opposes a dam to the overflow of subversive theories threatening

---

40 Letter of August 25, 1958 (Archives J. Maritain).

Archbishop of Milan

Christian dogma, we find unhoped-for compromises and exhortations to encourage positive research, both Scriptural and scientific." The term "unhoped-for compromises" attracted the attention both of those who found themselves comforted in their opinions, and those in some Roman circles who were highly critical because they regarded it as treason against the pope and his views. The following regret was also noticed: "Maybe, in the past, we have too often cried scandal when some brave pastor has attempted an unheard-of and courageous opening. Risk is part of the pastoral art..."

Pius XII died the following October 9 at Castel Gandolfo, after three days of suffering. A diplomat reported that Archbishop Montini rushed to the papal residence on the evening of the 9th to see the dying pope one last time. Sister Pascalina,[41] who had served Pius XII for many years and did not get along with Archbishop Montini when he was Substitute, allegedly forbade him from entering the room: "She gave the pretext that the doctors prohibited visits from strangers, to avoid tiring the sick man."[42] If the story is true, Archbishop Montini must have been hurt to see himself treated as a stranger. When, the next day, he was able to see the mortal remains of the pope, he is supposed to have murmured: "How I wished him well. And yet we did not understand each other."

A few weeks later, the conclave to elect the new pope was about to open. Although Archbishop Montini was not a cardinal, it turned out that some (notably the French cardinals) had considered promoting his candidacy. Nothing, canonically, forbids the election of a pope who is not a cardinal; although the last such case was in the fourteenth century. But the vast majority of cardinals were hostile to such a possibility. When Benny Lai[43] asked Cardinal Siri about rumors of the possibility of the election of the archbishop of Milan, the reaction was pronounced:

> The face of Siri darkened immediately, and he interrupted me: "Oh! No, not that!" he cried. And he showed me his right hand, upon which there was a ring that was missing a stone. "A few minutes ago," he explained to me, "someone came to hold a

---

41 Sr Pascalina Lehnert (1894–1983) was a Sister of the Holy Cross Menzingen and had been Pope Pius XII's housekeeper and secretary since he was nuncio in Bavaria. See *His Humble Servant: Sister M. Pascalina Lehnert's Memoirs of Her Years of Service to Eugenio Pacelli, Pope Pius XII* (South Bend, IN: St Augustine's Press, 2014); Fr Charles Theodore Murr, *The Godmother: Madre Pascalina, a Feminine Tour de Force* (N.p.: Independently published, 2017).
42 T. Breza, *La Porte de bronze*, 409.
43 Benny Lai (1925–2013) was an Italian journalist and Vaticanologist.

strange conversation with me. I understood that he had come to test the waters in view of a Montini candidacy. I hit the table with my fist so hard that I broke this stone. If Montini were a cardinal, then . . ."[44]

The conclave was hotly disputed. On the first ballot, there appear to have been two votes for Montini. But the names of Siri, Aloisi Masella,[45] and Agagianian,[46] of Armenian origin, were those that came up most often. Cardinal Roncalli was eventually suggested, as a compromise, and elected, on the eleventh ballot, on October 28. He chose the name of John XXIII, interrupting the series of Piuses that had continued throughout the nineteenth and twentieth centuries. But he confirmed Msgr Tardini as the head of the Secretariat of State, to reassure those who did not want a brutal rupture with the preceding papacy.

On November 4, the coronation took place in Saint Peter's Basilica. Beforehand, John XXIII wrote a letter to Archbishop Montini to announce that he would hold a consistory soon, and that he and Tardini would be the first cardinals named. The pope asked the archbishop of Milan to keep this secret until the official announcement.[47] By this thoughtful courtesy, the new pope showed his desire promptly to repair what seemed in some eyes to be an injustice on the part of his predecessor. It was also a mark of special esteem, and the first in a series of favors demonstrating that John XXIII saw in Montini his successor.

On November 17, the official announcement of the creation of twenty-three cardinals took place. In addition to Montini and Tardini, who were at the head of the list of the newly promoted, prominent names included Cicognani, apostolic delegate to the United States and friend of Montini; Döpfner,[48] archbishop of Berlin; König,[49] of Vienna;

---

44 Lai, *Les Secrets du Vatican*, 59–60.
45 Card. Benedetto Aloisi Masella (1879–1970) was an Italian Cardinal who served as Prefect of the Discipline of Sacraments (1954–1968) and as Chamberlain of the Roman Church (1958–1970). He attended the Second Vatican Council and voted in the 1963 conclave that elected Pope Paul VI.
46 Card. Gregorio Pietro Agagianian (1895–1971) was an Armenian cardinal and head of the Armenian Catholic Church (1937–1962). He also served as one of the four moderators at the Second Vatican Council (1962–1965), alongside Suenens, Lercaro, and Döpfner.
47 Letter of November 4, 1958, in *Giovanni e Paolo*, 100.
48 Card. Julius Döpfner (1913–1976) was the archbishop of Munich and Freising (1961–1976). He was elevated to the cardinalate in 1958. As archbishop, he took part in the Second Vatican Council (1962–1965) and was on its Board of Presidency. He was considered as having liberal positions and supported ecumenism.
49 Card. Franz König (also spelled Koenig, 1905–2004) was archbishop of Vienna,

Cushing,[50] of Boston. Many of these men would play important roles in the next council. The consistory was held on December 15.

On January 25, 1959, John XXIII announced his intentions of reforming Canon Law, holding a synod of the diocese of Rome, and convoking an ecumenical council, to a restricted circle of cardinals who had met for a religious ceremony at Saint Paul Outside the Walls. The last of these intentions caused a sensation. In the history of the Church, only twenty ecumenical councils had been called; the last was the First Vatican Council, which had notably proclaimed the dogma of papal infallibility, and which had been interrupted by the siege of Rome in 1870. Pius XI, in 1923, and Pius XII, in 1948, had thought of reconvening this interrupted council and continuing its work; they studied questions that had since hung in suspense, and considered other problems with which the Church had since been faced. But both popes abandoned the idea, after having had commissions discreetly work on the project.

The announcement of January 25 was presented by John XXIII himself as born of an "inspiration." The expression was taken up by journalists and some historians. In fact, if there was an inspiration, it was not sudden, but had been meditated for a long time: he had spoken about it for the first time to his secretary, Msgr Capovilla,[51] in the preceding November.[52] The very day of the official announcement, the Vatican Press Office issued a press release specifying that "The Holy Father does not intend that the Council have for its sole end the well-being of Christians, but he wants it to be equally an invitation to separated communities to search for that unity for which so many souls today aspire over the whole face of the earth." From the next day, Cardinal Montini, in a press release published in *L'Italia*, enthusiastically announced this council to his diocese as "a historic event of the first degree ... great today for tomorrow; great for the people and for human hearts; great for the whole Church and for humanity."

Austria (1956–1985) and President of the Secretariat of Non-Believers (1965–1980). John XXIII created him a cardinal in 1958; he was one of the most influential figures at Vatican II.

50 Card. Richard Cushing (1895–1970) was archbishop of Boston from 1944 to 1970. He was made a cardinal by John XXIII in 1958.

51 Card. Loris Francesco Capovilla (1915–2016) served as personal secretary to John XXIII (then Patriarch of Venice) from 1953 until the latter's death in 1963. He was consecrated archbishop by Paul VI in 1967 and created a cardinal by Pope Francis in 2014.

52 Msgr L. Capovilla, "Reflections on the Twentieth Anniversary," in *Vatican II by Those Who Were There* (London: Geoffrey Chapman, 1986), 116.

The council was not to begin until four years later. In the meantime, the work of preparatory commissions at the Vatican would be multiplied by the propositions and suggestions made by French and German-speaking theologians in particular. In May 1959, one of the first such memorandums was submitted, by the theologian Otto Karrer,[53] on ecumenism in the next council. Notably, he asked that no new dogmas be proclaimed, and counseled an affirmation of episcopal collegiality; he also suggested that the vernacular language be introduced into the liturgy. Significantly, he addressed this memorandum to the bishops of his own country, Germany; to Msgr Charrière,[54] who was in charge of ecumenism for the Swiss episcopacy, and to Cardinal Montini, who would increasingly appear to be one of the key figures of the future council.

On May 17, an Ante-Preparatory Commission for the Council was created, under the leadership of the Secretary of State, Cardinal Tardini. It was composed of different members of the Curia. Its principal duty was to ask all the cardinals, archbishops, and bishops of the world, and the Superiors General of the religious orders, their "wishes" concerning the subjects to discuss and the reforms to undertake. The following month, John XXIII specified his intentions in the encyclical *Ad Petri Cathedra* (June 29, 1959). He convoked a council of the whole Church to promote "truth, unity, and peace." "The principal end of the Council," wrote the pope, "will consist in promoting the development of the Catholic faith, the moral renewal of the Christian life of the faithful, and the adaptation of ecclesiastical discipline to the needs and ways of our times."

The Ante-Preparatory Commission received 2,109 responses from bishops and religious superiors from all over the world. Among the most frequent requests, albeit in varying proportions from region to region were: a dogmatic proclamation of the Virgin Mary as Mediatrix or Co-redemptrix; a condemnation of Communism and Secularism; and the introduction of the vernacular language into some parts of the liturgy. The response of Cardinal Montini, in Latin, was collected like the others in large volumes. Curiously, this has never been translated or published in Italian, or in other languages; yet this constitutes a highly

---

53 Fr Otto Karrer (1888–1976) was a German ecumenist, theologian, and philosopher of religion who published many spiritual writings and translations. His studies led him into a crisis in 1923, causing him to resign from the Jesuit order and join the Evangelical Lutheran Church. However, a few weeks later he left and returned to the Roman Catholic Church but was limited in his actions as a priest.
54 Bishop François Charrière (1893–1976) was the bishop of diocese of Lausanne, appointed by Pope Pius XII. He was ordained in 1917 and authored several religious works, including *Truths of Forever* (1944) and *La physionomie des heures canoniales* (1941).

important document for understanding what the archbishop of Milan expected of the Council.[55]

This response stands out in relation to those of his colleagues in the Italian episcopacy. Concerning the preparation of the Council, he suggested that some "contradictory conferences" be organized between Catholics and Orthodox, Anglicans, and Protestants to confront each other's opinions (he proposed Milan as the place of these Catholic-Protestant conferences). He called for no condemnation of dangerous doctrines, instead proposing definitions of "the supernatural end of the human race and of each man" and "grace and its means for salvation," the better to fight "against the conception of materialist humanism which easily dominates worldly minds." He did not want new dogmatic definitions in Marian theology but, without specifically aiming at piety towards the Virgin Mary, he wrote:

> Theological and biblical foundations must be given to Christian piety, to Christian piety must be rendered its theological and biblical bases. Those forms of piety that are not healthy, given to diverse often arbitrary devotions, and that lend themselves to the detriment of liturgical piety and authentic religious sense must be tempered.

He also identified himself as a partisan of the "audacious" introduction of the vernacular language into the liturgy. Finally, to insure the effectiveness of the ecumenical council, he suggested "a series of particular councils following one after the other in the nations and regions" afterwards.

PREPARATION OF THE COUNCIL

It would be a mistake to represent the archbishop of Milan as unreasonably optimistic, or as having unlimited confidence in the world. At the end of 1959, in a long private letter addressed to John XXIII, he revealed a very realistic vision of things:

> The number of adversaries of the name of God seem to grow and be strengthened; secularism and anticlericalism return imperiously to the world; moral license, especially in the press and in popular entertainment, grows dominant, insolent, and

---

55 *Acta et Documenta Concilio Oecumenico Vaticano II apparando*, Series I (Antepræparatoria), vol. II, pars III (Vatican: Typis Polyglottis Vaticanis, 1960), 374–81. We would like to thank Philippe de Gavriloff for translating this long response.

unchecked; ideas and currents of a doubtful goodness agitate and divide the very ranks of those who should illustrate and defend the Christian name.[56]

A short while later, during a minor synod of his diocesan clergy, he painted a catastrophic image of the situation and recognized that the Great Mission had not provided the expected result: "The impulsion of religious fervor incited by the mission of the city in 1957 has not had the positive effects that we expected. The religious situation of the city is alarming." To cite some numbers: only 2.5% of youth from fifteen to twenty-five participated in the Catholic Action movement (the GIAC); the number of priestly ordinations was in freefall (eighty-nine in 1955, thirteen in 1960). Following the Great Mission, some reforms had been enacted to try to attract the Milanese to the churches (or keep them there): the celebration of the Sunday Mass in the evening was authorized, a pamphlet explaining what the Mass is was published and distributed. Nothing had sufficed to arrrest the decline in religious practice. The Milanese went about their lives more and more without concern for the teachings of the Church.

In politics as well, the archbishop was perplexed. Throughout Italy, the bishops were worried. In March 1959, Aldo Moro had been elected Secretary of the Christian Democrats. He had declared himself in favor of "openness to the left," by which he meant the entry of socialists into the government majority. He also planned to reaffirm the "secularism" of the party and render it independent of ecclesiastical authorities. To try to prevent this "openness to the left," numerous bishops individually, then the Italian Episcopal Conference (under the leadership of Cardinal Siri), issued warnings. Cardinal Montini, in spite of his friendship for Moro, was not going to disassociate himself from the whole of the episcopacy. On May 21, 1960, he addressed, by mail, a letter to each of the priests of his diocese on the subject of "openness to the left." The complete text was also published by two Catholic newspapers in Milan. The political alliance of the Christian Democrats with the socialists was declared impossible, because the socialists were "still incapable of liberating themselves from Marxism, still full of prejudice and hostility against religion, still imbued with materialism and anticlericalism." Yet this letter was much more moderate in tone than those published by other bishops; it is to be noted that the archbishop of Milan did not exclude

---

56 Letter of December 22, 1959, published in *Giovanni e Paolo*, 116.

the possibility, "if we judge that the circumstances have changed, to give you other instructions." Openness to the left is not dismissed, except "in the present moment and in the form currently foreseen." This was essentially what happened in 1963: after he became pope, the former archbishop of Milan enabled Aldo Moro to form a government with the support of the socialists.

On the following June 5, the preparatory commissions of the Council were created. There were ten, including a Theological Commission, a Liturgical Commission, and a Commission for the Missions, each set up to prepare the "schemas," that is to say, the texts that would be submitted to the Council for discussion, amendment, and voting. Three secretariats were also added: a secretariat for dealing with the questions touching on the press and modern means of communication; a technical and administrative secretariat; and a secretariat for the unity of Christians that rapidly assumed a dominating role in the development of the entire project. A central commission, presided over by the pope, supervised all of these organizations. Each commission was presided over by a cardinal, and made up of members chosen from among the bishops, priests, and religious who were competent in the matter to which each commission was devoted; also, there was a small number of "consultors," experts who could be consulted if necessary. In total, around forty cardinals (including some Eastern Patriarchs) from every country in the world presided over or were members of these preparatory commissions. Until June 1962, they held regular sessions; the results of their efforts were then submitted to the Central Preparatory Commission. Cardinal Montini did not directly participate in this work; he would not be named to the Central Commission until a year and a half later, in November 1961. This absence must not be seen as a forced separation of which he was the victim, but rather his own deliberate will to distance himself from the preliminary technical discussions, which were devoted to organizational issues. Further, although he was not a member of any preparatory commission, he was kept informed of the developments by three of his confidants whom he had asked John XXIII to appoint to important positions: Fr Carlo Colombo, his private theologian, member of the Theological Commission; Msgr Giovanni Colombo, member of the Commission for Studies and Seminaries;[57] and Fr Bevilacqua, member of the Liturgical Commission.

---

57   A few months later Msgr G. Colombo became auxiliary bishop of Milan, replacing Bishop Pignedoli, who was named apostolic delegate for West-Central Africa.

PAUL VI: THE DIVIDED POPE

Cardinal Montini seems to have adopted a wait-and-see attitude that would be even more notable during the first session of the Council, as if he was on standby for the papacy. When the creation of the preparatory commissions was announced, he was outside Italy, having left for a thirteen-day tour of major cities in the United States and Brazil. If this was not a pre-electoral campaign in view of a future conclave, it was at least a means of making contact with two important heads of state, and the cardinals of the North and South American continents. The pretext of the voyage had been an invitation to visit Brazil, [58] offered barely a month before, by President Kubitschek. [59]

On June 3, Cardinal Montini left Milan, in the company of his faithful secretary, Father Macchi. [60] After a stop of a few hours at the nunciature in Paris, they boarded a flight for the United States. They spent a day in New York, where they were the guests of Cardinal Spellman. Next they went to the University of Notre Dame, in Indiana. At the time there were six thousand students. Cardinal Montini was to receive a doctorate *honoris causa*, at the same time as other dignitaries, including the President of the United States, Eisenhower. [61] He had a conversation with him on the great political problems of the day, then gave the president a bronze statuette representing an angel breaking a chain. Eisenhower saw in it the symbol of the combat of the "free world" against oppression. Then the voyage continued towards Chicago and Boston, where Cardinal Montini met successively with Cardinals Meyer [62] and Cushing, visited colleges, hospitals, and diocesan organizations, and met Catholics of Italian origin. Then there were stops in Philadelphia, Washington (including meetings with various diplomatic and political personalities at the apostolic delegation), and New York again.

In Brazil, where he arrived on June 11, he was welcomed by the head of state. At the airport of Brasilia, a military detachment and several

---

58   In gratitude for an enthusiastic speech by the cardinal, at the Brazilian consulate in Milan, in honor of the new capital of the country, Brasilia.
59   Juscelino Kubitschek (1902–1976) was President of Brazil (1956–1961). He had the capital transferred from Rio de Janeiro to Brasilia.
60   He gave an account of the voyage in the review *Diocesi di Milano* 7 (August 1960): 3–35.
61   Dwight D. Eisenhower (1890–1969) was a Republican politician and the thirty-fourth President of America (1953–1961). During the Second World War, he was the supreme commander of Allied forces in Western Europe and led the D-day invasion of Nazi-occupied Europe.
62   Card. Albert Meyer (1903–1965) was archbishop of Chicago (1958–1965) and was elevated to the cardinalate in 1959. He participated in the first three sessions of Vatican II and was on the Board of Presidency.

ministers awaited him. He was received by President Kubitschek, and was awed by the capital, with its avant-garde architecture. The journey continued, with stops at São Paulo, where he was received by Cardinal Carlos Carmelo de Vasconcellos Motta,[63] and at Rio de Janeiro. In this city, he received another doctorate *honoris causa*. He also met again with people he had known in Rome, including Alceu Amoroso Lima,[64] a writer and friend of Maritain's; and Msgr Hélder Câmara, who had him visit a *favela* where he had developed a social assistance project. On June 16, Cardinal Montini left for Milan.

Although he was not among the first members of the preparatory commissions, the archbishop of Milan followed the work closely, and organized study sessions in his diocese. Over time, as the opening of the Council drew closer, the cardinal became more and more optimistic. In August 1960, during a course on "cultural *aggiornamento*" organized by the Catholic University of Milan, he declared:

> This council, unlike many of those which have preceded it, is being called in a moment of peace and fervor in the life of the Church. It does not have to resolve worrying or distressing internal problems; instead, uniquely, it has been convened to continue internal progress. No heresies, schisms, or dramatic difficulties at the heart of the Church will assemble the bishops around the pope; instead they are meeting out of their desire to enjoy the Church's own internal unity, their obligation to make the Church's own vitality more effective, and the need for sanctification and internal growth.

Less than a year before he was still speaking of an "alarming situation." Was this a glaring inconsistency in his thought? It seems likelier that the situation in Milan appeared exceptional, and unique to that diocese, and that he still hoped that the Council would lead to a major international renewal.

Such sentiments prevailed among numerous bishops and theologians. It was not necessary to be a member or consultor of a commission to

---

63   Card. Carlos Carmelo de Vasconcellos Motta (1890–1962) was a Brazilian prelate who served in a variety of ecclesiastical posts in his homeland. He was ordained in 1918 and consecrated in 1932. He was made an archbishop in 1935 and a cardinal in 1946.
64   Alceu Amoroso Lima (1893–1983) was both a journalist and an activist who also founded Brazilian Christian Democracy. In 1928, he converted to Catholicism which ultimately resulted in his taking charge of Catholic Action in Brazil. He was known for being strongly opposed to fascism and promoted freedom of the press during the military dictatorship.

make one's voice heard and thus contribute to forming public opinion. The Swiss theologian Hans Küng published *The Council and Reunion* in 1960 as well.[65] This volume outlined his personal views on what the next council should do. The internal reform of the Church was the preliminary condition for unifying Christians, he explained. "Criticism, that is to say, vehement criticism, can be a duty." The reform to be undertaken was not "simply an internal reform of hearts, nor a mere exterior reform of abuses"; instead it must express "new creative structures." This clearly contradicted what John XXIII had wished: "a salvific reform of Christian morals." Amongst the supposed deviations to be extirpated, Küng counted "legalism," "Marianism," and "papalism." While restraining himself from defining a "plan of renovation," he discussed a series of "possibilities": not looking for the Council to resolve controversial theological questions nor define new Marian dogmas, but rather making a "revaluation of the episcopacy" the axis around which all the other reforms (liturgical, disciplinary, etc.) would turn. The work, prefaced by Cardinal König, archbishop of Vienna, for the German edition, and by Cardinal Liénart,[66] for the French translation, would cause reverberations internationally.

Did Cardinal Montini read this book? It does not seem so; the work is not included in his library. Nonetheless the author was not unknown to him. "I knew the cardinal of Milan at the end of the fifties; we have commiserated much," remembered Hans Küng.[67] It is possible that the ideas expressed by the author of *The Council and Reunion* were not unknown to the archbishop of Milan. Indeed, some of them were echoed in the response of Cardinal Montini to the Ante-Preparatory Commission.

These preconciliar ties between a bishop and a theologian were not exceptional, numerous other examples could be cited. Theologians and experts would anticipate or reinforce, as the case may be, the bishops in their ideas. Very soon there would appear a division within the Church,

---

65 Hans Küng, *The Council and Reunion*, trans. Cecily Hastings (London: Sheed and Ward, 1961). Fr Küng (1928–2021) was a Swiss priest and ecumenical theologian. His public rejection of papal infallibility led to the loss of his right to teach Catholic theology in 1979. Although a friend of Pope Benedict XVI, he criticized his former colleague on many points, including the lifting of the excommunication of the bishops of the Society of Saint Pius X in 2009.

66 Card. Achille Liénart (1884–1973) was a French cardinal, elevated in 1930, who served as the bishop of Lille (1928–1968). He was a prominent liberal figure at the Second Vatican Council and was on the Board of Presidency. He also formed a part of the 1963 papal conclave that elected Pope Paul VI.

67 Hans Küng, letter to the author, November 19, 1991.

which was quickly picked up by the press, between "reformers," "progressives," "innovators" on one side, and "conservatives," "traditionalists," or "anticonciliarists," on the other.

In the spring of 1961, Cardinal Montini traveled, privately this time, to Ireland. His old friend from the Ecclesiastical Academy, Antonio Riberi, had been named nuncio to Dublin two years before. Another friend of his youth, Amleto Cicognani, was to succeed Cardinal Tardini the following July as Secretary of State, after Tardini's death. There is hardly any doubt that the archbishop of Milan convinced John XXIII to name one of his own allies to this very important post. At the end of this same year, John XXIII proceeded to nominate new members to the preconciliar commissions and secretariats, notably Cardinal Montini, who was named to the very important central commission. It had already held two sessions of several days each; it would hold five more up through June 1962. The archbishop of Milan took the floor around sixty times.[68] In this commission the conflicts between opposing cardinals were sometimes intense. The task at hand was to examine and amend all the schemas prepared by the ten specialized commissions. A few of Cardinal Montini's interventions may be highlighted: he was opposed to attributing the title of Mediatrix to the Virgin Mary, judging the title "inopportune and even harmful"; he supported the abolition of book censorship;[69] then there was his position on Communism. On this subject, Cardinal Montini insisted that "our discussion be rational, not insulting." It was essential to adopt a new attitude towards the Communists, who had experienced "our severity, but not our charity." "Patience," he concluded, "is necessary for us. Our faith will triumph if it is patient . . ."

Another hotly disputed question involved "religious liberty" versus "religious tolerance." There was here more than a difference of vocabulary between the two expressions. The Central Preparatory Commission

---

68 The principal interventions of the members of this commission during this period and those of Cardinal Montini have been collected in *Interventi nella Commissione Centrale Preparatoria*.

69 The Church required that books touching on matters of faith and morals receive ecclesiastical authorization prior to publication. If a book should contain a theological error, the author would be notified in writing and given the opportunity to correct the text or to demonstrate how the text was theologically acceptable as it stood. Some terms used in this process are *nihil obstat* ("nothing hinders": notice by the censor that the work contains nothing meriting censorship), *imprimi potest* ("it may be printed": authorization from a religious major superior for the publication of the work of one of his or her subjects), *imprimatur* ("let it be printed": authorization from a bishop for the publication of a book).

was presented with two texts on the same subject. That of the Theological Commission affirmed the traditional doctrine: error (all religious confessions other than Catholicism, that is) has no rights; in consideration of the common good other confessions can only be tolerated; the state can accord civil liberty to other religions, but must recognize, by a concordat for example, the spiritual rights of the Church, and ultimately favor them. The other schema on religious liberty discussed in the Central Commission was prepared by the Secretariat for Unity and presented an entirely different point of view: religious liberty is a right which man possesses by nature and which no state can constrain. Cardinal Montini aligned himself with the second point of view but did not want it defined "in a theoretical and absolute way, but rather in a practical manner." This question would be fiercely debated and, during the Council, it expanded into every session, year after year, before a final formulation was found, in the last weeks of the Council, that still faced strong opposition.

The liturgy was another subject debated by the Central Commission. Cardinal Montini had closely followed the work of the Pontifical Commission for the Reform of the Liturgy created by Pius XII in 1948, presided over by Cardinal Micara;[70] its secretary was Fr Bugnini.[71] On occasion, Montini had served as intermediary between this commission and Fr Bevilacqua, addressing to him documents for examination.[72] But the responsibility of this commission was not a complete reform of the liturgy. Its work principally concerned renovating the Easter Vigil (1951) and the liturgy of Holy Week (1955). The Preparatory Commission for the Liturgy, created in 1960, had a much more ambitious remit. Presided

---

70   Card. Clemente Micara (1879–1965) was an Italian cardinal, appointed by Pope Pius XII in 1946, who worked for the Holy See as an ecclesiastical diplomat. He was also the Vicar General of Rome (1951–1965).
71   Archbishop Annibale Bugnini, CM (1912–1982) had worked for liturgical reforms since the 1940s. He was among the primary authors of Vatican II's Constitution on the Liturgy *Sacrosanctum Concilium* and secretary of the Consilium for implementing this constitution from 1964 until 1969, at which time it was incorporated into the newly formed Congregation of Divine Worship. Bugnini served as secretary of this congregation until he was "exiled" as Apostolic Pro-Nuncio to Iran. Paul VI consecrated him titular archbishop of Diocletiana in 1972. Describing the way things were done in the Consilium, Fr Louis Bouyer spoke of "the maneuvers of the mealy-mouthed scoundrel that the Neapolitan Vincentian, Bugnini, a man as bereft of culture as he was of basic honesty, soon revealed himself to be" (Bouyer, *Memoirs*, 219). For a complete biography, see Yves Chiron, *Annibale Bugnini: Reformer of the Liturgy*, trans. John Pepino (Brooklyn: Angelico Press, 2018).
72   *Notiziario* 3 (May 1981): 17.

over by Cardinal Gaetano Cicognani,[73] it had Fr Bugnini for Secretary and counted amongst its members or consultors numerous specialists on the liturgy who promoted radical reforms: Fathers Bevilacqua, Capelle, Jungmann, Botte, Gy, and Canon Martimort.[74] The archbishop of Milan had followed their work closely, thanks to Fr Bevilacqua, and he had received ten or so of the consultors of this commission in Milan, on February 9, 1961. From the testimony of one of these: "He spoke to us straightaway of the vernacular language as something upon which he had profoundly reflected and which he considered important: 'I think that the time is ripe.'"[75] This preparatory commission was attached to many other reforms; some of its members worked on particular special subjects: the concelebration of Mass, the communion of the faithful under both species, the simplification of the liturgical vestments, the reform of the liturgical calendar.[76] If some of them already dreamed of reforming the *ordo* of the Mass itself, or of writing new canons, they did not mention any of this in the prepared schema. The final version of the schema was examined by the Central Preparatory Commission in March and April 1962. Cardinal Montini made a long intervention in support of introducing the vernacular language into the Mass (excluding the Canon itself). Having become pope, he would authorize a much more profound and radical liturgical reform. Yet while he was still archbishop of Milan, he had in a sense announced his intention in a Lenten letter addressed to the clergy and faithful of his diocese, at the beginning of the year

---

[73] Card. Gaetano Cicognani (1881–1962) was the brother of Card. Amleto Cicognani. To date, they were the last pair of brothers in the College of Cardinals. Gaetano served as Prefect of the Apostolic Signatura (1954–death) and was elevated to the cardinalate by Pope Pius XII.

[74] Dom Bernard Capelle, OSB (Paul Capelle Henry de Faveaux, 1884–1961), ordained in 1906, was a monk of Maredsous from 1918. He was elected as the second abbot of Mont-César (1928–1952). He was a proponent of the Liturgical Movement, especially of the liturgical use of the vernacular language. Fr Josef Andreas Jungmann (1889–1975), an Austrian Jesuit, was one of the most influential figures in the Liturgical Movement. Fr Bouyer notes that although he was an excellent historian of the Roman missal, he never celebrated a Solemn Mass (Bouyer, *Memoirs*, 220–21). Dom Bernard Botte, OSB (1893–1980) was a monk of Mont-César in Louvain and a contributor to the Liturgical Movement. He joined the CPL in 1948 and directed the Institut Supérieur de Liturgie from 1956 to 1964. Fr Pierre-Marie Gy (1922–2004), a French Dominican ordained in 1948 and a university professor at the ICP, played a large role in the liturgical reform of the Second Vatican Council. He was later to spar with Joseph Ratzinger over liturgical questions.

[75] P.-M. Gy, "Msgr Bugnini et la réforme liturgique de Vatican II," *Revue des sciences philosophiques et théologiques* (April 1985): 315.

[76] Archbishop Annibale Bugnini, *The Reform of the Liturgy 1948–1975*, ch. 2.

1962.[77] Writing about the necessary "internal reform" of the Church, he announced: "She will take care *to update herself* in casting off, if necessary, this or that old royal cloak resting upon her sovereign shoulders to dress herself in the simpler clothes that modern taste demands."

At the end of the seven plenary sessions, the Central Preparatory Commission had completed a great deal of work. "Sixty-five schemas had been discussed; the results of the discussions had been collected in four volumes of more than four thousand pages . . ."[78] The opening of the Council was set for October 11, 1962. Cardinal Montini then confided to a confidant: "We are not ready, we still need three years of preparation."[79] The texts which were going to be presented to the bishops and superiors of orders from all over the world were numerous — too numerous according to some; no plan of the whole had been previewed.

Before the Council began its work, the archbishop of Milan undertook another major voyage, in Africa this time. There were several reasons: his former collaborator, Msgr Pignedoli, had been named nuncio two years before as Apostolic Delegate in West Central Africa; further, the Diocese of Milan had opened a mission in what was then Rhodesia in 1961, near the shores of the Zambia, where a consortium of Milanese businessmen had just finished a giant dam. Also, over the course of the meetings of the Central Preparatory Commission, he appears to have become particularly attached to Bishop Hurley,[80] bishop of Durban. On religious liberty, and the separation of Church and state, this South African had expressed opinions close to those of Cardinal Montini.

The voyage in Africa lasted from July 19 to August 10; the archbishop of Milan was the first European cardinal to visit the continent. In Rhodesia he visited the Italian mission of Kariba and the missionary post of Chirundu, which had recently been founded, and gave the sacrament of Confirmation to a large group of young Africans. In South Africa,

---

[77] John XXIII had just published an apostolic constitution *Veterum Sapientia* dedicated to the defense of Latin and dictating concrete measures to ensure that it would always be studied by the clergy.
[78] Msgr Giuseppe Colombo, "Presentazione," in *Interventi*, VI.
[79] Cardinal Giovanni Colombo, *Ricordando*, 155.
[80] Bishop Denis Hurley, OMI (1915–2004) was a South African member of the Missionary Oblates of Mary Immaculate. He was named Vicar Apostolic of Natal and bishop of Durban in 1946. When his see was elevated to the Archdiocese of Durban, he became its first archbishop. He was known for his strong opposition to apartheid and for his work on the English translations of the Novus Ordo Sacramentary and Liturgy of the Hours in the International Commission on English in the Liturgy (ICEL).

Cardinal Montini was able to see the practical application of the politics of apartheid. If he restrained himself while there from condemning the apartheid state in public declarations, he intended to make a "gesture" to mark his disapproval: he went into a black neighborhood of Johannesburg to bless the first stone of a church that was to be built there; and he did not meet with the political authorities of the country, even though at his next stop in Nigeria, his first visit was to the head of state. In Nigeria, under the guidance of Msgr Pignedoli, he toured the different regions of the country, visiting missions, schools, and hospitals kept by religious; he celebrated Mass for Catholic communities, who were a minority in the country. Then the trip ended with a visit to multiple cities and sites in Ghana. Upon returning to Milan, Cardinal Montini would say, in a televised interview, that this voyage had been "an extraordinary experience, which has marked me profoundly." Then, in a message addressed to his faithful, he eulogized African Christianity, with its songs, its dances, and its spontaneity, and compared it with some sorrow, as he admitted, to the religiosity of the Milanese who "have fallen somewhat in the intensity of their faith."[81]

FIRST SESSION

As the Council was just about to open, Cardinal Montini committed an error which had repercussions. He was sometimes prone to let himself be swept away by emotion and act without reflection. A young Spanish student had been tried before a military tribunal for having thrown a homemade bomb at a statue of General Franco, and for distributing tracts calling for other students to demonstrate in favor of the minors on strike. Some Milanese students spread the news that the student and several minors had been condemned to death. They went to find their archbishop and asked him to intervene. Without verifying the facts, he addressed a telegram to Franco asking for pardon for the condemned, and had it published in the Italian press although it had not yet been received by its addressee. General Franco was deeply unhappy, all the more because the tribunal had in fact pronounced no death sentence. The Spanish newspapers published statements of protest, on October 9, and General Franco addressed a very severe letter (of which the precise contents are unknown) to Cardinal Montini. But the faux pas of the archbishop of Milan was quickly forgotten. Two days later the Council opened.

---

81 Account of this voyage and discourses in Pasquale Macchi, "Il Cardinale di Milano in Africa," *Diocesi di Milano* (December 1962): 605–25.

John XXIII had thought for a long time that one session of a few weeks would suffice for examining all the prepared schemas and then voting on them, and that the Council could be finished before Christmas. In fact, four sessions were necessary, and it would not end until December 1965.[82]

On October 11, more than two thousand bishops and superiors from the whole world were assembled in Saint Peter's Basilica. Among the "Council Fathers," according to the expression which became increasingly popular, numerous bishops of Communist countries were conspicuous by their absence: no Catholic bishop of the USSR, Romania, China, or North Vietnam had been able to come to Rome. Many amongst them were in prison or lived in hiding. In other Communist countries, their participation had been authorized in very low numbers. On the other hand, thirty-one non-Catholic "observers" were present, among whom were the pastors Schütz and Thurian. Anglican, Orthodox, and Protestant communities had been invited to send representatives. These representatives did not intervene in the debates; hence the description "observers." Nonetheless, they would became more and more numerous (ninety-three at the end of the Council) and over the course of the sessions they played an important role. Every Tuesday, some bishops, experts, and theologians would meet with them. Fr Congar recounted: "We discussed with them either the text the Council was studying at that moment, or the one it was going to address the following week. After the document or the problem was presented, they made their observations known."[83] At the end of the first session of the Council, Bishop Willebrands[84] would say to the leader of the Anglican delegation: "The presence of observers here is very important. You have no idea how much they have influenced the work of the Council."[85]

The different Orthodox churches had refused to send observers to this first session, except one, the Russian church. The principal agreement to send two observers had been given by Bishop

---

82 The present biography is not intended to serve as a history of the council. In addition to the History of Vatican II (Maryknoll, NY: Orbis/Leuven: Peeters, 1995–2006), this book makes use of the chronicles written or assembled by various journalists and theologians who were present (Caprik, Congar, Fresquet, Laurentin, Wenger, Wiltgen). Our presentation of the four sessions will be limited mainly to the role played by Cardinal Montini, who, prior to the second session, became Paul VI.
83 Congar, Une vie, 144.
84 Card. Johannes Willebrands (1909–2006) served in the Secretariat for Promoting Christian Unity under Card. Bea from 1960 to 1989, succeeding as president upon the latter's death in 1969. He was consecrated in 1964, created cardinal in 1969, and served as archbishop of Utrecht and Primate of the Netherlands 1975–1983.
85 J. R. H. Moorman, "Observers and Guests of the Council," in Vatican II by Those Who Were There, 166.

Nikodim,[86] who oversaw Foreign Affairs of the Orthodox Church, during a meeting with Cardinal Tisserant,[87] on the preceding August 13, at Metz. The bishop of this city revealed that a condition had been imposed by Msgr Nikodim: "that guarantees be given concerning the apolitical attitude of the Council."[88] What guarantee could it be, other than an assurance that Communism would not be condemned explicitly by the Council? The promise was kept. Also worthy of note was the presence, as an observer, of Jean Guitton, the only Catholic layman present at this first session. Cardinal Montini had asked John XXIII to invite him.

In addition, the Council was attended by qualified, credentialed theologians who did not participate in the Council debates directly, but were there to be consulted by the Council Fathers and by the Commissions on difficult subjects. There were two hundred the day of the opening of the Council; by 1965, they would number more than four hundred. Many of them played a determining role in writing the texts that were finally adopted. Some of them had been sanctioned in previous years (Congar, Lubac), others were going to become famous by their involvement in the Council (Ratzinger),[89] all saw their ideas triumph. Each important bishop asked for at least one theologian of his acquaintance to be appointed an "expert" (*peritus* in Latin): Cardinal Montini asked for Fr Bevilacqua; Cardinal König, Fr Rahner;[90] Msgr Dell'Acqua asked for Fr Morlion to be recognized and credentialed as a *peritus*. Others, notably Fathers Chenu and Schillebeeckx,[91] did not obtain this title and were forced to content themselves with playing an unofficial (though still important) role in the proceedings.

---

86   Bishop Nikodim (1929–1978) was a Russian Orthodox metropolitan bishop of both Leningrad and Novgorod (1963–1978). He was ordained at the age of 31, making him the youngest bishop in the world at the time (1960). He also went on to be one of the six presidents of the World Council of Churches.
87   Card. Eugène Tisserant (1884–1972) was a French curial prelate who held a variety of posts including Dean of the College of Cardinals (1951–1972), Grand Master of the Equestrian Order of the Holy Sepulcher of Jerusalem (1960–1972), Prefect of the Congregation of Ceremonies (1951–1967), Librarian of the Vatican (1957–1971), and Archivist of the Vatican Secret Archives (1957–1971).
88   Interview of Msgr Schmitt with the daily *Le Lorrain*, February 9, 1963.
89   Card. Joseph Ratzinger (1927–) was a peritus of Card. Frings (Cologne, Germany). He distinguished himself by taking up the torch of the *nouvelle théologie*. He was consecrated archbishop of Munich and Freising and Paul VI created him a cardinal in 1977. He reigned as Pope Benedict XVI from 2005 until his resignation in 2013.
90   Fr Karl Rahner (1904–1984) was a German Jesuit theologian known for his intricate neoscholastic studies and his theory of the "anonymous Christian."
91   Fr Edward Schillebeeckx (1914–2009) was a Belgian Dominican theologian of the *nouvelle théologie* movement.

On October 11, in his opening speech, which was largely (according to Msgr Carlo Colombo) inspired by the archbishop of Milan, John XXIII denounced the "prophets of doom who always predict the worst, as if the end of the world were nigh."[92]

> They assert repeatedly that if you compare our age with times past, it has declined into something worse; they behave as though they have nothing to learn from History — the teacher of life — and act as though everything went smoothly and to everyone's advantage in the days of earlier Councils (as far as Christian doctrine, morality and the true freedom of the Church were concerned).[93]

The pope was going to draw a large number of Council Fathers into his optimistic vision of the world. "The principal concern of the ecumenical council," he also affirmed, "is that the sacred deposit of Christian doctrine be conserved and proposed in a more effective manner."[94] The doctrine must "be studied and explained in the way which our times require."[95] The speech was in Latin; some understood and translated it thus: "by using modern methods of research and the literary forms of modern thought."[96] It is more than a nuance of translation. Was it about presenting the immovable doctrine of the Church for a new era, or about adapting this doctrine by using the categories of modern thought and accounting for ideological evolutions? This dilemma would split the Council into two great tendencies.

The ecumenical council, a complex organization, was regulated by highly precise rules. The two thousand Council Fathers met each morning

---

92 Pope John XXIII, Discourse, October 11, 1962, in AAS 54 (1962): 789 —"ab his rerum adversarum vaticinatoribus, qui deteriora semper prænuntiant, quasi rerum exitium instet."

93 AAS 54 (1962): 789 —"dictitant nostra tempora, si cum elapsis sæculis comparentur, prorsus in peius abiisse; atque adeo ita se habent, quasi ex historia, quæ vitæ magistra est, nihil habeant quod discant, ac veluti si, superiorum Conciliorum tempore, quoad christianam doctrinam, quoad mores, quoad iustam Ecclesiæ libertatem, omnia prospere ac recte processerint."

94 AAS 54 (1962): 790 —"Quod Concilii Oecumenici maxime interest, hoc est, ut sacrum christianæ doctrinæ depositum efficaciore ratione custodiatur atque proponatur."

95 AAS 54 (1962): 790 — The full phrase reads, "This certain and immutable doctrine, to which faithful submission is expected, must be studied and explained in the way that our times require" ("Oportet ut hæc doctrina certa et immutabilis, cui fidele obsequium est præstandum, ea ratione pervestigetur et exponatur, quam tempora postulant nostra").

96 Wiltgen, Inside Story, 6.

in "general congregations" to examine the text (or schema) drafted in the preceding months by the preparatory commissions. Under well-determined conditions, some Council Fathers could take the floor to approve or criticize the schema and propose modifications. Votes were cast on both the parts of the schema and then the whole of it. Three formulas could be used: *placet* (approbation of a text), *non placet* (refusal), or *placet juxta modum* (consent under condition of modification). As long as a schema was not adopted by a majority of two thirds, it was discussed again and modified. Specialized commissions (ten in total) were entrusted with writing the new version of the schemas, taking into account the opinions expressed and the proposed amendments. If a schema was voted by a two-thirds majority, it would then be promulgated by the pope and would become a "constitution," a "decree," or a "declaration" for the whole Church.

The pope did not preside at the Council in the general congregations, except in a few instances. But a closed-circuit television permitted him to follow the meetings. The debates of the Council were directed by the Council Presidency, which was composed of ten cardinals. A Secretary General, Msgr Felici,[97] coordinated everything; his work would be essential throughout all four sessions.

The first general congregation took place on October 13. This day was marked by an incident that showed the intention of a coalition of certain European bishops not to allow the Roman Curia to run the Council. The ten council commissions were to be designated. Composed of twenty-four members each, of whom two-thirds were to be elected by the Council Fathers and a third named by the pope, they were to carry out the important work of redoing the texts after their examination in general congregation. As they were about to proceed to the vote, Cardinal Liénart, bishop of Lille, France, and member of the Council Presidency, took the floor. The coalition wanted to avoid the simple renomination of those bishops who had been members of the preparatory commissions. He asked that the vote be postponed so that the over two thousand Council Fathers could get to know each other and establish lists of candidates. It was immediately approved by Cardinal Frings,[98] another member of

---

[97] Card. Pericle Felici (1911–1982) was a conservative Italian Catholic prelate, holding various offices in the Roman Curia (1947–1982). He was created a cardinal in 1967 and was the Secretary General of the Second Vatican Council (1962–1965), where he identified with conservatives who wished to retain curial control.

[98] Card. Joseph Frings (1887–1978) was a German cardinal and archbishop of Cologne (1942–1969) who was viewed as a significant Catholic figure who had been resistant to the Nazi regime.

the Council Presidency. Both were strongly applauded; finally, it was decided to end the session and to postpone the vote to three days later.

This first thunderclap at the Council was not an isolated intervention but the result of a coordinated action by a few. Paul VI himself would later admit to Jean Guitton that the intervention of Cardinal Liénart had been decided a few days before during the course of a restricted meeting of six or seven cardinals, of whom he was one.[99] From October 13 to 16, the campaigning that permitted the different episcopacies to establish lists of candidates took place. Of the thirty-four lists presented, the Frings-Liénart list, representing the "progressive" tendency, won by a landslide, obtaining almost half of the seats in the commissions.

Cardinal Montini, although implicated in the Liénart "conspiracy," was very discreet during this first session; and therefore we will not dwell at length on the course of this one. John XXIII had put a small house adjoining Saint Peter's Basilica at the disposal of the archbishop of Milan. This special favor allowed Cardinal Montini to see the pope discreetly, and also just as discreetly to receive visits within the Vatican from bishops, *periti*, and theologians.

John XXIII, feeling that illness would soon take him and that the archbishop of Milan would succeed him, is supposed to have counseled him to avoid engaging in the debates and to maintain a neutral appearance. Whatever truth there might be in this explanation, it may be noted that Cardinal Montini only held the floor twice during this first session. The first time, November 11, was during discussions of the schema on the liturgy. He gave his full approbation, while reassuring those who were worried by the dispositions of the text. In fact, this schema left the door open to numerous changes.

When the end of the session was approaching, in December, only the first chapter of the schema on the liturgy had been adopted by a large majority. All the other schemas presented (on Revelation, on the Unity of Christians, on the Church, on the Means of Social Communications) had been the subjects of passionate debate and were returned to the commissions to be modified. But sometimes these returns for review involved no little pressure. The schema on Revelation, for example, presented by Cardinal Ottaviani, was strongly contested by some bishops, who found it too abrupt in its definitions and lacking in open-mindedness towards Protestants. Although unofficial, two counter-projects on the subject had already been prepared by two experts: Fathers Rahner and

---

99   Guitton, *Paul VI secret*, 96.

Daniélou.[100] In spite of this opposition, the necessary two-thirds majority to return the whole schema to its commission was not obtained. On November 20, three prominent adversaries of the text, Cardinals Montini, Meyer, and Léger[101] went to find John XXIII and ask him to put the text aside. The pope acquiesced and announced, the next day, that the text would be withdrawn and that a mixed commission (composed of members of the Theological Commission and members of the Secretariat for Unity) was charged with preparing a new schema on Revelation.

In short order, Cardinal Montini scowled on the unfolding of the Council. On October 18, less than a week after proceedings began, he wrote a letter to Cardinal Secretary of State Cicognani, rather than addressing himself directly to His Holiness, so as to not seem to question the pope. "Compelled by other bishops," he wrote, he complained that the Council did not have an "organic, ideal, and logical plan." He proposed one: it is around the theme of the Church that the Council should be "polarized." From this time on, he thought that the Council would need three sessions to do its work well. The first would conclude with a definition of "what the Church is," the second should address the question of "what the Church *does*" (in different fields: liturgy, morality, the missions, etc.), the third session should be dedicated to the study of the relations of the Church with the world (with "separated brethren," states, the world of culture, other religions, and the "enemies of the Church"). The Council would then conclude with some solemn canonization — to emphasize the communion of saints — and by some gesture of charity (gift to the poor, solemn pardon). This letter, which for a long time was not known except to a highly restricted number of people, prefigured, in many ways, the line which the Council would follow once the archbishop of Milan became pope.[102]

This keynote address took numerous ideas from another plan that Cardinal Suenens, in April 1962, had addressed to John XXIII after

---

100 Card. Jean Daniélou (1905–1974) was a French Jesuit and theologian, whom Paul VI created a cardinal in 1969.
101 Card. Paul-Émile Léger (1904–1991) was a Canadian cardinal, elevated in 1953, and archbishop of Montreal (1950–1967). He had initially joined the Jesuit novitiate but was deemed too emotional to be allowed to continue so he was transferred to Valleyfield diocese once he had been ordained a priest in 1929. He displayed leadership during the Second Vatican Council, focusing mostly on ecumenism and freedom of thought within the Church.
102 The letter was not known until November 1983 by its publication in Notiziario 7, 11–14.

consulting with Cardinals Lercaro, Döpfner, and Montini. These two plans were also an implicit condemnation of the schemas developed by the preparatory commissions. It was therefore only gradually that they were revealed at the end of the first session — for the first time, on December 2, in an article by Cardinal Montini in *L'Italia*. Since the opening of the Council the archbishop of Milan had regularly published "Letters of the Council" in the Catholic newspaper of his city to recount the proceedings of the Council. In a new letter he expressed several criticisms of the session, which was going to end soon, qualifying the seventy-odd preparatory schemas as "immense and excellent, but heterogenous and unequal material that would require courageous editing and classification." He also expressed disdain for the abundance of oral interventions of the Council Fathers and the "collective diversity of tendencies and currents" which had appeared. Two days later, in general congregations, Cardinal Suenens took the floor to ask that the next session revolve "around a central theme which may efficiently orient its development: namely, the Church." On December 5, Cardinal Montini intervened in his turn, for only the second time during that council session, so that he was listened to attentively. He firmly supported Cardinal Suenens's intervention of the previous day. On the 5th and the 6th, after these two extraordinary discourses, John XXIII announced an upheaval of the Council: a coordinating commission would be created to unite the other commissions and follow their work (it included Cardinals Suenens, Léger, Lercaro, Montini, and Döpfner), and more importantly, the seventy some schemas to be studied would be reduced to seventeen. That implied a complete overhaul of the existing schemas, except those on the liturgy and the means of communications, which were already being reviewed. On the other hand, a new schema (Schema XIII) was to be prepared, "On the principles and the action of the Church for promoting the good of society," which would become the famous Pastoral Constitution on the Church in the Modern World *Gaudium et Spes*.

    The long work of the preparatory commissions was thus almost completely swept away. Reporting on this first session, Hans Küng could declare: "No one who was here for the Council will go back home as he came. I myself never expected so many bold and explicit statements from the bishops on the Council floor."[103]

---

103   Cited in Wiltgen, *The Inside Story*, 60.

Statue of Paul VI by Raffaele "Lello" Scorzelli, unveiled in Brescia in 1984

Giorgio Montini (1860–1943), father of Giovanni Battista Montini

Giuditta Montini (née Alghisi, 1874–1943), mother of Giovanni Battista Montini

Giuditta, holding Giovanni Battista in her lap, with older brother Lodovico

The church where Giovanni Battista was baptized: Pieve di Concesio

Family photo of the Montinis: Giovanni and Giuditta, with their three sons

The Montini brothers: Francesco, Giovanni Battista, and Lodovico

G. B. Montini after receiving his diploma in 1916, with friends

On the day of his priestly ordination: May 29, 1920

Fr Montini with FUCI students

Maria Faina, Giovanni Battista Montini, and Igino Righetti, *president of* FUCI

Fr Montini with his parents

Msgr Montini of the Secretariat of State, with Pope Pius XII

Alcide De Gasperi: leader of Christian Democracy

As Archbishop of Milan

With Pope John XXIII

Formal portrait after being created cardinal by John XXIII (February 1959)

The cardinal archbishop of Milan

With brothers Francesco and Lodovico in 1960

On the day of Montini's election to the papacy: June 21, 1963

Cardinal Ottaviani places the tiara on Paul VI at the papal coronation: June 30, 1963

"A lightweight tiara, in the shape of a missile, of white metal made by Fiat..." (p. 174)

Paul VI in pontifical regalia, including the fanon and gloves

John F. Kennedy visits Paul VI: July 2, 1963

Presiding at the Second Vatican Council, with Cardinal
Ottaviani and Master of Ceremonies Enrico Dante

Offering Mass in a Roman chasuble, accompanied by Msgr Dante

Aldo Moro and his family visit with Paul VI (1964)

Paul VI on pilgrimage in the Holy Land (January 1964)

At the River Jordan (1964)

Offering Mass in the Holy Land (1964)

Patriarch Athenagoras I of Constantinople and Paul VI in the Holy Land (1964)

Mass in Italian (except the Canon) and versus populum: Rome, March 7, 1965

Addressing the United Nations in New York: October 4, 1965

At the closing of the Second Vatican Council: December 8, 1965

Anglican Archbishop of Canterbury Michael Ramsey
and Paul VI embrace in Rome (1966)

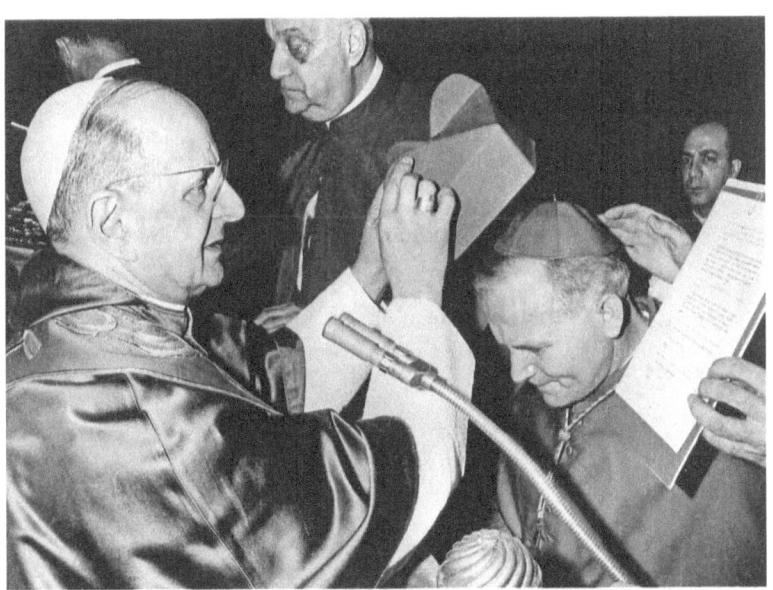

Karol Wojtyła's elevation to the cardinalate (1967)

The pope's pilgrimage to Fatima for the fiftieth
anniversary of the apparitions: May 13, 1967

In the year of Humanae Vitae (1968)

The pope with his close friend Jean Guitton

Jacques Maritain, confidant and ghostwriter for Paul VI

Montini's long-time spiritual director Giulio Bevilacqua

In Bogotá, Colombia (1968)

At the World Council of Churches headquarters in Geneva (1969)

Greeting Milton Obote, president of Uganda, in the first-ever papal trip to Africa (1969)

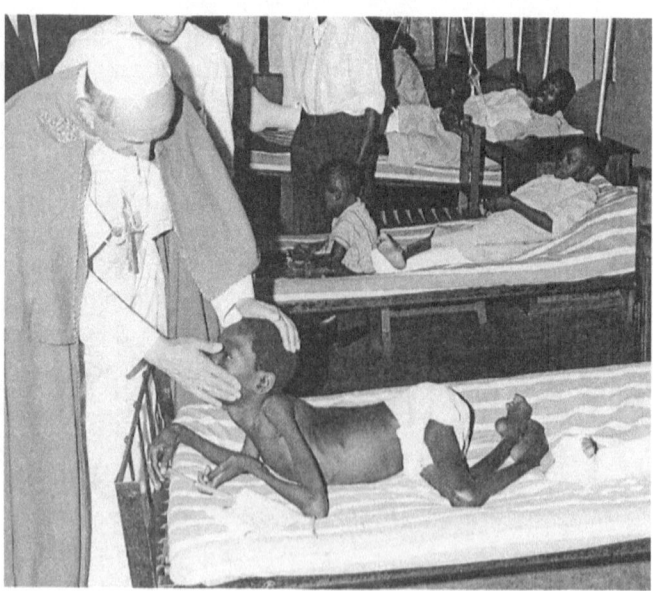

During the visit to Uganda (1969)

Greeting workers (exact date unknown)

With President Nixon in Rome: September 29, 1970

With Annibale Bugnini, Secretary of the Consilium for liturgical reform

Cardinal Léon-Joseph Suenens, a major leader of the "progressives"

Archbishop Marcel Lefebvre at a traditional Latin Mass

Joseph Ratzinger's elevation to the cardinalate (1977)

Another photo with Joseph Ratzinger

Meeting with Bishop Oscar Romero, about six weeks before the pope's death (1978)

One of some twenty-five portraits painted by Dina Bellotti (1911–2003)

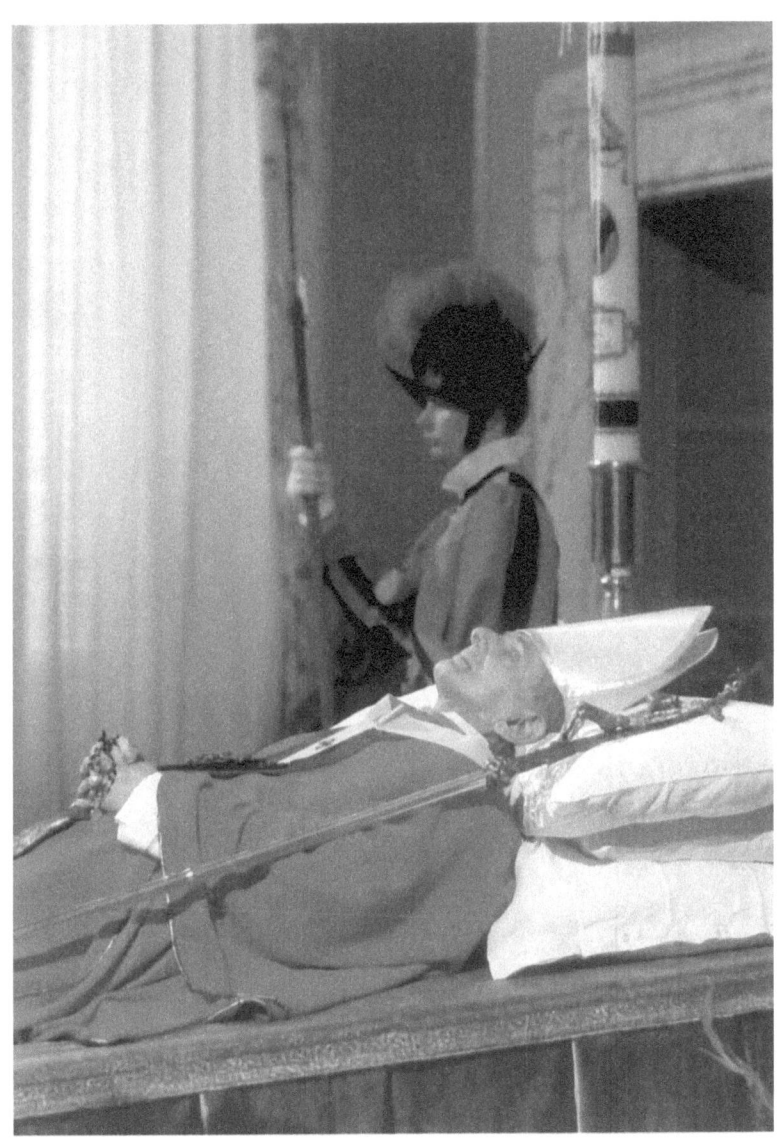
The body of Paul VI lying in state

7
The Pope of the Council

AFTER THE FIRST SESSION OF THE COUNCIL, the bishops returned to their dioceses. The pope invited them to study the distributed schemas, and those that would be sent to them, before the opening of the next session, in September 1963. Each bishop returned home profoundly marked by the experience: a worldwide assembly of bishops frankly discussing essential religious subjects. So much freedom, boldness, and controversy was terrifying to some, but thrilling to others. After three months of absence, they found that the faithful and clergy had also closely followed the events, thanks to the media which played an essential role in publicizing the themes and discussions of the Council. Impatient, unsettled, or satisfied with the upheavals they foresaw, they began to speak out, just as the spirit of the Council encouraged them to do. Some bishops began to warn against a revolutionary interpretation of the Council, which was spreading to include many members of the clergy. For this reason, Cardinal Montini addressed a sharply worded letter to his priests and, beyond them, to the faithful, on Palm Sunday 1963. "Our reforms," explained the archbishop of Milan,

> ought to consist less in an indulgent attitude towards our century's lifestyle, as if we ought to become tasteless salt deprived of burning yet salvific effects: vigorous affirmations of our original and autonomous life, such as it flows from the Gospel and from the concrete interpretation that we give the ascetic experience and law of the Church. To speak, for example, of the sunset of the "Constantinian age," of "ideological pluralism," or to oppose the "spiritual" Church to a "juridical" Church is all extremely dangerous, because all this merely authorizes vague and imprecise concepts, while flattering subversive impulses and fueling false hopes. Accusing the exercise of pastoral authority of "paternalism," demanding a freedom of thought and conduct that is stripped of prejudices..., all that is not constructive and misleads spirits that are hungry for sincerity and religious fecundity.

PAUL VI: THE DIVIDED POPE

Cardinal Montini, in the months following the first session of the Council, multiplied this sort of warning in his discourses. The same concern not to stand by and watch while the faithful strayed down dangerous paths made him ban a lecture by Jean-Marie Domenach at this time.[1] Then serving as director of the review *Esprit*, he had been invited by the Catholic University of Milan to give a lecture ("It was on a general subject and had no polemical character"). Cardinal Montini asked the university authorities to cancel this invitation. No doubt he acted not out of personal animosity towards Domenach but out of fear that existentialism would favor atheism too much.

On another subject, ecumenism, he was equally cautious. During the first session of the Council, he made the acquaintance of one of the observers, the Protestant theologian Cullmann.[2] He had numerous conversations with him; a friendship developed between the two men that would continue after the archbishop of Milan became pope. Having returned to his diocese, Cardinal Montini continued to correspond with Cullman, since the unity of Christians was so close to his heart. But he showed both affectionate haste and yet prudence when he spoke of this subject to his faithful. During the annual Week of Prayer for Christian Unity,[3] he gave a speech demonstrating this balance between the desire for reuniting non-Catholic communities to the Church and the necessity of preserving the integrity of the Faith: he said that Catholics must make

> every effort to straighten the way to the union of Christians in the one Church: to study, to forget the offenses of the past, to widen "the place for charity," to sacrifice the things that can be sacrificed, to wait with patience, to encourage efforts, etc. Do we not know that to welcome brothers we must go to meet them with affectionate and humble haste, and with that great and unbreakable truth of the Faith which saves, not with equivocal irenicism, but with the fullness of faith and obedience?

---

1 Letter of J.-M. Domenach to the author, January 13, 1992. Jean-Marie Domenach (1922–1997) was a French intellectual and writer, known for his left-wing Catholic views.

2 Oscar Cullmann (1902–1999) was a Lutheran theologian. Aside from his ecumenism, he is known for his work in eschatology and Christology.

3 The Week of Prayer for Christian Unity is an octave celebrated from January 18, the old Feast of the Chair of Saint Peter in Rome, until January 25, the Feast of the Conversion of Saint Paul. Catholics participated (and some still do) by celebrating during the octave the votive Mass for the end of schism.

Should we interpret all of the archbishop of Milan's warnings, during the first months of 1963, as a sort of strategic retreat before the coming conclave which everyone knew was looming, so that he would not appear too liberal, and scare off the moderate cardinals who would be his future electors? These political calculations, which are not to be dismissed, do not take into account the future pope's characteristic prudence. Audacity and prudence together, "prophetic gestures" towards non-Catholic religious leaders alternating with more reserved texts, were typical. In areas other than ecumenism, the same ambivalence could be observed.

VOCABOR PAULUS

Everyone knew that John XXIII had been very ill for some months. In November 1962 his health deteriorated. Since April 1963, according to the director of the Vatican Press Office, preparations were underway to announce his death to the press and inform them of the subsequent conclave.[4] In this same month, he promulgated his last great encyclical, *Pacem in Terris*, in which he explained his conception of international peace. This naturally followed his 1961 encyclical on social peace, *Mater et Magistra*. The pope also evoked, according to an expression that has become famous, "the signs of the times," boldly predicting a better future for mankind. Among these he did not hesitate to place the Universal Declaration of the Rights of Man of the UN, which he considered "as a step towards the establishment of a juridical-political organization of the world community."

His public appearances made his decline obvious. When, on May 31, a sudden collapse in the pope's health was announced, Cardinal Montini rushed to Rome to see the dying man one last time. John XXIII was sedated, and on a ventilator. When the worst seemed to have past, the cardinal returned to Milan. According to his secretary, on his deathbed John XXIII announced the name of his successor: "My successor, in my opinion, will be Cardinal Montini. It is for him that the votes of the Sacred College should be cast."[5]

On June 3 John XXIII died. Three days later, in the funeral oration he pronounced at the Duomo, Cardinal Montini gave an account of the completed pontificate which appeared to many as a program of what was about to begin: "It is no longer behind, it is no longer to him that we

---

4 Wiltgen, *The Inside Story*, 70.
5 Cited by P. Dreyfus, *Jean XXIII*, 401.

now look, rather it is to the horizon that he opened for the progress of the Church and of history. His tomb cannot enclose his legacy, nor death smother his spirit." This legacy is the "internal ecumenism" through collegiality that ought to take place ("collaboration suitable to the episcopal body, not exercising governance, which remains certainly personal and unique, but sharing the responsibility for the whole Church"), and a "double external ecumenism": reunion of the "so many factions of separated Christians" into the Church and the diffusion "of peace among peoples and social classes, of civil peace over the whole world."

Everyone understood that Cardinal Montini was ready to carry on this legacy and his name always appeared high on the lists of *papabili* that began to be published in Italy and abroad. But his name was far from enjoying unanimous approval. Among those terrified by the first months of the Council, worried by the evolution of minds even within the Church, there was a search for a cardinal who could be firm and authoritatively reaffirm the traditional doctrine; thus, as in 1958, the name of Cardinal Siri made the list of favorites. In the progressive ranks, Cardinal Lercaro also represented a serious rival for the archbishop of Milan.

On June 16, on the eve of his departure for the conclave, Cardinal Montini wrote to his old master Bevilacqua: the Church now needs an "effective and wise" pope; he also added: "Certainly not myself, as the habit of designating prefabricated popes could insinuate."[6] These declarations, and others like it, should deceive nobody. According to Jean Guitton, from the age of fifteen or twenty, Montini had known that one day he would become pope; as time went on and the possibility became closer, he was divided between two sentiments: humility, which caused him to reject the idea, and ambition, which on the contrary made him wish for the office.[7]

It cannot be said that he did all he could to refuse the papacy. On the contrary, if he did not necessarily launch an electoral campaign, it at least appears that several discreet meetings took place before the opening of the conclave so that bargains could be discussed. On the afternoon of June 16, Cardinal Montini left Milan and went to Rome. He lodged at first with the Sisters of the Child Mary, whose protector he was; then, the next day, to avoid the pre-conclave turmoil, he inconspicuously retreated to Castel Gandolfo, at the home of his friend

---

6   Letter of June 16, 1963 published in *Notiziario* 3 (May 1981): 25.
7   Guitton, interview.

The Pope of the Council

Bonomelli, the Director of the Pontifical Villas, who would recall: "I took my meals with him. He had then a very great mastery of himself. He was his usual self."[8]

Bonomelli's testimony does not tell the whole story. Cardinal Montini received a visit from Cardinal Spellman, archbishop of New York, an old friend. His American journey in 1960 had allowed him to become better acquainted with the five American and two Canadian cardinals; the North American votes were his. Another meeting took place on June 17, at the convent of the Capuchins of Frascati, not far from Castel Gandolfo. Besides Cardinal Montini, the heads of five episcopal conferences were there: Cardinal Liénart for France, Frings for Germany, Suenens for Belgium, König for Austria, and Alfrink[9] for Holland.

A more mysterious meeting, one in which the interested party does not seem to have participated, was held at Grottaferrata, in a villa belonging to a business lawyer by the name of Umberto Ortolani,[10] who had been closely tied to Cardinal Lercaro.[11] An agreement among the cardinals (whose names are unknown) is supposed to have been made on Montini's candidacy.

On June 18, Cardinal Montini was back in Rome. He went to the Benedictine Abbey of Saint Priscilla and celebrated Mass there. The abbey's Mass registers attest that Cardinal Lercaro was also in residence. It is possible that Cardinal Montini informed his potential rival of the support he had from the Americans, and from some European cardinals as well.

On the afternoon of June 19, the cardinals entered the conclave. With eighty cardinals present, it was the largest conclave in history. Fifty-four votes were needed to be elected. The votes began the next day. Six ballots were needed to elect Cardinal Montini (not four or five,

---

8 Cited by Guitton, *Journal*, 548.
9 Card. Jan Alfrink (1900–1987) was a Dutch cardinal and archbishop of Utrecht (1955–1975). During this time, he became the apostolic vicar of the Catholic military vicariate of the Netherlands (1957). He was also one of the cardinal electors that elected Pope Paul VI (1963) and they worked out disputes between the Dutch Church and the Vatican.
10 Umberto Ortolani (1913–2002) was an Italian businessman and banker who was known for his interest in the Vatican's Institute for Works of Religion. Pope Paul VI awarded him the title of papal chamberlain, but Pope John Paul II revoked this in 1983.
11 Lai, *Les Secrets du Vatican*, 127, from a speech given by G. Andreotti; and M. Short, *Inside the Brotherhood*, 163. Ortolani would be named "Gentleman of His Holiness" a month after the election of Paul VI.

as has been claimed). Although all the French and American cardinals voted for him on the first ballot, as did some of the European cardinals, votes were also dispersed between Siri, Lercaro, and Antoniutti[12] (Ottaviani's candidate), and some were cast for non-Italian cardinals (Suenens, Agagianian). This diversity demonstrates the impossibility of manipulating a conclave of eighty cardinals like a drill team; the "grand electors" did not suffice by themselves to orient the body of votes. A papal election is not merely political; when a large number of votes fall on a candidate, the other cardinals may see in this a demonstration by the Holy Spirit, making them see it as their duty, for the good of the Church, to withdraw. Cardinal Siri finally reasoned thus, and told others to vote for Montini. On the second day of the conclave, June 21, late in the morning, he was elected with sixty votes. The cardinals had made a choice that went beyond his person; it was the choice of a spirit. The choice for Montini had been in a great part determined by

> the underlying sentiment that the Church was likely headed towards a crisis which the Council had created, so that it needed a regulator with whom all sides could associate in order to broker a resolution. On this view, the career of G. B. Montini doubtless played a key role: despite having worked in the Curia, he did not represent the Roman Curia in the politicized sense of the term; he was close to Pius XII, who distanced himself from him; and he was recognized by John XXIII, who did not hide the fact that he considered him a likely successor. G. B. Montini incarnated a synthesis of the times past.... The conclave was arguably looking for a regulator who was also an alchemist.[13]

To the Dean of the College of Cardinals, who asked him whether he accepted his election to the Throne of St Peter, Cardinal Montini responded with his episcopal motto: *Accepto in nomine Domini* (I accept in the name of the Lord); to the other ritual question on the name he had chosen, he responded: *Vocabor Paulus* [I will be called Paul].

There was no surprise when Cardinal Ottaviani announced the election to the crowd gathered in Saint Peter's square about midday. But his choice of name was surprising: Paul VI. The last pope to have borne this name was from the illustrious Borghese family, in the early

---

12   Cardinal Ildebrando Antoniutti (1898–1974), Italian nuncio to Spain (1953–1962), created cardinal in 1963, Prefect of the Congregation of Religious (1963–1973).
13   P. Levillain, "Le pontificat de Paul VI," in *Paul VI et la modernité dans l'Église* (Rome: École Française de Rome, 1984), XVIII.

seventeenth century. This Paul V[14] had applied the decisions of the Council of Trent,[15] and canonized Saint Charles Borromeo; under his pontificate the first condemnation of Galileo also took place. But it was rather in reference to Saint Paul that the new sovereign pontiff had chosen his name — Saint Paul, whose writings he had studied at length during his time at FUCI, the "Apostle to the Gentiles" who had carried the Gospel to the Greeks and Romans. One of his friends noted at the time in his journal: "Very deft choice of name: there could not be two 'Pope Johns.' To re-use the name of Pius would have been interpreted as indicating a return to Pius XII, in reaction against John XXIII. 'Paul' was without danger."[16]

Soon the new pope came to the loggia of the basilica to give his first *Urbi et Orbi* benediction, to the Eternal City and to the world, but without speaking. Then he returned among the cardinals until the next day; a banquet was held. In a spirit of humility, it is said, he wanted to take his place among them, as during the conclave. The next day he took possession of the papal apartments, on the third and fourth floors of the Apostolic Palace: on the fourth, the private apartment included a bedroom, an office (with, next door, a small office for his secretary), a chapel, and a dining room; between the third and fourth floors, there was a library where Paul VI installed his thousands of books and a large armoire filled with family photos and letters; on the third floor was the official apartment which included an office and reception rooms. In this solemn setting Paul VI's daily life would continue until his death. Out of concern for his personal comfort and his fondness for modern art, which he shared with his faithful personal secretary, Fr Macchi, he

---

14 Pope Paul V (1550–1621) was born Camillo Borghese in Rome. He was the head of the Catholic Church and ruler of the Papal States from 1605 to 1621. He protected Galileo from persecution by instructing Cardinal Bellarmine to provide him with a certificate that allowed him to continue his studies. He used this certificate in his defense in 1633.

15 The Council of Trent (1545–1563), the nineteenth ecumenical council and one of the most important in the history of the Church, was called in response to the Protestant Revolt. This council held twenty-five sessions which covered almost all major doctrines of the faith, with seventeen doctrinal decrees; it formally defined the canon of Sacred Scripture. The effects of the Council were widespread, affecting Catholic life and practice from top to bottom. It set in motion diverse reforms such as the unification of the liturgy with careful corrections to all liturgical books, the publication of a universal catechism, a standardized text of the Sacred Scriptures, and the establishment of regional seminaries.

16 Card. Jacques Martin, extract of "Journal" published in *L'Osservatore Romano* (French edition), May 14, 1991.

commissioned numerous works in the following months, calling mostly upon decorators and artists from Milan. In the apartments the heavy garnet-colored tapestries and the gilded furniture were replaced by light toned fabrics and furniture in a modern design. Green plants and works of contemporary art combined to give a less solemn touch to the high rooms. The papal chapel was also entirely renovated: the marble floor, a glass ceiling, stained-glass windows, the way of the cross, even the tabernacle; all was redone in a modern style that resolutely broke with the anterior style.

Paul VI, who had never known poverty in his life, enjoyed a degree of comfort. To avoid descending to the Vatican gardens and disturbing the papal guards in charge of surveillance, he had a terrace installed on the roof of the Apostolic Palace for his daily walk, and a small elevator for direct access from his apartment. Another small act of papal sovereignty: on his first evening in the pontifical apartments, he was annoyed by the murmur of fountains in Saint Peter's Square, and asked for them to be stopped. As long as he was pope, they were turned off nightly at eleven o'clock, and restarted in the morning.

The day after his election, the new pope began the first in-depth meetings with the cardinals, who were henceforth his subordinates as well as his collaborators. The night before, Paul VI had indicated to his old friend Cicognani that he would keep him in post as Secretary of State. The Substitute Dell'Acqua was also maintained in his position. The new sovereign pontiff did not intend to cause any ruptures. In the same spirit, the next day he successively received in audience two tradition-minded cardinals, Ottaviani and Siri. Each, at the conclave, had attempted to block his election, and each was in a position to become an obstacle to the policies that the new sovereign pontiff was going to enact: Ottaviani, who, as Secretary of the Congregation of the Holy Office, had the right to an audience with the pope, at least three times per month, and was also President of the Doctrinal Commission of the Council; Siri, archbishop of Genoa, and President of the Italian Episcopal Conference. Both offered to resign from their duties; Paul VI refused and confirmed them in their respective functions.[17] The two cardinals, during the entire pontificate, neglected no opportunity to make their opposition known to the pope about various texts and decisions, but also remained obedient servants.

---

17 Resignation of Ottaviani evoked by E. Cavaterra, *Il prefetto del Sant'Offizio*, 73; that of Siri by Lai, *Les Secrets du Vatican*, 135–36.

June 22 was also the day when the new sovereign pontiff addressed the world for the first time. The cardinals reunited around him in the Sistine Chapel; his speech was broadcast by Vatican radio and republished by newspapers throughout the world. This was a much-anticipated speech, since there was a rumor that some in the Curia and many Italian bishops did not want the Council to be resumed. Paul VI reassured those who feared such a cessation: "The preeminent part of Our pontificate will be occupied by the continuation of the Second Vatican Ecumenical Council, towards which the eyes of all men of goodwill are turned." He also clearly affirmed the objective of working for "peace among peoples" and for the unity of Christians. To reassure the adversaries of such a direction, the pope affirmed, in a traditional way, that this peace "is not only the absence of warring rivalries or armed factions, but a reflection of the order willed by God, Creator and Redeemer"; the unity of Christians will be made "in Rome, in the paternal home which gives honor and exalts with a new splendor the treasures of their history, their cultural patrimony, and their spiritual heritage."

The guarantees given to conservatives, and the reassuring declarations for both sides, were accompanied by consultations that better indicated what was going to be this papacy's orientation from the beginning. As mentioned above, on June 22, Cardinals Siri and Ottaviani were received and confirmed in their posts. Paul VI, through the intermediary of his private theologian, Carlo Colombo, asked Father Congar for his impression on the evolution of the conciliar work. The next day, he gave a lengthy audience to Cardinal Suenens, the man of the "plan" which had upturned the Council. Paul VI shared with the Belgian cardinal his intention to give a "sure direction" to the Council and to break off the immobility and the disorder of the first session. Remarkably, he wished to name the cardinal as his personal representative (with the title of "legate") to the Council.[18] Other reforms were also mentioned, especially that which would oblige the bishops and cardinals to leave their positions at seventy-five years of age. Paul VI remarked that this would be very useful for his envisioned renewal of the Curia.[19] The reform would soon be announced.

On Sunday, June 30, the solemn coronation ceremony took place. Because of unprecedented crowds, for the first time in the history of

---

18 M. Maccarrone, "Paolo VI e il Concilio: Testimonianze," Rivista di Storia della Chiesa in Italia (January-June 1989): 108.
19 Cardinal Suenens, Souvenirs et Espérances, 121.

papal coronations in Rome, the ceremony took place entirely outside of Saint Peter's Basilica. About one hundred countries were represented, most by their sovereign or head-of-state. It was a long and solemn ceremony during which the pope was carried on the *sedia gestatoria*. The epistle and the Gospel were sung in Latin then in Greek, a sign of unity. The pope spoke in nine languages over the course of his address, alternating between strong words ("We will defend the Holy Church against the errors of doctrine and practice which come as much from inside as from outside the Church, and threaten her integrity and hide her beauty") and optimistic visions (the modern world "also works through grace and the spirit"). Then came the coronation properly speaking. Cardinal Ottaviani placed on the head of the sovereign pontiff a tiara that had been designed according to his instructions: tapered and not heavily ornate like that of his predecessors. In *Témoignage chrétien*, Father Sainsaulieu described it thus, drawing out all its significance: "A tiara that is ancient, a tiara that is monastic, the tiara of Benedictine pope-reformers. A tiara from before the time of the three crowns, a lightweight tiara, in the shape of a missile, a tiara of white metal made by Fiat and almost smooth. Lastly, a tiara of the twentieth century, which drives its nail into the *Syllabus*."[20]

This tiara, a bit richer than this commentator said, was ornamented with fleur-de-lys at its base and set with gems. Paul VI was soon to abandon it definitively in one of those spectacular "gestures" that would punctuate the whole of his pontificate.[21]

RESUMPTION OF THE COUNCIL

Three days before the coronation, the Secretary of State announced that the date for the reopening of the Council was set for September 29. To prepare for this second session, Paul VI had the coordinating commission assemble twice during the summer, on July 3 and August 31. As he had indicated to Cardinal Suenens, he wanted to give a new cohesion to the Council to advance his desired reforms rapidly. On the other hand, he wished, as much as possible, to unify the two tendencies that had been seen at the first session: the "majority" (reformist or revolutionary) and the "minority" (traditional).

---

20 A reference to the *Syllabus of Errors* promulgated by Pope Pius IX on December 8, 1864, which condemned eighty heretical propositions, including rationalism, socialism, communism, and liberalism.
21 Similarly, he renounced the grand, ornate *ferula* of his predecessors for a crozier-cross made by the sculptor Scorzelli, from whom he would commission other such items.

On July 13, he held his first general audience. These audiences would remain important throughout his papacy, and as he gradually ceased publishing encyclicals, his speeches to the faithful and to pilgrims featured the most personal expression of his thought, not the large directive documents, which were more technical and administrative and, although covered by his authority, were the work of the congregations. These audiences took place each Wednesday, except on feast days, or when there was some serious impediment (a voyage, illness, or his Lenten retreat). To receive increasing numbers of the faithful on Wednesdays, the construction of an audience hall behind the Holy Office, to the left of Bernini's colonnade, was planned in 1964. In the name of the pope, Father Macchi closely supervised construction: the modern-styled trapezoidal building was inaugurated in 1971 and can welcome up to twelve thousand people standing.

Paul VI spent the month of August at the pontifical residence in Castel Gandolfo, discreetly receiving visitors (among whom was Cardinal Siri). A very personal text, written during this stay, allows a glimpse of his spiritual attitude a few weeks after his election as pope. He had not lost any of his sensitive and emotional temperament: "Everybody is my neighbor," he wrote. "What goodness is necessary! Every meeting should provoke a demonstration [of it]. Sympathy for all, love of the world, *dilexit mundum*. Prayers and universal love. Constant, vigilant initiative for the good of the other: papal policy." But he was also keenly aware of the enormous responsibilities now weighing on him, and the immense solitude in which that placed him; from now on, he would be accountable to God alone:

> I must recognize that both my position and my task are mine alone, characterizing me, rendering me inexorably responsible before God, before the Church, before humanity. The position is unique. This is to say that it places me in an extreme solitude.... As Jesus was alone on the Cross.... I and God. The conversation with God becomes full and immeasurable.[22]

This conversation with God could not subtract from his duties as head of the Church. This month of August was taken up with important modifications of the rules and the organizational structure of the Council that was soon to reopen. To allow the work to continue at a more rapid rhythm, and to enhance control of the flow of meetings, it

---

22 Cited by P. Macchi in *Notiziario* 1 (Christmas 1979): 51 & 53.

was decided that a refusal or postponement of the schemas could take place with a simple majority and no longer a two-thirds majority, which was still required for the approbation of a text. The Council Presidency was enlarged to twelve members, with three new members: Cardinals Meyer, Siri, and Wyszynski. The nomination of a conservative cardinal, and another who had known the Communist gulags, was reassuring to some, until it was realized that these nominations were purely formal, or at least were merely honorific. Four *moderatores* (moderators or, more precisely, governors) were named to direct the work of the general congregations: Cardinals Döpfner, Lercaro, Suenens, and Agagianian. The first three were prominent leaders of reformism. The Council Presidency seemed, for all intents and purposes, useless. These moderators, officially above the fray, were in fact going to control proceedings tightly. It is to be noted that, in this system, the pope retained his possibility of intervention in the debates, notably through the intermediary of the Council's General Secretary, Felici.

Lastly, on September 21, a week prior to the reopening of the work of the Council, Paul VI addressed the Roman Curia in an important speech. He praised the work of the heads of congregations who were present, then obliquely announced the creation of a council of bishops from all over the world that would be involved "in the responsibilities of Church government"; he also announced his project of reforming the Curia. These two projects would come to fruition four years later.

On September 29 the second session of the Council opened. Over the preceding weeks, Cardinal König and the envoys of the Secretariat of State had taken steps behind the scenes to convince Communist governments to allow more Catholic bishops to come; their efforts bore little fruit. No bishops from North Korea, China, North Vietnam, Poland, or the Baltic States were present; the other bishops from Marxist countries showed up in restricted numbers. Non-Catholic observers, on the other hand, were more numerous than in 1962. The Orthodox patriarchates, despite efforts by Athenagoras I of Constantinople,[23] had again refused to send representatives (the Russian Orthodox church was an exception). As if to compensate for this absence, on November 20 Paul VI wrote to Patriarch Athenagoras. It was the first direct contact at the highest level between Orthodox Christians and Catholics for centuries. Paul VI said that he was "anxious about all things concerning

---

23   Athenagoras I (born Aristocles Matthew Spyrou, 1886–1972) was the Greek Orthodox Patriarch of Constantinople from 1948 to 1972.

the union of Christians and all that can contribute to reestablishing concord among them all."

Lay Catholics were also more numerous. This time, Jean Guitton was not alone at the general congregations: twelve other laymen from around the world (mainly directors of international Catholic organizations) were present, with the title of "auditors." The description was only partly accurate: although the auditors did not take the floor during general congregations (with a few exceptions), several of them participated actively in the work of conciliar commissions, and helped write some of the texts. Further, after an intervention on the part of the pope, the press became better informed of developments through press conferences organized each day. A journalist, Fr Wenger, editor-in-chief of *La Croix*, who had connections with Msgr Villot, was even able to assist at all the sessions.[24]

In his discourse for the opening of the second session, Paul emphasized the ecumenical orientation that the Council ought to take. As was his custom, he proceeded with a double affirmation: the necessity of guarding the integrity of the Catholic Faith, all the while recognizing the spiritual riches that the "separated brethren" had preserved. Another declaration of the pope equally pleased the observers: the Church should ask pardon for the offenses that she committed in the past and she is ready to pardon those that she has suffered. This theme of reciprocal pardon would become one of the leitmotifs of Paul VI's ecumenical strategy.

The second session was devoted to the examination of several schemas, all of which would undergo important modifications and be returned to the commissions to be rewritten.

The schema on the Church came first. The question of collegiality was immediately the focus of debate. Was the supreme government of the Church to be exercised by the pope alone or should the bishops, successors of the Apostles, be considered as forming a college which had the right to govern continuously the whole Church with the pope? Two conceptions clashed: that of a personal-monarchic government of the Church and that of a collegial, so to speak aristocratic, government.

---

24 Fr Antoine Wenger (1919–2009) was a French priest of the Augustinians of the Assumption. He directed *La Croix* from 1957 to 1969. He was also a Patristics scholar who taught at the Institut Catholique. Cardinal Jean-Marie Villot (1905–1979) served as one of the undersecretaries at the Council, as archbishop of Lyon (1965–1967), as Prefect of the Congregation of the Council (i.e., of the Clergy, 1967–1969), as Secretary of State (1969–1979), and as President of the Pontifical Council *Cor Unum* (1971–1978). He was created cardinal in 1965.

On this question, several bishops, notably Archbishop De Proença Sigaud, Archbishop Lefebvre, and Bishop Luigi Carli[25] defended the traditional doctrine of papal primacy and the subordinated character of episcopal power. To orient the debates, Cardinal Suenens announced, on October 15, that a text would be distributed the next day on these questions, and also on the question of the permanent diaconate. The procedure was highly unusual: the General Secretary of the Council had not even been informed in advance. Cardinal Suenens appears to have acted with the permission of Paul VI, but without having previously submitted the text to be distributed. When the pope heard about it, he judged the definition of collegiality that it gave to be too bold. He asked that this text not be distributed to the Council Fathers. Three thousand copies had already been printed; he had them burned. Despite this, the text became known, because a moderator passed it to a newspaper, *L'Avvenire d'Italia*, for publication. During a meeting organized a few days later by the pope, a new text was drafted in the form of a questionnaire this time.[26] These were submitted to the vote of the Council Fathers as the starting point of new discussions, the two questions bearing on collegiality receiving several hundred negative votes. A majority voted in favor of the following formulation: the college of bishops "enjoys full and sovereign authority over the whole Church, together with its head the Roman Pontiff and never without this head." The simple fact of recognizing the bishops' authority over the whole Church, even with strict restrictions, appeared a victory for the partisans of collegiality. The day after the vote, Fr Congar wrote: "The Church has made, peacefully, its October Revolution."[27] Nevertheless, the debate cropped up again a short time later and would not end until two years later, during the fourth session, after another personal intervention of the pope. But already the partisans of collegiality had won this round.

Another debate, in which the pope was indirectly implicated, involved the Virgin Mary. A schema had been prepared on the subject. When it

---

25   Archbishop Geraldo de Proença Sigaud (1909–1999) was a Brazilian prelate who served as the archbishop of both Jacarezinho (1947–1960) and Diamantina (1960–1980). He orchestrated and delivered a petition signed by 213 Fathers that demanded the condemnation of Communism, Marxism, and socialism. Archbishop Luigi Carli (1914–1986) was ordained a priest in 1937, consecrated bishop of Segni in 1957, and finally served as archbishop of Gaeta from 1973 until his death. He was part of the steering committee of the Coetus Internationalis Patrum which was an influential minority group of conservatives at the Second Vatican Council.
26   Maccarone, "Paolo VI e il Concilio," 108.
27   Republished in Yves Congar, *Le Concile au jour le jour: Deuxième session*, 115.

was presented in assembly, several voices were raised (sometimes in the name of an entire episcopacy, especially Germany) to demand that the Virgin Mary not be made the object of an isolated conciliar text but be included in a vaster schema, that on the Church.

According to Fr Congar, the concern was "to avoid any increase in a separate Mariology"; in other words, they did not want a dedicated schema lest new titles be attributed to the Virgin Mary, especially those of "Mediatrix of All Graces" and "Co-Redemptrix." Otherwise, the Protestants would consider such a separated text as a supplementary proof of Catholic "Mariolatry." Paul VI sided with this concern. As mentioned above, when he was still a cardinal, he had spoken against attributing new titles to the Virgin Mary. Otherwise, a few days before the vote on whether or not to include the text, in a ceremony at the Basilica of Saint Mary Major, the pope expressed his desire for the Church to recognize the Virgin "as its Mother, as its Daughter, as its Sister chosen from amongst all others." This amounted to standing against an isolated schema. The day of the vote, despite the opposition of numerous bishops, notably the Spanish bishops, a majority voted that the Virgin Mary be relegated to the final chapter of the schema on the Church.

The question of collegiality was raised again during discussions on the schema concerning bishops and the government of dioceses. Cardinals Ottaviani and Browne[28] took a resolute stand against it. The organization and power of the episcopal conferences were also discussed. Some expressed the fear that they would endanger the individual authority of bishops; others on the contrary thought that on the national level the exercise of power could no longer be solitary but must be collegial. Finally, the pope's suggestion to the Curia a few months before to "associate the episcopacy in the responsibility and the government of the Church" was mentioned. Some suggested that this take the form of a "permanent synod" of bishops from around the world who would assist the pope with governing. To this end, a petition was circulated asking the pope to create a "council of bishops." One hundred and fifty signatures were collected. But the pope did not intend to submit to this pressure. He did not want the Council to determine the organization of such an important institution; also, he would soon announce that he had entrusted the study of this project to a specialized commission.

---

28   Card. Michael Browne (1887–1971) was an Irish priest of the Dominican Order. He was ordained in 1910 and was created cardinal in 1962 by John XXIII. He was a conservative who expressed opposition to reformatory schemes when he attended the Second Vatican Council (1962–1965).

At this session a long schema on ecumenism was presented containing, curiously, three chapters on relations with the "separated brethren," but also a chapter on religious liberty and another chapter on the Jews. These were grouped together in a single text because all of them were the concern of the Secretariat for Unity, directed by Cardinal Bea. But it was decided that the three subjects would be studied separately. The text on the Jews originated with the historian Jules Isaac,[29] who approached John XXIII in June 1960. He had asked the pope for "the modification of Christian teaching concerning the Jews,"[30] so that the Jews would no longer be considered responsible for the death of Christ, or spoken of as being culpable of "deicide." John XXIII had delegated the study of this question to Cardinal Bea.

Only during the following sessions would these texts on the Jews, religious liberty, and ecumenism develop their final form, and only after considerable debate.

It should also be mentioned that during the last days of November a petition was issued by two Brazilian bishops, Msgr De Proença Sigaud and Msgr De Castro Mayer,[31] asking that the question of Socialism and Communism be included in the agenda of the next session. The petition was signed by more than two hundred Council Fathers from forty-six nations, and was delivered to the Secretary of State so that it would be communicated to the pope. Other similar attempts at intervention would be made, without success as we shall see.

On December 3, at the request of Paul VI, two of his friends, the lay auditors Vittorino Veronese and Jean Guitton, were allowed to speak before the Council on the role of the laity and ecumenism respectively. The second session would soon draw to a close. Only two schemas had been adopted in their entirety, after having undergone redrafting. On December 4, Paul VI solemnly promulgated them: one, today all but forgotten, was in the form of a decree (*Inter Mirifica*, on the concerns and problems of social communications); the other, which would be applied in very diverse and unexpected ways, was on the liturgy (the Constitution *Sacrosanctum Concilium*).

---

29 Jules Isaac (1877–1963) was a French Jewish historian who sought to show that the roots of anti-Semitism were in the supposed anti-Jewish bias in the Gospels and Christian theology.
30 J. Isaac, interview in *L'Arche* 69 (October 1962).
31 Bishop Antonio de Castro Mayer (1904–1991), a Brazilian, was bishop of Campos until his resignation (1949–1981). He was excommunicated for co-consecrating, together with Archbishop Lefebvre and without papal mandate, four bishops for the Society of St. Pius X in 1988.

The same day the pope made a spectacular announcement: the following January, he would go to the Holy Land. The announcement stupefied the two thousand Council Fathers, who applauded enthusiastically.[32] For centuries no pope had left Italy, except when forced to do so by war or invasion. Paul VI declared that he wanted to go on pilgrimage to the places where Christ had lived. This journey would quickly become an "ecumenical voyage."

FIRST VOYAGE

The worldwide opinion of Paul VI as the travelling pope was largely forged by this pilgrimage to the Holy Land. It all originated in a letter addressed to the pope in August 1963 by a former worker-priest who had settled in Palestine, Fr Paul Gauthier.[33] He had founded the "Companions of Jesus the Carpenter" and established a religious community in Nazareth. He invited the pope to come to the Holy Land. The idea slowly grew in the mind of Paul VI. On September 21, in a personal note, he sketched what could be a pilgrimage to the Holy Land, with an air of "simplicity, of piety, of penitence, and of charity."[34] In October he asked his secretary, Macchi, and Msgr Jacques Martin,[35] from the Secretariat of State, an old friend, to travel there, in the greatest secrecy, to study the arrangements for the trip. As neither one spoke English, the indispensable language for negotiating with the Israeli and Jordanian authorities, the Substitute, Msgr Dell'Acqua, suggested that they include an American cleric who was working at the Secretariat of State, Paul Marcinkus.[36]

---

32 This spectacular announcement to the Council and the world eclipsed a major political event which took place on the same date: the creation, under the leadership of Aldo Moro, of a Christian Democrat coalition government, that is to say, one with the support of socialist deputies. In 1962, the Italian episcopal conference, presided over by Cardinal Siri, had warned against such a coalition if the platform was not defined. Moro had gone ahead, announcing an "opening to the left" without condition of the political program.
33 Paul Gauthier (1914–2002) was a French theologian and humanist known for his significant contributions to Liberation Theology. He travelled to Palestine (1957) to live with and help some of the poorer populations of the world.
34 Cited by Cardinal Martin, "Les voyages de Paul VI," in Paul et la modernité, 318.
35 Card. Jacques Martin (1908–1992) was a French cardinal who attended the Pontifical Gregorian University and received a doctorate in theology. He was ordained a priest in 1934 and was elevated to the cardinalate in 1988. He accompanied Pope Paul VI on his pilgrimage to the Holy Land in 1964.
36 Archbishop Paul Marcinkus (1922–2006) was an American archbishop and president of the Vatican Bank (1971–1989). While studying canon law at the Gregorian University, he became friends with Giovanni Battista Montini and completed special tasks for the Vatican. Notably, he foiled an assassination attempt by a deranged priest on Pope John Paul II in 1982.

This latter would soon play an important role in papal voyages and in the finances of the Vatican.[37]

Paul VI asked them to insist on the uniquely spiritual character of the voyage he wished to take in these two countries, which had been in conflict for the preceding twenty years. Jerusalem had been cut in two; no Arab country recognized the borders of the Hebrew State; the Holy See maintained diplomatic relations with neither Israel nor Jordan; the problem of Palestinian refugees had not been resolved: so many elements demanded caution and prudence. This voyage was not to allow for any political interpretation. Also, the pope kept himself from pronouncing the word "Israel" even once, or giving the title of "President" to the head of the Jewish State.

The pilgrimage, even before it began, would take on an additional character. When Patriarch Athenagoras, head of the Orthodox Church, learned through the press that Paul VI was going to the Holy Land, he decided that he wanted to meet him there. The Holy Land was the ideal place for a meeting on "neutral" ground, or rather on sacred ground. Since 1954, Athenagoras had been communicating messages of this sort, initially to Pius XII: "I want to meet the pope. I cannot now go to Rome as you understand, but I am ready to go to meet him in any other place." The patriarch communicated this message verbally through a theologian interested in ecumenical questions, Fr Duprey,[38] who made it known to the Substitute of the Secretary of State, Montini.[39] Ten years later, as pope, he received the same appeal, and decided to respond favorably, so he asked Fr Duprey to travel to Constantinople to regulate the protocols to be observed during meetings.

On Saturday, January 4, 1964, Paul VI left Rome for Jordan. He invited his master Fr Bevilacqua to participate in the trip. Cardinals Cicognani, Secretary of State, and Tisserant and Testa[40] accompanied him. Cardinal Bea was not able to participate in the voyage: the project of the declaration on the Jews that he had prepared for the Council had been strongly

---

37 Cardinal Martin, interview with the author, February 21, 1992.
38 Bishop Pierre Duprey (1922–2007) wanted to be a priest from a young age. He left Nazi-occupied France in 1940 for Tunisia and joined the White Fathers in 1942. He was ordained a priest in Carthage (1950) and received a doctorate in Eastern Christian studies from the Pontifical Oriental Institute in Rome. He became a bishop in 1990.
39 Msgr P. Duprey, letter to the author, March 16, 1992.
40 Card. Gustavo Testa (1886–1969) was an Italian curial prelate who had worked for the Secretariat of State in various roles (1920–1959), including Apostolic Delegate to Jerusalem, Palestine, Transjordan, and Cyprus (1948–1953).

contested in Arab countries. For the personal security of the pope, sixty agents of the SIFAR, the Italian intelligence agency, accompanied him.[41] As the plane carrying the pope and his entourage flew over foreign countries, the pope had messages sent to their heads of state by radio. The custom would be maintained in future travels. At the airport of Amman, the pope was received by the King of Jordan and the Oriental Catholic patriarchs. The voyage continued by car towards Jerusalem, with a stop by the shore of the Jordan, then at Bethany. In the Holy City, at the Damascus Gate, an enormous crowd awaited the pope. When the pontifical cortège arrived, the security service was overwhelmed. Paul VI was not able to give his planned speech, and walked through an indescribable crowd across the old city along the Via Dolorosa, following the Way of the Cross which led to the Church of the Holy Sepulcher, on Golgotha. This Way of the Cross could not be completed as planned: the pope was supposed to carry a wooden cross and stop at each station to pray, but was unable to do it. Pressed by the crowd, he stumbled on the stairs of the alleys. Arriving at the Church of the Holy Sepulcher, he celebrated Mass, "there where Christ consummated his sacrifice"; at this moment, he said in a speech after his return to Rome, he felt "gripped by emotion and tears." Then he went to the Apostolic Delegation where he received visits from the Greek Orthodox Patriarch of Jerusalem and the Armenian Orthodox Patriarch of Jerusalem. After this he went to the Church of Saint Anne to meet with six of the Oriental Catholic patriarchs. Finally, late in the evening, he went to Gethsemane, to the Basilica of the Agony, built on the site where Jesus had prayed before the Passion.

The next day, Sunday, January 5, he went into Israeli territory. At the border he was welcomed by President Shazar.[42] The pontifical cortège went through Galilee. The pope stopped at Nazareth (where he celebrated Mass in the Church of the Annunciation), at Cana, at Tabgha, at the shore of the Lake of Tiberias (where Peter cast his nets and Jesus walked on water), at Capharnaum, and at Mount Tabor. That evening, as he left Israeli territory to return to the Apostolic Delegation, he again greeted President Shazar and the Israeli authorities. In this short speech, he defended Pius XII, who was then the center of a controversy concerning his attitude during the war.[43] "Everyone knows," affirmed Paul VI,

---

41 Msgr Dell'Acqua, closely aligned to Father Morlion and his espionage activities, obtained this support from the SIFAR.
42 Zalman Shazar (1889–1974), a Hasidic Jew from modern-day Belarus, was president of Israel from 1963–1973.
43 A 1963 stage play, *The Deputy*, by Rolf Hochhuth, popularized the thesis of Pius

what he did for the defense and the safety of all those who were in trial, without any distinction. And yet, you know, there is desire to cast suspicions, and even accusations against the memory of this great pontiff. We are happy to have an occasion to affirm, on this day, and in this place, that there is nothing more unjust than these attacks on such a venerable memory.

At that same time, Cardinal Tisserant had gone to pray in the name of the pope at Yad Vashem, in the crypt built in memory of the Jewish victims of Nazism and had lit six candles in memory of the six million Jews who had disappeared during the war. On returning to the Apostolic Delegation, Paul VI received Patriarch Athenagoras. Having come from Constantinople, he was not able to represent all of the Orthodox; indeed, some other Orthodox patriarchs had been reticent, or even hostile, about the meeting. But everyone recognized him as the first of the patriarchs; thus, his meeting with the pope took on an exceptional importance. Paul VI multiplied his gestures of friendship towards Athenagoras, taking him by the hand, and demonstrating his great emotion. During their first meeting, they spoke in French, and decided to create a commission in which Catholic and Orthodox theologians would meet and discuss the questions which separated them. "We will have discussion, we will search for the truth," said Paul VI. At the end of the meeting the pope offered a golden chalice to Athenagoras, as a symbol of the communion which the pope wished to see soon reestablished between the two Churches. Then they recited together the *Pater*, one in Latin, the other in Greek. The extraordinary, highly emotional character of this meeting led some to believe that the union of Catholics and Orthodox was close at hand. The remainder of this pontificate made it clear that grave theological obstacles remained.

On Monday, January 6, Paul VI went to Bethlehem, celebrating Mass where Jesus was born. From there he gave an important message to the Church and the world, featuring themes that would be at the center of his fifteen-year-long papacy. He notably declared: "We must give the Church's life a new mode of feeling, willing, acting; to have her redis-cover a spiritual beauty under all its aspects, in the fields of thought and word, in prayer and the methods of education, in art and canonical

---

XII's "silence" on the Jewish genocide during the war. In May of that year, Cardinal Montini defended the memory of Pius XII in an article sent to the English journal *The Tablet*. The article appeared a few days after his election as pope. He also decided to publish the archives of the Holy See relative to this controversial period: these are the ADSS cited above.

legislation." This announced renewal for the rediscovering of a "spiritual beauty," which the Church was supposed to have lost in all aspects, was bold. Few paid any attention to it. In the message to the world, as well, Paul VI employed new language. "We know," he declared,

> that modern man takes pride in doing things by himself; he invents new things and achieves stunning things. But all these achievements make him neither better nor happier; they do not offer man any radical, definitive, or universal solution to his problems. Man, We also know, fights against himself; he knows atrocious doubts. We know that his soul is invaded by shadows and besieged by suffering. We have a message for him that we believe to be liberating. And We believe Ourselves all the more authorized to propose that it is fully human. This is the message of the Man to mankind.

This was stunning language in the mouth of a pope, particularly in his insistence on the "humanity" of Christ, and therefore of the Church. Jesus, explained the pope, called himself "the Son of Man":

> he is the firstborn, the prototype of the new humanity; he is the brother, he is the companion, he is the friend *par excellence*.... There is no value which he did not respect, enhance, and redeem. There is no human suffering he did not understand, share, and value. There is no human need — excluding any moral imperfection — that he has not assumed and experienced in himself.

This was the new image of Christ that the pope began to spread. The traditional doctrine of Christ as divine Savior and Redeemer was not forgotten; it could be found in other passages of the discourse pronounced in the Holy Land; but Paul VI believed that a new language would be better heard by contemporary man.

On the way back towards Jerusalem, he stopped at the residence of the Orthodox Patriarch of Jerusalem, on the Mount of the Ascension. He was to meet Patriarch Athenagoras again, returning the visit he had made the previous evening; the protocol had been reviewed to ensure that everything took place at a level of equality. In his allocution the pope alluded to the "divergences of doctrinal, liturgical, and disciplinary order" which would need to be "examined," but insisted on "fraternal charity" which "can and must progress forward, starting now." At the end of the meeting, the patriarch offered an *encolpion* (a pectoral chain bearing a small icon) to the pope. The *encolpion* is the symbol of episcopal authority for the Orthodox. Paul VI did not hesitate to place it around his neck. Then the pope and the patriarch read, alternating in Latin and Greek, a passage of the Gospel of John and, on the initiative of Paul VI, they blessed the assembly together.

Then, upon returning to the Apostolic Delegation, the pope held short meetings with the Anglican archbishop of Jerusalem, the Anglican bishops of Jordan, Lebanon, and Syria, and also with the Grand Mufti of Jerusalem, who had come to bring him the salutations of the city's Muslim community. During this journey, Paul VI had the idea (as an "illumination," he will say) of an ecumenical center of studies to be headquartered in the Holy Land. Catholics, Protestants, and Orthodox could study the great theological questions together there. On returning to Rome, he would have this project realized. The Holy See bought some land at Tantur, between Jerusalem and Bethlehem, and Paul VI asked the Protestant theologian Cullmann to prepare the program of studies. The pope closely followed the construction of this center, discussing with Cullmann on several occasions the activities to be planned, and in 1972, the Ecumenical Institute of Theological Research opened its doors at Tantur.

Before leaving the Holy Land, Paul VI had a message of peace sent to the representatives of all the non-Catholic communities that had observers at the Council, heads of state across the world, and the directors of large international organizations. In total there were over two hundred forty telegrams; this initiative demonstrates the euphoria generated by this first papal pilgrimage.

THE POPE OF DIALOGUE

Paul VI, the traveling pope, also wanted to become the pope of "dialogue," a word he cherished above all others. Dialogue implied becoming receptive to everyone, listening to adversaries, and meeting them if necessary. It was just as much a way of being that sought to be charitable as it was an intellectual attitude. Often, although not always, he will appear to have made concessions, while resting firm on the position which he held. This was why, shortly after his return from the Holy Land, he successively received in audience two bishops who had shown themselves to be among the most vigorous defenders of traditional doctrines during the second session of the Council. On February 3, 1964, Msgr De Proença Sigaud gave the pope a document signed by five hundred and ten archbishops and bishops of seventy-eight countries, imploring him to acquiesce to a request made by the Virgin during the apparitions at Fatima: that the pope in union with the bishops of all the countries in the world should consecrate the world to the Immaculate Heart of Mary, especially Russia that she be converted. Paul VI refused this solemn consecration, but in order not to seem like he left this request unheeded, the following November 21, during the third session of the Council, he "entrusted the human race" to the Virgin Mary and give her the title of "Mother of the Church."[44]

Another audience accorded to a "minority member" was on February 7. Msgr Carli, bishop of Segni, one of the great adversaries of collegiality, complained of an abuse of authority committed by the moderators during the second session. He gave the pope a memorandum indicating all the personal interventions of the moderators that had, in his eyes, manifestly favored the progressive tendency of the Council. Paul VI undoubtedly read the report attentively; but he did not directly intervene with the moderators; instead he simply transmitted the memorandum of Msgr Carli to the General Secretary of the Council.

For all that, Paul VI was not unconscious of the potential dangers represented by certain passages in the schemas being redrafted. Theologians including Cardinal Browne shared with him their worries concerning the definitions of collegiality contained in the text on the Church that would be presented at the next session of the Council. On May 18, Paul VI received the General Secretary in audience and shared with him twelve modifications which he wanted to see introduced into the schema on the Church. They consisted notably in affirming the power of the pope more clearly. It was a wish, not an order. Some modifications were rejected, notably where it was affirmed that the pope "is responsible only before God."[45] Paul VI often suggested or asked; rarely did he give orders or impose his will. As we shall see, he will manifest unbreakable firmness on few subjects: the liturgy, the celibacy of priests, and birth control.

A telling example of this desire for dialogue, to the point of obsession, is his first encyclical: *Ecclesiam Suam*. On August 5, 1964, on the eve of the publication of this text, he specified that this first solemn

---

44 This title was conceded to satisfy a request of the Polish bishops, communicated to the pope on September 15 by Cardinal Wyszynski, and as an act of good-will towards those who had tried, in vain, to insert the title of "Mediatrix" for the Virgin Mary in the schema on the Church.

45 Statement of A. Wenger, "Mgr Villot et le concile Vatican II," in *Le Deuxième Concile du Vatican* (Rome: École Française de Rome, 1989), 255–56.

teaching of his papacy should "take the form of a conversation and a confiding, a manifestation of our sentiments and of our thoughts." This encyclical is, as his private theologian has remarked, "perhaps the most spontaneous" of all those he wrote, "revealing the deepest preoccupations animating him in the beginning of his papacy."[46] He had asked Jean Guitton to suggest ideas for this first encyclical. In November 1963 the French philosopher proposed reflections for an encyclical on the "truth." The pope was not at all satisfied with the theme. He preferred that of "dialogue." He asked for new reflections on the subject from Guitton, and also from Jacques Maritain.[47] Paul VI would have liked to entitle this encyclical "On Dialogue." But such a title appeared too bold for a teaching of the pontifical magisterium. The theme itself was approached solely through the prism of the Church: the consciousness which the Church should take of herself, of her mission; the renewal she should undergo; the dialogue with which she should engage the world. This last part was in a sense the announcement of a council schema on "The Church and the world in the present time" which was to be presented during the third session of the Council, and of which one of the principal artisans was Msgr Guano,[48] with whom he had had ties since his days at FUCI. The central idea of the encyclical was that dialogue is the most appropriate means, for the Church, in current circumstances, to exercise her apostolic mission. Paul VI saw this zone of dialogue as involving three concentric "circles": the "separated brethren" (non-Catholic Christians); then the believers in other religions; and lastly the non-believers. Despite this focus, it was not about conforming to the mentality of the world. The pope warned against "naturalism" and against "relativism, which finds a justification for everything and puts everything on the same level, thus sapping away the simple and absolute value of Christian principles."[49]

Atheism and Communism were not passed over in silence under the pretext of dialogue, however. It may even be thought that, in a certain

---

46 C. Colombo, "Un Papa che ha tanto amato," *Vita e Pensiero* 62 (1979): 68.
47 Guitton, interview.
48 Bishop Emilio Guano (1900–1970) was ordained a priest in 1922, before his appointment as bishop by Pope John XXIII (1962). He was also vice-assistant of FUCI (1933–1955) and let his religious views be influenced by the French and German Catholic theology of the time.
49 It should be noted that John XXIII had created, for the first circle, a Secretariat for the Unity of Christians; on May 19, 1964, a few weeks before the encyclical was promulgated, Paul VI created a Secretariat for Non-Christians, the second circle; at last, in 1965, for the third circle, Paul VI created a Secretariat for Non-believers.

sense, the pope responded positively to those who had signed and submitted the petition pleading with him to include Communism on the agenda of the Council. The Church had agreed to not condemn Communism at the Council, but the pope, in his first encyclical, a non-conciliar text, intended "to condemn all systems of thought that negated God and the Church — systems often identified with economic, social, and political regimes, and among them Atheistic Communism in particular" and to pay homage to "the Church of Silence."[50] But he specified also that there was "no exclusion *a priori* with regard to those who profess these systems and adhere to these regimes."

What is more, he continued to hope for a "dialogue." Herein lies one of the paradoxes of Paul VI's pontificate. This pope, who did not hesitate to condemn atheism, Marxism, or communism, had engaged in a policy of dialogue with Communist governments; it was called *Ostpolitik*, a policy of openness towards the East. John XXIII was the first to have taken this route by secretly negotiating to obtain the release of the Ukrainian Archbishop Slipyj,[51] who had been imprisoned for decades. He also received Khrushchev's[52] son-in-law at the Vatican; and in May 1963 he sent Msgr Casaroli,[53] of the Secretariat of State, to begin talks with the Hungarian and Czech authorities. Paul VI did not break with this policy: he intensified it. It is a question, he will explain one day, of remaining "firm" in the "application of principles" while being "ready for honest and loyal agreements that are compatible with these principles."[54] In the encyclical described above he clearly indicated that dialogue with the Communist authorities appeared to him "very difficult to achieve,

---

50 The Church of Silence refers to that part of the Mystical Body of Christ that has been forced into clandestine silence by Communist persecution, as is still the case in China.
51 Card. Josyf Slipyj (1893–1984) was the Ukrainian Greek Catholic Metropolitan of Galicia and archbishop of Lviv (1944–1984). He promoted the creation of a Ukrainian patriarchate, but Paul VI instead created the new office of major archbishop for him. Paul VI would make him a cardinal in 1965.
52 Aleksei Adzhubei (1924–1993) was a prominent Soviet journalist and husband of Khrushchev's daughter, Rada. Nikita Khrushchev (1894–1971) took control of the USSR after the death of Joseph Stalin in 1953 as the First Secretary of the Communist Party of the Soviet Union (1953–1964) and then Premier (Chairman of the Council of Ministers of the Soviet Union, 1958–1964). He carried on the Cold War through some of its tensest years, including the Cuban Missile Crisis.
53 Card. Agostino Casaroli (1914–1998) was an Italian priest and diplomat for the Holy See. He became both a Cardinal-Priest and Cardinal Secretary of State (1979–1990) during John Paul II's pontificate. He was widely regarded as a diplomat able to negotiate tactfully with regimes hostile toward the Church.
54 Discourse to the Sacred College, June 21, 1976.

not to say impossible," especially because, for the two sides, the word "dialogue" did not have the same meaning, or correspond to the same realities; also all open dialogue was at risk of being used by Communist governments in propaganda.

Despite all this, dialogue with the Communist world continued. The encyclical, with its pessimistic considerations, was published on August 6, 1964; shortly afterwards, on, September 15, the signature of an agreement between the Holy See and the Hungarian government was announced. It was the first time since the advent of Communism in Europe that such an agreement was reached between a Communist state and the Church. Msgr Casaroli, then Under-Secretary of the Congregation of Extraordinary Ecclesiastical Affairs, had been its architect. In years to come he would sign agreements with other Communist countries. These accords were very limited. The Hungarian government authorized the Holy See to name six bishops in dioceses that had in some instances been vacant for decades. In return, these bishops were required to take an oath of fidelity "to the people and the Constitution." There was no shortage of problems: would the Church be free to pick candidates of her choice? Time would demonstrate this not to be the case. There were, in different Eastern countries, candidates who were imposed by governments, and at their service thereafter. Meanwhile, many of the restrictions imposed on the Church had not been lifted: religious instruction in schools was still not authorized; religious orders saw their freedom of operation strictly limited; numerous diocese remained without a bishop; finally Cardinal Mindszenty[55] had taken refuge in the American embassy at Budapest in 1956, and remained there to avoid being arrested again. Was this Hungarian agreement, the first of its kind, too costly for the Church? Certain cardinals thought so. Msgr Casaroli, to defend himself politically, was compelled to make clear in the days that followed that the required oath of fidelity for the Hungarian bishops would be taken *sicut decet episcopum* ("as is worthy of a bishop," that is to say, keeping safe his liberty to not act against the faith and his conscience). Whatever it was, this accord, as the *New York Times* described it, marked the beginning of a "new era" between the Vatican and the Communist world.

---

55   Card. Joseph Mindszenty (1892–1975) was a Hungarian cardinal and archbishop who was granted the title of the Prince Primate. His opposition to both fascism and communism was extremely strong. He was arrested and tortured as a result of his anti-communist views and was freed eight years later in the Hungarian Revolution (1956). He then sought political asylum in the American embassy in Budapest.

"BLACK WEEK"

On September 14, 1964 the third session of the Council opened. Lay auditors were even more numerous than during the second session, as were non-Catholic observers (this time, several Orthodox patriarchates sent representatives). In his opening speech, Paul VI reaffirmed papal primacy; however, he also wished that the prerogatives of the episcopacy be reaffirmed. It was already clear that the question of collegiality was yet again going to be at the center of debate. Between the two sessions, in *Divinitas*, in the *Revue de droit canonique*, and in *La Pensée catholique*,[56] the opponents of this doctrine expressed themselves with force. The night before his speech, a long "private note" expressing severe criticism of the chapter on collegiality in the schema on the Church and signed by about twenty cardinals, several bishops, and about ten general superiors had been handed to the pope. From his personal notes, it appears that Paul VI perceived this note as an affront and considered it a "maneuver."[57] He chose to let the Council first debate the subject again.

The debates of the third session will not be described here in detail. They involved many subjects: the Church; religious liberty; ecumenism; Revelation; the apostolate of the laity; religious; missions; seminaries; and the Church in the modern world. Only Paul VI's direct interventions will be discussed.

First there were a few carefully planned "gestures," which this introverted pope liked so much. On September 23, the feast of Saint Andrew, Paul VI was present for the Mass celebrated before the Council by Cardinal Marella.[58] A venerable relic, the head of Saint Andrew, was there. It had been taken to Rome in the fifteenth century to save it from destruction by the Ottomans who had invaded Greece. Paul VI announced that the relic would be returned to the Orthodox, in token of friendship.

Another even more spectacular gesture took place on November 13. The pope was again present at the Mass before the Council, which was being concelebrated that day by the Oriental Catholic Patriarchs. After the ceremony, he descended from his throne and deposited his tiara on

---

56 *Divinitas* and *La Pensée catholique* are both theological journals. The *Revue de droit canonique* is a canon law journal published by the University of Strasbourg.
57 Cited by G. Caprile, "Paolo VI e il Concilio," *L'Osservatore Romano*, September 19, 1982.
58 Card. Paolo Marella (1895–1984) was a delegate of the Holy See whom Pope John XXIII elevated to the cardinalate in 1959. He studied at both the Pontifical Roman Seminary and La Sapienza University. From 1977 until his death in 1984, he was the vice-dean of the College of Cardinals.

the altar, announcing that he made a gift of it to the poor of the world. It was a symbolic gesture in favor of Third World countries (he was traveling to India a few weeks later) but it was also, in the minds of many, a renunciation of the temporal power that this triple crown represented. The tiara was not in fact sold: it was given to Cardinal Spellman, who displayed it in his cathedral in New York, then at the Vatican's pavilion at the 1964 World's Fair (held in New York), and at last at the Shrine of the Immaculate Conception near the Catholic University of America in Washington, D. C. The bishops of the world were invited to offer a sum of money for the poor.

The first of the subjects discussed during this third session was religious liberty. American cardinals were its most ardent defenders. Cardinal Cushing, who had shunned the preceding sessions because he could not understand the interventions in Latin, had come from his diocese in Boston specifically to defend the proposed schema: "The whole subject of religious liberty can be summarized in two propositions," he declared. "Firstly, in her whole history the Catholic Church has always insisted on her own liberty in civil society and before public powers. Secondly, in these days, this same civil liberty, which she has always demanded for herself, the Church now also champions for other churches and their members, in reality for every human person . . ." The adversaries of religious liberty, Cardinal Browne, Msgr Parente,[59] Archbishop Lefebvre, and Msgr De Castro Mayer, recalled the traditional doctrine on the matter: only the Catholic religion possesses the whole truth, therefore she alone possesses specific rights; other Christian confessions or religions are in error, and can only be tolerated by the state. The state, furthermore, cannot pretend to be entirely separated from the Church; it cannot pretend to be neutral in religious matters, and must recognize the "rights of God" and the Catholic religion. For these opponents of the concept, the right to religious liberty was dangerous, because it was too subjective, individualist, and prone to favor indifferentism. Moreover, to proclaim religious liberty as an equal right for each individual to profess the religion he judged to be true would necessarily lead, in all countries, to discontinuing recognition of the Catholic religion as the "religion of state." The result thereafter would be the separation of Church and state.

---

59 Card. Pietro Parente (1891–1986) was an Italian theologian who worked in the Holy Office. He frequently wrote for *L'Osservatore Romano* and was known for his forthright style. In fact, he was considered too outspoken by Pope Paul VI to be made Prefect of the Congregation for the Doctrine of the Faith (1965). He was created a cardinal in 1967.

Partisans and adversaries of religious liberty supported two completely antagonistic points of view. Paul VI, who was not present for the debates, intervened awkwardly. He asked his personal theologian, Msgr Colombo, to take part in the debate. Msgr Colombo defended the principle of religious liberty as an inalienable right of the individual; but he also thought that it was necessary to review the proposed text to specify its foundations. This was in recognition of the fact that the doctrine as set out had not been clearly formulated. After a few further interventions, the text was therefore returned to its commission to be rewritten. On October 9, it was announced that "by superior order," that is to say at the request of the pope, this highly contested text would not be examined again at this session, and would be reviewed not only by the Secretariat of Unity that had initially proposed it, but also by Msgr Colombo and three opponents of the declaration (Cardinal Browne, Archbishop Lefebvre, and Reverend Father Fernández[60]). On October 11, fifteen cardinals (including Cardinals Suenens, König, Liénart, Rugambwa,[61] and Alfrink) addressed a letter of protest to the pope that was published in *Le Monde* a few days later. The pope then retreated from his position and announced that the three opponents to the text would not take part in its revision after all. Another text was distributed on November 17; the votes were to be cast on the 19th. In turn the opponents of the text circulated a petition, which received one hundred forty-three signatures (including those of Cardinal Larraona,[62] Archbishop Lefebvre, and Msgr Carli), asking that the votes be deferred to the next session, as there was too little time for the new text to be examined. On November 19, the Council Presidency agreed with them. There was an uproar in the Council hall; insults were hurled. A new petition was circulated, calling for an immediate examination of the

---

60 Fr Ancieto Fernández Alonso (1895–1981) was a Spanish priest, philosopher, theologian, and master general of the Order of Preachers. He was a professor at the Angelicum and was the founder and president of the Spanish Confederation of Religious (CONFER) from 1954–1962. He also participated in the Second Vatican Council (1962–1965).
61 Card. Laurean Rugambwa (1912–1997) became the first African cardinal of the Catholic Church, elevated in 1960. He was born in Tanzania, studied in Uganda at the Regional Grand Seminary of Katigondo, and was ordained a priest in 1943. He also served as archbishop of Dar es Salaam (1968–1992). He was a progressive member of the Second Vatican Council, important in implementing modern reforms. He was part of the 1963 papal conclave that elected Paul VI.
62 Card. Arcadio Larraona Saralegui (1887–1973) was a Spanish Claretian elevated to the cardinalate in 1959 who then served as Prefect of the Sacred Congregation of Rites (1962–1968), where he assisted in preparing the liturgical reform that would produce the *Novus Ordo*.

text. It received four hundred eleven signatures; Cardinals Meyer, Ritter,[63] and Léger went to carry it directly to the pope. Paul VI did not want to contradict a decision of the Council Presidency. The text on religious liberty was not discussed or presented for voting again until the next session.

The day of the 19th was only one of the memorable days of what has been called the "Black Week" (November 14–21). That same week, Paul VI intervened twice, this time in an authoritarian manner, in the writing of two important texts. First was the text on collegiality. The final proposed version still contained ambiguities and sentences which could be interpreted in a sense restricting the authority of the pope. Paul VI, alerted by Cardinal Larraona, spokesman of several other cardinals and bishops, had a text written which provided, in precise terms, some clarifications. On November 16, this text, called the Nota praevia or "Preliminary Note," was read in assembly by the Secretary General. This preliminary note affirmed clearly that the college of bishops exercised its authority only by the consent of the pope. It may be noted that the introduction of this note permitted the chapter on collegiality, and then the schema on the Church in its entirety, to be approved by an immense majority of the Council Fathers. Almost all of the opponents of collegiality had been reassured by this last-minute addition imposed by the pope.

The schema on ecumenism had similar problems. It had been voted on chapter by chapter. There were also lively debates. Some feared that the text conceded too much to Protestants. Then, after the text had been voted chapter by chapter, on November 19, the Secretary General of the Council announced that "by superior authority" some *modi* (changes) had been introduced in different passages. They had been written, on the request of the pope, by Father Ciappi,[64] consultant of the Holy Office and theologian of the Papal Household. These modifications constituted a "regression," in the eyes of Fr Congar. Where the voted text said that the Protestants "find" God in the Scriptures, it now said: they "look for" God in the Scriptures...[65]

---

63 Card. Joseph Ritter (1892–1967) was archbishop of Indianapolis, Indiana (1934–1946) and then of St. Louis, Missouri until his death in 1967. John XXIII created him a cardinal in 1961.
64 Card. Marin Luigi Ciappi (1909–1996) was an Italian who served five different popes as their personal theologian (1955–1989). In 1977, he was elevated to the cardinalate. He taught moral and dogmatic theology at the Angelicum and additionally was the Dean of the Theological Faculty (1935–1955).
65 It is to be noted that the pope had suggested forty *modi*; only nineteen were retained by the Secretariat of Unity responsible for the text — proof that the pope made minimal efforts to impose his views.

This third session ended on November 21 with the solemn promulgation of the Dogmatic Constitution on the Church *Lumen Gentium*, and the decrees on ecumenism, and on the Oriental Churches, and by the proclamation of "Mary, Mother of the Church" discussed above. Disillusionment was widespread. The pope, by his more or less authoritarian intervention, had disappointed those who saw audacity in him. The attribution to Mary of the title "Mother of the Church" disgruntled those who worried about an excess of "Mariolatry," as well as the Protestant observers. Several non-Catholic observers made highly critical public declarations. On December 8, Oscar Cullmann addressed a letter to Paul VI expressing his regret that the restrictive *modi* had been introduced in the text on ecumenism. The pope was sensitive to these criticisms expressed by this Protestant theologian and friend. He responded to him in a long personal letter, and advised him to go see Cardinal Bea for further explanation.[66]

BETWEEN DOUBTS AND WORRIES

The third session of the Council was short compared to the preceding ones, because the pope was to make his second major trip. The organization of a Eucharistic congress in Bombay, at the beginning of the month of December, gave him the opportunity to go to India. There he could comfort the Catholics who were by far the minority (about five million in a country of four hundred forty million inhabitants), but also proclaim Christianity to a mostly Hindu population. The evening before his departure, an Italian Catholic writer in an article brought his attention to the existence of texts by the Indian poet Rabindranath Tagore[67] who had sought to "construct a bridge between the philosophy of the Upanishads and the Gospel." Upon reading this article, Paul VI immediately sent a telegram to the author of the article to learn more about these texts — an exceptional gesture for a pope. Perhaps also the pope remembered the project of his now-deceased friend, Msgr Rampolla del Tindaro who, in the thirties, had dreamed of a large-scale project to evangelize India.

---

66 Letters published by G. Stella, "Paul VI e O. Cullmann," *Notiziario* 6 (May 1983): 7–20. In the preceding November, during a homily, Paul VI had made a polemical point against liberal Protestantism and Modernism. Certain non-Catholic observers were unhappy with it, notably Pastor Boegner. When he learned of it, the pope sent his theologian, Msgr Colombo, to explain his thoughts more fully to Pastor Boegner.
67 Rabindranath Tagore (1861–1941) was a Bengali Brahmo Hindu polydisciplinary artist who was the first non-European to win the Nobel Prize in Literature.

This trip would also allow him to see a Third World country which, at that time, had not yet put an end to regularly recurring famines. Msgr Marcinkus, who had shown his efficiency in arranging the pilgrimage to the Holy Land, was put in charge of this one as well. On December 2, the pope left Rome for Bombay. Upon his arrival at the airport in the afternoon, the Vice-President of India, Zakir Husain,[68] and several ministers awaited him. The pope promptly adopted the Hindu gesture of welcome, the *namaste* (hands joined before the forehead), and gracefully donned the traditional necklace of welcome that was offered to him. From the airport to the center of Bombay, over almost fifty miles, an enormous crowd had gathered. Tens of thousands of curious onlookers, almost all Hindus. Stunned and amazed by this multicolored sea of joyful, shouting people, who threw flowers in his way, the pope continually blessed them, with his arms outstretched. Later, he would say to his secretary Fr Macchi that he had then an intuition that this crowd of Asians would become Christian in the future, and that they would put the Gospels into practice better than Westerners because in a way they already lived the Beatitudes.[69]

Arriving in Bombay, he went to the principal square of the city, the Oval, where the Eucharistic congress was taking place. He gave a lengthy greeting to the faithful who awaited him, and prayed with them; then he went to the cathedral, where he celebrated Mass. He was to reside at the archbishop's palace in the city. The evening of his arrival, a reception was offered for the Indian political authorities. Two hundred and fifty religious extremists had been arrested before his arrival as a preventative measure, for fear of an attack. When he learned of it, Paul VI was disturbed. During the reception he asked the Minister of Information, Indira Gandhi,[70] to free them. She informed the pope that they already had been. Immediately, with his perennial concern to go to meet his would-be enemies, he said to the minister: "Then will you let them know that I am ready to shake hands with them." The reply made the front page of the Indian newspapers the next day.

On December 3, at the archiepiscopal palace, he received representatives of non-Christian religions. He emphasized the tasks they had

---

68 Zakir Husain (1897–1969) was a Pashtun Muslim from Punjab, India who served as the country's Vice President from 1962 to 1967 and then as President until his death.
69 Father Macchi, *Notiziario* 1 (Christmas 1979): 27.
70 Indira Gandhi (1917–1984) was the first and to this date only female Prime Minister of India, serving in office twice, from 1966–1977 and from 1980 until her assassination in 1984. She was the daughter of Jawaharlal Nehru who was the first prime minister of India.

in common: "You also are engaged in combat against the evils which darken the life of countless persons in the world: poverty, hunger, sickness.... We must not meet as simple tourists, but as pilgrims who are going to look for God, not in edifices of stone, but in the heart of men." This immanentist discourse would be counterbalanced the next day by a frankly evangelizing discourse. Then he received the representatives of the non-Catholic communities of India, about forty Anglican bishops and priests with their head, the Anglican bishop of Bombay. In the evening, before three hundred thousand faithful assembled in the Oval, he celebrated Mass and proceeded to consecrate six bishops from five continents, the better to symbolize the universality of the Church: a Belgian, an Indian, two Africans, an Australian, and a South American. During his homily, to affirm his dialogue with non-Christians, he cited two Hindu texts, one evocation of the "Lord" by Tagore, and a passage from the Upanishads on the truth.

To Indian Catholics he had wanted to teach the virtues of dialogue. The next afternoon, an outdoor Mass had been planned in a poor section of Bombay. Paul VI made himself a missionary to the Hindu majority that was present. During his homily, he notably declared:

> We have come in this hospitable land as a pilgrim, to honor Our Lord in the Holy Eucharist. If you ask: "What is this pilgrim? What are his motives and his intentions?" We respond: We are a servant and a messenger of Jesus Christ, placed by Divine Providence at the head of his Church, as the successor of Saint Peter, the prince of the Apostles.... We come to you as a messenger of Jesus Christ and of his teachings.

Next he visited some orphanages, hospitals, and a professional school. In a hospital where dying children were admitted, he took a meal in the company of the least weak patients among them. Then, after a reception at the city hall of Bombay, he presided at the end of the afternoon over a Mass in the Antiochian Rite at the Oval. In the evening, he held a press conference. On this occasion he pronounced a solemn message to the world, exhorting the nations to "cease the arms race and to dedicate their resources and their energy instead to fraternal assistance to developing countries." The appeal was launched when the Americans were multiplying the deployment of troops to Vietnam as a barrier against Communism. What is more, he launched it from a "Non-Aligned" country (officially neutral in the "Cold War") that was still close to the USSR. His appeal was judged harshly by much of the international press; it was deemed unrealistic. Paul VI wanted this appeal from Bombay to be officially transmitted to the General Secretary of the UN, U Thant,[71] so that it might have the greatest possible reverberation.

The next day, after a Mass for altar boys in the Cathedral of Bombay, a visit to the Marian sanctuary of Bandra (a place of pilgrimage since the sixteenth century), and a visit to the seminary of Goregaon, Paul VI boarded the plane for Rome. As his personal physician, Fontana,[72] remarked to journalists, during this travel marathon, Paul VI, who looked so fragile, had proved, at more than sixty-seven years of age, to be "highly resilient."

On his return to Rome, the pope discovered an atmosphere of doubt and uncertainty that had been generated by the last difficult days of the third session of the Council. Among even the cardinals, the divisions were great. The council texts then hanging in suspense, notably those on religious liberty and the Church in the modern world (with its numerous practical implications), had created factions which seemed impossible to reconcile. The pope was greatly troubled. After Christmas, he asked his secretary Father Macchi, the man of confidential missions, to go to France to consult with Jean Guitton and Jacques Maritain in his name. Fr Macchi went to fetch Jean Guitton in Paris, and then they went together to Toulouse where Jacques Maritain had retired to a community of the Little Brothers of Jesus. It was on December 27. There they discussed the different questions which had divided the Council assembly. Jacques Maritain proposed to write memoranda for the pope on some of them. The following March, Maritain sent four texts to Paul VI, on subjects that at times go beyond the conciliar problems themselves: "On the notion of truth"; "Religious liberty"; "The apostolate of the laity"; and "Common prayer and private prayer: the vernacular language and sacred texts: studies."[73] The first two only reinforced Paul VI's determination to have the Council adopt a declaration on religious liberty. Maritain insisted on the right for each individual to think freely, even in religious matters, without the state being able to

---

71   U Thant (1909–1974) was a Burmese Buddhist statesman and the third Secretary General of the UN (1961–1971). He organized negotiations between US President Kennedy and the Soviet premier Khrushchev to bring a peaceful end to the Cuban Missile Crisis of 1962.

72   Dr Mario Fontana (1904–1979) was Pope Paul VI's doctor. Dr Fontana and his assistant, Dr Renato Buzzonetti, signed Pope Paul VI's death certificate at the papal summer residence of Castel Gandolfo.

73   Memoranda preserved in the J. Maritain Archives; the second and fourth are unpublished.

contradict him. "The state," wrote the philosopher, "no longer has any right to intervene in matters of the conscience." It was a legitimization of the separation of Church and state — a separation which Paul VI had always supported. The memorandum on the liturgy was more critical. But, on the whole, Maritain's reflections were well received. Certain practical suggestions were implemented, such as the abandonment of Latin for the teaching of philosophy and theology in seminaries and Catholic universities.

The divisions over important points of doctrine during the third session of the Council were only one aspect of a Church in full upheaval. The council proceeded towards a general revision of the doctrine and discipline of the Church. This revision did not always involve change, but was often interpreted as such. In numerous countries, especially in Europe and the Americas, a growing proportion of the clergy seemed impatient to see the application of reforms that had been decided, or merely envisioned, in Rome. A bold declaration from a bishop or expert could be considered an open door to a reform. For some faithful and clergy, a suggestion or a project initiated at the Council immediately became a demand; the critique of an institution or a point of doctrine in Rome soon became a virulent contestation in Paris or New York. What has been called the "crisis of the Church" began to manifest itself openly. It was no longer a matter of isolated controversial acts or writings, but a spirit that was spreading, fueled by a multitude of declarations, pronouncements, and decisions. It was a crisis whose magnitude was only going to be made more manifest by the diversity of its aspects. It was a crisis of faith: theologians undermined and questioned fundamental beliefs; many new opinions were spreading amongst the clergy and the faithful. It was a crisis of the priesthood: the clergy was becoming ever more controversial and politicized, questioning its priestly identity, and those abandoning the clerical state were ever more numerous, and vocations ever rarer.

The warning signs began to multiply in these years. One of the bestsellers in France of the beginning of the year 1965 was a book by Michel de Saint-Pierre:[74] *Les Nouveaux Prêtres* [The new priests]. In this sociological novel, written after researches among the clergy in the "red" quarter of Paris, Michel de Saint-Pierre focuses on the clergy of a large suburban parish. A priest, Paul Delance, finds himself confronted with "progressive"

---

74 Michel de Saint-Pierre (1916–1987) was a French writer and journalist. He was an ardent Catholic, royalist, and defender of the Traditional Mass, as will be noted.

confreres, influenced by Marxism. The accommodating attitudes of a certain type of clergy and the danger of abandoning spirituality is brilliantly presented therein. In a few weeks, the book sold over two hundred thousand copies. But it also incited fierce controversy: the author was dismissed as a "Fascist." There had been a rupture among the French clergy and faithful alike between "conciliarist reformists" on one side and "integralist reactionaries" on the other.[75] Michel de Saint-Pierre, in the beginning of February 1965, addressed an open letter "To our bishops and our priests," which was published a few days later by Jean Madiran,[76] editor of the journal *Itinéraires*, who would soon become one of the leaders of what has been called "traditionalism." In this appeal, Michel de Saint-Pierre and Jean Madiran asked the bishops to intervene to "recognize the rights of the great number of priests and faithful within the whole Christian community that are being excluded from Catholic social and institutional life under the accusation of 'integralism,' 'anti-Communism,' 'Marian devotion,' and other similar pretexts." But this appeal had no effect. Soon other subjects, notably the new catechisms and the new Mass, would divide the Church more radically still, in France and other countries.

Michel de Saint-Pierre's appeal was read by Paul VI; the copy preserved in his library attests that it was read pencil in hand. His immediate reaction remains unknown, but perhaps a response to Michel de Saint-Pierre and Jean Madiran may be glimpsed in one of the declarations of the pope, a few months later, to the French bishops: "No soul of good will who remains strongly attached to the Church should be able to complain legitimately of being held at arm's length, or not being heard, understood, or loved by his pastors" (November 22, 1965).

Michel de Saint-Pierre's book was one of those warning signs that would multiply in the months and years to come. The Pope was not unaware of this escalating crisis. If he refused to take authoritarian disciplinary measures to condemn books and their authors, in the last two sessions of the Council he repeatedly gave more or less solemn warnings. It is also likely that at this time, he hoped that the as-yet-unfinished Council would finally and rapidly bear good fruits and that the disorders

---

75 Two works were immediately written on the affair: Pierre Debray, *Le Dossier des nouveaux prêtres*, and Michel de Saint-Pierre, *Sainte Colère*.

76 Jean Madiran (1920–2013) was a French nationalist and traditionalist Catholic writer, often using the pen name Jean-Louis Lagor. He co-founded *Itinéraires* (1956), which was a review of Catholic themes with heavy criticism of reforms within the Catholic Church and especially after the Second Vatican Council.

and controversies would therefore be short-lived. Such turmoil and uncertainty weighed heavily on him. On February 1965, three months after the end of the third session, during a Wednesday general audience, he pleaded pathetically in public:

> The pope too needs reassurance.... The pope has his sorrows, which come before all else from his human insufficiency, with which, at every instant, he finds himself confronted and almost conflicted by the enormous and excessive weight of his duties, his problems, his responsibilities. Sometimes it reaches the point of agony.

One week later, on February 25, Paul VI held his first consistory. Twenty-seven cardinals were created, thus increasing the number of members of the Sacred College to one hundred and three.[77] The names of the newly promoted reflected, in a great number of instances, the affinities and preoccupations of Paul VI. Some had been long associated with the pope: his old teacher Fr Bevilacqua; Father Journet, author of a treatise on the Church which he often cited, and a friend of Maritain's; Giovanni Colombo, who had succeeded him as archbishop of Milan; or again Jean Villot, whom he had known since the thirties at the Secretariat of State, who was one of the under-secretaries of the Council and was going to be named archbishop of Lyon. There were also particular homages: Léon-Joseph Cardijn,[78] founder of the *Jeunesse ouvrière chrétienne* (Young Christian Workers — JOC); Msgr Duval,[79] archbishop of Algiers, who, after Algerian independence (which he had encouraged), had taken Algerian citizenship (while maintaining his French citizenship), and promoted dialogue with the Muslims; Msgr Slipyj and Archbishop Beran,[80]

---

77 Since the sixteenth century, the Sacred College had never numbered more than seventy members (in reference to the seventy elders of Israel who assisted Moses). John XXIII exceeded this number, as have all popes since.
78 Card. Léon-Joseph Cardijn (1882–1967) was a Belgian cardinal who founded the JOC (*Jeunesse ouvrière chrétienne*). He was famous for dedicating his life to social activism, for which he achieved numerous recognitions, as he strove to improve the life of the working class, particularly by sharing the Gospel's core messages with them.
79 Card. Léon-Étienne Duval (1903–1996), a Frenchman in Algeria. He was archbishop of Algiers (1954–1988) before being elevated to the cardinalate (1965). He is notable for championing the independence of Algeria and promoted peace amongst the people of different religions living there.
80 Cardinal Josef Beran (1888–1969), from Bohemia; he was imprisoned in the Dachau concentration camp by the Nazis. In 1946 he was consecrated archbishop of Prague and Primate of Czechoslovakia. He was placed under house arrest by the Communist government (1949–1951) and then imprisoned until 1963, with an

two bishops of the "Silent Church" who had known Communist prisons before being exiled to Rome. Lastly, as a novelty, three Eastern Catholic Patriarchs also received the dignity of cardinal.

During this consistory, Paul VI recalled the role which the cardinals were called upon to play: "You will be Our cooperators and Our counselors in the government of the Holy Catholic Church." It is difficult to determine which specific decisions of the pope were influenced by any specific cardinal. From among the new cardinals, three facts, on diverse yet important subjects, should be noted. Firstly, the counsel given to Paul VI by Cardinal Cardijn to read Naissance des prêtres-ouvriers [Birth of the worker-priests][81] by the ex-priest Émile Poulat, then just published. This advice dates to June 1965 (a note in the book preserved in Paul VI's library attests to it). The following October, the French episcopacy was again officially authorized to restart the experiment of the worker-priests, which had been banned for years. Is it not likely that Cardinal Cardijn and the book by Émile Poulat, which is so full of erudition and nuance, contributed to the decision? Cardinal Bevilacqua, according to one of Paul VI's confidants, influenced the pope concerning priests who abandoned their ministry. Cardinal Colombo judged that Paul VI was "magnanimous beyond measure" with the priests who asked to be relieved of their priestly functions and reduced to the lay state; he guessed that Cardinal Bevilacqua had encouraged the pope to be as indulgent as possible.[82] The third attested influence was Cardinal Journet's, on the question of religious liberty. Although he did not doubt that this doctrine was based on solid foundations, Paul VI worried about finding an adequate formulation. Cardinal Journet's intervention on this subject during the fourth session lent weighty authority to the doctrine, and rallied the support of many who had been hesitant or skeptical about it up to that point.

In the months preceding its opening, this fourth session worried Paul VI greatly. His concern to see the Council to a serene and fruitful completion mixed with the fear aroused in him by international events led him to sign an all-but-forgotten encyclical, Mense Maio [In the month of May], on April 29, 1965. Days before the month of May,

---

interdiction upon exercising his episcopal duties. He was exiled to Rome in 1965 as part of the pope's negotiations with the Communists. Beran resisted at first but resigned for the good of his flock. Paul VI made him a cardinal in 1965. He spoke at the last session of the Second Vatican Council on the issue of religious liberty.

81   Émile Poulat, Naissance des prêtres ouvriers (Paris: Casterman, 1965).
82   Cardinal G. Colombo, Ricordando G. B. Montini, 57.

a month traditionally dedicated to the Virgin Mary, the pope asked the faithful to pray to the Virgin in a "particularly grave hour" for the Church: "heavy duties remain for the next session which will close the Council. Then will come the no less important phase of putting the Council's decisions into effect." This was also a potentially dark time in the wider world: the pope deplored the development of war practices "in flagrant contradiction with the moral sense and usage of civilized nations": "guerilla warfare, terrorism, hostage-taking, and reprisals against unarmed populations." To obtain peace in the world and in the Church, the pope recommended prayer, and particularly the recitation of the Rosary, because "peace is not simply the result of our human activity; it is also and above all a gift of God."

At the approach of the opening of the fourth session, the warnings multiplied still further. In May 1965, for example:

> Whoever sees in the Council a relaxation of the prior teachings of the Church, towards her faith, her tradition, her asceticism, her charity, her spirit of sacrifice, and her adhesion to the Word and the Cross of Christ, or worse still, an indulgent concession to the fragility and fluid, relativistic mentality of a world without principles and without any transcendent purpose — a sort of convenient, undemanding Christianity — will be making a serious mistake.

About that same time, Paul VI wrote his last will and testament, dated June 30. This is a surprising undertaking for a man who had only been pope for two years; it is less so for someone who was going to turn sixty-eight, was in fragile health, and could sometimes already feel his strength declining.[83] On the other hand, it is known that the thought of death had accompanied him throughout his existence. Shortly after the writing of his will, he wrote a moving "meditation on death," which shows a pope who wished to be discharged of his responsibilities, which he thought too burdensome:

> The hour comes. I have seen it coming for some time. Still more than physical fatigue, which at every moment is ready to overwhelm me, the drama of my responsibilities seems to suggest my departure from this world as a providential solution, so that Providence can manifest itself and lead the Church towards a better world.... It seems fairly clear that I must be

---

83 Two brief additions will be made to this will in 1972 and 1973.

called to the life to come so that I may be replaced by one who is stronger, who is not constrained by the present difficulties.[84]

The will itself opens with a long prologue, striking in its enthusiasm and thanksgiving, in which the pope gives thanks for the "earthly pilgrimage" he has completed, for the masters and the friends he has had the privilege of knowing. Its dispositions as such are brief: the faithful private secretary Macchi was named the executor of the will, Francesco and Lodovico inherited the "movable assets and real estate in my possession," the Holy See was named universal inheritor of the rest. The funeral was to be "pious and simple" ("let the catafalque be omitted"), the tomb "in real earth." The final recommendations testify yet again to the pope's grave concern for the Church. It could be believed that he was not certain he would see the end of the Council in this life: "Let it be carried to a good end," he wrote, "and let the faithful execution of the prescriptions be foreseen." Above all this testament includes two warnings, which are to be considered his precise thoughts on two subjects of importance: ecumenism and the relationship between the Church and the world. On ecumenism: "Let the work of coming closer to the separated brethren be continued, with deep understanding and patience; with great love; but without deviating from true Catholic doctrine." On the relationship between the Church and the world: "Let no one suppose himself to be useful to it by taking on its thoughts, manners, or tastes, but rather by studying it, loving it, and serving it." This last counsel was a difficult and delicate task. Paul VI knew this, surely: he had suffered from it, and sometimes not only did he not know how to halt deviations but even, in certain decisions and in certain words, may have seemed to encourage them. In this sense also he was a "divided pope."

Uncertainty and warnings dominated a great part of 1965, as if the pope wanted to ward off the upheavals taking place in the Church, upheavals which the Council, and his continuation of it, had helped to accelerate. Outside of a few important points,[85] the Council did not propose new doctrines likely to disturb Catholics; however, in the six years since its announcement, it favored a climate of interrogation, reevaluation, and sometimes radical controversy. About ten days before the opening of the fourth session, Paul VI wanted to intervene solemnly

---

84 "Meditation de Paul VI sur la mort," *La Documentation catholique*, October 7, 1979.
85 In the motu proprio *Ecclesia Dei Adflicta* (July 2, 1988), John Paul II admitted the "innovation" of certain "points of doctrine" defined by Vatican II.

with regard to one of the central doctrines of the Catholic Faith that was the object of contestation and erroneous opinions, not only in the midst of the Council, but also among theologians and clergy, especially in Holland. On September 3, he published the encyclical *Mysterium Fidei* on the doctrine and worship of the Holy Eucharist.[86] The pope said that he was "worried and preoccupied" by "certain opinions which trouble the minds of the faithful [and] cause a great confusion of ideas related to the truths of the faith." He vigorously condemned the following theories: "communal" Mass being held of greater worth than private Mass; the terms "transignification" or "transfinalization" better expressing the Eucharistic mystery than "transubstantiation"; or, worst of all, "Our Lord Jesus Christ [being] no longer present in the consecrated hosts remaining after the celebration of the Mass." On all these points, the pope reaffirmed the traditional doctrine by relying on the definitions of previous councils, and abundantly citing the Fathers of the Church. He exhorted the promotion of Eucharistic worship by reminding the faithful of the benefits of the Mass, daily communion, and visits to the Blessed Sacrament. This encyclical, which firmly restated the traditional doctrine, did not halt the spread of false theories and scandalous practices in years to come, but at least it encouraged some bishops and theologians to try to oppose them.

He gave one last speech expressing his concerns, just two days before the opening of the last session of the Council. He went to the underground basilica of the ancient catacombs of Saint Domitilla and, during the Mass he celebrated, he gave a lucid and severe sermon on Communist regimes and the fate they were planning for the "Church of Silence." The Soviet news agency TASS[87] saw it as a "provocation." The pope had notably declared:

> We pray today in a special way. Between the Church of the catacombs and the Church that today is suffering and barely surviving in the countries of atheist and totalitarian regimes there are real and evident analogies.... They try to asphyxiate the free religious life of nations and individuals, and the deliberate intention — even if it is not admitted — is the hope

---

86   This encyclical had been preceded by two remarkable trips: in August 1964, Paul VI had gone to Orvieto for the celebrations commemorating the eighth centenary of the Eucharistic miracle of Bolsena, and three months before the publication of the encyclical he had insisted on assisting at the Eucharistic congress in Pisa.

87   Russian News Agency TASS (Информационное агéнтство Росси́и ТАСС) was a major Russian state-owned news agency founded in 1904.

of making it die. They progressively inhibit the recruitment of clergy, which is already so decimated; when they cannot lead the clergy, religious, and faithful to "collaborate" with the regime, they throw up obstacles to normal pastoral government; they monopolize all the means that totalitarianism has at its disposal: the press, culture, education, and recreation, to withdraw the youth from the Church and to impose Marxist doctrine on them.

This clear-sightedness did not prevent him from wanting to continue dialoguing with Communist governments and negotiating with them, often acquiescing to the payment of a high price, in the hope of obtaining some degree of increased liberty for the faithful behind the Iron Curtain.

FOURTH SESSION

On September 14, 1965 the fourth session of the Council opened. Some hoped that there would be a fifth, but very rapidly Paul VI made it known that the Second Vatican Council would come to an end absolutely in the following December. A few days before the opening of this final session, the pope had a telegram sent to Jacques Maritain, to thank him for a parcel,[88] saying that he was "avid [for] advice in obviously agonizing circumstances."[89] Maritain arrived in Rome a few days later, on the 11th, and would be a low-key guest of the pope's in Castel Gandolfo. Did their discussions bear on the declaration on religious liberty which was going to be presented for a vote again in the following days? Did Maritain meet with other persons besides the pope, notably Cardinal Journet, his friend, who was preparing to make a bold declaration in favor of religious liberty? Surely yes. In any case Paul VI is known to have asked Maritain to prepare some "messages" to be read at the end of the Council.

This fourth session was the most complicated. Eleven schemas were still to be examined, discussed, and put to the vote. During the opening assembly, Paul VI wanted to summarize, as it were, the purpose of the Council at the very moment when two important texts, one on religious liberty and the other on "the Church in the modern world," were going

---

88   They were manuscripts of a work which Maritain had just finished, *Le Mystère d'Israël* and some other essays, which he thought could be interesting to the pope at the moment when the text on the Jews was going to be discussed at the council.
89   Telegram, September 4, 1965 (Archives J. Maritain).

to be discussed. "The council is a solemn act of love for humanity," he declared. The two major texts being drafted, as discussed above, had to show that "this outlook towards the world will be one of the principal acts of the session about to begin: once again and above all, love; love for the men of today, whoever they may be, wherever they may be, love for all . . ." The Church was thus well removed from a council for the condemnation of errors or for doctrinal correction, as some had hoped and thought necessary. The pope had confidence in man and refused to despair of the world. In the weeks to come, this confidence will appear almost as an act of faith in the expressions of still more innovative speeches.

Paul VI also generated surprise in announcing the creation of a new institution: a synod of bishops. During meetings of the Central Preparatory Commission, and later on in the Council sessions, such an organization had been repeatedly requested, notably by Cardinal Alfrink. This synod, according to some, would take the form of a permanent mini-Council; according to others, it would act as a sort of "bishops' council" to lead the Church with the pope. In announcing the creation of such an organization himself, Paul VI proved his dexterity. He drew up the rules for it the next day in a *motu proprio*.[90] This synod would have neither executive nor legislative powers: it would act solely as a consultative body. It would not be permanent but temporary, and could be convoked by the pope whenever he thought it necessary for the Church.

Other than the cardinals who were heads of the dicasteries, and the Eastern Catholic patriarchs, who automatically held membership in this synod by rights, the bishops would be elected by their peers, with the pope reserving to himself the designation of fifteen percent of the members. The pope alone could decide the agenda for the synod, and reserved the right to designate the synod's President-Delegate, secretaries, and relators. During the pontificate of Paul VI, the synod would meet five times, sometimes with rancorous debates.

During the last session of the Council, Paul VI rarely imposed his will. The first assemblies focused on religious liberty. Adversaries and partisans faced off. Other than the above-mentioned intervention of Cardinal Journet, which was likely inspired by the pope, the interventions in favor of this declaration by three cardinals from "the Church

---

90 *Motu proprio* means "by his own initiative" and is analogous to an American president's executive order, except that, since it comes from the Roman Pontiff, it has the force of law.

of Silence" (Slipyj, Beran, and Šeper[91]) are noteworthy. On September 20, the debate was officially closed. One hundred twenty-seven Council Fathers and a few cardinals formally pleaded with the pope to allow the debate to continue, and to ensure that the text would be revised by theologians who did not all hold the minority opinion. Paul VI refused their request and, on the next day, had an "orientation vote" taken, that is, a gauge of the general approbation of the text, under condition of "ulterior detail work." The result was decisively approbative: of the 2,222 votes, 1,997 approved the text, 224 opposed it.

This preliminary vote is explained by the fact that the pope would be visiting the headquarters of the UN, in New York, only a few days later. A first general approbation of religious freedom was necessary for the pope to present himself before the representatives of the world with a new doctrine that Cardinal Journet had summarized: "the regime of Christendom" is over, the Church and "civil society" are two entirely distinct orders, and in the temporal order the freedom to profess the religion of one's choice must be recognized for all "except if it truly destroys public order."

On October 4, the pope was able to leave for the UN with the "passport" of religious liberty in his pocket. On the eve of his departure, he exceptionally granted a long interview to the major Italian daily paper Il *Corriere della Sera*. Asked about Italian politics, and the relationship between the Church and the Italian state, he responded clearly and forcefully: "We desire Italians to make their own way freely." This was an unmistakable assertion of his desire to allow complete freedom to the Christian Democrats who were then in control of the government (for two years his friend Aldo Moro had led a coalition with the support of the Socialists).

The pope went to the UN at the invitation of the Secretary General, U Thant, for the twentieth anniversary of the international organization's founding. Thant had been receptive to the pope's appeal voiced in Bombay the preceding year, and immediately invited the pope to address the UN General Assembly. The Holy See was not a member of the UN, but held a permanent mission with the rank of observer since 1964. On the morning of October 4, Paul VI arrived in New York accompanied by seven cardinals, who were with him as representatives of the Council.

---

91 Card. Franjo Šeper (1905–1981) was the Croatian archbishop of Zagreb and Primate of Yugoslavia (1960–1969) and Prefect of the Congregation for the Doctrine of the Faith (1968–1981).

Millions of New Yorkers lined the roads along the papal cortège's route from Kennedy Airport to Saint Patrick's Cathedral. The pope had asked to pass through the poorest neighborhoods of the city, Harlem, and Little Puerto Rico. After a short ceremony at Saint Patrick's, Cardinal Spellman led the pope into the surrounding streets so he could greet and bless the crowds awaiting him. Then, in the afternoon, Paul VI held a meeting in the Waldorf-Astoria hotel with President L. B. Johnson.[92] They spoke for almost an hour about the great international problems of the day. America was engaged in the Vietnam War; a UN-imposed cease-fire had just halted a bloody conflict between India and Pakistan. "The means of promoting the cause of peace" were also discussed. No concrete results appear to have been produced by this high-level meeting.

In the afternoon, he went to the UN headquarters, passed through the "Meditation Room"[93] and presented himself before the General Assembly. Numerous people awaited the pope, including the representatives of one hundred and seventeen countries (only Albania's representatives refused their invitations). Before six to seven thousand people Paul VI gave a speech in French that has become famous. Speaking in the name of the Church but also in the name of non-Catholic communities, he presented himself as an "expert on humanity." In this role he had come to provide "a solemn and moral ratification": the UN is "the necessary means of modern civilization and world peace." His speech was not merely a homage paid to an organization which was then being severely criticized for its incapacity to maintain peace in the world. It was also a recognition of the principles on which it had been founded: The Universal Declaration of the Rights of Man. There again, through the voice of Paul VI, the Church implicitly recognized a doctrine explicitly condemned by successive popes at the end of the eighteenth and in the nineteenth century. Yet at the end of his speech, without seeming to criticize the ideology of the Rights of Man, Paul VI recalled that "the edifice of modern civilization must be constructed

---

92 Lyndon B. Johnson (1908–1973), a Democrat, succeeded John F. Kennedy to the White House after the latter's assassination in Dallas in 1963; he won the following election, staying in office until 1969. He was the architect of the "Great Society" legislation aimed at expanding public assistance to minorities to win them over to the Democratic Party.

93 Constructed to allow representatives of the UN, regardless of religion, to meditate in a single place. Did Paul VI pray in this syncretist location, which contained a sort of altar to an "unknown god," or did he only pass through it? The minutes of the visit of the pope preserved in the archives of the UN only mention his passing through.

on spiritual principles, the only ones capable not merely of supporting but also of enlightening and giving life": those of Christianity. This last reference was only made discreetly. Later Paul VI will tell Jean Guitton: "I was not there to evangelize. My speech was situated on another plane, I would even say: on the plane of Socrates. I was looking for what was just and reasonable, equitable and salutary — what all responsible men should think."[94]

The pope also called on the UN to accept new countries among its members. The pope named none, though everyone understood that he was alluding principally to Communist China; a few days later at the UN, France declared itself in favor of such an admission, the first Western country to do so. This speech was certainly full of audacity. Lastly, the pope made a passionate exhortation for peace: "Never again one against another, never, never again!... Never again war, never again war!"

At the end of his speech, Paul VI conversed for a few minutes with Gromyko,[95] Minister of Foreign Affairs for the Soviet Union. It was the first time that the head of the Catholic Church met with a Communist official of this rank. Other such meetings would follow in the years to come.

After receiving representatives from Protestant and Jewish communities at the Holy Family Church, located near the UN headquarters, the pope went to Cardinal Spellman's residence. In the evening, he celebrated a Mass in Latin (with readings and homily in English) at Yankee Stadium, before one hundred thousand people. At last, after a rapid nighttime visit to the Vatican pavilion at the New York World's Fair, he reboarded the plane for Rome late the next morning.

Upon his return, the pope wished to go immediately to Saint Peter's Basilica where the session of the Council continued. He received a triumphal welcome. Through the morning papers, the Council Fathers had learned of the pope's speech at the UN; upon the recommendation of Cardinal Liénart it was decided that this speech should be included in the official acts of the Council.

The last weeks of the Council were taken up with discussions and votes on the final texts: constitutions, decrees, and declarations. Here it

---

94 Guitton, *Dialogues*, 147.
95 Andrei Gromyko (1909–1989) was a Soviet communist politician during the Cold War, known in the West as Mr Nyet ("Mr No") because of his frequent use of his veto in the UN security council. He served as both Minister of Foreign Affairs (1957–1985) and on the Presidium of the Supreme Soviet (1985–1988).

is worth mentioning a few important decisions taken by Paul VI, but which did not necessarily appear to be from him at the time. The first was in the days preceding his voyage to New York. On September 29, Msgr Zoghbi,[96] Melchite Patriarchal Vicar for Egypt, arguing from a principle of Eastern theology, took a stand in favor of remarriage after divorce in certain cases. This intervention caused a great sensation in the Council hall; it called into question the principle of the indissolubility of marriage. Cardinal Journet shared his concerns with Paul VI, who asked him to defend the traditional position of the Church on the subject. With the help of Fr Wenger for the historical part, Cardinal Journet prepared his response throughout much of the night and, by the intervention of Paul VI with the Secretary General of the Council, was able to take the floor the next day, before all the scheduled speakers, to defend the indissolubility of marriage.

Paul VI's second intervention occurred during the debate on "The Ministry and Life of Priests." Some Council Fathers wanted to plead in favor of the marriage of priests. The press had already discussed this question repeatedly. Several bishops, including the presidents of some episcopal conferences, were worried that under the pressure of the media the Council might examine the question heatedly, stirring up new divisions. In light of this concern, on October 10, Paul VI addressed a letter to the Dean of the Council Presidency asking that this question not be discussed by the Council, and voicing his determination to defend the celibacy of priests as an "ancient, sacred, and providential law." One year before, October 23, 1964, Paul VI had acted the same way on the question of "birth control" (whether contraception should be authorized). These questions were the focus, in years to come, of two encyclicals.

When the oft-reworked text on Revelation was again brought up, the pope had three modifications he wished to be introduced transmitted to the Secretariat of the Council. Not all were fully accepted by the competent commission, proof that the pope could not always impose his will.

Another area in which the pope intervened, this time entirely secretly, was the non-condemnation of Communism. As was mentioned above, a condemnation of Communism had been requested by numerous bishops during the Ante-Preparatory Commission's consultations. Since then, new requests and efforts in this direction had been made — all in vain,

---

96   Archbishop Elias Zoghbi (1912–2008), born in Egypt of Lebanese parents, was consecrated in 1954 by the patriarch Maximos IV. He assisted at all four sessions of Vatican II and cultivated ecumenical relations with the Greek Orthodox.

because the Church, during the meeting at Metz, had agreed to not condemn Communism at the Council. John XXIII, and subsequently Paul VI, both felt bound by this agreement. When the text on "The Church in the Modern World" was examined, Archbishop Garrone,[97] its relator, explained that it did not include a judgement on Communism because "this mode of proceeding conforms with the pastoral aims of the Council and the express will of John XXIII and Paul VI." Some final efforts were made all the same. On September 29, three hundred thirty-two Council Fathers, or four hundred fifty according to other sources, signed a text asking for the condemnation of Communism; Archbishop Lefebvre and Msgr De Proença Sigaud gave it to the Council Presidency to be transmitted to the under-commission tasked with writing the passage on atheism. On October 18 a group of bishops who had been expelled from Marxist countries addressed, directly to the pope this time, a petition formulating the same request. Finally, on November 15 and 16, a new amendment circulated, receiving two hundred and nine signatures, because the first text had been "forgotten" among other papers and had not been examined in time. So many efforts could not fail to be taken into consideration. The commission responsible for the final editing of the text contented itself with adding a footnote with references to earlier condemnations.

It has recently become known that on November 26, a meeting was held around the pope to make a decision. Paul VI sided with the opinion of Cardinal Tisserant, who remained faithful to the promise he had made at Metz and deemed it preferable not to use the word "Communism" and to rest content with merely recalling earlier condemnations.[98]

The council was drawing to a close. On November 18, the pope had entered the Council assembly to deliver a speech announcing the next steps to be taken after the Council: the Curia would be reformed; the Congregation of the Holy Office would have a new organization; and the first synod of bishops would be called in 1967. This same day he announced that the formal causes would be opened for the beatification of his two predecessors: Pius XII and John XXIII. This was a deft

---

97 Card. Gabriel-Marie Garrone (1901–1994) was Prefect of the Congregation of Catholic Education (1968–1980). He studied at both the Pontifical Gregorian University and the Pontifical French Seminary. He was elevated to the rank of Cardinal-Priest of Santa Sabina (1967) and took part in the conclaves that elected Pope John Paul I and Pope John Paul II.
98 V. Carbone, "Schemi e discussioni sull'ateismo e sul marxismo nel Concilio Vaticano II," *Rivista di Storia della Chiesa in Italia*, 44 (1990): 58–59.

The Pope of the Council

maneuver: certain Council Fathers wanted John XXIII to be canonized, by acclamation, in full council. To open a process of canonization permitted avoidance of a practice that had been exceptionally rare, even in the first centuries of the Church. In simultaneously introducing the cause of Pius XII, Paul VI made it known that he took upon himself a double heritage, a twofold political line as it were.

On December 4, there was a ceremony of farewell for non-Catholic observers at the Basilica of Saint Paul Outside the Walls. For them as much as for the Catholic Church, Vatican II had been a historical event. Effectively the Council had constituted for the Church "a 180-degree turn in the direction of ecumenism." The non-Catholic communities professing Christ were recognized as "churches" in their own right, and in all the texts of the Council care was taken not to overlook their positions.[99]

The ceremony at Saint Paul Outside the Walls, therefore, was a sort of fond farewell to "churches" with which there had been a great deal of rapprochement over the last four years. Paul VI, at Jerusalem, had already prayed with the Orthodox Patriarch Athenagoras. This time, he prayed with Orthodox, Anglicans, Protestants, and other representatives of various communities. Prayers alternated with songs; prayers in French, English, Greek, and Latin. Was this truly "prayer in common," or was it merely simultaneous praying? In his speech Paul VI seemed to leave the choice to the observers who surrounded him. "Your departure," he said, is going "to create a vacuum"; he admitted that he felt this separation "with sorrow." He held a positive tone with hope for the future: "If no decision has been made in ecumenical matters, one ought not to underestimate that which has been done during the Council." He ended in recounting a parable by Solovyov[100] on the unity of the Church: a man, in a convent hallway, searched all night for the door to his room; only in the morning did he realize that it was open. Thus, for the "separated brethren": they have only to push the door of the Church to come home.

The next day Paul VI invited one of these observers, Oscar Cullmann, to his table, along with a lay auditor, Jean Guitton, and an expert, Fr de Lubac — three men with whom he was very friendly. During the meal, Father Macchi delivered a telegram from Constantinople: Patriarch Athenagoras had agreed to lift the mutual excommunications

---

99   Hans Küng, "An ecumenical inventory," in *Vatican II by Those Who Were There*, 26.
100 Vladimir Solovyov (1853–1900) was a Russian sophiologist who favored mending the East-West schism.

which, during the eleventh century, had sealed the separation between Catholics and Orthodox. This by no means reestablished unity between Catholics and Orthodox: important doctrinal differences remained. For Paul VI it was nonetheless a victory of "charity." This solemn lifting of the excommunications was officially announced on the last day of the Council, December 7, after the last text had been promulgated by the pope. The same day the *motu proprio* was published reforming the Sacred Congregation of the Holy Office, which had been repeatedly called for during the Council, sometimes with a certain virulence. The Holy Office was accused of acting with "obscurantism" and, in the examination of suspected doctrines and writings, for proceeding with methods "reminiscent of those of the Inquisition." The Holy Office would henceforth be called the Sacred Congregation for the Doctrine of the Faith, but Cardinal Ottaviani remained at its head. It would be responsible for "making clear the rationale of definitions and laws," while "correcting errors and returning those who have gone astray to the right path." Possible sanctions would be taken after consultation with the bishops of the regions concerned, and after giving the interested parties the opportunity to defend themselves orally or in writing. A short time later, the *Index of Forbidden Books* was suppressed.

This same December 7, Paul VI gave a final message to the Council which was about to end. Over the four years of the Council, the Church had been very occupied with man,

> man as he truly presents himself in our era, living man, man entirely occupied with himself, man who makes himself not only the center of all that interests him, but who dares to think himself the principle and reason behind every reality — a tragic man, the victim of his own drama; a man who is both sinner and saint.

The pope continued: "The old story of the Samaritan has been the model of the Council's spirituality. A sympathy without limits has entirely invaded it.... We also, We more than anyone, We hold the cult of man." The expression was shocking and even scandalous.[101] Paul VI had justified himself in advance on the same day by declaring: "Whoever closely observes this prevailing interest of the Council for human and

---

101 Fr Georges de Nantes made it the center of his case against Paul VI "for heresy, schism, and scandal," *Liber accusationis in Paulum sextum* (n.p.: Contre-Réforme catholique, 1973).

temporal values cannot deny that such an interest is due to its pastoral character...: loving man to love God." As did the Samaritan, the Council has had pity on man, using charity towards him rather than severity; "it has reflected more on his positive facets than on his negative facets." It did not want to condemn errors or give definitions, rather it wanted to be "pastoral."

On December 8, on the threshold of Saint Peter's Basilica, seven "messages of the Council" were read and given to representatives of the seven groups to whom they were addressed: "to leaders," "to men of thought and science," "to artists," "to women," "to workers," "to the poor, the ill, to all who suffer," "to the youth." Paul VI would say to Jean Guitton that these seven messages were "as the seven trumpets of the Apocalypse." The pope had asked Jacques Maritain and Jean Guitton to prepare these messages. Some required no adaptation. Maritain was responsible for the message to leaders; Guitton composed the message to women. Others had to be reviewed and rewritten.[102] Maritain, who drafted the message to men of thought and science, brought back fifty copies that he sent to those whom he judged to be the principal French intellectuals of the day. This final ceremony was not particularly noticed in the public forum. After four years of debates, surprising announcements, and spectacular initiatives of the pope, it was as if attention was no longer directed towards Rome, but towards the changes which the Council was going to cause in the different countries to which the bishops returned. All returned from the Council transformed. How many among them now accepted ideas and reforms that they would never have contemplated four years before? The first promulgated council document, on the liturgy in 1963, had already been translated into act by numerous highly visible reforms, and had not yet produced all its effects. The final documents adopted, those on religious liberty and "The Church in the Modern World," had met with great resistance[103] and portrayed a new vision of "the relationship between the Church and the world."[104]

---

102 Guitton, interview.
103 During the definitive votes — that is to say, those made just before promulgation by the pope — seventy Council Fathers had still voted against religious liberty, and seventy-five against "The Church in the World." The same texts each received more than 2,300 positive votes.
104 With regard to religious liberty, one of the principal theologians of the Council, Fr Congar, recognized: "It cannot be denied that a text like this does *materially* say something different from the Syllabus of 1864, and even almost the opposite of propositions 15 and 77–79 of that document." *Challenge to the Church: The Case of Archbishop Lefebvre*, trans. Paul Inwood (Huntingdon, IN: *Our Sunday Visitor*, 1976), 44.

Despite the great concern he had expressed throughout the year 1965, Paul VI was confident. In his interview with *Corriere della Sera* in October he had affirmed: "Besides the crisis of faith in the world, there is not, happily, a crisis of the Church." At this date, therefore, he still thought that the Church would be rejuvenated by the Council, and would be able to respond to this "crisis of faith." The crisis of the Church, however, had already begun and was going to grow. A few years after the Council, he would admit to the archbishop of Milan: "We were hoping for a springtime, and a storm has come."[105]

---

105   Cardinal G. Colombo, *Ricordando*, 194.

8

Between Reforms and Voyages

THE COUNCIL HAD ADOPTED GENERAL TEXTS, which only rarely indicated practical measures. According to the instructions, there were two institutions that would pursue the envisioned reforms: the Roman Congregations, which were often centuries old, and the more recently formed national episcopal conferences, many of which were created in the year following the Council. Paul VI had authority over both, but it quickly became apparent that he neither could nor would impose his views, and that the Roman Congregations and the episcopal conferences could easily find themselves in conflict, and thus create a climate of uncertainty and confusion. One of the first examples of this difficult "three-player game" arose in the weeks immediately following the Council.

On January 25, 1966, the Congregation for Seminaries and Universities published an instruction that Latin was to be retained in the seminaries for the celebration of Mass and for the recitation of the Breviary. Cardinal Lercaro, responsible for the liturgical reform then in progress, complained to the pope, as did several French bishops. Among them was Cardinal Villot, then archbishop of Lyon. When he met with the pope the following February 22, he shared his concerns. He received a reassuring response, as a confidant testifies: "Paul VI could not disavow the Congregation for Seminaries and Universities. He said simply that the instruction was not imperative, but only indicative."[1] In the French seminaries, Latin was very soon able to disappear from the liturgical offices.

In any case, this congregation received a new prefect, and was entrusted to a Frenchman. In this same month of February, Paul VI called upon Archbishop Garrone, who had intervened during the Council to call for a reform of seminaries, to direct it. He was named "to get things going."[2]

THE LITURGICAL REFORM

The liturgical reform that Vatican II called for, and its implementation during the pontificate of Paul VI, constitutes without a doubt the

---

[1] Wenger, Le Cardinal Villot, 55.
[2] Card. Gabriel-Marie Garrone, interview with the author, February 21, 1992.

Council's deepest change in the life of the Catholic Church. It is also the most obvious change, and it gave occasion to the greatest number of excesses and deviations. It most directly concerned all Catholics and affected everyone intimately, clergy as well as the faithful. It was the most controversial, and met with the strongest resistance. Paul VI followed this liturgical reform step by step with scrupulous attention, because he had longed for this reform for decades. One of the artisans of this reform has said: "Nothing was decided, much less promulgated, without Paul VI being aware of it. He received the plans, which he annotated with his own hand, making his preferences clear and sometimes also his demands or refusals, so much so that sometimes real crises were created."[3]

While he was a cardinal at the Central Preparatory Commission and then during the first session of the Council, Paul VI had intervened in favor of such a reform, promoting a limited introduction of the vernacular in the ritual of the Mass. Having become pope, he was able to promulgate the constitution on the liturgy which the Council had just passed in December 1963. It envisaged a revision of the Mass ritual and other rites, the limited introduction of the vernacular and of concelebration, with faculties given to local ecclesiastical authorities to extend their usage. But even before this text was adopted, Paul VI had Cardinal Lercaro prepare a list of reforms which could go into effect immediately. Finally, it was deemed preferable to wait for the promulgation of the constitution. On December 4, 1963, it was definitively voted by a very large majority: 2,147 votes in favor, 4 against. On the following January 25 the organization responsible for its implementation was created: the *Consilium ad exsequendam Constitutionem liturgicam «Sacrosanctum Concilium»*. The Consilium was presided over by Cardinal Lercaro, who, in the preceding years, had become well-known on account of various liturgical initiatives in his diocese. The secretary of the Consilium was Fr Bugnini: he had been, during the preparatory period of the Council, the linchpin of the Liturgical Commission. He had been removed from it during the first session of the Council; thanks to Paul VI, he returned to favor and would play a central role in the ongoing reform.[4] The Consilium counted amongst its leaders the master of Paul VI, Father Bevilacqua, and among its consultors (or experts with a vote), who would play an essential part in its work, number some of the key

---

3   Martimort, "Le rôle de Paul VI dans la réforme liturgique," 64.
4   Archbishop A. Bugnini has published an indispensable documentary work on the subject: *La Riforma liturgica (1948–1975)*; English edition: *The Reform of the Liturgy: 1948–1975*, trans. Matthew J. O'Connell (Collegeville, MN: The Liturgical Press, 1990).

figures of the postwar Liturgical Movement: Fathers Botte, Bouyer, Gy, Jungmann, Feder, and Lanne,[5] and Canon Martimort. Experiments and instructions were going to follow one after the other in rapid succession while the revision of the rites of the Mass and of the other sacraments were being prepared. In June 1964 a first "experimental" Mass took place at the Abbey of Saint Anselm in Rome — the text of the Mass was not yet altered, but two important innovations had been introduced. The Mass was celebrated by multiple participants (the Abbot Primate of the Benedictines, Benno Gut,[6] surrounded by twenty religious) who were facing the faithful; they consecrated one large host, which they shared. Soon afterwards, on the following September 26, a long instruction was published prescribing the most important reforms, namely the use of the vernacular language in certain parts of the Mass (not only the readings of the Epistle and the Gospel, but also for the Ordinary: the Kyrie, Gloria, Credo, Sanctus, and Agnus Dei). It also recommended the construction of altars separated from the wall "so that clergy can easily go around them and celebrate towards the people."[7]

These instructions were to be observed beginning on March 7, 1965, the first Sunday of Lent, but already in some countries, particularly France, the vernacular had been introduced into the Mass several months before.

That Sunday, in a parish of Rome, Paul VI celebrated Mass in Italian for the first time in this manner: only the Canon of the Mass was still in Latin; he was turned towards the faithful throughout. This same day he stated the reasons for such a rupture:

> This Sunday marks a date to be remembered in the spiritual history of the Church, because the vernacular has officially entered into liturgical worship.... The Church makes a sacrifice in renouncing Latin, a sacred, grave, beautiful, highly expressive, and elegant language. She has sacrificed centuries of tradition, and of unity of language for an aspiration towards ever-greater universality.... That is for you, the faithful, so that you may

---

[5] Fr José Feder (1917–1989) was a French Jesuit and liturgist. Emmanuel Lanne (1923–2010) was a monk at the Benedictine abbey of Chevetogne and during the Second Vatican Council a member of the Secretariat for Christian Unity. He was also a co-editor of a number of the decrees, including the one on ecumenism *Unitatis Redintegratio*.

[6] Card. Benno Gut (1897–1970) was a Swiss cardinal who served as Prefect of the Congregation for Divine Worship (1969–1970). In 1959, he was elected as the fourth Abbot Primate of the Benedictine Confederation.

[7] A modified *Ordo Missæ* would be published in January 1965, taking these instructions into account.

better know how to unite yourselves to the prayer of the Church, so that you may know how to pass from the state of simple spectators to that of participating and active faithful.

This abandonment, partial for the moment, of Latin had raised some concerns. The disappearance of Latin meant the loss of the universal language of the Church, and the risk of seeing the mystery of the Mass lose its sacrality. It was in Norway that the first groups for the preservation of Latin in the liturgy were formed. In France, Bernadette Lécureux published a work, *Le Latin, langue de l'Église*, which met with great success.[8]

Not long afterwards, in December 1964, an association was founded in Paris for the defense and the development of Latin liturgy and Gregorian chant: Una Voce.[9] The initiative began with Georges Cerbelaud-Salagnac,[10] editor and Secretary General of the Association of Catholic Writers (though he was acting in a personal capacity). Una Voce, which would win the support of musicians including Maurice Duruflé and Olivier Messiaen,[11] and writers (Jean Dutourd, Gustave Thibon, and Jacques Vier, among others),[12] garnered a certain degree of success and numbered up to twenty thousand members.

The spreading use of the vernacular in long swaths of the Mass over the course of 1965 did not go without criticism. Ten days after vernacular Masses took effect, Paul VI responded severely, during a public

---

8   Bernadette Lécureux, *Le Latin, langue de l'Église* (Paris: Pierre Téqui, 1998). Bernadette Lécureux (1913–2011) was a French author who was born and died in Brest, France. She was awarded the Knight of the Legion of Honour award. A similar work was published in 1966 by Marie-Madeleine Martin, *Le latin immortel*; recently an English translation has appeared: *Immortal Latin* (Waterloo, ON: Arouca Press, 2022). An equivalent in Italy was Tito Casini's 1967 polemic *The Torn Tunic: Letter of a Catholic on the "Liturgical Reform"* (Brooklyn, NY: Angelico Press, 2020, repr. of 1967 English ed.).
9   G. Cerbelaud, interview with the author, March 16, 1992.
10   Georges Cerbelaud-Salagnac (1906–1999) was a French historian, writer, and journalist with many works and awards to his credit, including the Biguet Prize (1983).
11   Maurice Duruflé (1902–1986) was a French musician and teacher known for his perfectionism and highly self-critical nature, only publishing a few compositions and continuously editing them after publication. Olivier Messiaen (1908–1992) was a French composer and organist.
12   Jean Dutourd (1922–2007) was a French novelist born in Paris. After escaping a World War II German war prison, he studied philosophy and entered the Resistance, taking part in the Liberation of Paris. Gustave Thibon (1903–2001) was a French philosopher and writer. He had started his literary career with an invitation from Jacques Maritain to write for the *Revue Thomiste*. Jacques Vier (1903–1991) was a French historian, literary critic, and writer.

audience, to those who complained: these critics, he said, "do not show a true devotion or an authentic sense of the significance and value of the Mass, but rather a certain spiritual sloth which makes them refuse the personal effort of understanding and participation..." (March 17, 1965). A few days later, however, one of his friends, Jacques Maritain, would make grave accusations against him. About this time, as has been mentioned above, the French philosopher addressed four memorandums to the pope. The longest centered on the liturgical reform underway.[13] Jacques Maritain was not opposed to this reform, but he criticized the way in which it was introduced. It led to a "loss of the sense of mystery." The translations authorized by the French bishops, in his eyes, featured too many platitudes and unfortunate translations. In the Credo he even noticed a formula that was "strictly speaking, heretical": the Latin *consubstantialem Patri* (consubstantial with the Father) was translated by "of the same nature as the Father," the formula that had been used by the Arian heretics of the fourth century.[14]

Paul VI did not respond personally to these criticisms made by his friend Maritain. He apparently did not intervene either with the French bishops' commission responsible for translations, since everything that Jacques Maritain judged to be faulty is still in use today. Instead, the pope left it to the Consilium to intervene. The Consilium ought to have "a directive role," he explained to its members; it was their job

> to supervise the experimental phase of the innovations..., to correct any deviations that might spring up here and there, to halt any arbitrary unauthorized practices which could cause disorders in the right disciplining of public prayer and even induce doctrinal errors. It is thus your duty to prevent abuses, to drive on the tardy and the reticent, to awaken energy, to favor good initiatives, to praise those who deserve it. (October 13, 1966)

Did the Consilium fully accomplish this mission? Evidently not. Often, by the admission of its members, it only "confirmed" decisions which the episcopal conferences had already made, and gave instructions relative to reforms already undertaken long before.[15] Focusing, as we are, only

---

13   Unedited memorandum of thirty-six type-written pages: "Common prayer and private prayer. The vernacular language and the sacred texts. Studies" (Archives J. Maritain).
14   The French philosopher Étienne Gilson made a similar remark in a resounding article published in *La France catholique* (July 2, 1965), "Suis-je schismatique?"
15   Martimort, "Le rôle de Paul VI," 65.

on the role of Paul VI in the liturgical reform, it must be remembered that his principal concern was to achieve, in all its aspects, the liturgical reform; his aim was the complete revision, in texts and actions, of the rite of the Mass and of all the other rituals. In October 1966, he had six non-Catholic "observers" added to the Consilium, including Pastor Max Thurian. Did these Lutheran, Anglican, and other observers contribute to the revision of the rites, notably that of the Mass? One of them said in self-defense: "Our role was to observe the work and to convey its fruits to our communities, not to influence in any way the work or the decisions of the Consilium."[16] All the same, it cannot be believed that they were merely mute spectators. When this Consilium presented, in 1969, a "New Mass," critics claimed that it had been "protestantized."

PURSUING DIALOGUE

The post-conciliar period is not only about the liturgical reform, but also the pursuit of "dialogue" with all: "separated brethren," communist countries, the whole world.

On March 23, Paul VI received Dr Ramsey, Anglican archbishop of Canterbury and primate of the Anglican Church. Dr Fisher, his predecessor, had been received by John XXIII, but only in a personal capacity.[17] This time it was an official visit, of the head of one Church to another. This meeting illustrates perfectly the spirit in which Paul VI planned to continue his post-conciliar ecumenical action. Dr Ramsey was received in the Sistine Chapel with these warm words: "We wish your first impression in crossing the threshold of our house to be that you arrive, not in a strange house, but in a house that you can always call your own." At the end of the afternoon there was another meeting, in the library, in the presence of Msgr Willebrands. The subjects discussed during this working session appear only vaguely in the official discourses. But the tone of the conversation could be faithfully reconstructed with ease.[18] Dr Ramsey proposed that a commission of Catholic and Anglican theologians be created to study the doctrinal questions continuing

---

16   Max Thurian, "Paul VI et les observateurs," 256.
17   Archbishop Geoffrey Fisher (1887–1972) was an English Anglican and the ninety-ninth archbishop of Canterbury (1945–1961). A key theme of his time as archbishop was Church unity; he worked to network and connect with other Christian churches. Michael Ramsey (1904–1988) was likewise the Anglican archbishop of Canterbury from 1961 to 1974 and was known as an Anglo-Catholic. He actively promoted the formation of some sort of unity between the Catholic and Anglican Churches, yet rejected the teaching of *Humanæ Vitæ*.
18   O. Chadwick, *Michael Ramsey: A Life*, 320–21.

to separate the churches; Paul VI accepted.[19] Dr Ramsey also discussed the problem of Anglican clerical ordinations, which the Catholic Church considers invalid; the pope agreed to reopen the dossier. Lastly the Anglican primate complained of the practices of the Catholic hierarchy in England: Anglican converts to Catholicism were rebaptized, and mixed marriages were only accepted with great difficulty. Paul VI responded that he would write to Cardinal Heenan,[20] archbishop of Westminster, to ask him not to demean Anglican baptisms.

The next day, March 24, there was another meeting, at the Basilica of Saint Paul Outside the Walls. After a common declaration, Paul VI asked Dr Ramsey to bless the assembly with him. The request was so unexpected that the Anglican primate did not understand it, and genuflected, believing that Paul VI wanted to bless him. The pope immediately raised him up. But the most dramatic moment was yet to come. Paul VI wanted to seal this first official visit of an Anglican primate with a "gesture" to move public opinion and demonstrate the goodwill of the Catholic Church towards Anglicans. Before departing he removed from his finger the episcopal ring which the people of Milan had offered him when he became their archbishop, and gave it to Dr Ramsey, who put it on his own finger.[21] This striking gesture was interpreted by many as an implicit recognition of the episcopal authority of Dr Ramsey, and thus of the Anglican ordinations. In fact, as was often the case with Paul VI, his attitude, warm words, and symbolic gestures far exceeded his actual thoughts. Although the Catholic hierarchy in England has had to be more supple towards the Anglicans according to the pope's demands; nevertheless, to the dismay of many ecumenists, never have the Anglican ordinations been recognized as valid.

Paul VI did not want to miss any occasion for dialogue in his relationships with governments, even those most hostile to the Church. Msgr Samoré,[22] then Secretary of the Section of Extraordinary Affairs, explained to a journalist:

---

19 It would be set up in 1969 under the name ARCIC (Anglo-Roman Catholic International Commission).
20 Card. John Carmel Heenan (1905–1975) was the archbishop of Westminster (1963–1975) and was created the Cardinal-Priest of S. Silvestro in Capite by Pope Paul VI (1965).
21 The gesture was premeditated. The pope had consulted Dr Ramsey's chaplain, Rev. John Andrew, in advance to know his ring size; but the Anglican primate was not aware of this.
22 Card. Antonio Samoré (1905–1983) was an Italian curial prelate. Paul VI gave him the red biretta in 1967 and appointed him Archivist and Librarian of the Holy See.

PAUL VI: THE DIVIDED POPE

The prayer of this pope could be: Lord, allow me to undo the sins of omission, the lost opportunities! Sometimes the pope tells me at the morning audience: "I thought of this last night; it must be done; I read this or that." And to hurry those of us who are at his service: "What can we do in this case? We must study the situation."[23]

This is how to understand his meetings with the authorities of Communist countries. On April 27, 1966, he had received Andrei Gromyko, Minister of Foreign Affairs for the USSR, the first Soviet official to be received at the Vatican since the Revolution. The following year he received Podgorny,[24] Soviet Head of State; then, in subsequent years, other Communist leaders: the Yugoslavian Tito[25] in 1971, the Romanian Ceaușescu[26] in 1973, the Bulgarian Zhivkov[27] in 1975, the Hungarian Kádár[28] and the Pole Gierek[29] in 1977. These official receptions complemented the negotiations carried out abroad by Msgr Casaroli, to establish diplomatic relations or at least arrive at some agreement. This Ostpolitik endeavored to obtain the minimal conditions of religious

---

23   A. Wenger, "Cinq audiences de Paul VI," Notiziario 18 (August 1989): 82.
24   Nikolai Podgorny (1903–1983) was a Soviet statesman who was both Chairman of the Presidium of the Supreme Soviet and Head of State of the Soviet Union (1965–1977). He was born into a working-class Ukrainian family and joined the Soviet Union's Communist Party (1930). He came to power in a coup, replacing the Soviet leader Nikita Khrushchev with himself and two others, making him the second most powerful man in the country, after Brezhnev.
25   Marshal Josip Broz Tito (1892–1980) was the first President of the Socialist Federal Republic of Yugoslavia (1953–1980). He had fought for the Austro-Hungarian empire during World War I and was captured by the Russians. He participated in the Russian Revolution, before helping to bring Communism to his homeland.
26   Nicolae Ceaușescu (1918–1989) was the general secretary of the Romanian Communist Party (1965–1989) and so, the penultimate communist leader of Romania. He also served as President (1974) and President of the State Council (1967) until he was overthrown and executed during the Romanian Revolution in 1989 due to claims of illegal wealth gathering and genocide.
27   Todor Zhivkov (1911–1998) was the Bulgarian President (1971–1989) and the secretary of the Bulgarian Communist Party's Central Committee (1954–1989), making him the longest-serving leader in any of the Eastern European Soviet nations. He resigned and was subsequently expelled from the party when Communist governments across Europe began to collapse in 1989.
28   János Kádár (1912–1989) governed Hungary as the General Secretary of the Hungarian Socialist Workers' Party from 1956 to 1988.
29   Edward Gierek (1913–2001) was a Polish communist politician and the de facto leader of Poland (1970–1980). He allowed communist Poland to be subject to Western influence, making the country more liberal, and is also known for his foreign loans economic policy, despite its ultimately failing and dragging Poland into economic turmoil.

practice for Catholics living in Communist countries: dioceses furnished with a bishop; guaranteed true freedom of worship; recognition of the spiritual jurisdiction of the Holy See over Catholics. But to obtain this minimum (which for example almost never ensured the right to religious education at school, or the existence of a Catholic press), the pope and his staff made certain concessions. The bishops were sometimes at the service of the Communist government. Even though agreements were publicly signed and subsequently used for government propaganda, their violation was not forcefully denounced by the Holy See. Lastly, Catholics in some countries did not benefit at all from this Ostpolitik: the Uniate of Ukraine were sacrificed or at least forgotten in favor of an understanding with the USSR and for ecumenical closeness with the Russian Orthodox; the Catholics of North Vietnam saw their plight subordinated to the pope's calls for peace. His frequent appeals for peace alternated between diplomatic maneuvers, solemn appeals, and prayer. On December 30, 1965, he officially addressed telegrams to the five heads of state directly implicated in the war in Vietnam (United States, China, USSR, North Vietnam, and South Vietnam), calling on them to engage in negotiations. A few months later, on September 15, 1966, he published an encyclical, *Christi Matri Rosarii*, in which he plaintively addressed all the governments of countries at war: "In the name of the Lord, We cry: Stop! You must meet; you must come to confer and negotiate in all sincerity." In the same text, he also recalled that Christ is the only "Prince of Peace," that peace must be begged for through prayer; he recommended once again the recitation of the Rosary.

SIGNS OF CRISIS

In October 1965, as we have seen, Paul VI still thought that the Church was not undergoing a crisis. In 1966 and 1967 he began to perceive things differently, although this did nothing to modify the general trends of his papal policy.

In July 1966, Cardinal Ottaviani, responsible for the Congregation of the Doctrine of the Faith, addressed a "circular" to the bishops of the entire world, as well as superiors of religious orders. It detailed a list of doctrinal errors: errors concerning Christ, and the Eucharist; the depreciation of confession; minimalization of the doctrine of original sin; ecumenical irenism; and religious indifferentism. Bishops and superiors were asked to indicate whether these were spreading among their clergy and the faithful, and also "to eliminate or prevent them." The responses of bishops in the different parts of the world are not known, though presumably these errors varied region by region. In any case, the French response, published in the press, shocked Paul VI. The response made collectively by the French bishops was intended to be optimistic; the pope judged otherwise: "This letter is an accusation against the French clergy.... [It] reveals a situation graver than what the inquiry of the Holy Office allowed us to suspect. This diagnosis in any case amply justifies the steps of the Holy Office. Poor clergy of France!"[30]

Paul VI must also have been sensitive to the alarm raised by his friend Maritain. Some weeks after Ottaviani's circular was distributed, by coincidence, he published a highly critical work, *The Peasant of the Garonne*.[31] Without rejecting anything of the Second Vatican Council or renouncing his "integral humanism," he fretted about the "neo-modernism which flourishes anew," speaking of "immanent apostasy" to describe the situation of certain sectors of the Church in France, and making himself a satirist to stigmatize "those priests who boast of no longer bending the knee before the tabernacle." In this book Maritain was cautious to distance himself from "integrism" (or "integralism"), "the worst offence to Divine Truth and to human intelligence"!

According to Guitton, the pope found the book "a bit too gloomy." However, the situation of France was far from exceptional. In this same month of October 1966, the bishops of Holland published a "Catechism" whose precepts, in many important points, were contrary to the traditional faith of the Church. The "Dutch crisis" had only just begun. At the beginning of the following year, some Dutch seminarians who were soon to be ordained priests wrote to the pope asking to be dispensed from celibacy. On February 14, after being informed of the matter, Cardinal Ottaviani addressed a letter to Paul VI encouraging him to remain firm on a rule which he himself had not wished to see debated by the Council. On the 17th, the pope responded to him emotionally, thanking his "former master and superior" for the encouragement and help "in the strong and faithful accomplishment of our difficult apostolic office."[32] This encouragement from Cardinal Ottaviani was undoubtedly not foreign to the determination shown a few months later by Paul VI in publishing

---

30 A. Wenger, "Paul VI et La Croix," in *Paul VI et la modernité dans l'Église* (Rome: École française de Rome, 1984), 758.

31 Jacques Maritain, *The Peasant of the Garonne: An Old Layman Questions Himself about the Present Time*, trans. Michael Cuddihy and Elizabeth Hughes (Eugene, OR: Wipf & Stock, 2011).

32 Letters published in Cavaterra, *Il Prefetto del Sant'Offizio*, 176ff.

the encyclical *Sacerdotalis Cælibatus*; in any case, the text was revised by the old cardinal. This fourth encyclical of the pontificate was entirely devoted to the defense of priestly celibacy, an imitation of Christ with a definite pastoral effectiveness and great eschatological significance.

A "HOLISTIC HUMANISM"

The encyclical on priestly celibacy — which did not however stop this rule from being questioned thereafter — had been preceded, three months earlier, by an encyclical that was considerably more groundbreaking, and had been much better received. That the same pope was able to publish two solemn texts of such different tones and spirits in the space of a few months shows how far there were two mindsets that coexisted in him, or even two personalities: one was religious, traditional, and quick to defend the great truths of dogma, as well as Church discipline; the other was humanist, sociopolitical, and innovative. Until the end of his papacy, neither can be said to have dominated the other. A cardinal who had known him well, particularly when the former was serving as intermediary between the pope and the Council, said of Paul VI: "He was a pope who suffered from a dichotomy, with his head to the right and his heart to the left."[33]

The encyclical that appeared in March 1967, *Populorum Progressio* [the development of peoples], had been germinating since the beginning of his papacy. From 1963 on, according to Cardinal Poupard,[34] who was then attached to the Secretariat of State, Paul VI had kept a dossier entitled: "On economic, social, and moral development. Study material for an encyclical on the moral principles of human development." Seven successive versions were drafted, each enriched by diverse consultations. The authors cited show that this encyclical was inspired to a great degree by contemporary authors: Fathers Lebret, Chenu, and de Lubac; Colin Clark[35] and Jacques Maritain. In making a direct reference to Maritain's

---

33   Cited by Lai, *Les Secrets du Vatican*, 168.
34   Card. Paul Poupard (1930–) is a French prelate who held various positions in the Roman Curia, including serving as the President of the Pontifical Council for Culture (1988–2007) and also briefly serving as President of the Pontifical Council for Interreligious Dialogue. He is a prominent scholar and author, with many of his works translated into several languages.
35   Colin Clark (1905–1989) was a British-Australian economist and statistician, best known for pioneering the use of gross national product (GNP) for studying national economies. He attended Oxford University, graduating in Chemistry (1928). Later in life, he taught statistics at Cambridge University, was the Director of the Institute for Agricultural Economics at Oxford University, and moved to Australia to work as an Economics Department Research Consultant at the University of Queensland, Australia, until his death.

Integral Humanism, Paul VI affirmed: "A holistic humanism must be promoted." "Holistic humanism" was defined as: "the integral development of the whole man, and of all men." The encyclical denounced "the exclusive search for possessions" to the detriment of "the growth of being"; "egotistical speculations" and the loss of capital; "liberalism without end"; "materialistic and atheistic philosophy"; and "neo-colonialism." He also saw, in "nationalism" and "racism," two obstacles of the same nature on the route towards "a fairer world structured more fully in universal solidarity." Revolutionary insurrection was to be rejected, "except in the case of self-evident and prolonged tyranny, would bring grave harm to the common good of the country." But when would these conditions be fulfilled, and who would determine that they were fulfilled and that it was necessary to start an insurrection? In the years to come, the movement of "liberation theology" or of "revolution" would rush through the doors opened by Paul VI. *Populorum Progressio* did not, however, preach revolution, but promoted the economic and social development of everyone. That was the solution, in the pope's eyes, for all the woes of the Third World, and the best guarantee of peace.

Outside the Church, there were mixed reactions to this encyclical. Financial circles generally criticized its principles, which they considered utopian, while its analyses were considered defective from an economic point of view. The *Wall Street Journal*, for example, pilloried the papal document. On the other hand, the Director of UNESCO, the General Secretary of the UN, and Patriarch Athenagoras, to whom the encyclical had been communicated, all congratulated the pope. The hierarchy of the Church unanimously praised the encyclical, which was in line with the last two encyclicals of John XXIII, but was more critical in its analysis of the economic and social world, and even more audacious. From Brazil, Msgr Hélder Câmara sent a telegram to the pope: "Thank you, Holy Father, in the name of the Third World." But the Church was not a society like any other; a façade of unanimity could hide wide divergences of opinion.

Paul VI had sent draft versions of his encyclical to the archbishop of Genoa, Cardinal Siri. The cardinal, who had been president of the Italian Social Weeks for many years, had a keen understanding of financial and economic circles: the pope wanted his opinion. Cardinal Siri judged the texts to be superficial and unrealistic. He sent them to different European economic experts for examination, without stating their origin. All were highly critical. As a result, the cardinal wrote to the pope: "It must be entirely redone. One would say that it is the reflections of a parish priest." But the pope did not dare contradict his own experts and counselors or rewrite the encyclical. *Populorum Progressio* appeared. According to Cardinal Siri, in the weeks that followed, some unfavorable reports arrived at the Vatican, not least from some governments. As a result the archbishop of Genoa was compelled to board a flight to Rome and take up the defense of the encyclical on Vatican Radio, in a spirit of obedience, and for the good of the Church...[36]

FROM FATIMA TO ISTANBUL

On May 13, 1967, Paul VI arrived in Fatima. This trip, contrary to the preceding visits to the Holy Land and to Bombay, was one that the pope made with great reticence. In 1917, at Fatima, the Virgin Mary had appeared several times to three young visionaries to deliver a message of conversion and penitence. She had particularly desired Russia to be solemnly consecrated to her: "If my demands are heeded, Russia will convert and there will be peace. If not, she will spread her errors through the world, provoking wars and persecutions of the Church." She had also confided to the little visionaries a "third secret" which, it was said, should not be revealed until 1960, because at that date it would be understood more clearly. The Church had recognized the authenticity of the apparitions, but in 1967, neither the solemn consecration nor the revelation of the "third secret" had taken place. The pope had the text of this "third secret" and it was his prerogative to reveal it.[37] John XXIII had read it; a few of his close collaborators (Cardinal Ottaviani) read it or at least were familiar with its essential outlines; but he had not given it much importance and did not reveal it on the indicated date. Paul VI also read it, but refused to reveal it. According to the testimony of Jean Guitton, the pope "was profoundly devoted to the Virgin, but at the same time he had a very modern, highly critical spirit... Paul VI had his own particular conception of apparitions."[38]

And so, when the Portuguese bishops asked him to come to Portugal for the fiftieth anniversary of the apparitions, he accepted, but against his inclinations. Upon his return, he would say to Jean Guitton that it was "a

---

36 R. Spiazzi, *Il cardinal Giuseppe Siri*, 136–37.
37 Brother Michel de la Sainte Trinité, *Toute la vérité sur Fatima*, vol. 3, "Le troisième secret." The author guessed that this "secret" was related to the crisis of the Church. In 2000, the Vatican released a text that was claimed to be the secret. Whether or not this text transmits in full the secret conveyed by Sister Lucy to the ecclesiastical authorities is still hotly debated.
38 Guitton, interview.

pilgrimage of penance" and "an act of humility."[39] Besides, Portugal was then led by Salazar,[40] who had led an authoritarian and corporatist regime since before the war. In going to Fatima, Paul VI did not want to appear to approve a regime so contrary to the democratic ideals he cherished.

He landed on Portuguese soil not in Lisbon but at a military airport, Monte Real, about thirty miles from Fatima. He declared straightaway that he came as a "pilgrim," and was not making an official visit to Portugal. At the Cova da Iria, the place of the apparitions, an enormous crowd awaited him, more than a million people. He celebrated Mass in Portuguese, in the rain, before fervent worshippers. At this Mass the Head of State and the head of the Portuguese government were present, along with about sixty cardinals and bishops, and also Sister Lúcia,[41] the last surviving visionary from 1917, who lived cloistered in a Carmelite convent.

At no point did Paul VI mention the apparitions or the "secret"; he prayed for peace. At the end of the Mass that he had celebrated before the crowd, he held a brief meeting with Sister Lúcia, who knelt before him. At one point, she expressed her desire to have a one-on-one meeting with the pope perhaps to bring up the famous "secret" and the consecration of Russia. According to the religious that was serving as their interpreter, Paul VI refused rather harshly: "Look, it's not the time. And then, if you want to communicate something to me, tell your bishop; he will communicate it to me; be confident in and obedient to your bishop."[42] Later, the pope held a short private meeting in French with Salazar, of which nothing is known. That very night he returned to Rome. If this rapid voyage to Fatima did not make him consider the apparitions in a new light, they did, however, leave the pope with a strong impression of the faith of the Portuguese. He told Guitton a few days later:

---

39 Guitton, *Journal de ma vie*, 575.
40 António de Oliveira Salazar (1889–1970) was Prime Minister of Portugal from 1932 to 1968. Having been formed as an economist, he established a corporatist government based on Catholic Social Teaching, which put end to the chaos that followed the overthrow of the Portuguese monarchy in 1910. He was a devout Catholic, negotiating a Concordat with the Holy See in 1940 and combating the anti-clerical Freemasons throughout his public life. See *Salazar and His Work: Essays on Political Philosophy*, ed. Brian Welter (Waterloo, ON: Arouca Press, 2021).
41 Sister Lúcia Dos Santos (1907–2005) was one of the three Portuguese children that saw Our Lady near Fatima, Portugal and the only one to converse with her. Later she joined the Discalced Carmelites (O.C.D). The other two children were Lúcia's cousins and died in childhood. Over the course of her life, she wrote six memoirs and several letters to clergy and lay people.
42 P. Almeida, "La rencontre de Paul VI avec sœur Lucie de Fatima," *La Documentation catholique*, July 2, 1967.

I could only summarize my impression in one word: I saw humanity. Yes, humanity, true humanity, in a state of simplicity, of prayer and of penitence. It was the sight of the final assembly, maybe the largest assembly of veritable true believers. I have never seen that in this world. Of course, at Bombay, there were millions of people, but they were merely curious people, and then they stretched out over twelve miles. There the assembly occupied a single valley, giving the impression that humanity, truly, was one.[43]

The following June 26, he held a second consistory during which he created twenty-seven new cardinals. Three of his friends, Antonio Riberi, whom he had known since the Ecclesiastical Academy, and Pierre Veuillot, and Angelo Dell'Acqua, who had worked with him at the Secretariat of State, received the cardinal's hat.[44] Msgr Garrone, who had entered the curia the preceding year, became a cardinal. Also to be noted was the entry into the Sacred College of the first Indonesian cardinal, Darmojuwono,[45] archbishop of Semarang, and of a Pole, Karol Wojtyła,[46] archbishop of Krakow, who had made his mark at the Council by his interventions in favor of religious liberty and for the important part which he had taken in editing the constitution *Gaudium et Spes*.

In July, the pope embarked on another voyage, the fifth of his papacy: a brief trip to Turkey, which was simultaneously a Marian pilgrimage (to Ephesus), a commemoration of the first great ecumenical councils of the Church, and an ecumenical meeting with Patriarch Athenagoras.

To facilitate the diplomatic negotiations for his visit to the mostly Muslim country, where Catholics numbered only a few thousand, he returned to the Turkish government the battle standard which had been captured from the Turkish fleet after their defeat at the naval battle of Lepanto[47] and which had been kept in Rome ever since. On July 25,

---

43 Guitton, *Journal de ma vie*, 575.
44 Cardinal Dell'Acqua was replaced at the post of Substitute of the Secretary of State by Archbishop Benelli.
45 Card. Justinus Darmojuwono (1914–1994) was archbishop of Semarang, Indonesia from 1963 to 1981.
46 Karol Josef Wojtyła (1920–2005) was auxiliary bishop of Krakow (1958–1964), then archbishop of the same see. Created a cardinal in 1967, he was elected pope in 1978 and took the name John Paul II.
47 The Battle of Lepanto was fought on October 7, 1571 in the Gulf of Patras between the fleets of the Ottoman Empire and the Holy League, a coalition organized by Pope St Pius V to defend the Christian West against the Muslim invasion. The Dominican pope had called for the recitation of the Rosary for a Christian

accompanied by several cardinals, Paul VI left Rome for Istanbul. His first visit was to the president of the Republic of Turkey, Cevdet Sunay,[48] with whom he met for ninety minutes. Doubtless the recent Israeli-Arab war was discussed, among other subjects. The preceding June, during the Six Days War, Israel had conquered Sinai, the Gaza Strip, the West Bank, the Golan heights, and East Jerusalem. Paul VI had then appealed for the declaration of Jerusalem as an "open city." When the war ended, the Holy See repeated its traditional position: that Jerusalem and the Holy Land should be placed under international control. Paul VI, at Istanbul, wanted to win the Turkish authorities over to this solution, and hoped that Turkey could plead his case to the Arab countries.

In the early afternoon, the pope went over the Bosphorus for an hour in the company of President Sunay. Then he visited the ancient Basilica of Santa Sophia, transformed into a mosque after the fall of Constantinople to the Muslims in 1453, then barred to worship by the Turkish authorities at the turn of the century and transformed into a museum. At the place of the altar where, in 1054, Cardinal Humbert[49] had placed the bull of excommunication of the patriarch of Constantinople, Paul VI knelt and made a silent prayer. As we have seen, this excommunication had been lifted at the end of the Council; the pope hoped this voyage would facilitate a reunion between Orthodox and Catholics. He held two meetings with Patriarch Athenagoras, one on the same day, in the Orthodox cathedral of Saint George, the other on the following day in the Catholic cathedral of the Holy Spirit. On this occasion, a letter from the pope was solemnly presented to the Orthodox patriarch. In it, he referred to the Orthodox churches and the Catholic Church as "sister Churches." As one ecumenist theologian has remarked, "this vocabulary was new in the mouth of a pope, but so was the theology that it supposed. Rome no longer presents herself as *mater*, situated above all the other

---

victory. Although the Muslims had the numerical advantage, at a crucial moment the winds changed in such a way that the Christians, led by Spanish and Venetian fleets, could win a decisive victory. In thanksgiving, the pope instituted the Feast of Our Lady of Victory, now celebrated as the Feast of Our Lady of the Most Holy Rosary.

48   Cevdet Sunay (1899–1982) was the Fifth President of Turkey (1966–1973).

49   Card. Humbert (c. 1000–1061), formally Humbert of Silva Candida, was a French Benedictine abbot who became a cardinal in 1051. He was well-known for his role in the excommunication of the Patriarch of Constantinople Michael I Cerularius (1054), which is treated as the definitive start of the "Great Schism" between the Roman Catholic and the Eastern Orthodox Churches, even though the Latin and Greek spheres had been drifting further apart for many centuries.

churches, but as a sister."⁵⁰ But union was far from being reached, and would certainly not be during his papacy. The ecumenical policy of Paul VI, with the Orthodox as with the Anglicans and Protestants, was always the same: reestablishment of "fraternal charity" through gestures and bold statements, filled with kindness, and once this prelude was over, a "sincere theological dialogue" to attempt to resolve the remaining doctrinal divergences. The aftermath was generally a disappointment for the ecumenists: the striking meetings at Jerusalem, Saint-Paul-outside-the-Walls, and Istanbul were not followed by the dreamt-of reunion of the churches, even if major concessions had been made by the Catholic Church.

The second leg of the Turkish voyage was to Ephesus and Izmir (ancient Smyrna). At Ephesus, one of the important places of the early Church, the tomb of Saint John the Apostle and the house of the Virgin were venerated. Saint Paul too had lived and was held captive in Ephesus, and the third ecumenical council was held there in 431. From there Paul VI wanted to address two messages, one to the Catholic patriarchs and bishops, the other to the Orthodox patriarchs, because "the inspired preaching of the Apostle Paul to the ancient churches of Asia has remained the common heritage of all Christians." During the visit to Ephesus, on the site where the Council of 431 had proclaimed the Virgin Mary "Mother of God," Paul VI became abstracted; motionless and mute, he seemed as though he might faint. Then after a moment's pause, he intoned the *Salve Regina*. Was this brief loss of awareness due to the fatigue of the trip and the intense heat of the Turkish summer, or to a mystical ecstasy? During his homily for the feast of the Assumption, which was a few days later, he seems to hold the latter thesis. Speaking of the pilgrimage to Ephesus, he said: "Something great, mysterious passed over our souls."

REFORM OF THE CURIA AND THE FIRST SYNOD

On August 15, 1967 the apostolic constitution *Regimini Ecclesiæ Universæ* was published. This may be considered "the most astonishing, most daring, most rigorously premeditated project and major historical decision of Paul VI, without which what was to follow would not have been possible."⁵¹ This was the reform of the Curia, that is to say, an overhaul of the functioning of all of the Roman congregations, the administrative departments of the Church. A Roman saying goes: "The popes pass, the

---

50   E. Lanne, "Hommage à Paul VI," *Irénikon* 3 (1978): 304.
51   R. Laurentin, "Paul VI et l'après-concile," in *Paul VI et la modernité dans l'Église*, 570.

Curia stays." The Curia was demeaned by its adversaries as conservative and sclerotic. Since the beginning of his papacy, as we have seen, Paul had announced his intention to reform it; the Council, in its majority, had also called for such a reform.

Following long preparatory work, numerous consultations, and the development of four successive projects, the planned reform was large-scale. Nominations to the congregations (whether for cardinals, members, or consultors) were to be for five-year terms, not for an undetermined period as before; the age limit of seventy-five years, previously imposed on bishops, was applied to all the members of the Curia, to allow for a rapid "renewal." Diocesan bishops could be named as members of the congregations, to internationalize their composition. The Secretariat of State was placed over the congregations and would be able to control their work. Hence the growth of the role that the Secretary of State would play in the years to come. The section of the Secretariat of State called "Extraordinary Affairs" became autonomous and received the name of Council for the Public Affairs of the Church (Msgr Casaroli remained in charge). Finally, a Prefecture was created for the economic affairs of the Holy See, to coordinate and control the different economic and financial organizations of the Vatican.[52]

This reform of the Curia was not accompanied by any immediate change in the heads of the congregations. Paul VI was not a man of great and abrupt upheavals. Over the course of the ensuing months, changes in personnel at last came about at the beginning of the next year. Cardinal Šeper, archbishop of Zagreb and partisan of the liturgical reform, was named to the head of the Congregation for the Doctrine of the Faith, replacing Cardinal Ottaviani, the old "soldier of the faith"; in 1969 Cardinal Villot was named Secretary of State to replace Cardinal Cicognani, who had long since passed the age limit; another Frenchman, Msgr Martin, was named prefect of the Apostolic Palace, an office which dealt principally with the delicate and very politically sensitive organization of papal audiences.

The reform of the Curia favored more direct control of the pope over the congregations, especially through the Secretariat of State, permitting a more rapid implementation of the reforms envisioned by the Council.

Among the reforms that had been requested, the creation of a synod of bishops had been granted by the pope during the council itself. But he

---

52 Except for the Vatican Bank, the IOR (Institute for Religious Works), which remained autonomous and was soon going to be confided to Msgr Marcinkus.

had reserved for himself the right to define its organization and operation. The first synod met during the month immediately following the reform of the Curia. From September 29 to October 29, the approximately two hundred participants (all the cardinal heads-of-congregations, elected bishops, and others designated by the pope) met to discuss different subjects: the revision of canon law, doctrinal questions, seminaries, catechesis, and the liturgy. The pope, who was not present for the debates, feared that the confrontations occasioned by the Council would be renewed. They were not. On the contrary, a fairly easy consensus seems to have been established. This may have been because the meetings were of the whole body, and not by language group, thus limiting the interventions, and because the subjects were too numerous.

The general tone of the work was optimistic. Msgr Wright,[53] bishop of Pittsburgh, summarizing the work on doctrinal questions, declared: "The synod reflects a sober spirit of alertness for the Church and for the people of God, but no one is sounding the alarm." He announced that "negative solutions" had been rejected, such as the establishment of lists of doctrinal errors to combat or "new formulations of the *Credo* or enumerations of the articles of the faith." It is, however, this last solution that Paul VI himself would choose one year later to reaffirm the faith of the Church against doubts and controversies. Otherwise, it was suggested that an "academy of theologians," of divergent theological schools, be created to assist the magisterium in the study of certain theological questions. The response would come in 1969 with the creation of the International Theological Commission.

Two events marked the synod. The first was the arrival of Patriarch Athenagoras in Rome, as the synod was reaching its close. Athenagoras was first received in Saint Peter's Basilica. Paul VI wanted to take his place beside the Orthodox patriarch on two exactly identical seats to mark their equality, in reference to the famous idea of "sister Churches" stated a few months prior in Istanbul. The celebration of a common Mass had even been envisioned, to seal the union of the two Churches, but the idea was abandoned following refusals by the Orthodox patriarchs of Athens and Moscow.[54]

The second event was the experimental presentation, before the

---

53   Card. John Wright (1909–1979), from Massachusetts, served as an auxiliary bishop of Boston (1947–1950), first bishop of Worcester until 1959, then bishop of Pittsburgh until 1969. Paul VI named him the Prefect of the Congregation for the Clergy and made him a cardinal in 1969.
54   Henri Fesquet, *Le Journal du premier synode catholique*, ed. Robert Morel, 158.

members of the synod, of a "new Mass." The liturgical reforms already in force so far concerned only the external aspects of the Mass: the abandonment of Latin as well as of certain gestures and prayers. From April 1967, the heart of the Mass, the Canon, which contains the Eucharistic Prayer, could be recited out loud and in the vernacular, but the text had not been modified. The "new Mass" was going to change that. The celebrant would henceforth be able to choose among four Eucharistic Prayers. From October 21, the synod studied these projects of the liturgical reform. The president of the Consilium, Cardinal Lercaro, held votes on various propositions. Most significantly, on October 24, the members of the synod were present, in the Sistine Chapel, for an experimental Mass or "normative Mass."[55] It was entirely in Italian, and celebrated by Father Bugnini, with the use of a new Eucharistic Prayer in the place of the ancient Roman Canon, as well as a significant reduction of the personal prayers said by the priest, a lengthening of the "liturgy of the word," and the suppression of further gestures and genuflections. The reactions of the synod to this experimental Mass were very mixed. All the more so because the Italian press at this time was echoing the complaints of different groups hostile to the liturgical reform taking place. A few days before this experimental Mass, Eric de Saventhem,[56] president of the International Federation *Una Voce*, which included national organizations from about ten countries, addressed an appeal to the synod to

> stop, without the slightest delay or equivocation, all experimentations on the rites of the Mass. In the current climate of the crisis of faith, these experiments can at best disguise, or otherwise even provoke, a rapid loss of the sense of the sacred, and thus compromise total and absolute faith in the Real Presence in the Eucharist.[57]

---

55 Bugnini, *The Reform of the Liturgy*, 346–59; in the remainder of ch. 24, Bugnini describes various other experimental Masses and the reactions to them on the part of various people, including Paul VI.

56 Eric Maria de Saventhem (1919–2005), also known as Erich Vermehren, was a prominent anti-Nazi, a member of the German military intelligence organization, Abwehr, who converted to the Catholic Faith in 1939 when he met his future wife, Countess Elisabeth von Plettenberg. She was a member of one of Germany's leading Catholic families. He was the first president of the Una Voce movement, founded in 1964.

57 The same month, Father Georges de Nantes launched a monthly review, *La Contre-Réforme catholique au XXe siècle* [The Catholic Counter-Reformation in the twentieth century], which began with an open letter to Paul VI, contesting his "project of a reform of the Church."

The normative Mass was criticized by some bishops of the synod. Cardinal Heenan, archbishop of Westminster, accused the Consilium of "technicism, intellectualism, and a lack of pastoral sense." Others shared that the many liturgical changes provoked weariness and disturbance among the faithful. Also, the "normative Mass" did not enjoy overwhelming approval: seventy-one members of the synod were favorable, forty-three were opposed, and sixty-two wanted modifications to be made. The Consilium had to modify its "new Mass."

The synod ended on October 29 without Paul VI being able to participate in the closing ceremony. For several weeks prostate pain had exhausted him and caused fevers. An operation was necessary; it took place on November 4. One of the rooms of his private apartments was transformed into an operating room. Dr Valdoni,[58] director of the polyclinic of the University of Rome, performed the surgical intervention surrounded by at least six other doctors. For several days the pope was unable to celebrate Mass; he watched, from the door of his room, as his secretary Father Macchi celebrated.

Paul VI was slow in recovering. The rumor spread that he had contracted cancer. He had not, but he was seventy years old; because of all the overwhelming activity since his election, his body was tired. In the beginning of December he finally appeared in public again, but it was not until several weeks later that he was able to take up his working audiences at a normal pace. This illness, the image of an exhausted pope that millions of people had seen on television or read about in the press, contributed to make Paul VI closer to the faithful: he was less cold and distant. Published that same year, the famous *Dialogues avec Paul VI*[59] of Jean Guitton also contributed to a better understanding of the personality and thought of the pope. Paul VI had authorized his friend to publish these "dialogues," which were not really such. The book was not a transcription of conversations, but the reconstitution of dialogues which had taken place over the years since the 1950s. The pope hoped that just such a book would be read on every continent. Effectively, the book was rapidly translated in thirteen countries, even as far as Japan.

---

58 Dr. Pietro Valdoni (1900–1976) was a renowned Italian surgeon and university professor, who had also treated John XXIII.
59 Jean Guitton, *The Pope Speaks: Dialogues of Paul VI with Jean Guitton*, trans. Anne and Christopher Fremantle (New York: Meredith Press, 1968).

9

From Humanæ Vitæ to the Gates of China

THE PONTIFICATE OF PAUL VI IS OFTEN thought of in two phases: one reformist, open, bold, featuring great voyages and major encyclicals; the other was more traditional, withdrawn, more prudent, and with more frequent warnings. 1968 would constitute the turning point of this pontificate. Such a distinct line of demarcation is hardly convincing. Although his last encyclical, which was very traditional in doctrine, was promulgated in 1968, one must consider that there are very novel texts, such as *Octogesimo Anno* in 1971. There were also important voyages to Latin America, Africa, and Asia. Ostpolitik would be pursued with the same intensity. There was, above all, the liturgical reform, which advanced steadily in spite of opposition, and would end with a "new Mass" imposed on the whole Church.

Paul VI began the year 1968 with an authoritative act: Cardinal Lercaro, archbishop of Bologna and president of the liturgical Consilium, was forced to resign from his two posts. Some commentators have tried to portray this as the first sign of a "conversion" of the papacy. In reality this resignation changed nothing of Paul VI's policy. To replace Cardinal Lercaro at the head of the Consilium he named Cardinal Gut, a Benedictine, who had been a member since its origin. To the archiepiscopal see of Bologna was named Msgr Antonio Poma,[1] a follower of Paul VI. Several reasons have been put forth to explain the forced resignation of Cardinal Lercaro. The pope, unhappy with the criticisms made of the "experimental" Mass during the synod, supposedly wanted to satisfy the adversaries of the liturgical reform by striking "the head." But this explanation is hardly satisfactory, because the composition of the Consilium was not modified and the same spirit continued to prevail in it with the pope's encouragement. Another explanation is possible. On

---

1 Card. Antonio Poma (1910–1985) was an Italian cardinal who served as the archbishop of Bologna (1968–1983). He was appointed the Cardinal-Priest of S. Luca a Via Prenestina in 1969. During his time as President of the Italian Episcopal Conference (1969–1979), he affirmed that support for Communism is incompatible with the Catholic Faith.

PAUL VI: THE DIVIDED POPE

January 1, 1968, Paul VI decided to celebrate, for the first time, a "Day of Peace," which would henceforth be celebrated on this date each year. It was to call for peace and have the whole Church pray for this intention. But, on this same day, Cardinal Lercaro, in a famous homily, vigorously condemned the American bombardments in North Vietnam. This public stance must have strongly displeased the pope, all the more because now we know that at the same time he had secretly sent representatives of the Holy See to the capitals of the countries involved in the war to propose the Lateran Palace in Rome as a possible place for negotiations. Cardinal Lercaro had thus committed a grave diplomatic fault. As he was older than seventy-five, it was easy to write off his forced resignation as a resignation imposed by the age limit.

1968 was above all marked by controversy on all sides, particularly in France but visible to different degrees in many countries. This controversy had affected the Church for several years already, but it was heightened even more by ongoing political and social controversies. The ecclesiastical hierarchy itself could sometimes be seen lending an indulgent ear to these calls to action. Two examples will illustrate the point.

Firstly, on March 19 Cardinal Suenens, archbishop of Malines-Brussels, addressed a letter to the pope asking him to submit the issues of priestly celibacy and birth control to the next synod.[2] But the pope had asked the Council to not address these two questions, reserving pronouncement on them to himself. As we have seen, the necessity of priestly celibacy had been solemnly reaffirmed in an encyclical, in June 1967. So was not the Belgian archbishop making an act of dissent, albeit covered with ecclesiastical diplomacy, by asking barely nine months later to have the question examined by a synod? Nevertheless, in 1971, Paul VI accepted the inclusion of this subject in the agenda of the synod.

Another controversy was developing in Holland. A new catechism for adults, De Nieuwe Katechismus,[3] had been published two years before, as mentioned above, containing, on several points, affirmations contrary to the Catholic Faith. Since 1966 Dutch Catholics had been pleading with the pope to intervene. Paul VI had chosen to act with gentleness and in 1968 the matter remained unresolved. Several commissions of theologians and of cardinals had successively convened to study the contested passages of the "Dutch Catechism." A list of necessary corrections was

---

[2] Letter published in Suenens, *Souvenirs et Espérances*, 158.
[3] English edition: *A New Catechism: Catholic Faith for Adults*, trans. Kevin Smyth (New York: Herder and Herder, 1967).

finally established in the first months of 1968. At last on June 27, the pope received Cardinal Alfrink, archbishop of Utrecht, and asked him to use his authority to impose the publication of the requested corrections on future editions of the work. At this date the "Dutch Catechism," which had already sold tens of thousands of copies in the Low Countries, was also available in translation in England, in the United States, and in Germany, and would soon be in France and in Italy. Cardinal Alfrink remonstrated, insisting on the difficulties of making such corrections. Finally, Paul VI caved in. Receiving Cardinal Villot in audience he told him:

> Cardinal Alfrink is greatly troubled; we should not create intolerable situations for the Dutch bishops; as a result we will content ourselves with publishing the clarifications of the cardinals' commission, without forcing the insertion of the corrections in the catechism: People of good faith will see where the truth is and what the Holy See desires.[4]

In fact, no "corrected" edition of the *New Catechism* appeared in Holland, and the modifications requested by the Holy See were published apart and presented as "recommendations."

Three days after receiving Cardinal Alfrink, Paul VI, at the end of a ceremony to close the Year of Faith and the celebration of the nineteenth centenary of the martyrdom of the Holy Apostles Peter and Paul,[5] solemnly proclaimed what has been called his "credo." It is sometimes presented, to minimize its importance, as a "personal profession of faith" concerning only Paul VI. In fact, the pope spoke as head of the Church. Ten years later, taking stock of his papacy, he said that he wanted to pronounce this profession of faith "in the name of the whole Church and wanted it to be the 'Credo of the People of God' to recall, reaffirm, and confirm the principal points of the faith of the Church."

The pope based his elaboration on the ancient formula of faith defined at the Council of Nicaea in 325. The pope said that it was a solemn re-affirmation of the twenty-century-old faith of the Church to respond to "the uncertainty which troubles certain modern milieus concerning the faith." These groups "do not escape from the influences of a world in profound mutation, in which so many certainties are contested or questioned.

---

4 Statement cited by Wenger, *Le Cardinal Villot*, 81.
5 The preceding June 25, Paul VI had solemnly announced that the bones and the tomb under Saint Peter's Basilica were indeed those of the Prince of the Apostles. This announcement came after almost thirty years of archeological research, conducted notably by Margherita Garducci.

We see even Catholics allowing themselves to be taken in by a passion for change and novelty." Beyond the detailed reaffirmation of the great dogmas of the faith, Paul VI insisted on the objectivity of truth: "The intelligence God has given us," he noted, "reaches that which *is*, and not merely the subjective expression of structures or of the evolution of the conscience." In an article written soon afterwards on this Credo, Father Daniélou contrasted it with the lack of definition of the Dutch catechism and proposed that it be considered as "a test of authentic faith, which would serve as an index to help evaluate the opinions spread in such books and articles."[6]

This solemn act, "without being a dogmatic definition properly speaking," the pope specified, was the accomplishment of his "mandate" as sovereign pontiff to "confirm in the faith." It is undeniable that in reaffirming the truth with such authority and clarity, Paul VI revived the courage of many, encouraging some to align themselves with him in defense of the faith. A theologian such as Father Daniélou, who rarely spoke on subjects outside his area of expertise, from this point forward began producing articles, books, and public declarations to defend the threatened faith and react against the errors that manifested a crisis in the Church which was now evident to all. Paul VI would himself multiply his discourses to warn against deviations and errors.[7] In the days following his proclamation of the Credo, he spoke out at a public audience against the conception of a "horizontal religion . . . of a merely philanthropic and social character." Some had tried to interpret his discourse of 1965 on the "new humanism" and the "cult of man," and his other speeches of this sort, as the beginning of a religion centered henceforth on man. Paul VI corrected and denounced

> a phenomenon to be observed among people who call themselves religious and Christian, which is an anthropocentric religion, that is to say, a religion oriented towards man as the principal center of interest. But religion should be, by its very nature, theocentric, and oriented first of all towards God, its principal and its ultimate end, and towards man as a secondary concern, who is conceived, desired, and loved according to his divine origin and consequently according to the relation and duties which flow therefrom.

---

6 Article reprinted in Daniélou, *Tests*, 36.

7 In 1970, Father V. Levi, whom Paul VI had asked a few years earlier to join the staff of *L'Osservatore Romano* to revamp its style, published a collection of the pope's speeches on this subject over 350 pages in length in Italy (and in a French translation from Éditions Fayard) entitled: *Face à la contestation*.

Less than a month after the profession of faith, the seventh (and last) encyclical of the pontificate, Humanæ Vitæ, appeared; its subject was birth control. Paul VI forcefully restated the ban on abortion, sterilization, and contraception, arguing that "this doctrine, which has been proclaimed many times by the magisterium, is founded on the indissoluble link which God has willed, and which man cannot break by his own initiative, between the twin meanings of the conjugal act: union and procreation."

This question of birth control had been removed from the Council by Paul VI. At that date, he seems to have still hesitated on how to respond to those who claimed a right to contraception. To the Editor in Chief of La Croix he then said, "Nothing has been said, because we do not know."[8] A commission, presided over by Cardinal Ottaviani, was established to deal with the question. It was soon divided, with a majority of its members favoring the authorization of contraception. Paul VI decided to dissolve this commission and entrust the file to a smaller committee, then to commissions that were more or less secret. Two theologians played a large part in these successive consultations and in the redaction of the encyclical: the private theologian of the pope, Msgr Carlo Colombo, and the French theologian Gustave Martelet.[9] Also consulted was Cardinal Wojtyła, author in 1962 of a book on these subjects, Love and Responsibility.[10]

In the pope's entourage, opinions were divided. Cardinal Suenens, for example, was of the opinion that the Church should not make a declaration on this subject, and should leave Catholics to decide for themselves following their consciences. In the weeks preceding the publication of the encyclical, there appear to have been interventions from various Western episcopacies with the pope to try to ensure that the text would not appear as an absolute interdiction. Jean Guitton has reported that Paul VI was divided between his "inclination," which was to accept contraception, and his "duty," which was to ban it to remain in continuity with the teaching of his predecessors, and avoid changing a law which had been observed until then by hundreds of thousands of Catholic families.[11] If

---

8   Wenger, "Paul VI et La Croix," 753.
9   Fr Gustave Martelet (1916–2014) was a French Jesuit priest and theologian who lectured at the Pontifical Gregorian University and took part in the Second Vatican Council. Much of his work is centered on the theme of Revelation and the Resurrection of Christ.
10 Karol Wojtyła, Love and Responsibility, trans. Grzegorz Ignatik (Boston: Pauline Books & Media, 2013).
11 Guitton, interview.

the pope had authorized the "pill," he would have been acclaimed as the "liberator of women." He did not hesitate to sacrifice popularity, and his encyclical was criticized — including by the bishops of some countries.

The Secretary of State had addressed a secret instruction to the bishops of the world asking them faithfully to echo the teachings of Humanæ Vitæ.[12] Not all seemed eager to respond to this solicitation. Around ten (mainly European) episcopacies made public declarations betraying reservations or even hostility. The French bishops published a pastoral note affirming: "[contraception] is always a disorder, but this disorder is not always culpable." Fr Karl Rahner in Germany, who had been so prominent during the Council, multiplied his declarations; Fr Bernard Häring,[13] who had preached the spiritual exercises at the Vatican before the pope during Lent of 1964 and who had been part of the first commission on conjugal issues, criticized this "typical case of a non-collegial exercise of the teaching power of the pope"; eighty-seven American theologians, under the leadership of Fr Charles Curran,[14] protested in a manifesto. Fr Antoine Wenger, who himself had defended the encyclical in La Croix as its Editor in Chief, recognized that "it was not easy to find columnists among the bishops or laity who were favorable to the encyclical."[15]

Paul VI was pained to see his pontifical magisterium questioned at the very heart of the ecclesiastical hierarchy in many Western countries. When an episcopacy such as that of Spain expressed its "sincere adhesion" to Humanæ Vitæ, he received the news "with much consolation," he would say, and had the Secretary of State address a letter of thanks to the president of the Spanish episcopal conference.

---

12 Revealed by The Times, September 4, 1968.
13 Fr Bernard Häring (1912–1998) was a German Catholic theologian and Redemptorist priest. He was conscripted into the Nazi army as a medic and was prohibited from exercising his priestly ministry. However, he still brought sacraments to Catholic soldiers. As a moral theologian he was perhaps best known for his three-volume work The Law of Christ, which enjoyed ecclesiastical approval.
14 Fr Charles Curran (1934–) was then professor of theology at the Catholic University of America. In the seventies, he began teaching that homosexual acts are morally legitimate. He was eventually banned from teaching Catholic theology in 1986 by the Congregation for the Doctrine of the Faith and dismissed from the Catholic University of America. He is now a professor at the Southern Methodist University in Dallas, Texas.
15 However, he did find laymen to defend it: Maurice Clavel, in Le Nouvel Observateur, appreciated the encyclical as "a breath of fresh air"; Jean Madiran, in Itinéraires, saluted a text that "smashed 'the collective conscience of humanity' in its current state of blindness and self-sufficiency."

It is noteworthy that the Third World countries, on the other hand, generally received the papal encyclical very favorably. In their eyes, to authorize the pill would be to adopt an antinatalist policy to halt demographic growth, which was the reflex of the rich counties who did not want to share their riches. Paul VI traveled to Colombia the month after the release of his encyclical and was able to see that it had been appreciated by the majority of bishops of Latin America.

This rapid voyage to Colombia, from August 22 to 24, had been planned for a long time. Two events allowed an opportunity for the pope to visit: the celebration, at Bogotá, of the Thirty-Ninth International Eucharistic Congress, and the opening at Medellín of the second conference of CELAM (Latin American Episcopal Conference). On August 22, at the airport in Rome, some members of the government, along with numerous civil and ecclesiastic dignitaries, came as usual to greet the pope before his departure. The evening before, troops of the Warsaw Pact had invaded Czechoslovakia to put an end to the "Prague Spring." Paul VI, in a short speech, could not keep silent about this event, and revealed his uncertainty: "We would be ready to suspend our journey immediately if we knew that our presence and our action could serve somehow to prevent the worsening of the evils that oppress that nation which is so dear to us, to avoid disastrous consequences..." But he very cautiously condemned the intervention: "We do not want to judge anyone, but how can we not begin to analyze the principles from which such troubles seem to flow?" In the face of this tragedy, Paul VI spoke, first from his heart, and then as a diplomatic adherent of Ostpolitik who did not wish to displease the Communist governments with which the Holy See was negotiating...

The pope had invited Roger Schütz, of the community of Taizé, to accompany him to Colombia, because he also wished to make this an ecumenical trip. Some Anglican, Orthodox, and Protestant "observers" participated at the International Eucharistic Congress. The evening of his arrival at Bogotá, the pope celebrated a Mass before seven hundred thousand faithful, and ordained one hundred and sixty-one priests and forty-one deacons. The next day he went by helicopter to Campo San José, about nineteen miles from Bogotá, where two hundred thousand peasants had assembled. His speech became famous by its daring exaltation of their condition:

> You are a sign, you are an image, you are a mystery of the presence of Christ. The Sacrament of the Eucharist offers us His

> hidden presence, living and real; but you also are a sacrament, that is to say a sacred image of the Lord amongst us: you are representative reflections, open and not concealed, of his human and divine face. You, dear sons, are Christ for us.... We love you with paternal affection.

The next day, he went to one of the poorest neighborhoods in the suburbs of Bogotá and, after having greeted the sick who had been brought to him, he celebrated Mass outside. Again, he spoke of "preference" towards the poor: "You, most dear sons, are the Lord's favorites! And thus, also the favorites of the pope, happy to be in your midst, to meet you, to comfort you, to bless you."

These statements, this insistence on a "preferential option for the poor," were often interpreted politically as an encouragement of the "Liberation Theology" which was beginning to spread in Latin America. This relatively new theological position, promoted notably by Gustavo Gutiérrez[16] and Fernando Cardenal,[17] claimed that the proclamation of the Gospel ought to go along with "liberation" from the economic and political structures which oppressed the people. However, on August 22, when Paul VI received, in the cathedral at Bogotá, the participants of the conference of CELAM, which was to open at Medellín in the next few days, he condemned recourse to violence. He reminded the bishops of Latin America of their threefold duties: spiritual, pastoral, and social (social, because the Church should be the "animator of civilization").

This assembly of one hundred and thirty-six Latin American bishops would define the major direction of activities for the Church on this continent for the years to come. The preparatory documents denounced chronic underdevelopment, singled out particular South American political regimes for censure, and claimed revolution to be legitimate in cases where those who were in power refused to undertake necessary reforms. This radicalism was not ultimately retained; but the assembly's final documents criticized the Western, that is to say liberal and capitalist, model of development, and popularized the concepts of "dependence" and "liberation." According to these, the Third World lived in "dependence"

---

16 Fr Gustavo Gutiérrez (1928–) is a Peruvian philosopher, theologian, and Dominican priest who is regarded as one of the founders of Liberation Theology.

17 Fernando Cardenal (1934–2016) was a Nicaraguan Jesuit and a Liberation Theologian. Because of his connection with the leftist Sandinistas, he was forced to leave the Society of Jesus. He was laicized by Pope John Paul II because his roles as government minister were incompatible with his priestly ministry and because of his insubordination.

on the West, which exploited its natural riches without ensuring, in return, its satisfactory economic development; as for "liberation," this ought to be non-violent but total, concerning all the aspects of human life, and ought to be enacted in light of the Gospel. These notions were in continuity with the encyclical *Populorum Progressio*.

"SELF-DESTRUCTION" OF THE CHURCH

Returning to Europe, the pope found a Church more obviously in crisis than ever. Every few weeks, as the year 1968 drew to a close, disputes and even sometimes public outcries surged and increased. On November 3, about fifty Parisian priests, who formed a group soon to be called "Exchanges and Dialogue," published an open letter entitled "Priests provoked by the world today in our 'situation.'" Asking themselves about themselves, "Priests of whom? Priests, why? Priests how?" they wanted "to design a new face for the priesthood" and thought that "it is time to 'speak through acts.'" They announced that some among them were going to take on paid employment alongside their priesthood, "as circumstances require, to make political choices or commitments, in trade unions or elsewhere," "to accept, with frankness and liberty, the possibility of married priests." Over the following weeks, more than six hundred priests, from Paris as well as the rest of the country, would sign this manifesto.

In December, another group of seven hundred forty-four priests and French laity addressed an open letter "to Paul, Pope" under the title "If Christ saw this." It was a global questioning of the Church, her wealth, her "juridicism," her "triumphalism," her treason against the Evangelical spirit, but also a personal accusation of the pope. Soon, thanks largely to a media campaign led by the weekly *Témoignage chrétien*, this open letter to Paul VI received more than four thousand signatures.

At the end of a speech in response to these public accusations against the pope, Father Daniélou and his 150-member audience sent the pope a telegram of "filial affection" and "moral obedience." A group of lay personalities (including E. Gilson, F. Mauriac, S. Fumet, G. Marcel, and A. Piettre[18]) addressed a letter to the pope in the same spirit, and a petition

---

18 Étienne Gilson (1884–1978) was a French philosopher who specialized in the tradition of Thomas Aquinas and was the leading scholar of the history of medieval philosophy in his time. He was nominated for the Nobel Prize in literature. François Mauriac (1885–1970) was a French journalist and writer who published many novels, plays, and poems, earning him the Nobel Prize for Literature (1952). As a Catholic writer, he grappled with some unpleasant modern-day realities. Stanislas Fumet

campaign was launched, collecting over a hundred and sixty thousand signatures. The division in the Church grew.

During this same December, worried that the works of two of them (H. Küng and E. Schillebeeckx) would be examined by the Congregation for the Doctrine of the Faith, thirty-eight theologians of the review *Concilium*, who were all professors in theology departments in Germany, France, Belgium, and other countries, made public a long declaration demanding that the "liberty of theologians and theology" not be questioned and that the procedures of examination of doctrines by the Congregation be modified. Among the signatories are found numerous theologians who counted at the Second Vatican Council, including Fathers Congar, Chenu, Rahner, and Ratzinger. They called upon their confrères to sign this manifesto. More than a thousand theologians finally rallied in support of this text that was so critical towards authority. Others, including Fathers Daniélou and de Lubac, who had also played an important role at the Council, refused to sign this declaration, finding it excessive.[19]

Such questioning of authority and such harsh criticism of the institutions of the Church struck a nerve with Paul VI. On December 7, receiving in audience a hundred of the students of the Lombard Seminary, he made a mournful speech, in which he admitted: "The Church finds herself in an hour of uncertainty, of self-criticism, one could almost say of self-destruction. It is a harsh, complicated internal upheaval, such as no one could have expected after the Council." This last qualification is not entirely true. The pope himself had not believed that the Council was going to unleash this crisis in the Church, as his declarations of 1965 bear witness. But even then, and for years before this, those who were referred to at the Council as the "minority" or the "traditionalists" were already worried about the first signs of this very crisis.

(1896–1983) was a writer and critic who was also a prominent "social Catholic." He took over as director of *Temps Présent* (1937) to which Jacques Maritain contributed. Gabriel Marcel (1889–1973) was a French Christian existentialist philosopher. He converted to Catholicism in 1929. André Piettre (1906–1994) was a French economist who studied Law at the University of Paris. Later in life, he taught political economy (1953–1976) and was elected president of the Congress of French-speaking economists (1955).

19 Other theologians had denounced, in this same year of 1968, dissent in the Church and doctrinal errors, while proclaiming their fidelity to the conciliar orientation: notably Hans Urs von Balthasar with his *Cordula ou l'épreuve décisive* (published in English as *The Moment of Christian Witness*) and Louis Bouyer with his *La Décomposition du catholicisme* (published in English as *The Decomposition of Catholicism*) — two works that Paul VI read attentively, as his personal copies, now preserved at Brescia, attest.

In the same speech, Paul VI also worried about the attitude he should take: "Many expect energetic and decisive interventions from the pope. But the pope does not believe that he should follow any program other than that of confidence in Jesus Christ; for He will calm the storm." To the very end of his papacy, the pope refused to discipline theologians who professed theories contrary to the Catholic Faith; he only intervened in dioceses in very rare instances. To all those prone to discouragement in the face of these upheavals, he counseled resignation. For example, when Cardinal Colombo, archbishop of Milan, asked him in 1969 for permission to relinquish his position, which had become too difficult because of disputes between some of the faithful and the clergy, Paul VI urged him to remain at his post: "It is necessary to love and to serve men pastorally as they are, even if they are very different from what they should be and what we want them to be: this applies especially to the youth, even our own, who suffer incredibly from transformations in trends of thought and modes of life..."[20]

THE POPE OF THE "NEW MASS"

Without a doubt, Paul VI will be remembered in history as the pope who led the Second Vatican Council to its conclusion — and as the one who gave the Church a "new Mass." After the hotly contested experiment of the "normative Mass" before the synod in 1967, the work of the Consilium continued towards developing a new rite. The pope repeatedly received Father Bugnini in audience; he read and reread the revised text of the Mass presented to him in September 1968, making precise annotations in the margins of the proposed texts, asking liturgists "to take into consideration, with a free and balanced judgement, these observations."[21]

The reforms that had already been authorized followed their course, with some excesses. Receiving the members of the Consilium in audience the following October 4, Paul VI shared his fears and expressed some criticisms: "In liturgical matters, the episcopal conferences sometimes willfully take themselves beyond reasonable limits. The result is that either arbitrary experiments are made or rites are celebrated in flagrant opposition to the rules established by the Church." When the archives are opened, it will finally be clear which specific episcopal conferences were particularly responsible for excesses, if this allusive criticism indeed

---

20   Letter published in Cardinal G. Colombo, *Ricordando G. B. Montini*, 83–84. At the end of 1970, again he had to exhort the ever more discouraged cardinal to stay in Milan.
21   Bugnini, *The Reform of the Liturgy*, 377.

suggests that some had to be called to order. It will also be known whether the Vatican's interventions were effective. For the moment it can be seen that in spite of the oft-denounced "arbitrary experiments" and excesses beyond "reasonable limits," the liturgical reform continued on. In the following November, the pope approved the new Order of Mass (hence the name by which it is frequently called: Novus Ordo Missæ). A few months later he asked again for final adjustments; then, during the consistory of April 28, 1969, at which he created thirty-three new cardinals,[22] he announced the forthcoming publication of the Novus Ordo Missæ. In the meantime, he replaced the head of the Secretariat of State. Cardinal Cicognani, long since past the age limit, gave way to Cardinal Villot. The nomination of a Frenchman to such an important post sparked some jealousy, even though he was not the first non-Italian to become Secretary of State. This nomination had been suggested, among others, by the Deputy, Archbishop Benelli,[23] who had known Villot well during his periods at the nunciature in Paris, then as observer for the Holy See at UNESCO. Although on paper he was President of the Council for the Public Affairs of the Church, Cardinal Villot, like his predecessor before him, allowed the Secretary of the Council, Msgr Casaroli, to take care of Foreign Affairs on his behalf. Cardinal Villot would maintain considerable influence over Paul VI until the end of the papacy. According to the rather blunt expression of Fr Macchi, after the nomination of Cardinal Villot Paul VI was *castrato* (castrated),[24] so strong was the impression of the new Secretary of State on an aging pope.

Dated April 3, Holy Thursday, the Novus Ordo Missæ was finally presented to the press on May 2. The Roman Missal codified by Saint Pius V was replaced by a missal which would soon be called the "Missal of Paul VI." There were innovations in form. Three new Eucharistic Prayers were added to the ancient Roman Canon; the celebrant was permitted to use, at his discretion, any of the four. The words of the consecration, which were identical in the four, had been modified. New Prefaces had also been introduced. Finally, in keeping with changes already under way

---

22 Among them were Archbishop Marty of Paris and Father Daniélou, who had made a name for himself by his campaigns against the "assassins of the faith." A thirty-fourth and a thirty-fifth cardinal were created, Msgr Trochta, a Czech, and Msgr Hossu, a Romanian, but their nominations were kept secret so as not to disturb ongoing negotiations with the Communist governments.

23 Card. Giovanni Benelli (1921–1982) was the Italian Cardinal-Priest of Santa Prisca, appointed by Paul VI in 1977. He became archbishop of Florence in 1977 and remained so until his sudden heart attack and subsequent death in 1982.

24 Cardinal Martin, interview with the author, February 21, 1992.

for several years, the gestures made by the celebrant were simplified; the altar was turned towards the faithful; and the local vernacular language was to be used.

The very conception of the Mass was altered as well: now it was defined as "the sacred synaxis, or the assembly of the people of God uniting under the presidency of the priest to celebrate the memorial of the Lord." This definition recalled nothing of the traditional definition of the Mass as a renewal of the sacrifice of the Cross and allowed one to believe in a solely spiritual presence of Christ. Instead, it was closer to the Protestant doctrine of the Eucharist.

This *Novus Ordo Missæ* would paradoxically win praise from various Protestants, while earning open or covert criticism from eminent members of the Catholic hierarchy. Max Thurian, of the Protestant community of Taizé, wrote some weeks after the publication of the new Ordo that it was "an example of a fruitful concern for open unity and dynamic fidelity, or true Catholicity: one of the fruits may be that non-Catholic communities could celebrate the Lord's Supper with the same prayers as the Catholic Church. Theologically, it is possible."[25]

Meanwhile, at Rome, a group of theologians and liturgists, among whom Fr Guérard des Lauriers[26] seems to have played a prominent role, produced a *Short Critical Study of the New Order of Mass* that June. Some cardinals were asked to present the text to Paul VI. Cardinal Siri refused, because he thought that a text promulgated by the pope had the force of law in the Church, and that in the spirit of obedience it should be upheld. Others were likely solicited. Only two, Cardinals Ottaviani and Bacci, agreed to present this critical study to Paul VI. They did so through a letter to the pope, which served as a preface for published editions of this *Breve esame critico del Novus Ordo Missæ*.[27] The cardinals indicated that they agreed with the critiques formulated in this study, affirming that the *Novus Ordo Missae* — considering the new elements, susceptible to widely different interpretations, which are implied or taken for granted — represents, both as a whole and in its details, a striking departure from the

---

25 *La Croix*, May 30, 1969.
26 Bishop Michel Louis Guérard des Lauriers (1898–1988) was a traditionally-minded Dominican theologian who became increasingly concerned about events taking place in the Church with the advent of the Second Vatican Council. He was consecrated a bishop in 1981 by Archbishop Pierre Martin Ngô Đình Thục and favored sedevacantism and sedeprivationism. He was later excommunicated.
27 Published in English as *The Ottaviani Intervention: Short Critical Study of the New Order of Mass*, revised and updated, trans. Rev. Anthony Cekada (West Chester, OH: Philothea Press, 2010).

Catholic theology of the Mass," and they pleaded with the pope to allow priests to use the Roman Missal of Saint Pius V.

These public criticisms were doubled by private censures that were then unknown to public option. For example, Cardinal Šeper, Prefect of the Congregation for the Doctrine of the Faith, realizing how much the second Eucharistic Prayer could lend itself to equivocal interpretations, declared to another cardinal: "I will never adopt this canon."[28] Countless associations of the faithful, in multiple countries, also made their voices heard; they asked for the abrogation of the new Ordo, or at least the preservation of the old, or even the maintenance of Latin in the use of the new Ordo.

The pope did not allow himself to be disturbed by these criticisms and concerns, particularly after he submitted the *Short Critical Study* to the Congregation for the Doctrine of the Faith, and received a response from Cardinal Šeper that comforted him, even though the cardinal himself was privately reticent about the matter: "The pamphlet *Breve esame* ... contains many superficial, exaggerated, inaccurate, biased, and false statements."[29] He only recommended a few modifications in vocabulary that the pope immediately requested. In the definition of the Mass, which Cardinals Ottaviani and Bacci judged dangerously incomplete, the formula "Eucharistic sacrifice" was added; some other expressions were changed; but overall, the *Novus Ordo Missæ* was not revised. It entered into force on November 30, 1969, the first Sunday of Advent. Country by country, the ancient Mass was either rapidly banned, or else authorized only on strictly-defined conditions.

The fight to preserve the "Traditional Mass" would be the focus of Archbishop Lefebvre's actions in the years to come. Paul VI would never back down.[30] On the contrary, the liturgical reform was continued. A few days after the publication of the new Ordo, the Consilium was integrated into the new Congregation of Worship, which continued the reform. This Congregation was directed by the same men: Cardinal Gut served as Prefect, Msgr Bugnini as Secretary. It proceeded not only to the revision of the rites of the other, as-yet unreformed sacraments (including confession and extreme unction) but also introduced still further new modifications to the liturgy of the Mass. It acted thus with the consent of the pope, but

---

28 Statement reported by Cardinal Oddi in *Trente Jours* (July-August 1991): 15.
29 Cardinal Šeper, letter dated November 12, 1969, cited in Bugnini, *The Reform of the Liturgy*, 287.
30 Paul VI stopped celebrating the ancient rite, but according to his private secretaries, when he celebrated Mass in his private chapel, he always used Latin.

sometimes against the expressed sentiment of a worldwide majority of bishops, as in the case of communion in the hand.[31] All bishops had been consulted on the opportunity of authorizing the distribution of the consecrated host into the hands of the faithful. 1,233 pronounced an unfavorable opinion, 567 a favorable opinion, 315 a favorable opinion with reservations. The majority of the bishops of the world were therefore hostile to a modification of tradition on this point. The Congregation for Divine Worship, at the request of Paul VI, nevertheless published an instruction which maintained communion on the tongue while allowing communion in the hand in countries where the practice had already been established, as long as there was a vote of the episcopal conference and the formal approval of the Holy See. Out of concern not to hinder the liberty of episcopal conferences, and anxious to respect diverse opinions, Paul VI refused to establish a common law for the Church on this matter, even though he was personally hostile to communion in the hand.[32]

FROM GENEVA TO KAMPALA

On June 10, Paul VI spent a day in Geneva. He wanted to greet this city that had an international role, but at the same time he did not want his visit in this majority-Calvinist city to appear as a provocation. Also, the trip was organized to disturb the daily life of Genevans as little as possible. The pope spent only a day in the city of Calvin. From the airport he went directly to the Palace of Nations. The International Labor Union (ILO) (where his brother Lodovico had worked in the twenties) was celebrating the fiftieth anniversary of its foundation. After his visit to the UN, Paul VI found a reason to salute another major international organization. Before the seventeen hundred delegates and experts in his audience, he gave a long speech in French. After mentioning some important figures of Swiss Catholicism, he indulged in some lyrical flights: "Never again work above the worker, never work against the worker, but always work for the worker; work at the service of man, the whole man, and for all men." The eulogy he made of the ILO was surprising:

> More than perhaps any other institution, you can contribute to a better future for humanity, simply in being actively and inventively faithful to your ideal: universal peace through social justice.... The voice of the Spirit resounds more than

---

31 Jean Madiran, "Le processus de la communion dans la main," *Itinéraires* (May 1972).
32 Cardinal Oddi, letter to the author, August 18, 1992.

elsewhere throughout this house that is open to the sufferings and troubles of workers.

After a rapid reception at the city hall of Geneva, he met with representatives of the Catholic clergy, the laity of some international Catholic organizations, and some former Swiss guards; then he went to the headquarters of the World Council of Churches. The Catholic Church, despite the wish of many ecumenists, was not a member of this group representing almost all the large Anglican, Protestant, and Orthodox communities. Paul VI recalled that such participation should not be foreseen. He also affirmed the unique character of his authority at the beginning of his speech:

> Our name is Peter. And the Scriptures tells Us what meaning Christ wanted to attribute to this name, what duty he imposed on Us: the responsibilities of the Apostle and of his successors.... And in what concerns Us, we are convinced that the Lord has given Us, without any merit of Our part, a ministry of communion.

Then he went to the lakeside La Grange Park, where sixty thousand Swiss Catholics waited for him to celebrate a Mass. Lastly, before leaving Geneva, he had a long meeting with the Emperor of Ethiopia Haile Selassie,[33] President of the OAU (Organization of African Unity), who hoped that the pope could play the role of mediator in the bloody conflict which was tearing Nigeria apart: the Nigerian-Biafran War.

With this hope in mind, a few weeks later Paul carried out a journey to Uganda, from July 31 to August 2. The trip, which had been announced several months before, was to coincide with the closing of the first symposium of African and Madagascan bishops, and to honor the twenty-two martyrs of Uganda, who had been canonized in 1964, in the first canonization of his papacy. But the efforts to bring peace to Nigeria would also become a major concern during this voyage.

At the airport of Entebbe, Paul VI was received by the president of Uganda, Apollo Milton Obote,[34] and four other African heads of state.

---

33 Emperor Haile Selassie I (1892–1975), an Ethiopian Orthodox and descendant of King Solomon, reigned from 1930 to 1973, losing the throne in a socialist revolution.
34 Milton Obote (1925–2005) was both the Prime Minister (1962–1966) and President (1966–1971 and 1980–1985) of Uganda before he was overthrown. During his time in power, he freed Uganda from Britain's colonial administration and obtained its independence (1962) but also marred his reputation towards the end of his time in power, with the repression and deaths of many citizens.

The evening of his arrival, he presided over the closing ceremony for the symposium of African and Madagascan bishops in the cathedral of Kampala. This symposium came nowhere near bringing together all the African bishops; few had come. This was an indication that, even on the religious level, African unity was far from being realized. Moreover, during this symposium, they were often openly severe towards the evolution of the Church in the West. They regretted that the flow of Western missionaries had been reduced in favor of major humanitarian projects from the international Catholic organizations; while they were not generally opposed to the new rite of the Mass, they wanted to maintain Latin in the liturgy, as a sign of unity in ethnically and linguistically divided countries.

The pope celebrated the Mass in Latin. But in his address to the bishops, Paul VI seemed on some points to swim against the tide of the symposium's general spirit. To these bishops who called for missionaries from the West, he announced: "You are henceforth your own missionaries." Against the conservatism of some in liturgical matters, he affirmed: "pluralism is legitimate, even desirable, where language, spirit, and culture are concerned." And he issued this command: "You can, you should have an African Christianity." The now famous expression legitimized what was already starting to be called the "Africanization" of Christianity; the term "inculturation" currently in wide use had not yet been coined. This "African Christianity" would be most ardently promoted by the archbishop of Kinshasa, Joseph Malula,[35] created cardinal at the preceding consistory. Cardinal Malula, who had been a member of every commission of the liturgical reform from before the Council until the Consilium, would later become the driving force behind the "Zaire Rite," in response to Paul VI's desire to see Africa bring to the Church "the precious and original contribution of negritude."

The next day, August 1, the pope celebrated a Mass before ten thousand people in a stadium in Kampala before consecrating twelve new African bishops. Then, before the Ugandan parliament, he delivered a "message to the Church of the people of Africa." A remarkable message, not least in that he favored the "liberty of national territories" defined thus: "civil independence, political self-determination, and liberation from colonization by other powers foreign to the African population." Even if no "foreign power" was named, everyone understood that Portugal and its

---

[35] Card. Joseph Malula (1917–1989) was a Congolese cardinal, elevated in 1969, who served as the archbishop of Kinshasa (1964–1989). He was a professor at the Minor Seminary of Bokoro.

colonies of Mozambique and Angola, and the white powers in Rhodesia and in South Africa, were meant. The pope, as tribune of decolonization, nonetheless rejected wars of independence: "Human relations should not be regulated by the struggle between forces unleashed for massacre and destruction, but by reasonable discussions supported by international institutions."[36] He also visited hospitals and community centers. That evening, at the nunciature where he was lodging, he received representatives from Islamic communities. He wanted to greet all the Muslims of Africa through them, and tell them of "his great respect for the faith they profess." This reception and the words he spoke met with criticism. The pope seemed to have forgotten that Islam was spreading in Africa from year to year, and that for several years Uganda had been welcoming Sudanese Christians and animists who had been forced to flee from their Muslim-dominated home country.

The last day of the trip was dedicated to the memory of the twenty-two Christians martyred at the end of the nineteenth century and canonized during the third session of the Second Vatican Council. Paul VI went to the site of their martyrdoms, at Namugongo, where an Anglican shrine had been built. Then he visited the Catholic shrine under construction, some distance away, and blessed the altar. During the Mass, which he celebrated on a small island, he baptized twenty-two catechumens. In the evening he returned to Rome, without having succeeded in bringing peace between Nigeria and Biafra, as he had hoped. At Kampala he had separately received delegations from the two warring countries; afterwards conversations had continued at the nunciature with Msgr Casaroli; all this was fruitless. This war, which had more than a million victims, including many children who died of hunger, would end in 1970 by the forced reintegration of Biafra into Nigeria.

A CHALLENGED POPE

A few weeks after his African trip, Paul VI called another synod of bishops. This synod, deemed "extraordinary" because it was composed mainly of the presidents of episcopal conferences and not of bishops elected by their peers, was to be devoted to the question of collegiality and the relations among episcopal conferences. This synod, more than the preceding one, would take place under the watchful eyes of the press. A few months earlier Cardinal Suenens had given a tantalizing interview

---

36   On July 1, 1970, however, he gladly received in audience at the Vatican the leaders of armed independence movements in the Portuguese colonies.

following up on a book he had written dedicated to "co-responsibility" in the Church.37 In this interview, which was presented as a "theological battering ram,"38 the cardinal denounced the "centralist, juridical, static, bureaucratic, and naturally essentialist tendency" still prevailing at Rome, and called on Paul VI to exercise his power in a more collegial manner, so that encyclicals and important pontifical texts would not be developed by the pope alone but in collaboration with all the bishops. He formulated criticisms on other subjects as well, notably on the naming of cardinals.

This stance received considerable coverage in the world press. It appeared all the more as a direct criticism of the pope's governance because its author was well known for having been one of Paul VI's confidants, notably at the Council. Cardinal Suenens immediately received the support of theologians such as Karl Rahner and Hans Küng, who published long articles in the press.

This synod, which was held from October 11 to 28, resulted in a conflict between two factions. One, represented prominently by Cardinal Daniélou, had decided that to counteract the Church's current crisis, it was necessary to support pontifical authority in all circumstances. The other side, without appropriating all the critiques of Cardinal Suenens, had concluded that the collegial exercise of power needed to be reinforced. A proposal circulated during the meetings, visibly encouraged by Cardinals Suenens and Pellegrino,39 to transform the way in which popes were elected: the bishops of the whole world would be represented at the next conclave by delegates. In the end, the synod did not propose any upheaval, but made suggestions which Paul VI partly enacted: a convocation of the synod every two years; and the creation of a limited permanent organization to follow up on matters between each synod.

Paul VI's authority was also challenged by what was starting to be called "traditionalism," particularly in France. From 1964, a priest, Father de Nantes, founder of a religious community inspired by the spirituality of Charles de Foucauld, accused Paul VI and the Council of professing "heresies."40 In his eyes the "cult of man" championed by the pope was

---

37 Cardinal Suenens, La Coresponsabilité dans l'Eglise (Paris: DDB, 1968). Paul VI read the book very attentively and left six handwritten notes in it.
38 The text of the interview, granted to Informations catholiques internationales (May 15, 1969), and the many reactions it provoked, have been collected by J. De Broucker, Le Dossier Suenens (Paris: Éditions universitaires, 1970).
39 Card. Michele Pellegrino (1903–1986) was the archbishop of Turin (1965–1977) and was made the Cardinal-priest of Santissimo Nome di Gesú by Pope Paul VI (1967).
40 Fr Georges de Nantes (1924–2010) was a Catholic priest who founded the League for Catholic Counter-Reformation (1967) to oppose the errors of the Second

particularly heretical, to say nothing of religious liberty as defined by the Council. The publications he oversaw — *Lettres à mes amis*, then *La Contre-Réforme catholique au XXe siècle* — were published at around twenty thousand issues each to subscribers in several counties. Fr de Nantes was disciplined for the first time in August 1966: the bishop of Troyes, where he resided, had declared a *suspensio a divinis* against him, meaning that he was banned from all religious functions, including the celebration of the Mass, in the diocese.[41]

Father de Nantes, contesting the sentence, demanded that his writings be examined by the Congregation for the Doctrine of the Faith. They were; their author was summoned twice to Rome to be heard by the Congregation, which finally published in August 1969 a "notification" which, curiously, did not condemn his theses but declared simply: "In rebelling in this way against the Catholic magisterium and the hierarchy, Fr de Nantes disqualifies the whole of his writings and activities." This "notification" against a theologian was the first the Congregation for the Doctrine of the Faith had made since the Council and the reform of the Holy Office. Other, generally progressive, theologians such as Hans Küng (whose works had already been examined by this date by the same Congregation) were never the object of any sanction during the pontificate of Paul VI. This resulted in the Congregation for the Doctrine of the Faith being accused of partiality.

In the "Dutch Catechism" affair, Paul VI demonstrated patience and, all things considered, great indulgence. From 1968 to 1970, the Church in Holland again made itself known in the eyes of the world as a controversial and progressive church; this time the pope would react with more firmness. In 1968, the "pastoral council of Holland" was opened, bringing together the country's eight bishops, representatives of the clergy, men and women religious, and lay faithful. In three years, this pastoral council held six sessions. At the end of the fifth session, in January 1970, it adopted a resolution calling for: the suppression of

---

Vatican Council and to promote traditional doctrine and worship. He was suspended *a divinis* in 1966 but continued to minister to his community. Blessed Charles de Foucauld (1858–1916) was a French nobleman and cavalry officer, who left the world to become a priest and hermit in the Algerian Sahara. He was martyred by Muslim Bedouins. He inspired the foundation of the Little Brothers of Jesus community.

41 Two months earlier, the permanent council of the French bishops had published a warning "against articles published particularly in the magazines like *Le Monde et la Vie*, journals like *Itinéraires* and *Défense du foyer*, bulletins like *Lumière*." It described these publications as challenging, "in the name of a fidelity to the past, the principles of the renewal currently under way."

obligatory celibacy for priests; the reintegration of married priests who had left the priesthood; and the ordination of men who were already married. On January 21, the Dutch bishops published a communiqué which noted these propositions, but left the final decision to the pope. The international press noisily reported these declarations. Paul VI, pained that the doctrine of priestly celibacy had been called into question yet again despite his repeated reaffirmations, reacted rapidly. On February 1, during the Sunday Angelus, he eloquently praised the "sacred celibacy of the priest" and, speaking to the faithful present in Saint Peter's Square, he alluded to the Dutch declarations: "We need your prayers, dear children, and you can certainly guess why." The next day, he addressed a public letter to Cardinal Villot on the subject of the pastoral council of Holland. Stating that he was "distressed" by the recent declarations on celibacy, he repeated his refusal to change the rule. The consecration of priests to Christ should be "without restriction, and without division, for the exclusive service of the Gospel." He refused to reintegrate priests who had married into the priestly ministry ("those who, after having put the hand to the plow, have turned back"). Also, he did not foresee the ordination of married men except in rare instances of "entirely particular necessities" and "in judging before God the good of the universal Church, which will not be disassociated from that of local churches."[42]

Coming a few years after the catechism affair, this situation generated suspicions about a schism between the Dutch church and Rome. Cardinal Villot met twice with Cardinal Alfrink, on "neutral ground," in Paris. Then the archbishop of Utrecht was received twice by the pope in July. Paul VI succeeded in obtaining from the Dutch bishops a declaration on the celibacy of priests, which marked a retreat relative to the previous statement. Paul VI, however, did not enact any sanctions or general measures against the church in Holland. Twice he imposed more "conservative" bishops on vacant episcopal sees instead of choosing from lists of three candidates proposed to him by the dioceses, as had been his practice until then. In December 1970, he named Msgr Simonis to Rotterdam and in January 1972, Msgr Gijsen to Roermond.[43] The Dutch

---

42 This letter had been written based on Cardinal Villot's own proposals. It was on his insistence that the pope finally accepted — after having first refused — a mention of the possibility of the ordination of married men (Wenger, *Le Cardinal Villot*, 110).
43 Card. Adrianus Johannes Simonis (1931–2020) served as bishop of Rotterdam (1970–1983) and then as archbishop of Utrecht (1983–2007). He was made a cardinal in 1985 and was a member of several curial departments. Bishop J. B. Matthijs Gijsen (1932–2013) was the Dutch bishop of Roermond (1972–1993) before

episcopacy from now on would be divided into two camps, a division which would endure well beyond the papacy of Paul VI.

To impose two episcopal nominations was, for Paul VI, a rare act of authority. At this same time, in November 1970, he was criticized for another authoritarian act. By a *motu proprio* dated November 21, *Ingravescentem Aetatem*, he decided that from the age of eighty the cardinals could no longer participate at the conclave to elect a pope. He had shared his plan with Jean Guitton, who made his disagreement clear: physical decline was not prejudicial to judgment and intelligence. In an affair as grave as the election of popes, the elderly, living symbols of wisdom and discernment, held their rightful place, especially at a time when the place of elderly persons should be more and more important in society thanks to the lengthening of lifespans. Paul VI did not give in to these arguments, and published his decree. Jean Guitton guessed that the pope acted thus "to diminish the weight of traditionalist cardinals in the next election."[44] This *motu proprio*, which was going to make 25 of the 127 cardinals lose the right to elect the pope, provoked public protestations from Cardinal Ottaviani — who had just turned eighty a few days before — and Cardinal Tisserant.

ALL THE WAY TO THE GATES OF CHINA

But Paul VI was no longer in Rome to hear these recriminations. On November 26 he took off for a fifty-thousand-mile tour of Asia and Oceania, his longest and last trip outside of Italy. The Philippines were his first port of call. On the way he made two brief stops, the first in Tehran where he held an hour-long conversation with the Shah of Iran in a hall at the airport, the second at Dhaka, in East Pakistan (now Bangladesh). This second stop, initially not planned, was added to the program when he had learned that a terrible cyclone had ravaged the country about ten days before, leaving more than a million dead. The pope gave a check of one hundred thousand dollars to the East Pakistani government, and another of the same amount to a representative of the Catholic community. He arrived in Manila on November 27, in the morning. Upon his descent from the airplane, he was the victim of an assassination attempt.[45] At the airport of Manila, a Bolivian painter,

---

becoming the bishop of the Diocese of Reykjavik in Iceland (1996–2007). He was against the liberal direction that the National Pastoral Council in Noordwijkerhout (1966–1970) was taking.

44 Guitton, interview.

45 In the preceding April, a minor incident took place during a short visit to

Benjamin Mendoza y Amor,[46] disguised as a priest, had succeeded in joining the welcoming committee. He attempted to reach the pope with a dagger, "for the sake of," he would later say, "showing that the faith consists in ignorance and hypocrisy." Accounts of the incident vary: either Cardinal Kim,[47] or President Marcos,[48] or Msgr Marcinkus, who organized the trip, succeeded in fighting off the assailant, who was promptly taken into custody by security services. The spokesman for the Holy See's Press Office hurried to publish a press release indicating that Paul VI had not been harmed. Actually, the pope's personal physician, who was part of the papal entourage, attested that the assailant did succeed in striking the sovereign pontiff:

> two strikes of the dagger to the right and the left of the jugular veins could have been fatal if Macchi had not immediately intervened in energetically restraining the arm of the aggressor. In this situation, Paul was equally saved from the blows by the protection of the stiff collar he wore to ease the pains caused by cervical arthritis.[49]

Paul VI spent three days in the Philippines, a majority Catholic country. He first spoke to one hundred and fifty thousand students from thirteen universities in the country, addressing them with a clear message: "Behold our message: God is light, Jesus Christ is the 'light of the world'; whoever follows him does not walk in the shadows." Then he spoke before an assembly of two hundred bishops from fifteen countries of Eastern Asia. He encouraged them not to "lose the truth and the unity of the faith"; instead they should defend doctrine and promote a "holistic humanism," which was described in *Populorum Progressio* as "the integral development of each man wholly and of all men." The Church, he explained, should be "the vanguard of social action." Then he received

---

Sardinia. Anarchists, some of whom came from Milan, had thrown rocks at the pope's car.

46 Benjamin Mendoza y Amor Flores (1933–2004) made an assassination attempt on Pope Paul VI in 1970. He was a Bolivian surrealist painter who posed as a priest to him to get close enough to the pope to attack him. He served 38 months in prison before returning to Bolivia.

47 Card. Stephen Kim Sou-hwan (1922–2009) was archbishop of Seoul (1968–1998). He was created cardinal in 1969.

48 Ferdinand Marcos (1917–1989) was the tenth President of the Philippines (1965–1986). He governed dictatorially, ruling under martial law for a large part of his presidency. He was a controversial leader, rumored to be involved in corruption and violence.

49 Witness of Dr Fontana reported by Lai, *Les Secrets du Vatican*, 186.

a South Vietnamese delegation. He wanted badly to visit their country, thinking that his presence could help to bring peace. Now he at least had an opportunity to transmit a message to Vietnam from nearby. He had no words of comfort for Vietnamese Catholics; instead the pope contented himself yet again with a call for negotiations, this time in the hope that Vietnam "tomorrow, thanks to the union of all forces, of all efforts, will be able to know, we are sure, better days." Was it not naïve to believe that the Communist government of North Vietnam could be disposed to this collaboration of "all forces"?

On November 29, the pope inaugurated a Catholic radio station, Radio Veritas, and addressed a long message to the people of Asia. He praised the diverse spiritual and religious traditions of Asia, which he saw as a defense against materialism and atheism, and made clear that "the message of Christ ... is not of a nature to cancel or diminish in any way the cultural and spiritual values which constitute your precious heritage."

From the second stop on his voyage, the Samoan Islands, Paul VI issued a new message, this time in favor of missions, calling for bishops to send missionaries, priests, and male and female religious, and asked "young boys and girls, whose souls, thirsting for truth, justice, and love, seek noble causes to defend," to become missionaries. Then he went to Australia. He visited the episcopal conference of Oceania, which consisted of seventy-two bishops. He made a passionate appeal on behalf of the unity of the Church, which should first of all be founded on the unity of the faith: "We cannot permit uncertainty, doubt, or equivocation when it comes to all that Revelation has communicated to us about God." He also celebrated Mass for the bicentennial celebrations of the foundation of Sydney. At the apostolic nunciature, he received a delegation of aborigines and took up the defense of their rights. At city hall, with representatives of the different religious confessions of Australia, he participated in an "ecumenical service" and recalled the terms of a recent declaration of the Secretariat for Christian Unity: Catholics should reject "doctrinal indifferentism," but also avoid "all triumphalism or appearance of confessional triumph." The trip continued in Indonesia where the pope arrived on December 3. In this country where Islam, Confucianism, Hinduism, Buddhism, and Christianity lived side by side, he congratulated such "collaboration and mutually enriching diversity." A Mass was then celebrated in a stadium before sixty thousand faithful, as well as representatives of non-Christian religions. In his homily he comforted the Catholics, who formed a very small minority in the country: "There

From Humanæ Vitæ to the Gates of China

exists in humanity a supreme, primal, irreplaceable need, which can be satisfied only by Jesus Christ..."

The next stage of the journey was Hong Kong. Paul VI had apparently planned to make an appeal to China, but dropped it at the last minute. Paul VI's attitude towards Communist China was marked by a goodwill that can today be considered exaggerated. In the 1960s, the Catholic Church in China was led by six bishops belonging to the "Patriotic Chinese Church," which had been created in the fifties, subjected to the authority of the Communist government, and condemned under Pius XII. The bishops (and thousands of priests) who rejected this "Patriotic" Church had been executed, imprisoned, or condemned to exile. It seems that Paul VI never considered this "patriotic church" schismatic. During the Council, learning that Fr Wenger was to go to China, he gave him an oral message for the archbishop of Peking, who was a member of the Patriotic Church: "The pope considers himself to be in a communion of faith and charity with the church of China, and his great desire was for her presence at the last session of the Council."[50] The message could not be transmitted, but Paul VI continued to demonstrate his benevolence, not only with regard to Chinese Catholics, but also to the government itself. He thought that a country of a billion inhabitants could not be banished from the international community. On January 6, 1967, celebrating the twentieth anniversary of Pius XII's institution of the ecclesiastical hierarchy in China, he did not hesitate to declare: "Today, the Catholic Church is still prepared to understand and favor, in its rightful expressions, the work of the present historical phase of [China's] transformation," although the country was then undergoing a terrible cultural revolution. During this 1970 Asian journey, he did not visit Taiwan, Nationalist China, to avoid offending Communist China. In his speech at Hong Kong, he encouraged the Catholics of this territory to persevere in the faith of their baptism and he concluded with an address to the whole Chinese continent: "For China as well, Christ is the master, pastor, redeemer full of love. The Church cannot silence this good word: the love which remains forever." The very day of this speech, in an "authorized" interview with an Italian daily, Msgr Casaroli made known that this speech was a gesture of good will, of openness with regard to the Communist government of Peking, and an appeal to all Chinese Catholics.[51]

---

50 Wenger, "Paul VI et La Croix," 755.
51 Il Giorno, December 3, 1970, cited by U. Floridi, Moscou et le Vatican.

The voyage ended with a short and final stage at Ceylon,[52] where for several years successive governments had limited the Church's field of action by nationalizing the Catholic schools, expelling nursing sisters from public hospitals, and halting the construction of religious buildings. Even here the pope wanted to preach reconciliation: "Make brotherhood unite you together in your social, economic, and political life, without any distinction of caste, faith, color, or language."

---

52   Modern-day Sri Lanka.

10

"The Storm that Batters Us"

IN 1968, DURING THE COURSE OF HIS VOYAGE TO Colombia, Paul VI, evoking the crisis in the Church, had borrowed an image with evangelical echoes: "From the top of the mystical barque of the Church, We feel the storm that batters us." This type of image recurs often in the pope's statements on the turbulence apparent in the Church. Soon afterwards, without changing the tone, he would no longer limit himself to lamenting theological deviations, liturgical excesses, or dissent originating from the progressive wing of the Church; he began to complain of attacks on his authority, attacks on Vatican II, and disobedience on the part of traditionalists. And thus, seemingly putting them on equal footing, he would set them against each other. In his speeches he criticized both sides in equal measure, sometimes with increasing bitterness. At the beginning of the seventies, he maintained his enthusiasm and hope of achieving some results in two areas: *Ostpolitik* and social issues.

PEACEFUL COEXISTENCE

Negotiations with the Communist governments of Eastern Bloc countries were undertaken, not to give a blank check to these regimes with respect to their policies, but in the hope of improving conditions for religious life. After bloody strikes in Poland at the end of 1970 that left forty-five dead and more than a thousand wounded and led to more than three thousand arrests, on February 14, 1971 Paul VI called for prayers for that country. He associated it in a lamentation that he poured over numerous countries and regimes: states

> tormented by civil war, or the negation of the fundamental rights of man (including that of religious freedom), or by unjust and cruel repression, or by the ideological and organized propaganda of hate and of the rivalry of citizens against citizens, by premeditated recourse to violence, by the utopia of radical and antisocial contestation, by the justification of revolution...

The pope also indicated that social peace is attainable only by "love of the people," and that is true only in reference to Christ.

At the same time, this sort of "crisis" in Eastern Bloc counties, or rather the crushing of rebellions against the Communist system, did not interrupt dialogue between the Holy See and Communist authorities. Every step that could induce goodwill from the Communist world towards the Holy See was taken. Not two weeks after the firmly anti-totalitarian discourse cited above, the Holy See officially joined the treaty for the non-proliferation of nuclear arms. The project for the treaty had been launched in 1967 during a conference on disarmament held in Geneva. Immediately Paul VI encouraged it. The Vatican, possessing neither an army nor any arms, is considered neutral territory; yet the pope insisted that the Holy See join this treaty, to show how the Church was involved in all the affairs of the world, and wanted to contribute to peace by all non-violent means. The Holy See could have officially made the pact in the United States or Great Britain. But Paul VI and Msgr Casaroli preferred that the admission be received in the Soviet Union, another signer of the treaty. This was meant to be a gesture of good will and homage towards the USSR, as well as an opportunity for a Vatican diplomat to visit Moscow for the first time since the Revolution. On February 25, in the Soviet capital, Msgr Casaroli signed a treaty which was one of the symbols of peaceful coexistence between these two powers.

Another gesture of good will towards a Communist government was made, a few months later, when Vatican diplomacy enabled Cardinal Mindszenty to leave Hungary. After the Hungarian uprising was crushed in 1956, he had found refuge in the American embassy in Budapest.

For the Communist government that had condemned him to prison before 1956, his presence on the nation's soil was a permanent risk of anti-governmental revolt. In their negotiations with the Holy See on the fate of Catholic Hungarians, the authorities in Budapest requested Cardinal Mindszenty's departure from Hungary, along with a list of draconian conditions. In July 1971, Paul VI sent a personal representative, Msgr Zágon,[1] to Cardinal Mindszenty to help enable his departure. The discussions were difficult. In leaving Hungary, the cardinal felt he might be betraying Hungarian Catholics, who were already so severely persecuted — all the more so because of the very severe conditions imposed on this departure: the cardinal had to leave the country discreetly without being able to greet the faithful one last time; while abroad he had to

---

1   Msgr József Zágon (1909–1975) was a Hungarian priest who studied theology at the Vienna University of Technology (1935), going on to receive his doctorate in 1938. He organized the Catholic Action of Hungarians in Rome.

abstain from all public declarations which could "damage the relations of the Holy See and the Hungarian government or be offensive for the popular Republic"; nor should he publish memoirs containing an account of his trial and imprisonment. Cardinal Mindszenty reluctantly accepted the conditions imposed on him and left Budapest forever in September, hoping that his departure would improve the situation of Hungarian Catholics. At Rome, Paul VI welcomed him splendidly, lodging him at the Vatican in a sumptuous apartment of Saint John's Tower and showering him with gifts and messages of esteem. The pope assured him that, although in exile, he remained the archbishop of Esztergom and the Primate of Hungary.

But the Holy See and Cardinal Mindszenty quickly fell into disagreement. When the primate asked to be able to name suffragan bishops to take care of the various Hungarian communities in exile, he was denied. In July 1973 the "Secretariat of the Catholic Committee for Peace" was created in Hungary to organize priests who were favorable to the regime, and to control the Church. The Holy See did not protest. Meanwhile, Paul VI, who had received the manuscript of Cardinal Mindszenty's memoirs and had read them, dissuaded him from publishing them. Then, on November 1, 1973, he asked the cardinal to renounce his archiepiscopal see. Cardinal Mindszenty refused. Had not the pope himself promised to allow him to keep his position? After another request by Paul and another refusal by the primate, on February 5, the decision of the pope to declare the archdiocese of Esztergom vacant and to nominate an apostolic administrator, Msgr Lékai,[2] to replace the deposed archbishop, was made public. The news sparked indignant commentaries in the press. The writer Giuseppe Prezzolini,[3] despite his ties to the pope, declared that there was "something Machiavellian in the deposition of the cardinal: *la raison d'État.*" Graffiti on the walls in Rome near the Vatican read: "The pope betrayed Cardinal Mindszenty." On February 6, the Primate of Hungry made a public declaration in which he made known that he had not resigned, but that the decision had been taken "unilaterally by the Holy See" and that "the

---

[2] Card. László Lékai (1910–1986) was a Hungarian cardinal, created by Pope Paul VI in 1976, who was the archbishop of Esztergom (1976–1986). Earlier in his life he was the private secretary of József Mindszenty who at the time was the bishop of Veszprém.

[3] Giuseppe Prezzolini (1882–1982) was an Italian journalist, editor, writer, and critic who cofounded the literary journal *Leonardo* (1903) before moving to the United States to teach. He wrote many books, including *L'arte di persuadere* (1907) and *The Legacy of Italy* (1948).

leadership of the Hungarian dioceses is in the hands of an ecclesiastical administration put in place and controlled by the Communist regime." The press office of the Holy See published a press release explaining that the decision had been made to allow the Church to secure her mission in Hungry. One year later, Paul VI named five new bishops in Hungary and, after the death of Cardinal Mindszenty, Msgr Lékai would be named archbishop of Esztergom and Primate of Hungary.[4]

POLITICAL PLURALISM

The year 1971 also featured a major papal document. Dated May 14, Paul VI published *Octogesimo Anno*, on the eightieth anniversary of Leo XIII's encyclical *Rerum Novarum* on social questions. Significantly, Paul VI chose to publish, not an encyclical, but an "apostolic letter" to Cardinal Roy, president of the Council of the Laity and of the Pontifical Commission for Justice and Peace. In *Octogesimo Anno*, Paul did not want to make a definitive pronouncement or "propose a solution that would have universal value," he wanted simply to propose some political and social "considerations and suggestions."

This text, which was not presented as obligatory teaching, and which did not define "Christian politics" (on the grounds that such politics do not exist), nonetheless played a substantial role in the political evolution of Catholics in numerous countries. It essentially recognized the legitimacy of political "pluralism" (the expression recurs many times in the text) among Christians. The pope reminded his readers that it was impossible to "accept the principles of Marxist analysis without recognizing their relation to the ideology"; nor was it reasonable to immerse oneself in "the practice of class warfare and its Marxist interpretations while neglecting to see the type of totalitarian and violent society to which this process leads." On the other hand, considering the attraction of Christians to "socialist movements and their various evolutions," Paul VI considered a "commitment" to this path possible "with the safeguarding of [Christian] values, especially liberty, responsibility, and openness to the spiritual, which guarantee the integral flourishing of man." The free market option was not excluded either, but it also required "an attentive discernment."

---

4 Another example of concession: in January 1973, Paul VI proceeded with four episcopal nominations in Czechoslovakia, following an accord with the government after ten years of negotiations. These nominations were contested, particularly because one of the bishops named, Msgr Vrana, had been a member of the "Movement of Priests for Peace," which was controlled by the Communist government.

This affirmation that "the same Christian faith can lead to different [political] commitments," including socialism, seemed to render the prior condemnations obsolete, notably those which Pius XI affirmed in 1931, in *Quadragesimo Anno*: "Religious socialism and Christian Socialism are contradictions: no one can be, at the same time, a good Catholic and a true socialist." This "contradiction" having been overcome, many Christians, supported sometimes by the ecclesiastical hierarchy, would commit themselves to promoting socialism. A few days before the apostolic letter appeared, a Jesuit, Fr Gonzalo Arroyo,[5] and eighty priests and religious founded the "Movement of Christians for Socialism" in Chile, becoming part of the campaign of "liberation theology." This movement soon spread throughout Latin America and Europe, and won the support of Msgr Méndez Arceo,[6] bishop of Cuernavaca, Mexico. The Chilean bishops, while affirming themselves not hostile to socialism, stated their opposition to an openly Marxist movement that did not exclude recourse to violence and held close ties to the Communist government of Cuba.

In France, on May 1, 1972, referring explicitly to Paul VI's "Letter to Cardinal Roy," the Episcopal Commission of the Working Class (*la Commission épiscopale du monde ouvrier*) published a long document affirming that "there is no incompatibility between the Gospel and a socialist type of economic and political system" and called for the discernment of "what in class warfare is the manifestation of dialectical materialism and what is simply a recognition of the oppression of workers and of a legitimate fight to obtain justice." It was certainly not a call to all the Catholics of France to come over to the socialist position, but it was a recognition of the legitimacy of political commitments in the Marxist parties and unions. This is just what many of the leaders of the Catholic movements (JOC and ACO[7] notably) would end up doing. At the elections, there was soon an observable shift to the Left in the regions of strong religious practice. In spite of a few isolated declarations to remind

---

5   Fr Gonzalo Arroyo (1925–2012) was a Jesuit known for his controversial political views that followed Liberation Theology, making and maintaining several contacts with progressive priest movements, agricultural worker's circles, and trade unions.
6   Bishop Sergio Méndez Arceo (1907–1992), a Mexican, was appointed bishop of Cuernavaca (1953–1983) and was known as an activist and human rights advocate. He graduated from the Pontifical Gregorian University of Rome.
7   *Action catholique ouvrière* (Workers' Catholic Action) was founded in 1950 as the older sibling of the JOC to bring the working masses to embrace and practice the Christian Faith.

the faithful of the dangers of Marxism, Cardinal Decourtray[8] recognized, in 1990, that during the 1970s the French episcopacy, "out of a concern for maintaining communion with the most committed . . . allowed itself to be dragged along by a certain degree of complicity."[9]

THE "MIDDLE WAY" OF PAUL VI

The 1970s also saw the development of the moderate, conservative, and "traditionalist" movements in the Church; these terms cover a wide variety of attitudes with regard to the pope.

On September 30, 1971, a new synod of bishops at Rome had made it clear that the divisions within the international episcopacy were grave. The synod centered around two themes: "the ministerial priesthood" and "justice in the world." The crisis of the priesthood was only one aspect, albeit a fundamental one, of the crisis in the Church: a drop in vocations, against a steep climb in the number of priests who abandoned the priesthood. The number of priests who left the clergy is difficult to ascertain. Several estimates place the number around thirteen thousand during the years between 1965 and 1978. Whatever the exact figure was, there was obviously a mass defection of a sort that the Church had not seen for a very long time. Some thought that in order to take a stand against the crisis of the priesthood, the Church should change its conditions. Certain members of the synod would support this position, hoping that clerical celibacy would no longer be an untouchable rule. Some publications joined in by waging a campaign on this front.

More than one hundred thirty interventions at the synod involved clerical celibacy. One of the most remarkable was that of Cardinal Wojtyła, who defended it, in the same spirit as Paul VI in his encyclical: "The connections between priestly celibacy, life, and ministry must be rigorously demonstrated. The priest finds his personal identity in the path of his consecration to God." But other voices made themselves heard, going so far as to claim on their behalf the breath of the Holy Spirit, in opposition to the institutions and rule of the Church and a theology inspired by a "preconciliar theology, stripped of the ecumenical spirit." On October 6, Paul VI came to speak forcefully before this divided synod:

---

[8] Card. Albert Decourtray (1923–1994) was archbishop of Lyon (1981–1994), Vice-president of the Episcopal Conference of France (1981–1987), and then President of the same until 1990. He was created cardinal by John Paul II in 1985.
[9] Interview in Figaro, January 5, 1990, republished by J. Bourdarias, Les Évêques de France et le marxisme.

> Is the hierarchy free to teach in religious matters only that which pleases it or that which pleases certain doctrinal currents, or more precisely anti-doctrinal [currents] of modern opinion? No. . . . We can never foresee the hypothesis of a change, of an evolution, of a modification whatsoever in matters of faith on the part of the Church. The Credo remains the same. On this level, the Church is rigorously conservative, and it is because of this that she remains forever young.

A crushing majority of the synod pronounced in favor of maintaining priestly celibacy, and did not follow those, including Cardinal Suenens and some French and Canadian bishops, who demanded that the Church authorize, at least in certain circumstances, the ordination of married men. This synod also gave Cardinal Slipyj an opportunity to recount how Catholic Ukrainians in the USSR were persecuted, and then to call "Vatican diplomacy" into question with respect to its prudence, its silence, and its politics of compromise.

Even if it ended by maintaining the rule of priestly celibacy, this synod had revealed the division in the Church and its hierarchy. Paul VI, until the very end of his papacy, tried to maintain unity among the bishops, welcoming the visits of all, even those who, such as Cardinal Suenens, were the most openly critical. This episcopal division, which was not at all new, manifested itself with all the more clarity and thus favored the formation of lay movements following Paul VI's preferred "middle way."

The year before the synod, a movement appeared calling itself the "Silent Ones of the Church." Founded by Pierre Debray,[10] they held their first meeting in November 1970, featuring more than nine thousand participants from all the dioceses of France, and delegations from eleven countries. More than a movement properly so called, it was for these "silent ones" who spoke up to "maintain a presence in the diocese and parishes." Willing to "work for the renewal of the Church as willed by the Council," they planned to oppose the "false reforms of the Church" and liturgical deviations (without forcing a return to the Mass of Saint Pius V, they wished to have the possibility of assisting at the Mass of Paul VI in Latin). One year later, on November 7, 1971, a few days before the end of the synod, the Silent Ones of the Church held a second assembly, at Strasbourg, which brought together five thousand delegates from organizations, movements, and publications representing three hundred

---

10 Sadi Louis Victor Couhé (pen name: Pierre Debray, 1922–1999) was a French anti-clerical-Communist-turned-Catholic-monarchist and prolific journalist.

fifty thousand Catholics from Germany, Austria, Belgium, Spain, Holland, Switzerland, and France. They addressed a message to Paul VI and "to the bishops in communion with him" (which left understood that some were not), to demonstrate their "total and indefectible fidelity" to the pope, and to rejoice in the results of the synod.

Almost the same day, November 6, in the same city of Strasbourg, Gérard Soulages[11] led a European colloquium of Catholic intellectuals. The focus was the duty of Catholic intellectuals in the face of the Church's current crisis. Cardinal Daniélou helped inspire this initiative. Also present were Jean Guitton, Gabriel Marcel, Jean de Fabrègues[12] and other personalities. Fathers Congar and de Lubac, Cardinal Journet, and the Protestant theologian Cullmann sent statements. Many of Paul VI's friends openly supported this budding movement. Moreover, the pope sent a telegram of blessing. "Fidelity" (to the pope and Vatican II) and "openness" (to distinguish themselves from "integralism" or "traditionalism") were combined to affirm the rejection of the "current debacle" and, at an hour when "the essence of the faith is a stake," the necessity for intellectuals "to exemplify that which had given life to the Church for two thousand years." In 1974 and headed by Gérard Soulages, this initiative was continued by the establishment of an association and a newsletter, taking up the original intuition: Fidélité et Ouverture (Fidelity and Openness).

At the same time, in a different spirit, Archbishop Lefebvre began an initiative which would epitomize, to the present day, the rejection of some of the reforms and teachings of Vatican II. Since 1963, when he participated at the Second Vatican Council as the Superior General of the Holy Spirit Fathers, he had thought about founding a traditionally-minded seminary. He sent a seminarian assistant, Christian Charlot, to ask Cardinal Siri, archbishop of Genoa, about possibilities in his diocese. Cardinal Siri approved of the project and promised his aid; however, he did not wish for such a foundation to be made in Genoa.[13] For a few years, Archbishop Lefebvre sent the young men who sought his formation to the French seminary in Rome and then to the Catholic University of Fribourg. By 1970, the candidates for the

---

11   Gérard Soulages (1912–2005) was a professor of philosophy in Châteauroux.
12   Jean de Fabrègues (1906–1983) was a traditional French journalist and intellectual. He was against both the idea of liberal democracy and far-right and far-left totalitarian regimes. During the 1930s, he was involved in the Young Catholic Right, a group which followed the views of people such as Jacques Maritain.
13   Spiazzi, Il cardinal Giuseppe Siri, 128–29.

priesthood and the seminarians coming from the French seminaries and abroad had become so numerous that he founded his own seminary at Écône in Switzerland and created the Priestly Fraternity of Saint Pius X. On November 1 of that year Msgr Charrière, bishop of Lausanne, Geneva, and Fribourg, officially approved the statutes of this Society, the members of which were destined to exercise their priestly ministry wherever they may be requested throughout the world. On February 18, 1971, Cardinal Wright, prefect of the Congregation of the Clergy, approved the fledgling project in his turn. But the refusal of Archbishop Lefebvre to accept the Mass of Paul VI would rapidly gain enemies, particularly among the French bishops.

This question of the Mass was not raised by Archbishop Lefebvre alone, as has been noted above. Founded independently of him, the *Una Voce* movement had petitioned over the course of several years that the faithful who so wished be permitted to assist at the Mass of Saint Pius V. An instruction of the Congregation for Divine Worship had fixed the date of November 28, 1971 as the date "from which one must obligatorily use the new *Ordo Missæ*," with an exception being made for old and sick priests. The announced disappearance of a centuries-old rite incited an initiative of great importance. A few months before the date fixed by this instruction, English writer Bernard Wall, professor at the University of Bologna G. B. Pighi, and professor at the University of Cologne Marius Schneider[14] issued a call to the Holy See in favor of a rite which belonged "to universal culture no less than to the Church and the faithful" and asked him carefully to "consider his terrible responsibility in the history of the human spirit, if he refused to allow the Traditional Mass to live on, even alongside other liturgical forms." This manifesto was signed by close to one hundred writers and artists from around the world, Catholics but also Protestants and Orthodox, including Agatha Christie, Graham Greene, Yehudi Menuhin, Jorge Luis Borges, Roger Caillois, Henry de Montherlant, Victoria Ocampo, and Augusto Del Noce.[15] This call, published in the *London Times*, then

---

14 Bernard Wall (1908–1974) was an English Catholic publisher and writer. Giovanni Battista Pighi (1898–1978) was a Latin scholar, academic, and poet who taught at many universities including the University of Bologna, where he taught for 22 years. Marius Schneider (1903–1982) was a German musicologist.

15 Agatha Christie (1890–1976) was an English writer known for her detective mystery novels, and a practicing Anglican; she received the first ever Mystery Writers of America's Grand Master Award (1955). Graham Greene (1904–1991) was a leading English and Catholic novelist of the twentieth century whose work delved especially into modern moral conundrums and trials of faith. Yehudi Menuhin

in other newspapers of the world, is said to have impressed the pope. Nonetheless, as was his habit, he did not want to contradict the decision of a congregation, and left it to the episcopal conferences of each country to decide whether or not to grant concessions. In November 1971, Cardinal Heenan, Archbishop of Westminster, authorized the Latin Mass Society, affiliated to the International Federation Una Voce, to use the ancient rite on "particular occasions," which remained undefined. Thereafter, all the bishops of England and Wales granted the authorization.[16] England gathered more signatures than any other country on the above-mentioned petition.[17]

In France, on the other hand, the Episcopal Conference allowed no authorization of this type. On October 27, 1972, Jean Madiran, editor of the journal Itinéraires, addressed a letter to Paul VI beginning "Give us back the Scriptures, the catechism, and the Mass,"[18] that is to say a faithful translation of the Bible, the teaching of the whole deposit of Faith, and the Traditional Mass. "We are more and more deprived of these," wrote J. Madiran,

---

(1916–1999) was a Jewish American violinist and conductor, much of whose performing career was spent in Britain; he was president of the International Music Council (1969–1975). Jorge Luis Borges (1899–1986) was an Argentinian writer and is very well known in both Spanish and world literature. Roger Caillois (1913–1978) was a French sociologist and author, known for his works on play and mimicry. Henry de Montherlant (1895–1972) was a French novelist and playwright; his most famous works include the series Les Jeunes Filles (1936–1939) and the play La Reine morte (1942). He was elected to the Académie Française in 1960. Victoria Ocampo (1890–1979) was an Argentinian writer most famous as a publisher of the literary magazine Sur; she was the first woman to be admitted as a member of the Argentine Academy of Letters (1976).

16 Annibale Bugnini records the granting of an indult for England and Wales in The Reform of the Liturgy, 297–98 and in his memoirs Liturgiæ Cultor et Amator: Servì la Chiesa (Rome: Edizione Liturgiche, 2012), 85–86; cf. Notitiæ 185 (1981): 589–611, at 606–8. The indult was signed on November 5, 1971, and allowed the bishops of England and Wales to authorize the former Missal (with the changes made in 1967) at their discretion. This was a response to the personal intervention of Cardinal Heenan, who on October 29 gave Paul VI a copy of the British version of the petition. Heenan quickly authorized two annual Masses at the high altar of his own cathedral, and a monthly Mass in the crypt. The use of the 1967 changes was in fact never enforced. [The information in this note and the next was kindly supplied by Dr. Joseph Shaw of the Latin Mass Society of England and Wales.]

17 Signatures of 57 UK-based figures were gathered for the petition by Alfred Marnau of the Latin Mass Society, and it was these which were published in The Times on July 6, 1971. Another 42 names were added when the same petition was subsequently republished in Italian.

18 Published along with commentaries by those who approved this appeal in Réclamation au Saint-Père (Appeal to the Holy Father), by Jean Madiran.

by a collegial, despotic, and impious bureaucracy which claims, rightly or wrongly, but which claims without contradiction that it is imposing itself in the name of Vatican II and Paul VI.... A party that you knew well when it played innocent and hid its plans, a party whose success has revealed it to be cruel and tyrannical, now diabolically dominates the Church's administration. This currently dominating party is that of submission to the modern world, of collaboration with Communism, of immanent apostasy. It holds almost all the command posts and reigns over the lax through intimidation, over the weak through persecution.

This open letter to Paul received widespread endorsement from individuals including Louis Salleron, American philosopher Thomas Molnar, the International Federation *Una Voce*'s president Éric de Saventhem, Marcel De Corte, Alexis Curvers, and Gustave Corção, but received no direct response from the pope.[19]

On a different plane, because this time it concerned the pope himself, was the billet of accusation which Fr de Nantes, founder of the Catholic Counter-Reform League, came to register at Rome in April 1973. In approximately one hundred pages, his *Liber accusationis in Paulum sextum* accused Paul VI "of heresy, schism, and scandal" and demanded that a canonical process be opened against the pope for the purpose of his deposition. The press office of the Holy See circulated a press release to denounce this "arrogant and fanatical gesture... devoid of seriousness and canonical foundation." Fr de Nantes and the delegation accompanying him were not allowed to hand the book directly to the pope; however, on April 11, during a public audience, a diplomat and friend of Fr de Nantes was able to place the *Liber* in the hands of Paul VI.[20] In the eyes of the pope such an accusation could only be rogue and this billet of accusations was not even examined by the Congregation

---

19   Louis Salleron (1905–1992) was a French Catholic writer and journalist who, with Jean Madiran, founded the conservative journal *Itinéraires* in 1956. Thomas Molnar (1921–2010) was a Catholic philosopher, historian, and the political theorist who authored over forty books on a variety of topics in religion, politics, and education. He received the Széchenyi Prize, awarded by the Hungarian President. Marcel De Corte (1905–1994) was a Belgian Catholic Thomistic philosopher. Alexis Curvers (1906–1992) was a French-speaking Belgian writer. Gustave Corção (1896–1978) was an engineer, writer, and journalist of Brazilian descent, known for his conservative thinking. He supported a dictatorship with the military intervention of 1964 as he opposed communism and Soviet influence.
20   *La CRC au XXe siècle* (April 1973).

for the Doctrine of the Faith, which had judged its author "disqualified" since 1969. Still this *Liber* was distributed in over ten thousand copies.

THE SPIRIT VERSUS "THE SMOKE OF SATAN"

The latter part of Paul VI's papacy was increasingly dominated by a spirit of abandonment, in the spiritual sense. From 1968, when he began to talk about the "self-destruction" of the Church, he gave himself to Christ, declaring: "How many times did Jesus say: 'Have confidence in God. Believe in God, believe in me!' The pope will be the first to follow this commandment of the Lord and abandon himself to the invisible but undeniable assistance which Jesus assures to His Church." In the 1970s, this attitude was even more prevalent. On June 21, 1972, for the ninth anniversary of his election, he cited lines from his personal notes — an unusual practice: "Perhaps the Lord called me to his service, not because I had some aptitude, not to govern the Church and save her from the present difficulties, but to suffer for the Church and so that it is obviously God and not another who guides and saves her."[21]

Eight days later came disillusionment, and a supernatural explanation for the crisis in the Church:

> By some crack, the smoke of Satan has entered the temple of God: doubt, uncertainty, difficulties, worry, dissatisfaction, and conflict have arisen.... We would have believed that after the Council would come a sunny day for the Church. But we have found new storms. We look to dig new abysses rather than fill them. What happened? We confide our thought to you: it is an adverse power, the devil, that mysterious being, enemy of all men, that supranatural thing, come to spoil and dry up the fruits of the ecumenical council and to prevent the Church from breaking forth in hymns of joy for having rediscovered the knowledge of herself.

The doctrines contrary to the faith that were circulated by theologians, the challenges from priests and the faithful, and the criticisms from part of the hierarchy continued to try his strength until they threatened to overwhelm him. His moral trials were aggravated by the physical decline

---

21 In a speech given in 1979, Father Macchi revealed that on some great solemnities Paul VI wore "a cilice with sharpened points." Jean Guitton doubted that these were very frequent (interview with the author, May 11, 1991). Whatever the case may be, can one not see here the mystical concern of Paul VI to suffer for the Church, compensating in his flesh for his weakness in governing the Church?

due to old age (he was racked with arthritis through the 1970s). At the approach of his seventy-fifth year, persistent rumors grew that the pope might resign. According to Jean Guitton, Paul VI seriously considered this possibility. He gave it up, however, because his confidants reminded him that, in the history of the Church, papal resignations were exceedingly rare. Also, his resignation might create a precedent that could oblige his successors to do as well. As he approached the age of seventy-five, he asked his Substitute of General Affairs, Archbishop Benelli, to dismiss the rumor in public before it spread any further. Yet he is known to have asked three members of his immediate entourage (Cardinal Villot, Msgr Martin, and Fr Macchi) to warn him if they realized that he was no longer in a state to carry out his duties.

It seems however that the difficulties that he faced in the government of the Church and the sense of abandonment to Divine Providence that was becoming his normal state of mind combined to reorient his preoccupations from the reforms of structures towards spiritual realities. René Laurentin[22] sees these last years of the papacy as a "pneumatological and mystical phase" (1972–1978), coming after a phase of expansion (1963–1967) then a phase of retreat (1968–1972). This delineation ignores the fact that during these last two phases the application of reforms, especially liturgical, was pursued without hesitation: was that not a continued "expansion"? Nonetheless, it must be recognized that in the final years of Paul VI, his decisions, declarations, and initiatives show that he was abandoning himself ever more to the Holy Spirit.

In this regard, his discovery of the Charismatic Renewal and his ever-warmer encouragements of the movement are significant. At the end of the 1960s the "charismatic" movement began to spread among American Catholic students. Modeled after Protestant Pentecostalism, it gives a prominent place in prayer to the invocation of the Holy Spirit. It essentially consists in praying for the "outpouring of the Spirit." This "outpouring" can have for exterior effects the manifestation of "charisms" in the believer: the gift of prophecy, power to heal, speaking in tongues, etc.

On Holy Thursday 1972, Cardinal Suenens, who had only just discovered the Charismatic Renewal, wrote a letter to Paul VI on the development of this movement in the Church. So far the pope was at best dimly

---

22   René Laurentin (1917–2017) was a French theologian who specialized in Mariology. He served in the French army in World War II, becoming a war prisoner before being ordained as a priest in 1946. He then studied at the Sorbonne (1952) and the ICP (1953) where he received a doctorate of Letters and a doctorate of Theology respectively.

aware of it. Then during an audience in February 1973, Cardinal Suenens again brought up the Renewal. The same day, during an afternoon public audience, Paul VI spoke with fervor of the "resounding manifestations" which can accompany the meeting with God. The pope became more and more interested in the movement, although he considered it necessary to be prudent concerning the extraordinary manifestations that occurred in charismatic prayer groups. From this month of February onwards, Cardinal Suenens wrote every three months to inform the pope about the developments in a movement whose protector he became. Eight months later he organized an international congress for Renewal near Rome and saw to it that twelve of its leaders were received in private audience by the pope, who encouraged them and invited them to discernment, "the gift of gifts." A few months later he did not hesitate to speak of an "epiphany of the Spirit" in the Church and, at the end of the year, he told the cardinals: "The life-giving breath of the Spirit has come to awaken in the Church her sleeping energy, to rouse dormant charisms." The summit of this approbation of the Charismatic Renewal took place on Pentecost 1975. The movement organized a pilgrimage to Rome. Fifteen thousand Charismatics from around the world (Catholics and Protestants alike) participated. They were able to attend the Mass celebrated by the pope in Saint Peter's Basilica. The next day, Cardinal Suenens received permission to concelebrate Mass with twenty bishops and 980 priests in the same basilica, this time for the Charismatics alone. After an hour of "murmured prayer," the pope arrived and spoke for a long time, hailing the Renewal as "a great opportunity for our time," which "ought to make the world young again . . . through joy, through hymns, through witness." A prolonged threnody of alleluias greeted the end of his allocution; Paul VI was overwhelmed to tears.[23]

This same year 1975 was also a Holy Year, as announced by Paul VI on May 9, 1973. The pope would say that this announcement was "inspired by the Holy Spirit" (May 23, 1973). He defined that this Holy Year should mean:

> The internal renewal of man: of man who thinks and who, in his effort to think, has lost the certainty of truth; of man who works and who, in his work, has felt that he was so turned towards the outside that he no longer had enough interior life; of man who plays and distracts himself in turning so much to

---

23   Daniel-Ange, *Paul VI*, 168–71.

means that excite his pleasure that he quickly falls into boredom and disillusionment. Man must be remade from within. Behold that which the Gospel calls conversion, penitence, *metanoia*.

The Church celebrates a Holy Year every twenty-five years. In announcing it for 1975, Paul was only conforming to a traditional rhythm. However, this celebration was criticized, notably by the European and North American bishops, as an outdated religious practice that ran the risk of accentuating Roman triumphalism and centralism, as well as papal adulation (because Catholic faithful from the whole world were invited to come in pilgrimage to Rome). But Paul VI did not let himself be disturbed by these criticisms, and did not modify the prescriptions attached to the celebration of the Holy Year: pilgrimages to the major basilicas of Rome, confession, and the granting of indulgences. To prepare the faithful for this exceptional Holy Year, he published two exhortations in 1973, one on Marian devotion, the other on reconciliation within the Church. In both texts, the pope noticeably insisted on the work of the Holy Spirit: in the history of salvation, in the Virgin Mary, and in the Church.

The Holy Year was a great success, although certainly difficult to quantify: six to twelve million pilgrims came to Rome (compared to fewer than three million during the preceding one in 1950). The pope was comforted by the high attendance of the faithful, multiplying his public audiences to be able to receive all the large groups and speak to them. On May 9, he published an apostolic constitution on Christian joy, *Gaudete in Domino*. Once more, he demonstrated how much he placed his confidence in the Holy Spirit and Providence. There was one clear allusion to the Charismatic Renewal — the text was dated on the feast of Pentecost: "Today the Spirit of Pentecost carries countless disciples of Christ along the paths of prayer in the joy of filial praise." He also strongly reaffirmed the conviction that Christ is constantly present in human history and the Church, despite her weakness and difficulties. Thus, one must be confident in the Lord.[24]

---

24 According to a curious anecdote recounted in several American and European publications, in 1975 Paul VI was supposedly kidnapped and replaced by a "double." This thesis depends on alleged apparitions of the Virgin (Bayside, New York) and messages that were supposedly transmitted there, as well as on revelations made by demons during exorcisms (in Germanic Switzerland and elsewhere), and on sonograms of the "two" voices of Paul VI. It is hard to see how the surviving members of the pope's family, all of his close collaborators, and the curial cardinals who frequently saw him could all have been either complicit or duped.

"THE CHURCH OF ALL AGES"

The end of Paul VI's pontificate was marked by what has come to be called the "Écône affair," which erupted at the end of 1974 and continued far beyond the pontificate to the present.

The year 1974 had been difficult for the sovereign pontiff. First because of the referendum concerning divorce, which the Church had lost. Divorce, which had been forbidden in Italy by the Concordat of 1929, was finally voted in by the Parliament at the end of 1970. Catholic movements had pressed for a referendum on the subject in May 1974. Cardinal Villot was hostile to the principle of such a referendum which, if the adversaries of divorce won the majority, would recall a generally accepted law and would create divisions in Italian society. Paul VI aligned himself with this point of view and attempted to find a middle-ground solution. The biographer and confidant of Cardinal Villot revealed: "Approaches were made to Aldo Moro, president of the Council, to revisit Article 34 of the concordat — dissociating, for example, the civil effects from a religious marriage: in the civil sphere, marriage could be dissolved by divorce, while for the Church it remained indissoluble."[25] Such a compromise could not work. Paul VI belatedly rallied to the idea of a referendum, but according to Cardinal Siri, he refused to launch a "crusade." The Italian bishops made a statement in opposition to divorce; certain Catholic organizations and hundreds of priests, on the other hand, made known that they favored its continuation. On May 12, 59.3% of Italians voted to maintain the law of 1970. It was a failure for the Church and a revelation of the profound secularization of Italian society.

The following September, when a new synod of bishops met in Rome, their subject, "The evangelization of the contemporary world," was visibly more relevant than ever. Paul VI had chosen Cardinal Wojtyła as the doctrinal reporter of this theme.[26] During discussions, it appeared that dechristianization and secularization were mainly problems confined to the West. The African bishops spoke more about the "indigenization" and "Africanization" of Christianity; those from Latin America emphasized the richness of the "popular religion," less intellectualist than Western controversies. The theme of "liberation" was also discussed. In the Apostolic Exhortation *Evangelium Nuntiandi*, which he drew out of the work of the synod, Paul VI mentioned the "generous Christians" who,

---

25 Wenger, *Le Cardinal Villot*, 200.
26 In 1976, he chose the same Cardinal Wojtyła to preach the traditional Lenten retreat at the Vatican, which was published in English as *Sign of Contradiction*.

sensitive to the dramatic questions involved in the problem of liberation, in their wish to commit the Church to the liberation effort are frequently tempted to reduce her mission to the dimensions of a simply temporal project. They would reduce her aims to a man-centered goal; the salvation of which she is the messenger would be reduced to material well-being. Her activity, forgetful of all spiritual and religious preoccupation, would become initiatives of the political or social order.[27]

This passage was directed not only at Christian movements engaged in revolution, but also at "liberation theology," which was particularly widespread among the Jesuits of Latin America.[28]

In November, the process that ended in the first sanctions against Msgr Lefebvre was set in motion.[29] Paul VI sent two "apostolic visitors," that is to say, two personal representatives, Msgr Onclin and Msgr Descamps,[30] to the seminary at Écône to interrogate Archbishop Lefebvre, the professors, and the seminary's approximately one hundred candidates to the priesthood, and report on the moral, religious, and intellectual situation of the establishment. This visit lasted three days; some of the visitors' statements shocked the seminarians. After the apostolic visit,

---

27   Pope Paul VI, Apostolic Exhortation *Evangelium Nuntiandi* (December 8, 1975), at vatican.va, §32: "Negare non possumus, revera, multos vel magnanimos christianos, intentos quæstionibus maximæ gravitatis, quas liberationis causa complectitur, cum cupiant Ecclesiam implicare ipso motu liberationis, sæpe cogitare et conari redigere eius munus ad limites alicuius negotii tantummodo temporalis; eius officia ad consilium ordinis anthropologici; salutem, cuius ipsa est nuntia, ad materialem prosperitatem; eius actionem ad incepta ordinis politici vel socialis, quavis cura spirituali et religiosa posthabita."
28   In 1972, Paul VI read, in an Italian translation, and annotated, the work of Fr Gustavo Gutiérrez, A *Theology of Liberation*.
29   See Bishop Bernard Tissier de Mallerais, *Marcel Lefebvre: The Biography*, trans. Brian Sudlow (Kansas City, MO: Angelus Press, 2004). We will mention here only the relations between the founder of the seminary of Écône and the pope. We refer also to the collection of documents: "La condamnation sauvage de Mgr. Lefebvre" [The illicit condemnation of Archbishop Lefebvre], *Itinéraires*, special number (December 1976) and other sources. Worthy of note in English is Michael Davies's three-volume set *Apologia pro Marcel Lefebvre* (Kansas City, MO: Angelus Press, 1979, 1983, and 1988), which, although it does not extend to the famous episcopal consecrations, covers with unusual thoroughness all the stages prior to that point, and is particularly valuable for its rich documentation, including many key writings of Lefebvre.
30   Msgr Guillaume Onclin (1905–1989), a writer and editor, was under-secretary of the Commission for the Revision of the Code of Canon Law. Bishop Albert Descamps (1916–1980) was a Belgian priest, university professor, titular bishop of Tunis, and auxiliary bishop of Tournai.

Msgr Lefebvre, on November 21, made a declaration, which was then made public, where he prominently stated:

> We adhere with all our heart, with all our soul to Catholic Rome, guardian of the Catholic Faith, and of the tradition necessary to maintain that Faith, and to eternal Rome, mistress of wisdom and of truth. We refuse, on the contrary, and have always refused to follow, the Rome of the neo-Modernist and neo-Protestant tendency which has clearly manifested itself both in the Second Vatican Council and after the Council in all the reforms issuing from it.

He had affirmed in conclusion: "We are resolved to remain faithful to the Catholic and Roman Church, to all the successors of Peter . . ."

Archbishop Lefebvre remained as yet unaware of the tone of the report made by Msgr Onclin and Msgr Descamps. Their declaration of 1974[31] became the center piece of the accusation. On February 13, then on March 3, 1975, the archbishop was summoned to Rome to be questioned by a commission of cardinals composed of Cardinal Garrone, Prefect of the Congregation for Catholic Education, Cardinal Tabera Araoz,[32] Prefect of the Congregation for Religious and Secular Institutes, and Cardinal Wright, Prefect for the Congregation of the Clergy. The Mass of Saint Pius V, which Archbishop Lefebvre planned to use exclusively in his seminary, was not in question, but rather his "attitude regarding the pope and the Council" and his November declaration, which he was asked to retract. He refused.

On May 6, the commission of cardinals sent a letter to Archbishop Lefebvre determining that his November declaration was "unacceptable in every way" and informing him that after the matter was referred to the pope, Msgr Mamie,[33] bishop of Lausanne, Fribourg, and Geneva, had been authorized to withdraw the canonical approval which his predecessor had granted to the Priestly Fraternity of Saint Pius X; by the

---

31   "Written in a sentiment of undoubtedly excessive indignation," as Archbishop Lefebvre later recognized, "Relation," *Itinéraires* 195 (July-August 1975): 138.

32   Card. Arturo Tabera Araoz, CMF (1903–1975) was a Spanish prelate ordained in 1928 for the Sons of the Immaculate Heart of Mary and consecrated bishop in 1946. He was created cardinal in 1969 and served as prefect of both the Congregation for Divine Worship (1971–1973) and the Congregation for Religious and Secular Institutes (1973–1975).

33   Bishop Pierre Mamie (1920–2008) was the Swiss bishop of Diocese of Lausanne, Geneva, and Fribourg (1970–1995). He attended the Collège Saint-Michel before being ordained a priest in 1946.

same motion all its foundations, beginning with the seminary of Écône, lost "the right to exist."

Who decided such a sanction? Archbishop Lefebvre never knew. Was it the commission of cardinals, Cardinal Villot, or the pope himself? It seems that after the two meetings with Archbishop Lefebvre, Cardinal Garrone, Prefect of the commission of cardinals, asked the pope to be relieved of the dossier. So, Paul VI had the declaration studied by Msgr Hanes of the Congregation for the Doctrine of the Faith. Then the decision was made, undoubtedly by the pope himself, to close the seminary of Écône.[34]

Archbishop Lefebvre appealed this sentence twice before the Supreme Tribunal of the Apostolic Signature, on grounds of irregularity of form. The tribunal declared itself incompetent and rejected the appeals. Before the sentence was known, the *Credo* association, founded at the beginning of the year by Michael de Saint-Pierre and devoted to uniting "the various tendencies" of "traditionalist Catholics," had decided to organize a pilgrimage to Rome on the occasion of the Holy Year, presided over by Archbishop Lefebvre. In spite of the order to dissolve the Priestly Fraternity of Saint Pius X and close the seminary of Écône, the pilgrimage continued, and took place without incident from May 24 to 25.

Archbishop Lefebvre was able to celebrate the Mass according to the Traditional Rite in the great Roman basilicas. To this date, the ecclesiastical hierarchy was not entirely hostile to Archbishop Lefebvre and his work. Without sharing all of his positions on the Mass or the Second Vatican Council, some tried over the course of several years to begin a reconciliation. One of the first among them was Msgr Thiandoum.[35] He had been, in 1947, the first African priest ordained by Archbishop Lefebvre, and he succeeded him to head the archdiocese of Dakar in 1962. From June 1975, without particular instructions from the Holy See, he met with the founder of Écône.[36]

On June 29, Archbishop Lefebvre went ahead with more ordinations of seminarians who had been formed at Écône. That same day Paul VI sent him a letter confirming the sanctions imposed in May and commanding him to accept the texts of the Second Vatican Council and the subsequent

---

34 Cardinal Garrone, interview with the author, February 20 & 21, 1992.
35 Card. Hyacinthe Thiandoum (1921–2004) was President of the Conference of Bishops of Senegal, Mauritania, Cape Verde, and Guinea-Bissau (1970–1987) and President of the Symposium of Episcopal Conferences of Africa and Madagascar (1971–1981). He was elevated to the cardinalate by Paul VI in 1976.
36 Cardinal Thiandoum, letter to the author, July 28, 1992.

reforms. Vatican II "holds no less authority than that of the Council of Nicaea, and under certain aspects is even greater," affirmed the pope. The Council of Nicaea in 325 had condemned the heresy of Arius, dogmatically affirmed the divinity of Christ, and defined the "Symbol of Nicaea," that is to say the first part of the Credo. The comparison was audacious and scandalized the traditionalists. Cardinal Villot himself, who knew about this letter before it was sent, criticized the comparison because the Second Vatican Council had not, as did Nicaea, promulgated dogmas, but was intended simply to be pastoral. Paul VI, however, insisted on maintaining this comparison because he did not want to lessen the importance of Vatican II and thus minimize the gravity of Archbishop Lefebvre's opposition.[37]

Until his death, Paul VI would demand only submission and obedience from Archbishop Lefebvre. During the summer, Archbishop Lefebvre met the confessor of the pope, Fr Dezza. He asked him to intercede in his favor with Paul VI for an audience. On August 27, after meeting with the pope, Father Dezza wrote to Archbishop Lefebvre that the Sovereign Pontiff

> awaits a response according to his desires to be able to then receive you in fraternal audience. He has tasked me with telling you "of his affection and affliction," but he considers that the decisions, which were taken after long reflection, were just and he expects that they will be accepted by Your Excellency, even if they do not seem justified to you.[38]

The term "submission" reappeared twice in another letter which Paul VI addressed to the prelate of Écône on September 8, threatening to sanction his "refusal of obedience." Archbishop Lefebvre, judging the measures taken against him to be unacceptable, was little disposed to abandon his work. This refusal resulted in the first condemnation of 1976. In a speech before the cardinals on May 24 of that year, speaking especially of Archbishop Lefebvre, Paul VI complained that:

> They cast discredit on the authority of the Church in the name of a Tradition for which only material and verbal respect is shown; they separate the faithful from the bonds of obedience to the See of Peter as well as to their legitimate bishops; they refuse the authority of today in the name of that of yesterday.

---

37   Wenger, Le Cardinal Villot, 142.
38   Fr Paolo Dezza, unedited letter to Archbishop Lefebvre, August 27, 1975.

In the same speech he called on the Catholic traditionalists to adhere to all the reforms initiated after Vatican II:

> In the name of Tradition itself we ask all of our sons and all the Catholic communities to celebrate, with dignity and fervor, the rites of the renovated liturgy. The adoption of the new *Ordo Missæ* is certainly not left to the free decision of priests or the faithful.... We command, in the name of that same supreme authority which comes to us from Christ, the same prompt submission to all the other liturgical, disciplinary, pastoral reforms ripened these last years by the application of the conciliar decrees.

In spite of these admonitions, the faithful were numerous in coming to Écône on June 29, to participate in the traditional ordination ceremony at the end of the academic year. A few days earlier, Archbishop Benelli had written again to Archbishop Lefebvre to ask him to "now abstain from conferring any ordinations" and he called him and his seminarians to "veritable fidelity to the conciliar Church." Archbishop Lefebvre went ahead and ordained around twenty priests, deacons, and subdeacons. On July 22, the Congregation for Bishops notified Archbishop Lefebvre that he had been suspended *a divinis*, that is to say that he was henceforth forbidden from saying Mass in public, from preaching, and from administering the Sacraments of Ordination, Confession, and Confirmation. Cardinal Villot favored a more restricted suspension, only forbidding him from priestly ordinations, while Paul VI wanted a more severe punishment.[39] The pope himself was not at peace with the sanction that he imposed: "I did not sleep last night," he said to Msgr Martin after the condemnation.[40]

Archbishop Lefebvre did not accept this sentence any more than he had accepted the dissolution of the Priestly Fraternity of Saint Pius X and its institutions the year before; all sanctions appeared to be unjustified. In the intervening time, he had asked on numerous occasions by letter that the pope to receive him in audience. Paul VI had always refused, insisting on Lefebvre's "submission" as a necessary condition.

On August 8, eight French nationals — Michael Ciry, Michel Droit, Jean Dutourd, Colonel Rémy, Michel de Saint-Pierre, Louis Salleron, Henri Sauguet, and Gustave Thibon[41] — addressed a letter to the pope asking

---

39 Wenger, *Le Cardinal Villot*, 147.
40 Cardinal Martin, interview with the author, February 21, 1992.
41 Michael Ciry (1919–2018) was a French artist, born into an artistic family. Even

him to reconsider the condemnation of Archbishop Lefebvre and to authorize "the Traditional Mass and the priesthood of all time."

On August 15, from Castel Gandolfo, Paul VI wrote again to Archbishop Lefebvre asking him to consider "the indefensible irregularity" of his position and "to break the illogical chain, which renders you estranged and hostile to the Church." On September 8 and 9 Jean Guitton came, as every year, to visit the pope. The Écône business was discussed.[42] Paul VI was outraged by the accusations brought against himself and the Council. He declared, "if there is later a schism, it is not I who will be responsible for it, but the insane and now morbid obstinacy of Archbishop Lefebvre, who is tearing apart and scandalizing the Church by his disobedience." When Jean Guitton suggested to him that to appease minds the Mass of Saint Pius V be allowed again in France, at least "during a probationary and provisionary period," Paul VI cried out, "Never!" Paul VI was ready to forgive if Archbishop Lefebvre would submit, but he added: "The condition is that Archbishop Lefebvre be sincere in his repentance. For I have every reason to believe that he is not sincere, that I would be duped by a submission." At last when Jean Guitton proposed himself as a mediator, Paul VI rejected the idea except if the philosopher went to Écône without saying that he was sent by the pope.

Paul VI had other harsh words for Archbishop Lefebvre: "He is a lost soldier.... He belongs in a psychiatric hospital.... He is the thorn of my papacy."[43] Jean Guitton thought that the pope, in this affair, was "ill informed."[44] That is also what Archbishop Lefebvre concluded after the audience which Paul VI suddenly accorded him on September 11. During this audience, which took place in the presence of Archbishop Benelli but without his intervention, Paul VI complained surprisingly that Archbishop Lefebvre had made the seminarians take an oath against the pope. The prelate of Écône assured him that no such thing had ever happened. The meeting was short; Archbishop Lefebvre sensed that the

---

as a child, he showed tremendous artistic potential and attended l'École Supérieure des Arts Appliqués Duperré (1934–1937). He illustrated books by many classical French authors and even Emily Brontë. Michael Droit (1923–2000) was a French novelist, journalist, and supporter of de Gaulle. Gilbert Renault (1904–1984) was a famous member of the French resistance to Nazi occupation and is remembered in France by one of his pseudonyms: Colonel Rémy. Henri Sauguet (1901–1989) was a French composer whose oeuvre contains operas, ballets, symphonies, concertos, and numerous other pieces.

42   Guitton, Paul VI secret, ch. XIII.
43   Guitton, interview.
44   Cardinal Oddi holds a similar opinion (letter to the author, August 18, 1992).

pope was personally wounded by criticisms about the Council and the conciliar reforms. The positions of the two seemed irreconcilable. One month after this meeting, which would be the last between Archbishop Lefebvre and Paul VI, the pope wrote the archbishop a long letter in which he posed the conditions for lifting the sanctions: he wanted him to adhere, "candidly to the Second Vatican Ecumenical Council and all its texts," "to recognize the legitimacy of the renovated liturgy, notably the Ordo Missæ, and Our right to require its adoption by the community of the Christian people," "to cease and retract the grave accusations or insinuations which you have brought publicly against Us, against the orthodoxy of Our faith and Our fidelity to the duties of the Successor of Peter, and against Our immediate entourage." Archbishop Lefebvre did not accept these conditions and the pontificate of Paul VI ended with no intervening solution.[45]

Even the theologian Hans Küng, who was opposed in every way to Archbishop Lefebvre, regretted the attitude of the pope. Soon after the pope's death, he wrote, "I was always pleased about the fact that Pope Paul VI excommunicated neither Archbishop Lefebvre nor the Traditionalists. Everything hung in suspense. It left a door open to reconciliation. I regret however that the pope did not permit them to celebrate the Traditional Mass."[46]

In the same article, Hans Küng wrote: "I am personally grateful to the pope for having protected me over the course of these years." It was not until the next papacy that the rebel theologian would be sanctioned. Two of his books, The Church[47] and Infallible? An Inquiry,[48] which contained opinions contrary to Catholic doctrine, were the object of an examination by the Congregation for the Doctrine of the Faith over several years. It was not until February 15, 1975, that it published a "Declaration" in which it listed the errors contained in these two books and asked the

---

[45] Some traditionalists went well beyond the position of Archbishop Lefebvre. For example, Fr Noël Barbara (1910–2002), a French priest and theologian, dedicated an entire issue of his review Forts dans la Foi to a demonstration that Paul VI is a "heretic, schismatic, and apostate," sent it to all the cardinals and patriarchs of the Church, and on November 19, 1976, in Rome, held a press conference which attracted widespread notice. Another movement began to appear: "sedevacantism," based on the premise that Paul VI could no longer be considered the legitimate pope.
[46] Hans Küng, "Der Papst hat seine Hand über mich gehalten," Die Zeit, August 11, 1978.
[47] Hans Küng, The Church, trans. Ray and Rosaleen Ockenden (New York: Sheed & Ward, 1967).
[48] Hans Küng, Infallible? An Inquiry, trans. Eric Mosbacher (London: Collins, 1971).

theologian "to not continue to teach these opinions." But none of his writings were banned, and he remained in his post as a professor of theology at the University of Tübingen. In later works, Hans Küng continued to assert positions contrary to the doctrine of the Church. Why did Paul VI show himself, in this case, to be so mild and indulgent? Doubtless because he had known the author for many years, since the end of the fifties as we have seen. He had read all his books attentively: the handwritten notes conserved in the works of his library bear witness to the fact. That he was not in agreement with the theses asserted by the author is certain. But to the Congregation for the Doctrine of the Faith, he recommended: "*Procedere con carità*" (proceed with charity), and Hans Küng attests also: "as far as I was concerned, he always refrained from disciplinary measures, and indeed prevented them."[49]

END OF THE REIGN

The last year of the papacy saw a pope who suffered from arthritis, had difficulty walking, and often had to be held up when he wanted to climb the stairs and when moving about. He had long been prone to think about death. To his long will of 1965, he added in 1972 and 1973 two codicils that did not modify the previous arrangements but repeated them or made precisions to better confirm them. The last "supplement to the arrangements of my testament" was very brief: "I desire that my funeral be very simple, and I desire neither special tomb nor any monument. Some intentions (good works and prayers)."

Beyond a few intimate spiritual notes, it is difficult to find access to the secret of his soul. As has been noted above, his confessor for a long time was Fr Bevilacqua, and his spiritual director was Fr Caresana. When Fr Bevilacqua died in 1965, a French Jesuit, Fr René Arnou,[50] professor of philosophy at the Pontifical Gregorian University, succeeded him. Then from 1969 until his death his confessor was Fr Paolo Dezza (subsequently a cardinal), whom he had known since 1927 and who had preached the Lenten retreat at the Vatican in 1967. Father Dezza habitually met with his penitent every week on Saturday evening.[51]

Psychologically, these last years seemed difficult enough, for a variety of reasons. The crises within the Church, which he had had so much difficulty admitting, could have felt like a personal failure or at least

---

49 H. Küng, letter to the author, November 19, 1991.
50 Fr René Arnou (1884–1972) was a French Jesuit who taught philosophy at the Pontifical Gregorian University.
51 Cardinal Dezza, letter to the author, October 4, 1991.

an unexpected consequence of a reform of the Church that he would never abandon. Also, he confided in a few friends about how he felt abandoned, even betrayed by some people whom he had trusted. It is difficult to say exactly whom he meant. Msgr Bugnini perhaps, but who else? Paradoxically he became closer to people whose theological and pastoral positions were far from his own, such as Cardinal Siri, whom he often summoned at difficult moments, and who came from Genoa to comfort him. Cardinal Siri would declare: "In the later years, I was perhaps his closest friend." The pope told him, "You are the only person to raise my morale. The others depress me. Come often to see me."[52]

Cardinal Siri seems to have been a determining factor in one of Paul VI's last important acts of leadership. The pope wanted, both out of personal conviction and following the wishes of those who desired that collegiality be better affirmed (notably Cardinal Suenens), to change how the sovereign pontiff was elected. The intended reform would have consisted in the papal election being the work not only of the cardinals, but also of the presidents of the episcopal conferences and bishops elected by their peers, or perhaps it might include the oriental patriarchs in the conclave. Cardinal Siri was opposed to this reform, and decided to react, first in an anonymous article in the theological journal he had founded at Genoa, *Renovatio*, then in person with the pope. The conversation lasted an hour and a half, he would later reveal.

> You would have said it was a ping-pong match. The pope would listen to my argument, opposing it with his dialectics. I held back one last objection. I told him that it would be an error to assimilate the cardinals designated by the pope with elected bishops. The former would not have to respond to anyone for their actions, while the latter would be obliged to answer for their decisions. These latter, I said, could be made to depend on conditions.

That final word made Paul VI grimace; finally he surrendered to the arguments of Cardinal Siri.[53] On October 1, 1975 the apostolic constitution *Romano Pontifici Eligendo* appeared. It did not modify the mode of the election of the pope, contrary to some expectations. The next pope would be elected, as popes had been for centuries, by the cardinals alone. The body of the sacred College was limited to one hundred twenty

---

52 Spiazzi, Il Cardinale Giuseppe Siri, 97 & 227.
53 Lai, Les Secrets du Vatican, 171.

members. As in November 1970, octogenarian cardinals could no longer participate at conclave (though nothing in the constitution prevented them from being elected pope).

A few months later, on November 29, 1975, the Congregation for the Doctrine of the Faith published a long "Declaration on Certain Questions of Sexual Ethics," which had been in preparation since 1968. Faced with the evolution of morals, it reaffirmed, on very precise points, traditional morality. It reasserted the ban on pre-marital conjugal relations, because they are a negation of the sacrament of marriage and because they almost invariably "exclude the perspective of the child." The declaration also reiterated condemnation of homosexuality and masturbation, because "the deliberate uses of the sexual faculty outside of conjugal relations essentially contradicts its finality." Of course, this text suffered widespread criticism from that section of public opinion that had been rallying for the "liberation of souls" for several years already.[54]

The publication of this text and the controversies that followed coincided with another controversy, concerning the membership of certain prelates in Freemasonry. At the beginning of 1976, a certain "International Committee for the Defense of Catholic Tradition" began to circulate lists of these supposed Freemasons, which were republished by different news outlets in Italy and other countries.[55] The lists specified, for the implicated names, the date of their alleged affiliation with the Freemasons. Among the names cited, several cardinals will be found (Baggio,[56] Liénart, Pellegrino, Poletti,[57] Suenens, Villot) and close associates of the pope (Fr Macchi, Fr Virgilio Levi;[58] Archbishop Mario

---

54   Personal attacks were made against the pope, famously by Roger Peyrefitte who accused Paul VI of being a homosexual. Exceptionally, the pope responded by mentioning "a certain journalist, little concerned with honesty, who spits out ridicule and spreads horrible and calumnious insinuations."

55   List republished in France, famously by G. Virebeau, *Prélats et Francs-Maçons*. There is reason to doubt the authenticity of these lists, and various related, purportedly Masonic documents. But perhaps other evidence exists. See, for more promising leads, Fr Charles Theodore Murr, *Murder in the 33rd Degree: The Gagnon Investigation into Vatican Freemasonry* (N.p.: Independently published, 2022). Fr Murr was the secretary of Card. Gagnon during the period in which the latter had been tasked by Paul VI with compiling a dossier of evidence.

56   Card. Sebastiano Baggio (1913–1993) was an Italian cardinal and President of the Pontifical Commission for Vatican City State (1984). He held an influential post in Rome as the Prefect of the Congregation of Bishops (1973–1984) where he had to select a list of candidates for episcopacy.

57   Card. Ugo Poletti (1914–1997) was an Italian cardinal, elevated in 1973 by Pope Paul VI. He also served as the Vicar General of Rome (1973–1991).

58   Fr Virgilio Levi (1929–2002) was ordained as a priest in 1952 and was editorial

Brini[59] who had been one of his secretaries in the forties), and above all that of Msgr Bugnini, the leading figure of the liturgical reform. These "revelations" would have hardly been the object of discussion for more than a few weeks, as has been the case with other more or less authentic revelations, if certain facts had not come to amplify the rumor. First of all, in the preceding years, Cardinal Heenan and the Grand Master of the National Lodge of France, Ernest van Hecke,[60] among others, had made discreet overtures to Paul VI in favor of the Church softening her stance on Freemasonry — specifically, that membership in "regular" Freemasonry be distinguished from secular and anticlerical Freemasonry, and that its members no longer be excommunicated. The Grand Master of the Grand Lodge of Austria has attested that Paul VI "had given the order in revising the CIC [Code of Canon Law] not to retain the canons referring to the excommunication of Freemasons, in particular canon 2335."[61] This revision of canon law was not finished until the pontificate of John Paul II, but under Paul VI, in 1974, a letter from the Congregation for the Doctrine of the Faith specified that, according to canon 2335, "only those Catholics who are part of associations acting against the Church" are excommunicated. Seemingly certain "spiritualist" Masonic obediences were no longer banned for Catholics. The Masonic lists which appeared in 1976 seemed to confirm, for some, that the Catholic Church and a branch of Freemasonry were drawing closer.

The other fact that fed the rumor was the eviction of Archbishop Bugnini: in January 1976 he was named nuncio to Iran. This exile of the main actor in the liturgical reform to a second-rate diplomatic post seemed to be a punishment. According to this theory, Paul VI separated himself from Msgr Bugnini because he supposedly learned that the latter was a Freemason.[62]

---

secretary (1967–1972), then deputy director (1972–1983), of L'Osservatore Romano. He edited various articles relating to Pope Paul VI, including Jesus of Paul VI (1985).
59   Archbishop Mario Brini (1908–1995) was ordained a priest in 1938 and was appointed as the titular archbishop of Algiza on October 14, 1961. Later, he became the Secretary of the Congregation for the Oriental Churches (1965–1982).
60   Ernest van Hecke (1883–1966) was the Grand Master of the French National Grand Lodge. He was born in Belgium and fought for that country in World War II before using his dual citizenship to move to France where he replaced the recently impeached Grand Master Pierre.
61   Kurt Baresch, Katholische Kirche und Freimaurerei (Vienna: Bundesverlag, 1983).
62   Archbishop Bugnini, in La Riforma liturgica, 101, defended himself against the accusation of being a Freemason, but he estimated that this accusation went a long way to explain the decision of Paul VI. For more details, see Chiron, Bugnini, 171–75; "New Interview with Fr. Charles Murr on Mother Pascalina, Bugnini, Paul

None of the other prelates accused of being a Freemason was disciplined. Some, such as Cardinal Villot, had formal retractions published in the same publications that had reproduced the accusatory list. This rumor, added to the general crisis which the Church was undergoing, came to darken the end of the pontificate.

"I DID WHAT I COULD"

If there is one area where the last years of Paul VI's reign appeared almost as enthusiastic as the first, it was ecumenism, even though no spectacular decision ever came of it. On December 14, 1975, for the tenth anniversary of the mutual lifting of the excommunications, the pope received an orthodox delegation, led by Metropolitan Melito of Chalcedon,[63] representing the patriarch of Constantinople. The patriarch addressed a letter to the pope in which he greeted him as the "first bishop of the Body of Christ by rank and in honor." The day of the meeting, after a Mass celebrated in the Sistine Chapel, Paul VI knelt down before the metropolitan and kissed his feet. It was an extreme gesture of humility imitating that of Jesus to His apostles on the evening of Holy Thursday. It was another spectacular gesture, but not a spontaneous one. The metropolitan had not been forewarned, but the pope had at least told Fr Macchi in advance. In his message for the patriarch of Constantinople, Paul VI declared: "The Catholic Church and the Orthodox Church are united by a communion so profound that very little is lacking for them to reach the common fullness of the Eucharist..." This bold declaration was much more optimistic than were the Catholic and Orthodox theologians who were studying everything that continued to separate the two churches. One year later, receiving members of the Secretariat for Christian Unity, the pope comforted them: "You must, cautiously, but without hesitation, go ahead, docile to the Holy Spirit who does not cease to guide you towards the whole truth," and he

---

VI, and Other Major Figures," *Rorate Cæli*, October 10, 2020; "Fr. Charles Murr on Vatican intrigues surrounding Cardinals Baggio, Benelli, Villot, and Gagnon," *Rorate Cæli*, December 18, 2020; cf. information coming via Fr Brian Harrison in "New historical evidence emerges in support of Bugnini's association with Freemasonry," *Rorate Cæli*, May 6, 2020.

63 Msgr. Melito of Chalcedon (1913–1989) was a prelate of the Eastern Orthodox Church, originally from Istanbul. In 1966, he was appointed the Metropolitan of Chalcedon, which he remained until his death. He was an important assistant of the Ecumenical Patriarch of Constantinople at the time and was favored to succeed him, but the Turkish government had him removed from the list of potential candidates in an attempt to retain control of the Patriarchate.

spontaneously declared that ecumenism was "the most mysterious and important enterprise of my pontifical ministry" (November 12, 1979).

This daring, which he displayed and encouraged, sometimes found itself halted by the reminder of realities that could not be neglected. Thus, when he received, April 28 and 29, 1977, Dr Coggan,[64] head of the Anglican community, Dr Coggan and Cardinal Willebrands would have liked a common Eucharistic celebration. The Anglican archbishop would not have concelebrated but would have attended the Mass from a seat of honor. Paul VI, it seems, was not disinclined but he asked the opinion of the Congregation for the Doctrine of the Faith, which was openly hostile to such a celebration, because too many points of important doctrine still separated the two churches.[65] Paul VI contented himself with a "liturgy of the Word" in the Sistine Chapel. This was to be his last great "ecumenical meeting." He knew it, and may have wanted to commemorate it by a historic act ...

Throughout 1977, Paul VI received the bishops of France, region by region, for their regular *ad limina* visits. Here again, he wished to deliver to them his ultimate message. The church in France was very sick. In December, to the last group he received, the pope shared his "sorrowful bewilderment" at the degradation of the religious situation in France:

> The problem of vocations and of sacerdotal formation; unacceptable liturgies everywhere; spiritual apathy in priests and male and female religious; the admission, by persons or organizations officially Catholic, of hypotheses or practices manifestly contrary to the faith or Christian ethics; in addition to all this, we have the courage to add: a certain anti-Roman complex ...

In the preceding months, several petitions from various laymen had reached him. The first, on the initiative of Michel de Saint-Pierre, and signed by different notable persons (Roland Mousnier,[66] Ivan

---

64 Archbishop Donald Coggan (1909–2000) was the Anglican archbishop of Canterbury (1974–1980). During his tenure, he was known for reviving morale within the Church of England and supporting women's ordination.

65 What is more, a new difference was added to the former doctrinal differences. Some Anglicans, including Dr Coggan, had stated their support for the ordination of women. The pope and Dr Coggan corresponded on this subject in 1975 and 1976, and the Congregation for the Doctrine of the Faith published a declaration recalling Catholic doctrine in October 1976.

66 Roland Mousnier (1907–1993) was a French historian who specialized in the early modern period, both in France and in other societies. He was a right-wing Catholic whose best known argument was that early modern France was a "society of orders."

Gobry,[67] Jacques Vier, Jean de Viguerie, Louis Salleron, Jean Dutourd, Jean-Marc Varaut[68] and others), asked that a papal legate be sent so that "you may know the truth of the situation of French Catholicism" and requested, among other things, the authorization of the Traditional Mass.[69] The second supplication originated with the group "Fidelity and Openness" of Gérard Soulages. It complained that in France there was no catechism bearing the formal approbation of the Holy See nor inspired by the "General Catechetical Directory" published in 1971 by the Congregation of the Clergy.[70]

Although Paul VI admonished the French bishops, he made no personal decision. In June, he separated himself from his very active Substitute, Archbishop Benelli. It was not a disgrace but a promotion: he was named archbishop of Florence, made a cardinal, and immediately seemed a likely *papabile*. Everyone knew that the pontificate was ending. When Jean Guitton met with Paul VI in September, the pope was sad, nervous, questioning himself with the passage from the Gospel: "When the Son of Man returns, will He still find faith upon the earth?" As if to reassure himself, the pope had added: "I have fought the good fight. I have run the race. I have kept the Faith.... I have done what I could."[71]

In November 1977, Cardinal Villot confided to Fr Wenger: "I have met with many cardinals to prepare for the interim period and the succession, because this cannot go on much longer. Aside from the pain of arthritis, there are abscesses."[72]

From Christmas to mid-January 1978, the ailing pope had to suspend his audiences. A final trial awaited him. In March, the leader of the Christian Democrats, Aldo Moro, was kidnapped by the Red Brigades. The pope had known him since his days at the FUCI and maintained contact with him, even when he led the government. The terrorists of

---

67 Ivan Gobry (1927–2017), a French essayist and philosopher, was professor of philosophy at the University of Reims for 27 years and created the Champagne Philosophy Society in 1970.
68 Jean-Marc Varaut (1933–2005) was a French Catholic lawyer and monarchist.
69 In February of this same year, Msgr Ducaud-Bourget (1897–1984), who until then had celebrated the Traditional Mass in the Wagram hall, occupied with some faithful the Parisian church Saint-Nicholas-du-Chardonnet. The SSPX has continued the Traditional Mass there since the death of Msgr. Ducaud-Bourget.
70 A few months later, at the synod of bishops devoted to catechesis, the same group will send a "File on the problem of catechesis" to each of the bishop-participants. It is John Paul II who developed the conclusions of this synod, which ultimately resulted in the publication of the *Catechism of the Catholic Church* in 1992.
71 Jean Guitton in *Notiziario* 1 (Christmas 1979): 28, and *Le Figaro*, August 9, 1978.
72 Wenger, *Le Cardinal Villot*, 211.

the extreme left who had taken Moro hostage demanded the liberation of political prisoners. On March 19, Paul VI called for the liberation "of him who is dear to us." On April 20 Aldo Moro, under the threats of his captors, wrote to the pope, asking him to intervene with the Italian government to meet his kidnappers' demands. Paul VI was ready to do it, but Cardinal Villot and Msgr Casaroli dissuaded him. Paul VI decided to attempt a personal appeal to the Red Brigades this time. On April 22, a few hours before the deadline fixed by the kidnappers, after having worked through part of the night, he had his famous call distributed: "To the men of the Red Brigades: I beg you on my knees: liberate Mr. Aldo Moro, simply, without conditions...; leave me to hope that there is still a sentiment of humanity in you that will prevail. I await the proof in prayer and love for you." Without their response, he made a final attempt. He offered them a large sum of money in exchange for Aldo Moro. Paul VI entrusted Macchi with contacting the terrorists, which he seemingly succeeded in doing, but without succeeding in convincing them.[73] Aldo Moro was murdered, and his body was found on May 9, not far from the headquarters of the Christian Democrats. Paul VI insisted on presiding over the funeral of his assassinated friend himself. He did not give a homily or speech; instead he read a sorrowful prayer. This poignant ceremony, this sickly pope with his drawn features, moved Italian public opinion, which suddenly seemed to unite in solidarity around Paul VI.

In the following months, his physical decline accelerated. His confessor recalled: "His spirit was clear, but nothing remained of his body. His strength declined day by day."

On August 3, after withdrawing as he did every summer to his residence at Castel Gandolfo, the last important audience he granted was to Sandro Pertini,[74] the Socialist leader who had been elected president of the Republic a few weeks before. The audience lasted for two and a half hours. There was some question of the concordat which both the Church and the Italian State wanted to revise. According to Pertini, Paul VI and he agreed to give "instructions to avoid useless intransigence" to the delegations that would engage in the negotiations on both sides.[75]

---

[73] G. Andreotti (President of the Council at the time of the events), interview, *Panorama*, March 13, 1988.
[74] Sandro Pertini (1896–1990) was the seventh President of Italy (1978–1985). He was a socialist who was strongly opposed to the Fascist totalitarian regime that existed in Italy in the twentieth century. He was also a journalist and a partisan who had a close personal friendship with Pope John Paul II.
[75] Witness of S. Pertini in *Notiziario* 5 (November 1982): 58.

On August 6, the feast of the Transfiguration, Paul VI died. In conformity with his wishes, his funeral was celebrated with extreme simplicity.

What judgment will History bear on his pontificate? Guitton, who was among those who knew him best and his friend for almost thirty years, makes a remark that historians ought to take into consideration: "Paul VI did not have the makings of a pope. He did not have that which is characteristic of a pope: resolve, the strength of resolve."[76]

Regardless of what future centuries will think of this pontificate, the Church, no longer concerned with the temporal success of the pope, nor even his "political" qualities, will perhaps judge that he was a saint. The cause for Paul VI's canonization is already open. On September 8, 1990, the postulator of the cause was named: Paolo Molinari,[77] already postulator of the cause of Pius XII. In 1992, Cardinal Ruini[78] officially opened the process of beatification.

Whether before the tribunal of history or in the judgment of the Church, Paul VI will not lack witnesses for the prosecution, nor advocates for the defense.

---

76 Guitton, interview.
77 Paolo Molinari (1924–2014) was an Italian theologian who published, among other books, *The Vocation and Mission of Joseph and Mary* (1992).
78 Card. Camillo Ruini (1931–) is an Italian cardinal and was both the president of the Italian Episcopal Conference (1991–2007) and the Vicar General of the Diocese of Rome (1991–2008). He studied at the Pontifical Gregorian University, obtaining degrees in philosophy and sacred theology. He was very active in the media as a social and political conservative.

ACKNOWLEDGMENTS

MY THANKS GO FIRST OF ALL TO THOSE WHO, HAVing known Paul VI, responded to my questions during interviews or by letter: Cardinals Paolo Dezza, Gabriel-Marie Garrone, Jacques Martin, Silvio Oddi,[1] and Hyacinthe Thiandoum; Msgr Pierre Duprey, Msgr Antonio Piolanti, Father Max Thurian, Father René Voillaume, Nicola Ciancio, Jean Guitton, Hans Küng, and Renato Papetti. Giuseppe Camadini, president of the Paul VI Institute; Jane B. Sealock, responsible for the FOI archives/Privacy Office of the American Department of Defense; and René Mougel, director of the Maritain Archives, facilitated my research: thanks be to them.

The following communicated useful information to me: Msgr Lorenzo Antonetti, Father Noël Barbara, Father Bruno Bosatra, Gilbert Callet, Msgr Vincenzo Carbone, Grégoire Celier, Georges Cerbelaud-Salagnac, Father Emmanuel du Chalard, Brother Charles-Eugène, Msgr Giuseppe Colombo, Pierre Debray, Jean-Marie Domenach, Father Gilberto Donnini, Father Joseph de Finance, Father Antonio Gliozzo, Father Peter Gumpel, Father Laurentius Koch, Bernadette Lécureux, Msgr Michele Maccarrone, Father Patrice Mahieu, Sister Maria Francesca of the Monastery of Saint Priscilla in Rome, Father Giacomo Martina, Father G. Michiels, Father Daniel Misonne, Father Petrus Novack, Father Christian Papeians de Marchoven, Father Stephan Petzolt, René Rancoeur, François Saint-Pierre, Father Joachim Salzeber, Eric de Saventhem, Gérard Soulages, Msgr Tissier de Mallerais, Beatrice de Varine, Nello Vian and Father Antoine Wenger.

My gratitude goes also to those who translated certain important texts: from German (Miraille Belliard and Véronique Wehrey), from Spanish (Hélène Curie-Seimbres), and from Latin (Philippe de Gavrilott).

---

1 Card. Silvio Oddi (1910–2001) was an Italian Prelate, created a cardinal in 1969. He was an ecclesiastical diplomat for the Holy See and Roman Curia and later became the head of the Congregation for the Clergy (1979–1986).

BIBLIOGRAPHY

ARCHIVES

Archives historiques du ministère des Affaires étrangères (France), series "Europe/ Saint-Siège"
Guerre 1939–1945, Vichy: 544 and 545.
Guerre 1939–1945, Alger/CFLN/GPRF: 1373, 1374, 1375.
Vichy/Saint-Siège: 555 to 559.
1944–1949: 534, 536 to 540.
1949–1955: 26-1-1.
Archives Jacques Maritain (Kolbsheim, France).
Department of Defense (United States)
FOI/Privacy Office: 204053, 213743, S-12803.
Paul VI Institute (Brescia).
Public Record Office (Great Britain)
FO 371/22441.
FO 371/23827.
Registries of guests or of Masses from the Abbeys of Einsiedeln, Ettal, Jouques (formerly rue Monsieur, Paris), Maria Laach, Mont-César (Louvain), and Saint Priscilla (Rome).

WORKS OF G. B. MONTINI–PAUL VI

Documents pontificaux de Paul VI. 17 vols. Saint-Maurice, Switzerland: Éditions Saint-Augustin, 1967–1980.
Insegnamenti di Paolo VI. 16 vols. Tipografia Poliglotta Vaticana. (Discourses published in their language of origin).
L'Eglise et les Conciles. Paris: Éditions Saint-Paul, 1965.
Vous les prêtres du Christ. Paris: Éditions Saint-Paul, 1969.
Face à la contestation. Paris: Fayard, 1970.
Lettere a un giovane amico: Carteggio di G. B. Montini con A. Trebeschi. Brescia: Editrice Queriniana, 1978.
Scritti giovanili. Brescia: Editrice Queriniana, 1979.
Colloqqui Religiosi. Brescia: Istituto Paolo VI; Rome: Edizioni Studium, 1981.
Coscienza universitaria. Rome: Studium, 1982. (First edition 1930.)
Giovanni e Paolo: Saggio di corrispondenza (1925–1962). Brescia: Istituto Paolo VI; Rome: Edizioni Studium, 1982.
Discorsi e scritti sul concilio, 1959–1963. Brescia: Istituto Paolo VI; Rome: Edizioni Studium, 1983.
Saggio di corrispondenza (1923–1977). With O. Marcolini. Brescia: CE. DOC., 1985.
Lettere ai familiari (1919–1943). 2 vols. Brescia: Istituto Paolo VI; Rome: Edizioni Studium, 1986.

Al mondo del lavoro (Discorsi e scritti, 1954–1963). Brescia: Istituto Paolo VI; Rome: Edizioni Studium, 1988.
Una rara amicizia G. B. Montini e M. Rampolla del Tindaro: Careggio 1922–1944. Brescia: Istituto Paolo VI; Rome: Edizioni Studium, 1990.
Interventi nella Commissione Centrale Preparatoria del Concilio Ecumenico Vaticano II. Brescia: Istituto Paolo VI; Rome: Edizioni Studium, 1992.

OTHER WORKS CONSULTED

There exists a bibliography of works and articles devoted to Paul VI: Pál Arató, Paulus PP. VI 1963–1978: Elenchus bibliographicus. Brescia: Istituto Paolo VI, 1981. The Paul VI Institute of Brescia publishes a review in which appear many of the unedited texts of G. B. Montini–Paul VI as well as testimonies: Notiziario. 54 numbers have been published since Christmas 1979.

COLLOQUIA

Paul VI et la modernité dans l'Église. Rome: École Française de Rome, 1984.
G. B. Montini arcivescovo di Milano e il Concilio œcumenico Vaticano II. Brescia: Istituto Paolo VI; Rome: Edizioni Studium, 1987.
Paolo VI e i problemi ecclesiologici al Concilio. Brescia: Istituto Paolo VI; Rome: Edizioni Studium, 1989.
Le Deuxième Concile du Vatican. Rome: École Française de Rome, 1989.
Paolo VI e il rapporto Chiesa-mondo al Concilio. Brescia: Istituto Paolo VI; Rome: Edizioni Studium, 1991.

GENERAL

(Anon.) . . . et pulsanti aperietur. Clarens, Switzerland: Fédération international Una Voce, 1980.
(Anon.) Livre blanc: Reconnaissance canonique du Monastère 1970–1990. Le Barroux, France: Abbaye Sainte-Madeleine, n.d.
(Anon.) "Paul VI et Maredsous." Lettre de Maredsous 3 (1978): 13–16.
(Anon.) Une Église du silence: Catholiques de Yougoslavie. Paris: Desclée De Brouwer, 1954.
Aarons, Mark, and John Loftus. Des Nazis au Vatican. N.p.: Olivier Orban, 1992.
Acerbi, Antonio. Chiesa e democrazia da Leone XIII al Vaticano II. Milan: Vita e Pensiero, 1991.
———. Actes et Documents du Saint-Siège relatifs à la Seconde Guerre mondiale. 12 vols. Vatican: Libreria Éditrice Vaticane, 1965–1981.
———. "Action catholique et fascisme." La Documentation catholique (1931), cols. 541–76, 771–896 and (1932), cols. 897–1024, 1219–80.
Alfrieri, Dino. Deux dictateurs face à face: Rome-Berlin 1939–1943. Paris: Les Éditions du Cheval ailé, 1948.
Ambrogiani, Pietro. Paul VI: Le pape pèlerin. N.p.: Solar, 1971.

Bibliography

Amerio, Romano. *Iota unum: A Study of Changes in the Catholic Church in the XXth Century*. Trans. John P. Parsons. Kansas City, MO: Sarto House, 2012.
André, Marie. *Les Martyrs noire de l'Ouganda*. Paris: Librairie Bloud & Gay, 1936.
Antonetti, Nicola. *La FUCI di Montini e Righetti: Lettere di I. Righetti ad A. Gotelli*. Rome: Éditrice A.V.E., 1979.
Antunès, Manuel. "Linhas mestras de un pontificado." *Brotéria* 107 (1978): 243–61.
Arnoulx de Pirey, Élizabeth. *De Gasperi: Le père italien de l'Europe*. Paris: Téqui, 1991.
Arrupe, Pedro. *Itinéraire d'un jésuite*. Paris: Le Centurion, 1982.
Arsan, Emmanuelle. *Épître à Paul VI sur la pilule*. N.p.: Éric Losfeld, 1968.
Aubert, Roger, ed. *Nouvelle Histoire de l'Église*. Vol. 5. "L'Église dans le monde modern (1848 à nos jours)." Paris: Éditions du Seuil, 1975.
Aubert, Roger. "Paul VI: un 'pontificate de transition.'" *Revue nouvelle* (December 1978): 613–28.
———. "Paul VI." *Catholicisme* 47 (1985), cols. 930–41.
Bendiscioli, Mario. "Paolo VI." In vol. 2 of *Dizionario storico del movimento cattolico in Italia*, 448–53. Turin: Marietti, 1982.
Bendiscioli, Mario, and Massimo Marcocchi. "La censura del S. Ufficio e 'L'Essenza del Cattolicesimo' di K. Adam." *Studi e memorie* 7 (1979): 95–147.
Bergerre, Max. *Quatre papes, un journaliste*. Paris: Téqui, 1978.
Besret, Bernard. *Confiteor: De la contestation à la sérénité*. Paris: Albin Michel, 1991.
Beyer, Jean. "Sens et rôle du droit ecclésial: La pensée de Paul VI." *L'Année canonique* 22 (1983): 25–36.
———. "Paul VI et le droit de l'Église." *Les Quatre Fleuves* 18 (1983): 43–75.
Blet, Pierre. "Pie XII et la France en guerre." *Revue d'histoire de l'Église de France* (July-December 1983): 209–32.
Bolado, Alfonso A. "Naturaleza y tiempo del Nacionalcatolicisimo." *Razon y Fe* (July-August 1986): 57–68.
Boland, André. "Paul VI." In *Dictionnaire de Spiritualité*, fasc. 76–77, col. 522–36. Paris: Beauchesne, 1983.
Bonnet, Serge. *A hue et à dia: Les avatars du cléricalisme sous la Ve République*. Paris: Cerf, 1973.
Bonneterre, Didier. *The Liturgical Movement: From Dom Guéranger to Annibale Bugnini*. Kansas City, MO: Angelus Press, 2002.
Borelli, Antonio A. *Fatima: Message de tragédie ou d'espérance*. N.p.: Éditions TFP, 1991.
Bourdarias, Jean. *Les Évêques de France et le marxisme*. Paris: Fayard, 1991.
Bourdarias, Jean, Bernard Chevallier, Joseph Vandrisse. *Les Fumées du Vatican: De Paul VI à Jean-Paul II*. Paris: Fayard, 1979.
Bouyer, Louis. *The Decomposition of Catholicism*. Translated by Charles Underhill Quinn. Chicago: Franciscan Herald Press, 1969.
———. *Religieux et clercs contre Dieu*. Paris: Aubier-Montaigne, 1975.
———. *Le Métier de théologien*. Paris: France-Empire, 1979.

Boyer, Charles. "Le pape Paul VI." *Esprit et Vie* (Dec. 14, 1978): 689–95.
Breza, Tadeusz. *La Porte de bronze: Chronique de la vie vaticane.* Paris: Julliard, 1962.
Bugnini, Annibale. *The Reform of the Liturgy: 1948–1975.* Translated by Matthew J. O'Connell. Collegeville, MN: The Liturgical Press, 1990.
Carrarel, Norbert. *La Vie du Concile.* Forcalquier: Robert Morel, 1966.
Calori, Carlo. "G.B.M. (oggi Paolo VI) studente." *La Rivista del Clero italiano* 8 (August 1970): 471–75.
Campanini, Giorgio. *Aldo Moro.* Paris: Beauchesne, 1988.
Caprile, G. *Il Concilio Vaticano II.* 6 vols. Rome: La Civiltà Cattolica, 1966–1969.
———. "Paolo VI e il concilio." *L'Osservatore Romano*, September 19, 1982.
Caprioli, Adriano. "Ritorno ad Agostino in Montini giovane." *La Scuola cattolica* 115 (1987): 267–95.
Carrier, Hervé. "Le pape Paul VI et l'Université grégorienne." *Gregorianum* 59/4 (1978): 653–57.
Casini, Tito. *The Torn Tunic: Letter of a Catholic on the "Liturgical Reform."* Brooklyn, NY: Angelico Press, 2020; repr. of 1967 English edition.
Caula, Carlo Felice. *Domenico Tardini (1888–1961).* Rome: Edizioni Studium, 1988.
Cavaterra, Emilio. *Il Prefetto del Sant'Offizio: Le opere e i giorni del cardinale Ottaviani.* Milan: Mursia, 1990.
Celier, Grégoire. *La Dimension œcuméinque de la réforme liturgique.* N.p.: Éditions Fideliter, 1987.
Chadwick, Owen. *Michael Ramsey: A Life.* Oxford: Oxford University Press, 1991.
Chelini, Jean. *Les Nouveaux Papes.* N.p.: Éditions Jean Goujon, 1979.
———. *L'Église sous Pie XII.* 2 vols. Paris: Fayard, 1983–1988.
Chenaux, Jean-Philippe. *Le Retour de la doctrine sociale de l'Église.* Lausanne: Centre patronal, 1991.
Chenu, Marie-Dominique. *Un théologien en liberté.* Paris: Le Centurion, 1975.
Ciancio, Nicola. *Vita con don Bosco.* Rome: Società Editrice Europea, 1991.
Clair, Romain. "Le pape Paul VI et l'abbaye Sainte-Madeleine." *Bulletin de l'abbaye d'Hautecombe* 111 (July-September 1978): 55–63.
Coache, Louis. *La Foi au goût du jour.* Paris: La Table Ronde, 1969.
———. *Vers l'apostasie générale.* Paris: La Table Ronde, 1969.
Colombo, Carlo. "Papa Paolo VI ed il Concilio Vaticano II." *Vita e Pensiero* 46 (1963): 535–41.
———. "Un Papa che ha tanto amato." *Vita e Pensiero* 62 (1979): 27–31.
Colombo, Giovanni. *Ricordando G. B. Montini.* Brescia: Istituto Paolo VI; Rome: Edizioni Studium, 1989.
Colombo, Giuseppe. *Omaggio a S.E. Mons. Carlo Colombo.* N.p.: H.C., 1991.
Comblin, Joseph. "El pontificado de Paulo VI." *Mensaje* 273 (1978): 609–15.
Congar, Yves. *My Journal of the Council.* Collegeville, MN: Liturgical Press, 2012. (Originally published in four volumes: 1963, 1964, 1965, and 1966.)

———. *Une vie pour la vérité: Jean Puyo interroge le P. Congar*. Paris: Le Centurion, 1975.
Coppens, Joseph. "In memoriam." *Ephemerides Theologicæ Lovanienses* (December 1978): 375–93.
Cremona, Carlo. *Paolo VI*. Milan: Rusconi, 1991.
Cripa, Romeo. "Paolo VI e la cultura contemporanea." *Coscienza* 8–9 (1978): 13–14.
Curvers, Alexis. *Pie XII: le pape outragé*. Poitiers: Éditions DMM, 1988.
Dahm, Paul. *Pie XII*. Paris: Elsevier, 1954.
Daniel-Ange. *Paul VI: un regard prophétique*. 2 vols. Paris: Éditions Saint-Paul, 1979–1981.
Daniel-Ropes. *Vatican II: Le concile de Jean XXIII*. Paris: Fayard, 1961.
Daniélou, Jean. *Tests*. Paris: Beauchesne, 1968.
———. *Et qui est mon prochain? Mémoires*. Paris: Stock, 1974.
De Broucker, José. *Le Dossier Suenens*. Paris: Éditions universitaires, 1970.
Defois, Gérard, ed. *Le Concile: 20 ans de notre histoire*. Paris: Desclée, 1982.
De Gasperi, Francesca. "Msgr Montini–De Gasperi: Testimonianza di un'amicizia." *Rivista di Storia della Chiesa in Italia* 33 (January-June 1979): 105–8.
De Jaeghere, Michel. "La maison Casaroli." *Le Spectacle du monde*, January 1991.
Deleclos, Fabien. *Jean-Paul Ier: L'espérance*. Brussels: Vokaer, 1978.
Delehaye, Philippe. "Paul VI et la Commission théologique international." *Revue théologique de Louvain* 4 (1978): 417–23.
De Rosa, Peter. *Vicars of Christ: The Dark Side of the Papacy*. London: Corgi Books, 1989.
Descamps, A.-L. "Pour un portrait de Paul VI." *Revue théologique de Louvain* 4 (1978): 395–406.
Devoghel, E. *La Question romaine sous Pie XI et Mussolini*. Paris: Bloud et Gay, 1929.
Dezza, Paolo. "Paolo VI e egli studi ecclesiastici." *la Civiltà cattolica* (April 21, 1979): 131–41.
Di Nolfo, Ennio. *Vaticano e Stati Uniti: 1939–1952*. Milan: Franco Angeli Editore, 1978.
Dizionario storico del movimento cattolico in Italia (1860–1980). 6 vols. (3 tomes). Turin: Marietti, 1981–1984.
Dorn, Luitpold A. *Paul VI: portrait familier en 100 anecdotes*. Paris: Albin Michel, 1970.
Dreyfus, Paul. *Jean XXIII*. Paris: Fayard, 1979.
Dupuy, André. *La Diplomatie du Saint-Siège après le IIe concile du Vatican*. N.p.: Téqui, 1980.
Durand, Jean-Dominique. *L'Église catholique dans la crise de l'Italie (1943–1948)*. Rome: École française de Rome, 1991.
Escoulen, Daniel. *François Marty: évêque en France*. Rodez: Éditions du Rouergue, 1991.

Eugène de Villeurbanne. *Illuminisme 67: Un faux renouveau, le pentecôtisme dit catholique*. Coligny: Verjon, 1975.

Falconi, Carlo. *Documents secrets du concile*. Paris: Éditions du Rocher, 1965.

———. *Vu et entendu au concile*. Paris: Éditions du Rocher, 1965.

Famerée, Joseph. "De Rerum novarum à Octagesima adveniens." *Nouvelle Revue théologique* (January-February 1982): 88–92.

Fanello Marcucci, Gabriella. *Storia di un'amicizia: G. B. Montini e Giuseppe Spataro*. Brescia: Edizioni Morcelliana, 1984.

Fappani, Antonio. *Giorgio Montini: Cronache di una testimonianza*. Rome: Edizioni Cinque lune, 1974.

Fappani, Antonio, and Franco Molinari. *Giovanni Battista Montini giovane, 1987–1944*. Turin: Marietti, 1981.

Felici, Pericle. *Il lungo cammino del Concilio*. Milan: Editrice Ancora, 1967.

Fesquet, Henri. *Le Journal du concile*. Forcalquier: Robert Morel, 1966.

———. *Le Journal du premier synod catholique*. Forcalquier: Robert Morel, 1967.

Fessard, Gaston. *Église de France, prends garde de perdre la foi!* Paris: Julliard, 1979.

Floridi, Ulisse, SJ. *Moscou et le Vatican*. Paris: France-Empire, 1979.

Fonzi, Fausto, ed. *Per il rinnovamento cattolico: La testimonianza di Luigi Piastrelli*. Brescia: Morcelliana, 1981.

Fouilloux, Étienne. "Paul VI." *Universalia* (1977): 445–46.

———. *Les Catholiques et l'unité chrétienne du XIXe au XXe siècle*. Paris: Le Centurion, 1982.

———. "Recherche théologique et magistère romain in 1952." *Recherches de science religieuse* (April-June 1983): 269–85.

Funditor. *Réponse à dom Oury sur "la messe de saint Pie V à Paul VI."* N.p.: Éditions Nouvelle Aurore, 1976.

Gamber, Klaus. *The Reform of the Roman Liturgy: Its Problems and Background*. Translated by Klaus D. Grimm. San Juan Capistrano, CA: Una Voce Press and Harrison, NY: The Foundation for Catholic Reform, 1993.

Garrone, Gabriel-Marie. *La Profession de foi de Paul VI*. Paris: Beauchesne, 1969.

———. "Paul VI et le concile Vatican II." (4 pages.)

———. *L'Église 1965–1972*. Paris: Le Centurion, 1972.

———. *50 ans de vie d'Église*. Paris: Desclée, 1972.

Gazeau, Roger. "Paul VI et les Bénédictins." *Lettre de Ligugé* 192 (1978): 20–25.

Gheorghiu, Virgil. *La Vie du patriarche Athénagoras*. Paris: Plon, 1969.

Gilbert, Maurice. "Paul VI: In memoriam." *Biblica* 4 (1978): 453–62.

Guintella, Paolo. "Il Papa del dialogo." *Il Mattino*, August 5, 1988.

Giovanetti, Alberto. "Pie XII et la défence de Rome." *La Documentation catholique* (July 1964), col. 1033–48.

Goldie, Rosemary. "La participation des laics aux travaux de Vatican II." *Revue des Sciences religieuses* (January 1988): 54–73.

Gonella, Guido. "Amico Maestro." *Studium* 74 (1978): 449–60.

Gouyon (Cardinal). "Les relations entre le diocèse et la conférence épiscopale." L'Année canonique 22 (1978): 1–23.

Graber, Rudolf. Athanasius and the Church of Our Time. Translated by Susan Johnson. Palmdale, CA: Omni Publications, n.d.

Graham, Robert A. "Espions nazis au Vatican pendant la IIe Guerre mondiale." La Documentation catholique (April 5, 1970): 331–36.

———. "Hitler voulait-il éloigner Pie XII de Rome?" La Documentation catholique (May 1, 1972): 427–34.

Grootaers, Jan. De Vatican II à Jean-Paul II. Paris: Le Centurion, 1981.

Guarnieri, Romano. Don Giuseppe De Luca: Tra Cronaca e storia. Rome: Edizioni Raoline, 1991.

Guasco, Maurilio. "Scritti e ricerche sul giovane Montini." La Rivista del Clero italiano (February 1981): 178–84.

Guelluy, Robert. "Le magistère 'ordinaire' de Paul VI." Revue théologique de Louvain 4 (1978): 407–16.

Guerini, Giuseppe. "G. B. Montini alunno del Lombardoi." L'Osservatore Romano, May 17, 1970.

Guerry, Émile. "Pourquoi nous dénonçons le livre Le Vicaire." La Documentation catholique (July 1964): 1009–32.

Guillou, Édouard. Le Canon romain et la liturgie nouvelle. N.p.: Éditions Fideliter, 1989.

Guitton, Jean. La Vierge Marie. Paris: Aubier, 1949.

———. Dialogues avec Paul VI. Paris: Fayard, 1967.

———. Paul VI et l'année sainte. Paris: Fayard, 1975.

———. Journal de ma vie. Paris: DDB, 1976.

———. Paul VI secret. Paris: DDB, 1979.

———. Portrait du père Lagrange. Paris: Éditions Robert Laffont, 1992.

Gy, Pierre-Marie. "Mgr Bugnini et la réforme liturgique de Vatican II." Revue des Sciences philosophiques et théologiques (April 1985): 314–19.

Hebblethwaite, Peter. "From G. B. Montini to Pope Paul VI." Journal of Ecclesiastical History 37.2 (April 1986): 309–20.

———. Jean XXIII: le pape du concile. Paris: Le Centurion, 1988.

———. John XXIII: Pope of the Century. New York: Continuum, 2000.

Hébrard, Monique. Les Charismatiques. Paris: Cerf; N.p.: Fides, 1991.

Hildebrand, Dietrich von. The Devastated Vineyard. Chicago: Franciscan Herald Press, 1973.

———. Trojan Horse in the City of God. Rev. ed. Chicago: Franciscan Herald Press, 1967.

Hochhuth, Rolf. The Deputy. Translated by Richard and Clara Winston. New York: Grove Press, 1964.

Hospital, Jean d'. Rome en confidence. Paris: Grasset, 1962.

———. Trois Papes au tournat de l'Histoire. Paris: Librairie Académique Perrin, 1969.

Houssiau, Albert. "La riforma liturgica." *Revue d'histoire ecclésiastique* (January-April 1984): 166–68.
Huber, Georges. *Paul VI*. Paris: Le Centurion, 1963.
Hubert, Bernard, ed. *Jacques Maritain et ses contemporains*. Paris: Desclée, 1991.
Jarlot, Georges. *Doctrine pontificale et histoire*. Rome: Presses de l'Université grégorienne, 1964.
———. *Doctrine pontificale et histoire*, t. 2, "Pie XI." Rome: Presses de l'Université grégorienne, 1973.
Juffé, Madeleine. *Paul VI*. Paris: Fleurus, 1963.
Kosicki, George W. "Pope Paul VI, Prophet of our Time." *Review for Religions* 37 (1978): 896–904.
Küng, Hans. *Concile et retour à l'unité*. Paris: Cerf, 1961.
Lai, Benny. *Les Secrets du Vatican*. Paris: Hachette, 1983.
Lanne, Emmanuel. "Hommage à Paul VI." *Irénikon* 3 (1978): 299–311.
Latreille, André. "Un évêque résistant: Mgr. P. M. Théas." *Revue d'histoire ecclésiastique* (April-June 1980): 284–321.
Laurentin, René. *Bilan de la session*. Paris: Éditions du Seuil, 1963.
———. *Bilan de la 2e session*. Paris: Éditions du Seuil, 1964.
———. *Bilan de la 3e session*. Paris: Éditions du Seuil, 1965.
———. *Bilan du concile*. Paris: Éditions du Seuil, 1966.
———. *Développement et salut*. Paris: Éditions du Seuil, 1969.
———. *L'Enjeu du concile*. Paris: Éditions du Seuil, 1962.
Lefebvre, Marcel. *Conférences spirituelles* (August 20, 1976; September 18, 1976; December 2, 1976). Écône, Switzerland: Séminaire Saint-Pie X, n.d. Unpublished recordings, except for that of September 8 in a special number of *Itinéraires*.
———. *I Accuse the Council!* Kansas City, MO: Angelus Press, 1982.
———. *Le Coup de maître de Satan*. Martigny, Switzerland: Éditions Saint-Gabriel: 1977.
———. *Non*. Interview by J. Hanu. N.p.: Stock, 1977.
———. *They Have Uncrowned Him. From Liberalism to Apostasy: The Conciliar Tragedy*. Kansas City, MO: Angelus Press, 1988.
Lehnert, S. Pascalina. *His Humble Servant: Sister M. Pascalina Lehnert's Memoirs of Her Years of Service to Eugenio Pacelli, Pope Pius XII*. South Bend, IN: St Augustine's Press, 2014.
Leiber, Robert. "Pie XII." *La Documentation catholique*, February 1, 1959.
———. "Pie XII et les Juifs de Rome." *La Documentation catholique*, April 2, 1961.
Lensel, Denis. *Le Passage de la mer Rouge*. Paris: Fleurus, 1991.
Leprieur, François. *Quand Rome condamne: Dominicains et prêtres-ouvriers*. Paris: Cerf, 1989.
Lesourd, Paul. *Qui est le pape Paul VI?* Paris: Les Éditions de Paris, 1963.
———. *La Vérité sur la crise de l'Église catholique vue de Rome*. Paris: La Table Ronde, 1969.

———. *Le Cardinal Mindszenty*. Paris: France-Empire, 1972.

———. *Paul VI*. Paris: France-Empire, 1978.

Levi, Virgilio. "Paolo VI e il Concilio." *L'Osservatore Romano*, October 10, 1982.

Levillain, Philippe. *La Mécanique politique de Vatican II*. Paris: Beauchesne, 1975.

Liénart, Maurice Emmanuel. *Vatican II: numéro spécial des Mélanges de science religieuse*. Lille, 1979.

Limagne, Pierre. *Éphémérides de quatre années tragiques (1940–1944)*. Lavilledieu/Ardeche: Éditions de Candide, 1987.

Lubac, Henri de. *Entretiens autour de Vatican II*. Paris: Cerf, 1985.

———. *Mémoire sur l'occasion de mes écrits*. Namur: Culture et Vérité, 1989.

———. *Vatican Council Notebooks*. 2 vols. San Francisco: Ignatius Press, 2015 and 2016.

Maccarrone, Michele. "Paolo VI e il Concilio: Testimonianze." *Revista di Storia della Chiesa in Italia* (January-June 1989): 101–22.

Macchi, Pasquale. "Adesso viene la notte." *La Prealpina*, August 6, 1988.

Madiran, Jean. *L'Intégrisme: histoire d'une histoire*. Paris: Nouvelles Éditions latines, 1964.

———. *L'Hérésie du XXe siècle*. Paris: Nouvelles Éditions latines, 1968.

———. *Réclamation au Saint-Père*. Paris: Nouvelles Éditions latines, 1974.

———. *Éditoriaux et Chroniques*. 3 vols. Poitiers: Éditions DMM, 1983–1984.

———. *Le Concile en question*. Poitiers: Éditions DMM, 1985.

McDowell, Bart. *Inside the Vatican*. Washington, DC: National Geographic Society.

Magister, Sandro. "I servizi segreti italiani spiano Paolo VI." *Espresso*, February 15 and 22, May 21, 1976.

———. *La Politica vaticana e l'Italia 1943–1978*. Rome: Editori Riuniti Politica, 1979.

Marchasson, Yves. *Les Papes du Xxe siècle*. Paris: Desclée, 1991.

Marcucci Fanello, Gabrielle. *Storia della FUCI*. Rome: Edizioni Studium, 1971.

Maria José de Savoy (Princess). "Forse avrei potuto entrare nella resistenza." *La Repubblica*, September 7, 1983.

Maritain, Jacques. *The Peasant of the Garonne. An Old Layman Questions Himself about the Present Time*. Translated by Michael Cuddihy and Elizabeth Hughes. New York: Holt, Rinehart and Winston, 1968.

Marsaudon, Yves. *Souvenirs et réflexions: un haut dignitaire de la franc-maçonnerie de tradition révèle des secrets*. Paris: Vitiano, 1976.

Martimort, Aimé Georges. "La réforme liturgique de Vatican II." *Les Quatre Fleuves* 21–22 (1985): 81–94.

Martin, Jacques. "Da minutante a Sostituto." *L'Osservatore della Domenica*, June 28 and July 5, 1970.

———. "Le Concile Vatican II vu de près." *L'Osservatore Romano* (French ed.), May 14, 1991.

———. "La Seconde Guerre mondiale vue du Vatican." *L'Osservatore Romano* (French ed.), September 24, 1991.

Martin, Malachi. *The Jesuits*. New York: Simon & Schuster, 1988.
Martina, Giacomo. "Paolo VI, la guida della Chiesa dell'esodo." *Coscienza* 10 (1978): 6–8.
Marty, François. "Paul VI, le pape du concile." *Le Figaro*, June 22, 1973.
Marty, Jean. *Avertissements de l'au-delà à l'Église contemporaine*. N.p.: Éditions Fideliter, 1989.
May, Georges. *L'Oecuménisme, levier de la protestantisation de l'Église*. N.p.: Éditions du Cèdre, n.d.
Mayeur, Jean-Marie, ed. *Histoire du christianisme*. Vol. 12, *Guerres mondiales et totalitarismes* (1914–1958). Paris: Desclée; Paris: Fayard, 1990.
———. "Magistère et théologiens sous Pie XII." *Les Quatre Fleuves* 12 (1980): 113–19.
Mehl, Roger. *Le Pasteur Marc Bœgner*. Paris: Plon, 1987.
Meyer, Bonaventure. *L'Église en danger*. Trimbach, Switzerland: Éditions Mariales, 1983.
Michel de la Sainte Trinité. *Toute la vérité sur Fatima*. Sainte-Parres-lès-Vaudes: Renaissance catholique; N.p.: Contre-Réforme Catholique, 1985.
———. *Pour l'Église: Quarante ans de Contre-Réforme catholique*. N.p.: Contre-Réforme Catholique, 1988.
Mindszenty, Joseph. *Mémoires*. Paris: La Table Ronde, 1974.
Miribel, Élisabeth de. *Giorgio La Pira*. Paris: DDB, 1992.
Molinari, Franco. "Entre prophétie et institution: le jeune Montini." *Communio* (November-December 1979): 62–68.
Monteilhet, Hubert. *Paul VI ou l'Amen Dada*. N.p.: Régine Deforges, 1978.
Montini, Giorgio. "Mon oncle le pape." *La Documentation catholique*, January 17, 1971.
Moro, Renato. *La Formazione della classe dirigente cattolica* (1929–1937). Bologna: Il Mulino, 1979.
Nantes, Georges de. *Liber accusationis in Paulum sextum*. N.p.: Contre-Réforme Catholique, 1973.
Onofri, Nazario Sauro. *Le due anime del cardinale Lercaro*. Bologna: Cappelli Editore, 1987.
Oury, Guy-Marie. "Paul VI et la réforme liturgique." *Esprit et Vie* 46 (1977): 620–22; 48 (1977): 649–54.
Padellaro, Nazareno. *Pie XII*. Paris: Julliard, 1950.
Pallenberg, Corrado. *Paul VI*. Paris: Buchet-Chastel, 1965.
Papin (Chanoine). *Le Dernier Étage du Vatican*. Paris: Albatros, 1977.
Peri, Vittorio. "Le radici italiane nella maturazione culturale di G. B. Montini." *Archivum Historiæ Pontificiæ* 22: 299–356. Publisher not indicated, 1984.
Picci, Mario, ed. *Don Giuseppe De Luca*. Brescia: Morcelliana, 1963.
Pie XI. *Actes de SS Pie XI*. 18 vols. Paris: Maison de la Bonne Presse, 1927–1945.
Pie XII. *Documents pontificaux*. 21 vols. Saint Maurice, Switzerland: Éditions Saint Augustin, 1952–1960.

Pontiggia, Virginio. "Le Fonti del pensiero di Paolo VI sulla liturgia." Notitiæ 265–66 (August-September 1988): 543–65.
Poulat, Émile. Église contre bourgeoisie. Paris: Casterman, 1977.
———. Catholicisme, démocratie et socialism. Paris: Casterman, 1977.
———. "Paul VI." Universalia (1979): 620–21.
———. Une Église ébranlée. Paris: Casterman, 1980.
———. Modernistica. N.p.: Nouvelles Éditions latines, 1982.
———. Catholicisme sous observation. Paris: Le Centurion, 1983.
———. L'Église c'est un monde. Paris: Cerf, 1986.
Poupard, Paul. Connaissance du Vatican. Paris: Beauchesne, 1967.
———. Le Pape. Paris: P.U.F., 1980.
———. Le Vatican. Paris: P.U.F., 1981.
———. Le Concile Vatican II. Paris: P.U.F., 1983.
Quidam. "Primizie di un sacerdozio." L'Osservatore Romano, May 17, 1970.
Rahner, Karl. Le Courage du théologien. Paris: Cerf, 1985.
Reina, Mario. "Une recherché italienne: les ACLI." Cahiers d'Actualité religieuse et sociale 81 (June 15, 1974).
Riccardi, Andreà, ed. Le Chiese di Pio XII. Bari: Editori Laterzi, 1986.
———.Il 'Paritio Romano' nel secondo dopoguerra (1945–1954). Brescia: Morcelliana, 1983.
———. Il Potere del Papa da Pio XII a Paolo VI. Bari: Editori Laterza, 1988.
———. "Roma 'Città sacra'?" Dalla Conciliazione all'operazione Sturzo. Milan: Edizioni Vita e Pensiero, 1979.
Richard, André. Signes pour notre temps: Fatima, Vatican II. Saint-Céneré: Éditions Saint-Michel, 1971.
Ricci, Jean-Claude. Les Mercredis de Paul VI. Paris: P.U.F., 1974.
Roche, Georges, and Philippe Saint-Germain. Pie XII devant l'Histoire. Paris: Robert Laffont, 1972.
Romanato, Gianpolo, and Franco Molinari. "Le Letture del giovane Montini." La Scuola cattolica 111 (1983): 37–78.
Rossi, Mario. "Mes rencontres avec Mgr. Montini." Témoignage chrétien, June 27, 1963.
Rouquette, Robert. "Paul VI héritier de Jean XXIII." Études 319 (1963): 245–59.
Roy, Jean. L'Année sainte de Paul VI. Paris: Téqui, 1974.
Saint-Pierre, Michel de. Les Nouveaux Prêtres. Paris: La Table Ronde, 1965.
———. Sainte Colère. Paris: La Table Ronde, 1965.
Salleron, Louis. La Nouvelle Messe. Paris: Nouvelles Éditions latines, 1970.
Schmidt, Stjepan. Agostino Bea, il cardinale dell'unita. Rome: Città Nuova, 1987.
Schneider, Burkhart. "Der Friedensappell Papst Pius XII vom 24 August 1939." Archivum historiæ pontificiæ 6 (1968): 415–24.
Serafian, Michael. Le Pèlerin. Paris: Plon, 1964.
Serrou, Robert. Pie XII, Le pape-roi. Paris: Perrin, 1992.
Short, Martin. Inside the Brotherhood. London: Grafton Books, 1990.

Siri, Giuseppe. *Orthodoxie, erreurs et dangers.* Paris: Civitec, 1962.
———. *Gethsemani: Réflexions sur le mouvement théologique contemporain.* Paris: Téqui, 1980.
Sittinger, A. *Complot au Vatican?* N.p.: D.F.T., 1983.
Sorge, Bartolomeo. "In memoria di Paolo VI." *La Civiltà cattolica* (September 2, 1978): 350–59.
Soulages, Gérard. *Fidélité et ouverture.* Tours: Mame, 1972.
———. *Dossier sur le problème de la catéchèse.* Paris: Téqui, 1977.
———. *Épreuves chrétiennes et espérance.* Paris: Téqui, 1979.
Spiazzi, Raimondo. *Padre Mariano Cordovani.* 2 vols. Rome: A. Belardetti, 1954.
———. *Il Cardinale Giuseppe Siri.* Bologna: Edizioni Studio Domenicano, 1990.
Spink, Kathryn. *Frère Roger de Taizé.* Paris: Éditions du Seuil, 1986.
Stacpoole, Alberic, ed. *Vatican II by Those Who Were There.* London: Geoffrey Chapman, 1986.
Suenens, Léon-Joseph. *Que faut-il penser du Reàrmement moral?* Paris: Éditions universitaires, 1953.
———. *L'Église en état de mission.* Paris: Desclée De Brouwer, 1958.
———. *Souvenirs et Espérances.* Paris: Fayard, 1991.
Tardini, Domenico. *Pie XII.* Paris: Fleurus, 1961.
Thomas, Joseph. *Le Concile Vatican II.* Paris: Cerf; Montreal: Fides, 1989.
Tisserant, Eugène. "Hommage à Paul VI." *L'Homme nouveau,* February 2, 1964.
Torrell, Jean-Pierre. "Paul VI et le cardinal Journet." *Nova et Vetera* 4 (1986): 161–74.
Vaussard, Maurice. *Histoire de l'Italie contemporaine (1870–1946).* Paris: Éditions du Seuil, 1950.
———. *Histoire de la Démocratie chrétienne.* Paris: Éditions du Seuil, 1956.
Vian, Nello. *Anni et Opere di Paolo VI.* Rome: Istituto della enciclopedia italiana, 1978.
Villain, M., ed. *L'abbé Paul Couturier, apôtre de l'unité chrétienne.* Lyon/Paris: Emmanuel-Vitte, 1954.
Virebeau, Georges. *Prélats et francs-maçons.* N.p.: Publications H.C., 1978.
Voillaume, René. *Retraite au Vatican avec sa Sainteté Paul VI.* Paris: Fayard, 1969.
Walsh, Michael J. "Pope Paul VI, 1897–1978." *Month* 239 (1978): 292–96.
Walter, Otto. *Pie XII, sa vie, sa personnalité.* Mulhouse: Salvator, 1950.
Weber, Jean-Julien. *Au soir d'une vie.* Paris: Le Centurion, 1970.
———. *Je me souviens...* Paris: Le Centurion, 1976.
Wenger, Antoine. *Vatican II: Première session.* Paris: Le Centurion, 1963.
———. *Vatican II: Chronique de la deuxième session.* Paris: Le Centurion, 1964.
———. *Vatican II: Chronique de la troisième session.* Paris: Le Centurion, 1965.
———. *Vatican II: Chronique de la quatrième session.* Paris: Le Centurion, 1966.
———. *Rome et Moscou: 1900–1950.* Paris: DDB, 1987.
———. *Le Cardinal Villot (1905–1979).* Paris: DDB, 1989.
———. *Les Trois Rome.* Paris: DDB, 1991.

Wiltgen, Ralph. *The Inside Story of Vatican II: A Firsthand Account of the Council's Inner Workings*. Formerly entitled *The Rhine Flows into the Tiber: A History of Vatican II*. Charlotte, NC: TAN Books, 2014.

Winowska, Maria. *Paul VI, Pape de l'Épiphanie*. Paris: Éditions Saint-Paul, 1965.

Zananiri, Gaston. *Paul VI et les temps présents*. Paris: Spes, 1966.

Zizola, Giancarlo. *The Utopia of Pope John XXIII*. Translated by Helen Barolini. Maryknoll, NY: Orbis Books, 1978.

BIBLIOGRAPHICAL COMPLEMENT FOR THE SECOND FRENCH EDITION (2008)

Adornato, Giselda. *Cronologia dell'episcopato di Giovanni Battista Montini a Milano*. Brescia: Istituto Paolo VI, 2002.

Alberigo, Giuseppe, ed. *History of Vatican II*. Maryknoll, NY: Orbis/Leuven: Peeters, 1995–2006.

Carcel Orti, Vicente. *Pablo VI y España: Fidelidad, renovacion y crisis (1963–1978)*. Madrid: B.A.C., 1997.

Chenaux, Philippe. *Paul VI et Maritain: Les rapports du "montinianisme" et du "maritanisme."* Brescia: Istituto Paolo VI; Rome: Edizioni Studium, 1994.

Chiron, Yves. "Il pontificato di Paolo VI." In *Storia della Chiesa*, vol. 10, 450–67. Milan: Jaca Books, 1995.

Del Noce, Augusto. *Pensiero della Chiesa e filosofia contemporanea: Leone XIII, Paolo VI, Giovanni Paolo II*. Rome: Edizioni Studium, 2005.

Etling, Mark G. *The Relevance of the Property Teaching of Pope Paul VI*. San Francisco: Mellen Research University, 1993.

Hebblethwaite, Peter. *Paul VI: The First Modern Pope*. London: Harper & Collins, 1993.

Hera Buedo, Eduardo de la. *La Noche transfigurada: Biografia de Pablo VI*. Madrid: B.A.C., 2002.

Macchi, Pasquale. *Paolo VI nella sua parola*. Brescia: Morcelliana, 2001.

Mahieu, Patrice. *Paul VI, maître spiritual*. N.p.: Le Sarment; Paris: Fayard, 1997.

Marchetto, Agostino. *The Second Vatican Ecumenical Council: A Counterpoint for the History of the Council*. N.p.: University of Scranton Press, 2010.

(Various authors.) *El hombre moderno a la busqueda de Dios, segun el magisterio de Pablo VI*. Brescia: Istituto Paolo VI; Rome: Edizioni Studium, 2002.

(Various authors.) *Pablo VI y España*. Brescia: Istituto Paolo VI; Rome: Edizioni Studium, 2001.

(Various authors.) *Paolo VI e l'ecumenismo*. Brescia: Istituto Paolo VI; Rome: Edizioni Studium, 2001.

(Various authors.) *Paolo VI e la collegialità episcopale*. Brescia: Istituto Paolo VI; Rome: Edizioni Studium, 1995.

(Various authors.) *Papa Pablo VI, profeta de la evangelizacion: Testimonios de obispos latinoamericanos*. Madrid: Edibesa, 2003.

BIBLIOGRAPHICAL COMPLEMENT
FOR THE FIRST ENGLISH EDITION (2022)

Bouyer, Louis. *The Memoirs of Louis Bouyer: From Youth and Conversion to Vatican II, the Liturgical Reform, and After*. Translated by John Pepino. Brooklyn, NY: Angelico Press, 2005.

Bunson, Matthew. *Saint Pope Paul VI: Celebrating the 262nd Pope of the Roman Catholic Church*. Irondale, AL: EWTN, 2018.

Chiron, Yves. *Annibale Bugnini: Reformer of the Liturgy*. Translated by John Pepino. Brooklyn, NY: Angelico Press, 2018.

Collins, Michael. *Paul VI: Pilgrim Pope*. Collegeville, MN: Liturgical Press, 2018.

Murr, Charles Theodore. *The Godmother: Madre Pascalina, a Feminine Tour de Force*. N.p.: Independently published, 2017.

———. *Murder in the 33rd Degree: The Gagnon Investigation into Vatican Freemasonry*. N.p.: Independently published, 2022.

Ottaviani, Alfredo, Antonio Bacci, and a group of Roman theologians. *The Ottaviani Intervention: Short Critical Study of the New Order of Mass*. Revised and updated. Translated by Anthony Cekada. West Chester, OH: Philothea Press, 2010.

Villa, Luigi. *Paul VI: Beatified?* 3rd ed. Oconomowoc, WI: The Apostolate of Our Lady of Good Success, 2018.

INDEX OF NAMES

Adam, Karl (Bavarian priest, theologian), 64
Agagianian, Gregorio Pietro (Armenian patriarch, cardinal), xiii, 144, 170, 176
Alessandrini, Federico (Italian editor of L'Osservatore Romano), 37, 107
Alfrink, Jan (Dutch archbishop, cardinal), xii–xiii, 169, 193, 207, 241, 259
Ambrose of Milan (Archbishop, Doctor and Father of the Church), 129
Ambrosetti, Giovanni (Italian, president of FUCI), 66
Andreotti, Giulio (Italian statesman, president of FUCI), 42, 72, 90, 101, 169 n11, 295 n73
Antoniutti, Ildebrando (Italian cardinal), 170
Arnou, René (French Jesuit, priest), 288
Arroyo, Gonzalo (Chilean Jesuit, priest), 269
Athenagoras I of Constantinople, 176, 182, 184–85, 213, 228, 231–32, 235
Augustine of Hippo (Roman-African bishop, Doctor and Father of the Church), 27, 51

Bacci, Antonio (Italian cardinal), 36, 251–52
Badoglio, Pietro (Italian Marechal), 85, 87–88
Baggio, Sebastiano (Italian, cardinal), 290, 291 n62
Barbara, Noël (French priest), 287 n45, 297
Barbey d'Aurevilly, Jules (French novelist), 34
Baroni, Augusto (Italian priest), 10
Bazoli, Luigi (Italian lawyer), 19
Beauduin, Lambert (Belgian Benedictine), 11 n28, 46

Benedict XV (Italian pope), xi, 25 n22, 27, 31 n40, 41 n18, 45 n31, 110 n70, 159 n89
Bendiscioli, Mario (Italian), 64
Benelli, Giovanni (Italian cardinal), 231 n44, 250, 277, 285–86, 294
Beran, Josef (Czech cardinal), 201–2
Bérard, Léon (French politician, lawyer), 79
Bernanos, Georges (French author, royalist), xx, 68, 131
Bernareggi, Adriano (Italian archbishop), 135
Bevilacqua, Giulio (Italian Oratorian, cardinal), 11, 13, 19, 27, 45–47, 50, 55 n54, 63, 67, 80, 120, 129, 132, 140–41, 154–55, 159, 168, 182, 201–2, 218, 288
Bidault, Georges (French politician), 93
Bigo, Pierre (French Jesuit, priest), xxii
Blanchet, Émile (French archbishop), 122
Bloch, Pierre (French politician), 92
Bonomelli, Emilio (Italian), 58, 85 n80, 169
Bonomi, Ivanoe (Italian lawyer, journalist, politician), 99
Borges, Jorge Luis (Argentinian author), 273–74
Borghino, Giuseppe, 101
Borgongini Duca, Francesco (Italian cardinal), 35, 53
Borromeo, Charles (Italian archbishop, saint), 129, 171
Bossuet, Jacques-Bénigne (French bishop), 6
Botte, Bernard (Benedictine), 155, 219
Bourdeillette, Jean (French diplomat), 106–7, 110
Bourget, Paul (French writer), 34, 294 n69
Boyer, Charles (French Jesuit, priest), 67, 108, 111, 137

Bouyer, Louis (French Oratorian), xiv, 11 n26, 94 n15, 136, 154–55, 219, 248 n19
Brini, Mario (Italian archbishop), 291
Browne, Michael (Irish Dominican, cardinal), 179, 187, 192–93
Buchman, Franck (American non-Catholic missionary), 122
Buenner, Denys, 10
Bugnini, Annibale (Italian archbishop), xiv, xxv, 154–55, 218, 236, 249, 252, 274 n16, 289, 291–92

Caillois, Roger (French sociologist and author), 273–74
Câmara, Helder Pessona (Brazilian archbishop), xxin19, 119, 151, 228
Capelle, Bernard (Belgian Benedictine, abbot), 155
Capovilla, Loris (Italian cardinal), 145
Carcel Orti, Vicente (Spanish priest), xxi
Cardenal, Fernando (Nicaraguan Jesuit, priest), 246
Cardijn, Léon-Joseph (Belgian cardinal), 201–2
Cardinale, Igino (Italian archbishop), 98
Caresana, Paolo (Italian priest), 10–13, 18, 27, 63, 66, 134, 288
Carli, Luigi (Italian archbishop), 178, 187, 193
Casaroli, Agostino (Italian cardinal), 189–90, 224, 234, 250, 256, 263, 266, 295
Casel, Odo (German Benedictine), 45
Castro Mayer, Antonio de (Brazilian bishop), 180, 192
Ceaucescu, Nicolai (Romanian Communist president), 224
Cerbelaud-Salagnac, Georges (French historian), 220, 297
Chamberlain, Neville (Prime Minister of the United Kingdom), 72
Chamoun, Camille (President of the Republic of Lebanon), 134
Charles-Roux, François (French Ambassador to the Holy See), 72, 77 n50

Charlot, Christian, 272
Charrière, François (Swiss bishop), 146, 273
Chenaux, Philippe (Swiss historian and biographer), xxii
Christie, Agatha (English author), 273
Ciano, Galeazzo (Italian, Minister of Foreign Affairs), 80
Ciappi, Marin Luigi (Italian cardinal), 194
Cicognani, Amleto (Italian cardinal), 40, 119, 144, 153, 163, 172, 182, 234, 250
Cicognani, Gaetano (Italian cardinal), 155, 182
Ciry, Michel (French painter, engraver, composer), 285
Clark, Colin (British economist), 227
Coggan, Donald (British, Anglican archbishop), 293
Colombo, Carlo (Italian bishop), 67, 134, 149, 160, 173, 243
Colombo, Giovanni (Italian cardinal), 131, 134, 149, 156, 201–2, 249
Colombo, Luigi, 41
Congar, Yves-Marie (French Dominican, cardinal), 107–8, 114, 121–22, 136, 158, 173, 178–79, 194, 215 n104, 248, 272
Corçao, Gustave, 275
Cordovani, Mariano (Italian Dominican friar, priest), 67, 111
Cottinelli, Giuseppe, 63
Couturier, Paul (French priest the Society of Saint Irenaeus), 108
Cullmann, Oscar (German Lutheran, theologian), 166, 186, 195, 213, 272
Curran, Charles (American priest), 244
Curvers, Alexis (Belgian writer), 84 n75, 275
Cushing, Richard J. (American cardinal), 145, 150, 192

Daladier, Édouard (French Prime Minister), 72
Dalla Torre, Giuseppe (Italian journalist), 46–47, 62, 70, 80, 113

Daniélou, Jean (French Jesuit, cardinal), 114 n86, 163, 242, 247–48, 250 n22, 257, 272
Darmojuwono, Justinus (Indonesian cardinal), 231
Debray, Pierre (pen name of Sadi Couhé, French writer), 171, 200 n75
De Corte, Marcel (Belgian philosopher), 275
Decourtray, Albert (French cardinal), 270
De Gasperi, Alcide (Italian Prime Minister), 40, 42, 47-48, 65, 85 n80, 87–88, 99–102, 112–13, 121
Dell'Acqua, Angelo (Italian cardinal), 98 n30, 159, 172, 231 n44
Del Noce, Augusto (Italian philosopher), xxiii–xxiv, 273
Delos, P., 109
De Luca, Giuseppe (Italian priest), 51–52
Descamps, Albert (Belgian priest), 181–82
Descartes, René (French philosopher), 44
De Stefani, Alberto (Italian politician), 87
Dezza, Paolo (Italian Jesuit, cardinal), 84, 284, 288
Dollfuss, Engelbert (Chancellor of Austria), 65
Domenach, Jean-Marie (French writer), 166
Döpfner, Julius (German, cardinal), xiii, 144, 164, 176
Dos Santos, Lucia, (Portuguese Carmelite sister), 230 n41
Dossetti, Giuseppe (Italian politician and theologian), 102
Doumic, René (French journalist), 34
Droit, Michel (French journalist), 285–86
Ducaud-Bourget, François (French Franciscan, priest), 34, 294 n69
Duprey, Pierre (French Holy Ghost Father, bishop), 182
Duruflé, Maurice (French musician), 220
Dutourd, Jean (French novelist), 220, 285, 294

Duval, Léon-Étienne (French-Algerian cardinal), 201

Eisenhower, Dwight D. (American President), 150
Evreinoff, Alexandre, 75

Fabrègues, Jean de (French journalist), 272
Fanfani, Amintore (Italian politician), 113
Farinacci, Roberto (Italian Fascist politician), 70, 80
Feder, José (French liturgist), 219
Felici, Pericle (Italian cardinal), 161, 176
Feltin, Maurice (French cardinal), 125
Féret, Henri-Marie, 107
Fernandez Alonso, Aniceto (Spanish Dominican, priest), 193
Fesquet, Henri, 235
Fisher, Geoffrey (English Baron, Anglican, Archbishop of Canterbury), 222
Fontana, Mario (doctor), 198, 261
Fouilloux, Etienne (French historian), 106–7, 122 n124
Franco, Francesco (Spanish Catholic Dictator), xxi, 157
Frei, Eduardo (Chilean politician), 109–10
Frings, Joseph (German cardinal), xii–xiii, 159, 161–62, 169
Fumet, Stanislas (French journalist), 247

Gaggia, Giacinto (Italian archbishop), 22
Galloni, Francesco, 12–13, 22, 28
Gandhi, Indira (Indian politician), 196
Garrigou-Lagrange, Réginald (French Dominican, priest), 108 n62
Garrone, Gabriel-Marie (French cardinal), 212, 217, 231, 282–83
Gasparri, Pietro (Italian cardinal), 25, 35, 46, 48
Gaulle, Charles de (French president), 68 n24, 89 n87, 91–93, 286
Gauthey, Christopher, 10
Gauthier, Paul (French priest), 181

Gedda, Luigi (Italian physician and activist), 100 n38, 102, 121, 131
Gemelli, Agostino (Italian Franciscan, priest), 104 n48, 133
Gerlier, Pierre-Marie (French cardinal), 111
Gierek, Edward (Polish politician), 224
Gijsen, J. B. Matthijs (Dutch bishop), 259
Gilson, Étienne (French philosopher), 221 n14, 247
Gobry, Ivan (French philosopher), 294
Gonella, Guido (Italian journalist and politician), 42, 62, 75, 77, 85, 87
Grandi, Dino (Italian Count, diplomat), 87
Grandmaison, Léonce de (French Jesuit, priest), 63
Grazioli, Angelo, 45
Greene, Graham (English novelist), 273
Gromyko, Andrei (Russian politician), 210, 224
Grosoli Pironi, Giovanni (Italian Count, politician), 20, 24
Guano, Emilio (Italian bishop), 188
Guardi, Luigi, 103
Guardini, Romano (German-Italian, priest), 63
Guarducci, Margherita (Italian archaeologist), 241 n5
Guasco, Maurilio, 126 n138
Guérard des Lauriers, Michel Louis (French Dominican), 251
Guérin, Hubert (French diplomat), 92–94, 120
Guitton, Jean (French philosopher), xi, xxiii n31, 8, 34, 69, 115–17, 120, 136, 159, 162, 168–69, 177, 180, 188, 198, 210, 213, 215, 226, 229–31, 237, 243, 260, 272, 277, 286, 294
Gut, Benno (Swiss Benedictine, cardinal), 219, 239, 252
Gutiérez, Gustavo (Peruvian Dominican, priest), 246, 281 n28
Gy, Pierre-Marie (French Dominican, priest), 155

Halifax, Edward (Edward Wood, 1st Earl of Halifax, English, politician), 72
Hanotaux, Gabriel (French historian), 6
Harcourt, Robert d' (French anti-Nazi polemicist), 62
Häring, Bernard (German Redemptorist, priest), 244
Harmel, Léon (French industrialist who experimented with Catholic social doctrine), 18
Hebblethwaite, Peter (British Jesuit, ex-priest turned journalist), xx
Hecke, Ernest van, 291
Heenan, John Carmel (English cardinal), 223, 237, 274, 291
Hefele, Karl Josef von (German bishop), 23
Hera Buedo, Eduardo de la, xx
Hildebrand, Dietrich von (German-Italian, philosopher), 64
Hitler, Adolf (Austrian Dictator of Germany), 61–62, 71–72, 75, 77, 80 n59, 84
Huber, Georges, 125 n135
Humbert (Byzantine Greek Patriarch, cardinal), 232
Hurley, Denis (South African archbishop), 156
Hussain, Zakir (Indian politician), 196
Huysmans, Joris-Karl (pen name of Charles Marie Huysmans, French writer), 34

Isaac, Jules (French historian), 180

John XXIII (Italian pope), xi–xii, xvii, xx, 36 n3, 94 n15, 97–98, 103 n45, 124, 127, 144–47, 149, 152–53, 156 n77, 158–64, 167, 170–71, 180, 188–89, 201 n77, 212–13, 222, 228–29; see Roncalli, Angelo
Johnson, Lyndon B. (United States President), 209
Joliot-Curie, Frédéric (French physicist), 106

Index of Names

Journet, Charles (Swiss cardinal), 141, 201–2, 207–8, 211, 272
Jungmann, Joseph Andreas (German Jesuit priest), 155

Kaas, Ludwig (German priest, politician), 80
Kádár, Janos (Hungarian Communist politician), 224
Karrer, Otto (German Jesuit priest), 146
Khrushchev, Nikita (Russian, USSR Communist Secretary), 189, 198 n71, 224 n24
Kim, Stephen S. H. (South Korean cardinal), 261
Kirschberg, Manfred (French doctor), 74
König, Franz (Austrian cardinal), xii–xiii, 144, 152, 159, 169, 176, 193
Kubitschek, Juscelin (Brazilian president), 150–51
Küng, Hans (Swiss priest), 152, 164, 213 n99, 248, 257–58, 287–88

Labourdette, Marie-Michel (French, Dominican priest), 108 n62
Lai, Benny (Italian journalist), 130 n7, 143
Lanne, Emmanuel, 219, 233 n50
Lapide, Pinchas (Austro-Israeli diplomat and historian), 84
La Pira, Giorgio (Italian politician), 88
Larraona, Arcadio (Spanish Claretian, cardinal), 193–94
Latreille, André (French historian), 93–94
Laurenti, Camillo (Italian cardinal), 45
Laurentin, René (French priest), 158 n82, 233, 277 n22
Lauri, Lorenzo (Italian cardinal), 30–31
Lebret, Louis-Joseph (French Dominican priest), xxii, 118, 227
Lécureux, Bernadette (French historian), 220
Lefebvre, Gaspar (French Benedictine priest), 46

Lefebvre, Marcel (French Spiritan archbishop), xx, 123, 178, 180 n31, 192–93, 252, 272–73, 281–87
Léger, Paul-Émile (Canadian Sulpician cardinal), xiii, 163–64, 194
Lekai, Lazlo (Hungarian cardinal), 267–68
Leo XIII (Italian pope), 8, 19 n9, 26 n25, 31 n40, 40, 44 n29, 116 n101, 268
Leprieur, François, 126 n137, 127 n140
Lercaro, Giacomo (Italian cardinal), xii–xiv, 141, 144 n46, 164, 168–70, 176, 217–18, 236, 239–40
Lesourd, Paul, 119 n116
Letamendia, P., 110 n68
Levi, Virgilio (Italian Substitute director of *L'Osservatore Romano*), 242 n7, 290
Levillain, Philippe (French historian), 170 n13,
Liénart, Achille (French cardinal), xii–xiii, 152, 161–62, 169, 193, 210, 290
Lima, Alceu Amoroso (Brazilian writer), 110, 151
Lio, Ermenegildo, xxii
Lizier, Pietro (Italian politician), 38
Loew, Jacques (French Dominican priest), 126
Loftus, John (American Army intelligence officer), 96–97
Longinotti, Giovanni Maria (Italian politician), 20, 24–25, 46, 48, 65, 85 n180, 90
Lubac, Henri de (French Jesuit cardinal), 108–9, 114–15, 136–37, 159, 213, 227, 248, 272
Luther, Martin (German Augustinian priest, excommunicated heretic), 44

Macchi, Pasquale (Italian archbishop), xxiii, 15 n35, 131, 150, 157 n81, 171, 175, 181, 196, 198, 204, 237, 250, 261, 276 n21, 277, 290, 292, 295
Madiran, Jean (pen name of Jean Arfel, French journalist), 200, 244 n15, 253 n31, 274–75
Magee, John (Irish bishop), 12

317

Maglione, Luigi (Italian cardinal), 73, 80, 82, 91, 105
Malula, Joseph (Congolese cardinal), 255
Mamie, Pierre (Swiss bishop), 282
Manfredini, Enrico (Italian archbishop), 134
Manziana, Carlo, 26, 32, 63, 90
Manzoni, Alessandro, 15, 17–18, 20
Marcel, Gabriel (French philosopher), 247–48, 272
Marchetti Selvaggiani, Francesco (Italian cardinal), 56, 58
Marchetto, Agostino (Italian archbishop), xxii n19
Marcinkus, Paul (American archbishop), 181, 196, 234 n52, 261
Marcolini, Ottorino (Italian priest), 90
Marcos, Ferdinand (Filipino President), 261
Marella, Paolo (Italian cardinal), 191
Maria José de Savoy (Belgian princess, Queen consort of Italy), 85
Maritain, Jacques (French philosopher), xxii, 43–44, 63, 94–98, 109–10, 127, 139, 141–42, 188, 198–99, 201, 206, 215, 220–21, 226–27, 248 n18, 272 n12
Martelet, Gustave (French Jesuit priest), 243
Martimort, Aimé-Georges (French priest), 118, 155, 218–19
Martin, Jacques (French cardinal), 70 n29, 77, 171 n16, 181–82, 250 n24, 277, 285
Martini, Angelo, 88
Masella, Benedetto Aloisi (Italian cardinal), 144
Massigli, René (French diplomat), 93
Matteotti, Giacomo (Italian politician), 33
Mauriac, François (French writer), 247
Mazzolari, Primo (Italian priest), 67, 141
Melito de Chalcedon (Turkish Eastern Orthodox Metropolitan), 292
Mendès-France, Pierre (French statesman), 113 n85, 131 n14

Mendez Arceo, Sergio (Mexican bishop), 269
Mendoza y Amor Flores, Benjamin (Bolivian painter), 261
Menna, Domenico (Italian archbishop), 18
Menshausen, Fritz (German diplomat), 76
Menuhin, Yehudi (American violinist), 273
Mercier, Désiré-Joseph (Belgian cardinal), 11
Meyer, Albert (American cardinal), 150, 163, 176, 194
Micara, Clemente (Italian cardinal), 154
Michel of the Holy Trinity (Brother), 229 n37
Mindszenty, Joseph (Hungarian cardinal, Venerable), 190, 266–68
Molinari, Franco (Italian writer), 19 n7, 58 n61
Molinari, Paolo (Italian), 296
Molnar, Thomas (Hungarian philosopher), 275
Monteilhet, Hubert (French writer), 130 n6
Montherlant, Henry de (French writer), 273–74
Montini, Francesca (Italian paternal grandmother of Pope Paul VI, born Buffali), 2 n3
Montini, Francesco (Italian, younger brother of Pope Paul VI), 7 n18
Montini, Gaetano, 1
Montini, Giorgio (Italian politician, father of Pope Paul VI), 2–5, 10, 13, 17, 19–21, 24, 31, 33, 41
Montini, Giorgio (nephew), 2–5, 10, 13, 17, 19–20, 24, 31, 33, 41, 58, 62
Montini, Giuditta (Italian mother of Pope Paul VI, born Alghisi), 3, 5–6, 9
Montini, Lodovico (Italian, older brother of Pope Paul VI), 1, 88, 101
Montini, Ludovico (Italian, paternal grandfather of Pope Paul VI), 10 n23

Index of Names

Morlion, Félix Andrew (Belgian Dominican), 98, 159, 183 n41
Moro, Aldo (Italian politician), xxiii, 42, 88, 101, 148–49, 181 n32, 208, 280, 294–95
Moro, Renato (Italian historian, nephew of Aldo Moro), 42 n20
Mousnier, Roland (French historian), 293
Muench, Aloisius (American cardinal), 96
Mussolini, Benito (Italian Prime Minister), 2 n4, 24, 30, 33, 38, 40–41, 46–47, 52–54, 70–72, 75, 80 n59, 85–88, 99–100

Nantes, Georges de (French priest and journalist), 214 n101, 236 n57, 257–58, 275
Nardini, Lionello, 10, 13
Nenni, Pietro (Italian politician and journalist), 88, 99
Neri, Philip (Italian Oratorian, priest, saint), 6, 63 n6
Newman, John Henry (English Oratorian, priest, cardinal, saint), 116
Nikodim (Russian Orthodox metropolitan), 159

Obote, Milton (Ugandan president), 254
Ocampo, Victoria (Argentine publisher and writer), 273–74
Oddi, Silvo (Italian cardinal), 252–53, 286 n44
Onclin, Guillaume, 281–82
Ormesson, Wladimir d', 77–79, 111, 113, 122, 127, 131
Orsenigo, Cesare (Italian archbishop and papal nuncio), 83
Ortolani, Umberto (Italian businessman), xiii, 169
Osborne, Francis D'Arcy G. (British diplomat), 68, 78, 80, 86
Ottaviani, Alfredo (Italian cardinal), 36, 49, 61, 66–67, 99, 102, 111, 125, 162, 170, 172–74, 179, 214, 225–26, 229, 234, 243, 251–52, 260

Pacelli, Eugenio: see Pius XII
Papen, Franz von (German diplomat), 61
Parente, Pietro (Italian cardinal), 192
Passerini, Angelo (Italian politician), 24
Paul V, born Camillo Borghese (Italian pope), 171
Pellegrino, Michele (Italian cardinal), 257, 290
Pertini, Sandro (Italian president), 295
Piastrelli, Luigi, 32, 38
Piazzi, Ugo (Italian politician), 37
Piettre, André (French economist), 247–48
Pighi, G. B. (Italian poet), 273
Pignedoli, Sergio (Italian cardinal), 80, 112, 136, 149 n57, 156–57
Pini, Giandomenico, 17
Pisani, Ernesto, 57
Pius X (Giuseppe Sarto) (Italian pope, saint), 8, 19, 22, 25 n22, 27 n31, 31 n40, 132, 152 n65, 180 n31, 273, 282–85
Pius XI (Ambrogio Damiano Achille Ratti) (Italian pope), 4 n9, 18 n4, 25 n22, 28–29, 31 n40, 40, 46–48, 53–54, 68–69, 71–73, 129, 145, 269
Pius XII (Eugenio Pacelli, Italian pope), xvii, 5, 35–36, 48 n43, 73–77, 81, 83–84, 86–87, 89–94, 96–97, 99–107, 110–12, 114–17, 119–21, 123–26, 129–31, 138, 141–43, 145–46, 154–55, 170–71, 182–84, 212–13, 263, 296
Pizzardo, Giuseppe (Italian cardinal), 25, 28–32, 35, 38, 49, 57–58, 61, 68, 98, 117, 126
Podgorny, Nikolai (Ukranian politician), 224
Poletti, Ugo (Italian cardinal), 290
Poliakov, Léon (Russian historian), 76
Poma, Antonio (Italian cardinal), 239
Pompilj, Basilio (Italian cardinal), 37–38
Poulat, Émile (French sociologist, ex-priest), xvii–xviii, 202
Poupard, Paul (French cardinal), 227

Prevotat, Jacques (French historian), 15 n35
Prezzolini, Giuseppe (Italian journalist), 267
Proança Sigaud, de (Brazillian archbishop), 178, 180, 186, 212

Rahner, Karl (German Jesuit theologian), 159, 162, 244, 248, 257
Rampolla del Tindaro, Mariano (Italian Indologist), 26, 28, 32, 64, 67, 87–88, 194
Ramsey, Arthur Michael (English Anglican archbishop), 222–23
Ratti, Ambrogio Damiano Achille: see Pius XI
Ratzinger, Joseph (German cardinal, future Pope Benedict XVI), xv, 108 n61, 155 n74, 159, 248
Rémy, Colonel (pseudonym of Gilbert Renault, French resistance fighter), 285–86
Riberi, Antonio (Italian cardinal), 26, 65, 75, 153, 231
Riccardi, Andrea (Italian politician), 37 n9
Richaud, Paul-Marie-Andre' (French cardinal), 122
Rigali, Justin Francis (American cardinal), xix
Righetti, Igino (Italian lawyer, activist), 38–39, 48, 53, 55, 66
Ritter, Joseph (American cardinal), 194
Rodhain, Jean (French priest), 89, 96
Roguet, A. M., 118
Ronca, Roberto (Italian archbishop), 56–57, 88, 99, 102
Roncalli, Angelo (Italian-Franciscan pope), 94, 117, 125, 137 n29, 141–42, 144
Roosevelt, Franklin Delano (American president), 78, 86
Rosmini, Antonio (Italian priest), 19
Rossi, Mario (Italian physician, activist), 104 n47, 130–31
Rotta, Angelo (Italian archbishop), 82

Rousseau, Jean-Jacques (French philosopher), 44
Roy, Maurice (Canadian cardinal), 137, 268–69
Ruffini, Ernesto (Italian cardinal), 103
Rugambwa, Laurean (Tanzanian cardinal), 193
Ruini, Camillo (Italian cardinal), 296

Sainsaulieu, A., 174
Saint-Laurent, Louis (Canadian Prime Minister), 120
Saint-Pierre, François (French writer), 4
Saint-Pierre, Michel de (French writer), 199–200, 283, 285, 293
Salazar, António de Oliveira (Portuguese Catholic statesman), 230
Salleron, Louis (French writer), 275, 285, 294
Samoré, Antonio (Italian cardinal), 223
Sapieha, Adam Stefan (Polish cardinal), 84
Sauguet, Henri (French composer), 285–86
Saventhem, Eric M. de, born Erich Vermehren (German activist, first president of Una Voce), 236, 275
Scaglia, G. B., xxii–xxiii
Schiavini, 131, 136
Schillebeeckx, Edward (Belgian Dominican priest), 114 n86, 159, 248
Schneider, Marius (German musician), 273
Schuster, Ildefons (Italian Benedictine cardinal), 29
Schütz, Roger (Swiss Protestant monk), 111–12, 116, 137, 158, 245
Scorzelli, Lello (Italian sculptor), xviii, 174 n21
Selassie, Haile (Ethiopian emperor), 254
Semeria, Giovanni (Italian priest), 19
Seper, Franjo (Croatian cardinal), 208, 234, 252
Shazar, Zalman (Israeli president), 183
Simonis, Adrianus (Dutch cardinal), 259

Index of Names

Sindona, Michele (Italian Mafia banker), 135

Siri, Giuseppe (Italian cardinal), 68, 125, 130, 140, 143–44, 148, 168, 170, 172–73, 175–76, 181 n32, 228–29, 251, 272, 280, 289

Slipyj, Josyf (Ukrainian cardinal), 189, 201, 208, 271

Solages, Bruno de (French priest), 110, 114

Solovyov, Vladimir (Russian philosopher), 213

Soulages, Gérard, 272, 294

Spadolini, Giovanni (Italian Prime Minister), 100

Spellman, Francis (American cardinal), 36, 120, 150, 169, 192, 209–10

Stabile, Francesco Michele, 104 n46

Stepinac, Aloysius (Croatian cardinal), 125

Storchi, Ferdinando (Italian politician), 103

Sturzo, Luigi (Italian priest, politician), 20, 31, 65, 121

Suarez, Emmanuel, 122

Suenens, Léon-Joseph (Belgian cardinal), xii–xiii, 137, 144 n46, 163–64, 169–70, 173–74, 176, 178, 193, 240, 243, 256–47, 271, 277–78, 289–90

Sunay, Cevdet (Turkish president), 232

Tabera Araoz, Arturo (Spanish cardinal), 282

Tacchi Venturi, Pietro (Italian Jesuit priest), 54, 75

Tagore, Rabindranath (Indian poet), 195, 197

Tanquerey, Adolphe (French Sulpician priest), 19

Tardini, Domenico (Italian cardinal), 36, 49–50, 67–68, 70, 73, 78, 80, 91–92, 94, 97, 99, 102, 123–24, 144, 146, 153

Taylor, Myron C. (American industrialist), 78

Teilhard de Chardin, Pierre (French Jesuit priest), 110

Testa, Gustavo (Italian cardinal), 182 n40

Théas, Pierre Marie (French bishop), 93

Thérèse of the Child Jesus (French Carmelite nun, saint), 4, 6, 34, 110

Thiandoum, Hyacinthe (Senegalese cardinal), 283

Thibon, Gustave (French philosopher), 220, 285

Thurian, Max (Swiss Taize subprior, converted to Catholicism, priest), 111–12, 116, 137, 158, 222, 251

Tisserant, Eugène (French cardinal), 159, 182, 184, 212, 260

Tito, Josip Broz (Yugoslavian president), 224

Tittmann, Harold H. (American delegate to the Vatican), 80, 86

Togliatti, Palmiro (Italian politician), 100

Tovini, Giuseppe (Italian lawyer and banker), 3–5

Trebeschi, Andrea (Italian lawyer), 5, 12–17, 20, 22, 24, 30, 90

U Thant (Burmese diplomat), 198, 208

Valdoni, Pietro (Italian surgeon), 237

Valeri, Valerio (Italian cardinal), 93

Van der Meersch, Maxence (French writer), 110–11

Varaut, Jean-Marc (French lawyer), 294

Vergine, Giovanni, 5

Veronese, Vittorino (Italian politician), 100, 103, 113, 121, 180

Veuillot, Pierre (French cardinal), 115, 122, 127–28, 231

Victor-Emmanuel II (Italian king), 1–2, 31 n40

Victor-Emmanuel III (Italian king), 33, 38, 85–87

Vier, Jacques (French historian), 220, 294

Villot, Jean (French cardinal), 177, 201, 217, 234, 241, 250, 259, 277, 280, 283–85, 290, 292, 294–95

Virebeau, Georges aka Henry Coston (French anti-Semitic journalist), 290 n55
Voillaume, René (French priest), 126

Wall, Bernard (English bishop), 273
Weber, Anton, 89
Weizsäcker, Ernst von (German politician), 90
Wenger, Antoine (French Byzantine priest), 177, 187 n45, 211, 217 n1, 226 n30, 243–44, 263, 294
Willebrands, Johannes (Dutch cardinal), 158, 222, 293
Wojtyła, Karol (Polish cardinal, future Pope John Paul II), 84 n72, 231, 243, 270, 280
Wright, John J. (American cardinal), 235, 273, 282
Wyszynski, Stefan (Polish cardinal), 125, 176, 187 n44

Zagon, Jozsef (Hungarian priest), 266
Zanotti, Clorinda, 4
Zhivkov, Todor (Bulgarian politician), 224
Zoghbi, Elias (Egyptian archbishop), 211
Zolli, Eugenio (Italian Catholic ex-Jewish Rabbî), 88–89
Zundel, Maurice (Swiss priest), 43

www.ingramcontent.com/pod-product-compliance
Lightning Source LLC
Chambersburg PA
CBHW030215170426
43201CB00006B/94